THE COMPLETE
FRANCIS OF ASSISI

PARACLETE GIANTS

ABOUT THIS SERIES:

Each Paraclete Giant presents collected works of one of Christianity's greatest writers—"giants" of the faith. These essential volumes share the pivotal teachings of leading Christian figures throughout history with today's theological students and all people seeking spiritual wisdom.

The Complete Paraclete Giant Series…

THE COMPLETE *CLOUD OF UNKNOWING*

THE COMPLETE FÉNELON

THE COMPLETE IMITATION OF CHRIST

THE COMPLETE *INTRODUCTION TO THE DEVOUT LIFE*

THE COMPLETE JULIAN OF NORWICH

THE COMPLETE THÉRÈSE OF LISIEUX

THE COMPLETE MADAME GUYON

THE COMPLETE FRANCIS OF ASSISI

For more information, visit www.paracletepress.com.

The COMPLETE

Francis of Assisi

His Life, The Complete Writings,
and *The Little Flowers*

Edited, Translated, and Introduced
by Jon M. Sweeney

 PARACLETE PRESS BREWSTER, MASSACHUSETTS

2015 First printing

The Complete Francis of Assisi: His Life, The Complete Writings, and The Little Flowers

Copyright © 2015 by Jon M. Sweeney

ISBN 978-1-61261-688-9

The photographs on pages 1, 195, and 261 are courtesy of April Love-Fordham.

The Paraclete Press name and logo (dove on cross) are trademarks of Paraclete Press, Inc.

Library of Congress Cataloging-in-Publication Data

The complete Francis of Assisi : his life, the complete writings, and The little flowers / edited by Jon M. Sweeney.
     3 volumes in 1 cm.— (Paraclete giants)
   Contents: book one. The road to Assisi : the essential biography of St. Francis / Paul Sabatier ; edited with introduction and annotations by Jon M. Sweeney—book two. Francis of Assisi : the essential writings (in his own words) / translated, introduced, and annotated by Jon M. Sweeney— book three. The Little flowers of St. Francis / [ascribed to] Brother Ugolino ; introduced, annotated, arranged chronologically, and rendered into contemporary English by Jon M. Sweeney.
   ISBN 978-1-61261-688-9 (paperback)
   1. Francis, of Assisi, Saint, 1182–1226. 2. Christian saints—Italy—Biography. 3. Francis, of Assisi, Saint, 1182–1226—Legends. I. Sweeney, Jon M., 1967– editor, translator, annotator. II. Ugolino, di Monte Santa Maria. III. Sabatier, Paul, 1858–1928. Road to Assisi. IV. Francis, of Assisi, Saint, 1182–1226. Works. Selections. English. V. Fioretti di San Francesco. English.
   BX4700.F6C632 2015
   271'.302—dc23
   [B]   2015013457

10 9 8 7 6 5 4 3 2 1

Published by Paraclete Press
Brewster, Massachusetts
www.paracletepress.com

Printed in the United States of America

To my children, Clelia, Joe, and Sima;
And to two professors, now gone, whom I loved:
Arthur F. Holmes and Paul L. Holmer

CONTENTS

BOOK TWO:
Francis of Assisi In His Own Words: The Essential Writings
Translated, Introduced, and Annotated by Jon M. Sweeney

BOOK THREE:
The Little Flowers of St. Francis
Brother Ugolino
*Introduced, annotated, arranged chronologically, and
rendered into contemporary English by Jon M. Sweeney*

CONTENTS

PART II – STORIES OF FRIARS FROM THE PROVINCE OF THE MARCHES

FOREWORD

In many ways, Francis of Assisi is easy to understand. The late medieval milieu notwithstanding, Francis's slow, awkward conversion, wrought with familial conflict of Shakespearean proportions, and his subsequent passion for living life with true Gospel simplicity, appeals to people of every era. We don't need much interpretation or explanation in order to quickly grasp the man and the message.

He surely seemed to be "a man after God's own heart," as his friend Pope Gregory IX put it in his bull of canonization nearly eight hundred years ago. Gregory went on to say that Francis was raised up "at the eleventh hour"—in other words, as the end of the day was nearing—to say something vital and critical to all of us with his life and work.

So, then, why would anyone require a book this fat to explain a man and a saint who seems to require no lengthy explanations? The simple answer: this collection is, most of all, for those who already love St. Francis and want to be in his company.

The three books combined here into one relay the man in the details of his biography, the concerns of his own personal writings, and the stories and legends attached to him in the early days of the Franciscan movement, and they point to his personality and spirit. On each of these four hundred plus pages, you will probably, over and over, remember what drew you to Francis in the first place.

Which is to say that this fat book is also ideal for someone new to the world's most popular saint. There is probably no better introduction to his life and spirit than through what you will discover in these pages. The biography by Paul Sabatier is the clearest one ever written, and the notes added in the margins elucidate some details that have come to light since the French scholar did his research a little more than a century ago. Then come the writings of the saint himself—and too often readers forget that Francis of Assisi wrote an innovative Rule for life, letters to friends, and other fascinating occasional writings including the "Canticle of the Creatures," the first poem penned in vernacular Italian and a daring, ahead-of-his-time interpretation of the world of creatures as part of God's kingdom. As for *The Little Flowers of Saint Francis*, it has had no shortage of readers over the centuries. This beautiful book has probably been introduced to more people in history than any other except for the Bible and *The Imitation of Christ*, and the edition here, unlike many others, organizes the stories in chronological order. With all of this, if you don't fall in love with the life of the little poor man from Assisi by the time you are done, perhaps you should have your heart checked! 1 Samuel 16:7, Matthew 6:21, Psalm 34:18.

Jon M. Sweeney
March 2, 2015
Feast of St. Agnes of Prague

BOOK ONE

The Road to Assisi

the ESSENTIAL BIOGRAPHY
of ST. FRANCIS

PAUL SABATIER

Edited with Introduction and Annotations by
Jon M. Sweeney

INTRODUCTION

———— ·◉· ————

Paul Sabatier (1858–1928) was the first modern biographer of St. Francis of Assisi. A French Protestant, Sabatier was motivated to write about the saint out of love for his unusual and creative life.

It can be a very personal and moving experience to write about the little poor man from Umbria. Over the centuries, many authors have been profoundly affected as they have "lived" with Francis while recounting his life. Nikos Kazantzakis, the twentieth-century Greek novelist, said that, while writing his novel *Saint Francis*, "often large teardrops smeared the manuscript."

It is not simply that Francis's ideals are worth recounting, but that his life was so extraordinary. He was fully human—like each of us in our awkwardness, insecurities, and fear—but he was also perhaps the purest example we have seen of a person striving to do what Jesus taught his disciples.

To write about Francis is to wish the same courage and heart into ourselves. This wishing—these good intentions—are often the stuff of our spiritual lives, as perhaps when we touch an icon, or wake up early before the rest of the house is awake to pray in solitude, or when we truly hunger for righteousness, as many of our liturgies say. Reading and writing about Francis can be our attempt, like a medium or sacrament, to enlarge our own capacities to be like him.

Paul Sabatier was born in the Cevennes, a mountainous region of southern France, in August 1858. He was educated in theology in Paris and after preparing for the ministry became pastor of St. Nicolas, Strasbourg, a post he held until he was almost forty. After a brief sojourn as pastor of St. Cierge back in the Cevennes he then devoted the rest of his life to historical writing and research. His book, *Vie de S. François d'Assise*, was first published in French in 1894. Thirty-two years later, a scholar of Franciscan studies wrote: "Countless thousands of readers have derived from . . . Sabatier . . . their first impulse towards interest in the saint, which has frequently developed into a complete surrender to his fascination and charm" (SETON, p. 252).

3

Sabatier's brother, the more famous of the two men, was old enough to be his father. Louis Auguste Sabatier (1839–1901) was a theologian and professor of dogmatics in the theology department at the University of Strasbourg and, later, was a member of the newly formed Protestant faculty in Paris. A Huguenot, Auguste found that his loyalty to French causes ultimately led to his being forced by the Germans to leave Strasbourg in the early 1870s. About fifteen years later, Paul Sabatier also fell out of favor with his German superiors, declining to become a German citizen, and left his pulpit in Strasbourg only to return in 1919 as a professor of church history. He dedicated his book on Francis to the people of Strasbourg. However, we might thank the Germans for forcing Sabatier into retirement from the active ministry (he was also plagued by health problems), leaving him the freedom and time to live in Italy, to do research, and to write his great biography.

Sabatier was moved by Francis, the man, and he wanted to create the first telling of his life that reflected the possibilities afforded by modern scholarship. He was the first person to scour the libraries of Italy to uncover original documents, and he employed textual and historical criticism as well as psychological insight. Modern scholarship, so-called, was new in Sabatier's time, in the second half of the nineteenth century. As a student, Sabatier listened to the lectures of the dynamic historian and critic Ernest Renan (1823–1892). It was Renan's groundbreaking—or notorious, depending on your perspective—work exposing naïveté in most precritical studies of the historical Jesus that motivated Sabatier to write his modern life of Francis, looking for the man amidst the layers of myth and legend. It was Renan who said: "No miracle has ever taken place under conditions that science can accept. Experience shows, without exception, that miracles occur only in times and in countries in which miracles are believed in, and in the presence of persons who are disposed to believe in them." Renan's book *Vie de Jésus* was published only thirty years before Sabatier's life of Francis; comparisons between the two works were inevitable. "So the sensation of delight or anger with which [Sabatier's] book was received is easy to explain" (BPL, p. 274).

These were the heady, early days of ultimate confidence in the power of science and logic to make faith unnecessary. But Sabatier did not follow Renan in discarding the reality of the mysterious. (Renan, for instance, explained Francis's stigmata as a deliberate hoax perpetuated by Brother Elias.) He did, however, accept the basic notion that many things can be seen only with eyes of faith; many realities may be understood only with a heart disposed to realize them.

Sabatier believed that to deny all of the miraculous in the lives of the saints was to deny a life-transforming faith. In the introduction to the first edition of his life of Francis, he separated himself from Renan, his teacher, when he wrote the following:

> Happily we are no longer in the time when historians thought they had done the right thing when they had reduced everything to its proper size, contenting themselves with denying or omitting everything in the life of the heroes of humanity that rises above the level of our everyday experiences.
>
> No doubt Francis did not meet on the road to Siena three pure and gentle virgins come from heaven to greet him; the devil did not overturn rocks for the sake of terrifying him; but when we deny these visions and apparitions, we are victims of an error graver, perhaps, than that of those who affirm them (SABATIER, p. XXX).

Sabatier's book was first published in French in 1894 (although early copies were distributed in the closing months of 1893), and quickly became a bestseller, almost unheard of for a work of its kind in those days. English, Swedish, German, and Italian editions followed within the next several years. When Sabatier died in the spring of 1928, forty-five editions had been published in the French language alone.

Scholarly reaction to the book was immediate and, most of it, favorable. Sabatier was quickly seen as one of his generation's most important historians. Both Catholics and Protestants admired the work, but the official Roman Catholic response was to condemn it. Historical and textual criticism applied to the legends of the saints was not looked upon favorably at the close of the nineteenth century. The book made the infamous Roman "Index" (*Index*

Librorum Prohibitorum) of forbidden books in the same year that it was first published.

Catholic authorities saw too much of a rebel in Sabatier's portrait of Francis. Always careful to portray this—the greatest of saints of the people—as a supporter of the Church, its doctrine, and hierarchy, popes and other staunch protectors of the faith have often proclaimed: "How foolish they are, and how little they know the saint of Assisi, who for the purpose of their own errors invent a Francis—an incredible Francis—who is impatient of the authority of the Church. . . . Let [Francis], the herald of the great King, teach Catholics and others by his own example how close was his attachment to the hierarchy of the Church and to the doctrines of Christ" (Encyclical Letter of Pope Pius XI, written in 1926 for the 700th anniversary of the saint's death; see SETON, p. 251).

Sabatier certainly shows us a Francis who is often going his own way. However, he is also careful to show both sides of the story, as when he wrote this passage: "One of Francis's most frequent counsels bore upon the respect due to the clergy. He begged his disciples to show a very particular deference to the priests, and never to meet them without kissing their hands. He saw only too well that the brothers, having renounced everything, were in danger of being unjust or severe toward the rich and powerful of the earth" (SABATIER, pp. 168–69).

As is true of any great work, Sabatier's life of Francis has given birth to hundreds of others, and also has enlightened his critics. Since the closing years of the nineteenth century there has been appreciation for Sabatier's book, but plenty of criticism as well. Many Franciscan scholars have disagreed with some of his conclusions, primarily the subtle ways in which the French Protestant portrays Francis as a forerunner of the Protestant Reformation of the sixteenth century. Other scholarly reactions have ranged widely. For instance, while some reviewers have deplored Sabatier's critical stance in reference to the Francis legends—thinking it wrong to view a medieval saint through a modern lens—others, including the popular medieval scholar and sometime critic of institutional religion G. G. Coulton, have taken Sabatier, his contemporary, to task for not being critical enough, for continuing to perpetuate credulity.

Sabatier's Francis is a gentle mystic and passionate reformer guided by an unwavering vision of fulfilling the ideals of Christ: the brotherhood of all people, evangelical poverty, and forgiveness, all with a Christ-filled intoxicating joy. An anti-intellectual at heart, Sabatier's Francis confounds the wise with his clarity of vision and dedicated praxis, and even occasionally by his holy foolishness. In Sabatier's book, the simple beauty of Francis's life and message is set clearly against the obscuring of that message in the years following the saint's death. The narrative builds to, and reveals, this eventual sadness. Francis the prophet is set against the priests of his day, and even against many of the Franciscan brothers and priests that followed in his footsteps.

Contemporary theologian Lawrence Cunningham writes: "Sabatier's mentor, Renan, once quipped that Jesus preached the Kingdom of God and the world ended up with the Catholic Church. Sabatier's biography was a variation on this theme: Francis had preached a lay Christianity bent on radical spiritual renewal, and Europe ended up with the Franciscan order" (CUNNINGHAM 1, pp. 865–68).

Sabatier also portrays Francis as an important forerunner of the Italian Renaissance. The "birth of the individual," long recognized as one of the key signposts of the Renaissance, is exemplified in the life of Francis. One Dutch scholar summarizes this, saying: "Perhaps Sabatier has contributed more than anyone to the shift in the nature and the dating of the concept of the Renaissance. It was no longer a growth of the mind . . . but a growth of the heart: the opening of the eyes and the soul to all the excellence of the world and the individual personality" (HUIZINGA, pp. 263–64).

Jacob Burckhardt, renowned historian of the Italian Renaissance, wrote a generation before Sabatier: "At the close of the thirteenth century Italy began to swarm with individuality; the ban laid upon human personality was dissolved; and a thousand figures meet us each in its own special shape and dress" (BURCKHARDT, p. 81). Burckhardt, however, does not in his secularism credit the revolution of spirit brought about by Francis with sparking a new individuality; for Burckhardt, the emergence of the individual in the early Renaissance period was the result, above all, of political change.

In his perspective on the life of Francis, Sabatier stood somewhere between the dry academics—Renan and Matthew Arnold, for instance, writing in the decades before Sabatier—and the absolutely devoted—Thomas of Celano, St. Bonaventure, and the other hagiographic and piously written "lives" of the saint. Since minutes after Francis's death—when the canonization process began in earnest and Assisi was quickly established as one of the most important places for tourism and pilgrimage in all of Christendom—until the late nineteenth century, the life of Francis was clouded in myth. *The Golden Legend*, a popular late medieval collection of tales from the lives of the saints, for instance, records this about Francis: "The saint would not handle lanterns and lamps and candles because he did not want to dim their brightness with his hands." Also: "A locust that nested in a fig tree next to his cell used to sing at all hours, until the man of God extended his hand and said: 'My sister locust, come here to me!' Obediently the locust came up and rested on his hand. 'My sister locust, sing! Sing, and praise your Lord!' The locust began to sing and did not hop away until the saint gave permission" (VORAGINE, p. 225).

Tellingly, Thomas of Celano, the first biographer of Francis, wrote in the prologue to his first life of the saint, "Pious devotion and truth will always be my guide and instructor" (ARMSTRONG, p. 180). Before Sabatier, historical evidence and hagiography were necessarily intertwined.

It is also important to realize, before reading Sabatier's book, that he stood in a long line of speculative Protestant tradition rich with disdain, even sarcasm, for the lives of the saints. For example, one popular Protestant book of the seventeenth century recounts "miracle" after "miracle" of Francis and the Franciscans only to show their ultimate foolishness. One sample miracle account reads this way:

> Frier Francis, in celebrating of mass, found a Spider in the Cup, which he would not cast away, but drank it off with the bloud, afterwards scratching his thigh, where he felt it itch, the Spider came out of his thigh without hurting the Frier.

And the interpretation reads this way:

Knave might have let this lie alone, for a Spider is not such poyson, as to deserve such a lie: For a cup of strong Wine without a Miracle is antidote enough against one (ALCORAN, pp. 59–60).

G. K. Chesterton, whose own book on Francis shows a deep level of personal understanding of his life, summarizes the many possible perspectives from which to write a modern life of St. Francis. Contrasting the viewpoints of the academics with those of the faithful, he writes: "A materialist may not care whether the inconsistencies are reconciled or not. A Catholic may not see any inconsistencies to reconcile." In his book, Chesterton opts for a perspective that is "sympathetic but skeptical," an approach similar to that of Sabatier.

Clearly, Sabatier loved his subject. But also as clearly, Sabatier was a thoroughly modern man who wanted to satisfy his own modern curiosities about miracles, influences, and conflict in Francis's life. The result is an engaging and fascinating portrait. Whereas, as Chesterton says—"Renan and Matthew Arnold were content to follow Francis with their praises until they were stopped by their prejudices"—Sabatier follows our subject throughout his extraordinary life, in all of its perplexities. It is Sabatier's passion for Francis that reassures us as we read his critical approach to the saint's life.

Sabatier became the leader, after a decade or so of mixed reaction, of a renaissance of interest in Francis. He corresponded with hundreds of students, readers, and scholars in several languages. He spent his last years back in the Cevennes in a villa near Chabrillanoux. At Sabatier's death in 1928, the Boston Public Library purchased his library from his widow. The 1931 volume of *More Books: The Bulletin of the Boston Public Library* announced the addition of the collection, summarizing the importance of Sabatier's *Life of St. Francis of Assisi*:

Sabatier's book brought back the reality of the "Little Poor Man" to multitudes. Once more, that strange figure in a small Italian town, who took upon himself to live the life of Christ and who succeeded in it better than any other person before or since, was before the public. Instead of the founder of a religious Order, Francis of Assisi became again "the jongleur of God"; a man who hated money and all other possessions, who prostrated himself before the meanest leper—who was so drunken with love and compassion for Christ that he could not distinguish his joy from his tears (BPL, p. 273).

No reader will understand the life of St. Francis without first understanding that religion—especially Francis's very personal faith—is to be understood intimately. Again, to use a phrase from Chesterton (because he is so accurate in these matters), "it is only the most personal passion that provides here an approximate earthly parallel" to understanding the life of Francis.

The primary difficulty that remains for any reader about to encounter Francis for the first time is this: Was Francis *real* in the sense that his life can have any relationship to the meaning of my own? I hope, at least for my own sake, that the answer is increasingly "yes." Francis's spirit lives on in extraordinary people today. Standing as we do with the benefit of hindsight, the similarities between the little poor man from Assisi and other notable spiritual figures, such as Mahatma Gandhi, for instance, are many. Despite different religious underpinnings, we can almost see Francis when we see photographs of the sandled, loin-clothed Gandhi negotiating with the rulers of Europe. In other contexts, Francis has been compared to Dorothy Day, founder of the Catholic Worker movement in twentieth-century America, and Mother Teresa of Calcutta, just to name a few. We each have the capacity to be a saint like him; Francis certainly believed so.

I hope that this book will serve as an informational and engaging introduction to the life of St. Francis for the reader interested in his life for the first time. But more important, I hope that *The Road to Assisi* will be a vehicle for you, the reader, to engage personally with Francis, the human being. As Nikos Kazantzakis summarized the meaning of Francis's life in the Prologue to his novel on the saint, each of us has "the obligation to transubstantiate the matter which God entrusted to us, and turn it into spirit."

What keeps the life and message of St. Francis from moving us to action? What keeps it from moving me to action, to change my life to be more like him? These questions are similar to those of art historian James Elkins, in the preface to his engaging book *Pictures & Tears*. Elkins wants to understand why art does not more easily "move" us. Allow me to quote one long paragraph in conclusion, with the hope that the parallels will be obvious:

> Our lack of intensity [in viewing paintings] is a fascinating problem. I'd like to understand why it seems normal to look at astonishing achievements made by unapproachably ambitious, luminously pious, strangely obsessed artists, and toss them off with a few wry comments. . . . What does it mean to say that you love paintings (and even spend your life living among them, as professionals do) and still feel so little? If paintings are so important—worth so much, reproduced, cherished, and visited so often—then isn't it troubling that we can hardly make emotional contact with them? (ELKINS, p. IX)

THE
ANNOTATED LIFE
OF
ST. FRANCIS OF ASSISI

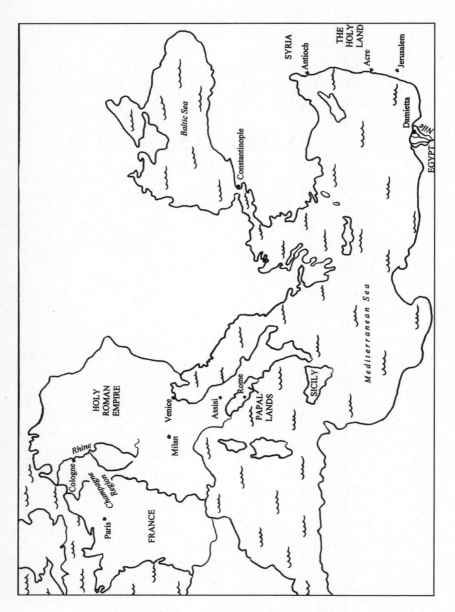

Italy, Central Europe, and The Holy Land ca. 1200 C.E.

CHAPTER ONE
His Youth and Family

Assisi is today very much what it was six or seven hundred years ago. The feudal castle is in ruins, but the aspect of the city is just the same. Its long-deserted streets, bordered by ancient houses, lie in terraces halfway up the steep hillside. Above it Mount Subasio proudly towers, at its feet lies outspread all the Umbrian plain from Perugia to Spoleto. The crowded houses clamber up the rocks like children a-tiptoe to see all that is to be seen; they succeed so well that every window gives the whole panorama set in its frame of rounded hills, from the summits of which castles and villages stand sharply out against a sky of incomparable purity.

He was born about 1182. The biographies have preserved to us few details about his parents. His father, Peter Bernardone, was a wealthy cloth-merchant. We know how different was the life of the merchants of that period from what it is today. A great portion of their time was spent in extensive journeys for the purchase of goods. Such tours were little short of expeditions. The roads being insecure, a strong escort was needed for the journey to those famous fairs where, for long weeks at a time, merchants from the most remote parts of Europe were gathered together.

Among all these merchants the richest were those who dealt in textile stuffs. They were literally the bankers of the time, and their

Sabatier's life of Francis was originally published in 1894. If written today, his first sentence would read: "Assisi is today very much what it was more than eight hundred years ago."

The original Assisan castle was built around the time of Charlemagne, who first razed, and then rebuilt, Assisi. When Francis was a teenager, a horde of Assisans stormed the castle, associated as it was with despotic power (whoever invaded or ruled Assisi took possession of it), and destroyed most of it. One hundred and seventy years later, the new rocca was completed. The castle was once called Rocca d'Assisi, the fortress of Assisi, and today, Rocca Maggiore ("larger castle").

Mount Subasio (4,230 ft.) gives foundation to the ancient city of Assisi. Most of the beautiful pink, grey, and white limestone of the Assisan buildings was originally quarried from Subasio. A national park sits atop Subasio today; tourists often climb to the top for the spectacular views.

heavy wagons were often laden with the sums levied by the popes in England or France. Bernardone often made these long journeys; he went even as far as France, and by this we must surely understand Northern France, and particularly Champagne, which was the seat of commercial exchange between Northern and Southern Europe.

He was not there at the very time of his son's birth. The mother, presenting the child at the font of San Rufino, had him baptized by the name of John, but the father on his return chose to call him Francis. Perhaps, indeed, the name was only a sort of grateful homage tendered by the Assisan burgher to his noble clients beyond the Alps.

Merchants, indeed, played a considerable part in the religious movements of the thirteenth century. Their calling in some sense forced them to become colporters of ideas. What else could they do, on arriving in a country, but answer those who asked for news? And the news most eagerly looked for was religious news, for people's minds were turned upon very different subjects than they are now. They accommodated themselves to the popular wish, observing, hearkening everywhere, keeping eyes and ears open, glad to find anything to tell, and little by little many of them became active propagandists of ideas concerning which at first they had been simply curious.

The importance of the part played by the merchants as they came

---

Not all of the medieval popes were located in Rome. From 1309 to 1377, the kings of England and France defied the Church in Rome and established a succession of seven popes who ruled from Avignon, in France. This was followed by "The Great Schism," when, from 1378 to 1417, two, and during one period, three, popes ruled, supported by differing factions of the Church.

Champagne is not just a bubbly wine. (Although it was at the Abbey of Saint-Pierre, in the province of Champagne, that Dom Perignon, Benedictine monk, invented bottled champagne in the early 1700s.) Champagne became a part of France about 90 years after Francis's death. As Sabatier mentions, for almost 200 years, beginning around 1150—or, at about the time of Peter Bernardone's birth—Champagne was the international center of European trade. Not far from Paris to the west, or the German cities of Mainz and Cologne to the east, the province of Champagne in northeastern France also sat strategically on the main north-south trade route between Flanders, on the North Sea, and the cities in the north of Italy. Merchants would gather from all over Europe, guaranteed safe travel by the counts of Champagne, to trade with each other; these sessions would last for as long as two months at a stretch.

and went, everywhere sowing the new ideas that they had gathered up in their travels, has not been put in a clear enough light. They were often, unconsciously and quite involuntarily, the carriers of ideas of all kinds, especially of heresy and rebellion. It was they who made the success of the Waldensians, the Albigensians, the Humiliati, and many other sects.

Thus Bernardone, without dreaming of such a thing, became the artisan of his son's religious vocation. The tales that he brought home from his travels seemed at first, perhaps, not to have aroused the child's attention, but they were like germs a long time buried, which suddenly, under a warm ray of sunlight, bring forth unlooked-for fruit.

The boy's education was not carried very far; the school was in those days overshadowed by the church. The priests of San Giorgio were his teachers, and they taught him a little Latin. This language was spoken in Umbria until toward the middle of the thirteenth century; every one understood it and spoke it a little; it was still the language of sermons and of political deliberations.

He learned also to write, but with less success; all through his life we see him take up the pen only on rare occasions, and for but a few words. In general he dictated, signing his letters by a simple T, the symbol of the cross of Jesus.

The part of his education destined to have the most influence on his life was the French language, which he may have spoken in his family. It has been rightly said that to know two languages is to have two souls. In learning the language of France the boy felt his heart thrill to the melody of its youthful poetry, and his imagination was mysteriously stirred with dreams of imitating the exploits of the French cavaliers.

His father's profession and the possibly noble origin of his mother raised him almost to the level of the titled families of the country. Money, which he spent with both hands, made him welcome among them. Pleased to enjoy themselves at his expense, the young nobles paid him a sort of court. As to Bernardone, he was too happy to see his son associating with them to be overly concerned as to the means. He was miserly, as the course of this story will show, but his pride and self-conceit exceeded his avarice.

Pica, his wife, a gentle and modest woman, about whom the biographers have always been too silent, would not despair of her son. When the neighbors told her of Francis's escapades, she would calmly reply: "I am very sure that, if it pleases God, Francis will become a good Christian." The words were natural enough from a mother's lips, but later on they were held to have been truly prophetic.

The son of Bernardone not only patterned himself after the young men of his age, he made it a point of honor to exceed them. With eccentricities, buffooneries, pranks, and prodigalities, he ended by achieving a sort of celebrity. He was forever in the streets with his companions, compelling attention by his extravagant or fantastic attire. Even at night the joyous company kept up their merrymakings, causing the town to ring with their noisy songs.

At this very time the troubadours were roaming over the towns of northern Italy and bringing brilliant festivities and especially Courts of Love into vogue. If they worked upon the passions, they also appealed to feelings of courtesy and delicacy; it was this that saved Francis. In the midst of his excesses he was always refined and considerate, carefully abstaining from every base or indecent utterance.

Already his chief aspiration was to rise above the commonplace. Tortured with the desire for that which is far off and high, he had conceived a sort of passion for chivalry, and fancying that dissipation was one of the distinguishing features of nobility, he had thrown himself into it with all his soul.

But he who, at twenty, goes from pleasure to pleasure with the heart not absolutely closed to good, must now and then, at some turning of the road, become aware that there are hungry folk who could live a month on what he spends in a few hours on frivolity. Francis saw them, and with his impressionable nature for the moment forgot everything else. In thought he put himself in their place, and it sometimes happened that he gave them all the money he had about him and even his clothes.

One day he was busy with some customers in his father's shop, when a man came in, begging for charity in the name of God. Losing his patience Francis sharply turned him away; but quickly reproaching himself for his harshness he thought, "What would I not have done if this man had asked something of me in the name of a count or a baron? What ought I not to have done when he came in the name of God? I am no better than a clown!" Leaving his customers he ran after the beggar.

Bernardone had been pleased with his son's commercial aptitude in the early days when the young man was first in his father's employ. Francis was only too proficient in spending money, but at least he knew well how to make it. But this satisfaction did not last long. Francis's companions were exercising a most pernicious influence over him. The time came when he could no longer endure to be separated from them; if he heard their call, nothing could keep him; he would leave everything and go after them.

All this time political events were hurrying on in Umbria and Italy. The rivalries between cities were strong, and Perugia, Assisi's neighbor to the west, was at this time at the apogee of its power, having already made many efforts to reduce Assisi to submission. It declared war on Assisi in 1202. An encounter took place in the plain about halfway between the two cities, not far from *Ponte San Giovanni*. Assisi was defeated, and Francis, who was in the ranks, was made prisoner.

The treachery of the nobles was not universal; a few had fought along with the people. It was with them and not with the *popolani* ("common people") that Francis, in consideration of the nobility of his manners, passed the time of his captivity, which lasted an entire year. He greatly astonished his companions by his

St. Bonaventure (c. 1220–1274), the most important of the second generation of Franciscans, adds this to the story: "But speedily recollecting himself, (Francis) ran after the poor man, charitably relieved his wants, and made a solemn promise to God that, from that day forth, he would never refuse alms to any that should ask them of him for the love of God."

Francis later turned his secular passion for the poetry of the troubadours to God's service. "All through the thirteenth [century], we find an increasing flood of popular religious works, competing...directly with the ordinary minstrel.... St. Francis had told his disciples to be God's gleemen—joculatores Dei. He himself is recorded to have preached one of his most remarkable sermons from the text of a French love-song: and one of his early disciples, Brother Henry of Pisa, resolved that 'the Devil should not have all the best tunes', and turned current love-songs into hymns" (COULTON, p. 529).

———— ◦◉◦ ————

The two cities of Perugia and Assisi are only sixteen miles apart, separated by the Tiber River, which, in ancient times, also divided the Roman and Etruscan empires. Even today, different dialects are nurtured in Perugia and Assisi, even though the Romans defeated the Etruscans in 283 B.C.E.

————————

When you read the actual writings of Francis, it is striking how he never talks about life before his conversion. Other famous saints in history refer often to their pre-converted lives—Augustine of Hippo and Teresa of Avila, for example. In contrast, the only references we have to Francis's early life are told by his biographers, beginning with Thomas of Celano. We also have accounts that originated as stories told and retold by those who knew him firsthand. Chronologically speaking, the first of these occurs in "When Francis and Rufino Preached in Their Breeches to the People of Assisi," a story collected in The Little Flowers of Saint Francis *and translated below on pages 168-169. It tells of an event that took place sometime between 1210-1215. After asking Brother Rufino to do something unnecessarily humiliating, Francis rebukes himself saying: "How did you become so bold, you, son of Bernardone, vile wretch? Brother Rufino was one of the most noble gentlemen in all of Assisi before he joined your small order, and you sent him there to preach to the people like a madman?" Francis then strips himself and makes his way to join his friend and fellow friar. The story offers little information about the saint's past, but communicates an important insight into how Francis regarded his previous station in life.*

———— ◦◉◦ ————

lightness of heart. Very often they thought him almost crazy. Instead of passing his time in wailing and cursing he made plans for the future, about which he was glad to talk to any one who came along. His fancy life was something that the songs of the troubadours had painted; he dreamed of glorious adventures, and always ended by saying: "You will see that one day I shall be adored by the whole world."

A compromise was finally arrived at between the counts and the people of Assisi. The agreement being made, the prisoners detained at Perugia were released, and Francis returned to Assisi. He was twenty-two years old.

CHAPTER TWO

Stages of Conversion
(Spring 1204–Spring 1206)

On his return to Assisi Francis at once resumed his former mode of life; perhaps he even tried in some degree to make up for lost time. Fetes, games, festivals, and dissipations began again. He did his part in them so well that he soon fell gravely ill. For long weeks he looked death so closely in the face that the physical crisis brought about a moral one.

Thomas of Celano (a companion of Francis who was also his first biographer) has preserved for us an incident of Francis's convalescence. He was regaining strength little by little and had begun to go about the house, when one day he felt a desire to walk abroad, to contemplate nature quietly, and so take hold again of life. Leaning on a stick he bent his steps toward the city gate.

The nearest one, called *Porta Nuova*, is the very one which opens upon the finest scenery. Immediately on passing through it you find yourself in the open country; a fold of the hill hides the city and cuts off every sound that might come from it. Before you lies the winding road to Foligno; at the left the imposing mass of Mount Subasio; at the right the Umbrian plain with its farms, its villages, its cloudlike hills, on whose slopes pines, cedars, oaks, the vine, and the olive-tree shed abroad an incomparable brightness and animation. The whole country sparkles with beauty.

Assisi is approximately 0.7 miles in length and half as wide, with the Basilica di San Francesco at the northwest end and the road to Foligno and Spoleto at the southeast. The medieval castle, Rocca Maggiore, stands on the north center edge, and the city gate of Porta Nuova at the southeastern.

Francis had hoped by this sight to recover the delicious sensations of his youth. With the sharpened sensibility of the convalescent he breathed in the odors of the springtime, but springtime did not come to his heart, as he had expected. Nature had for him only a message of sadness. He had believed that the breezes of this beloved countryside would carry away the last shudders of the fever,

21

and instead he felt in his heart a discouragement a thousandfold more painful than any physical illness. The miserable emptiness of his life suddenly appeared before him; he was terrified at his solitude, the solitude of a great soul in which there is no altar.

Memories of the past assailed him with intolerable bitterness. Seized with a disgust of himself, he found that his former ambitions seemed to him ridiculous or despicable. Francis went home overwhelmed with the weight of a new suffering.

In such hours of moral anguish we seek a refuge either in love or in faith. By a holy violence he was to arrive at last at a pure and virile faith, but the road to this point was long and sown thick with obstacles, and at the moment at which we have arrived he had not yet entered upon it; he did not even suspect its existence. All he knew was that pleasure leads to nothingness, to satiety and self-contempt.

He knew this, and yet he was about to throw himself once more into a life of pleasure. The body is so weak, so prone to return to the old paths, that it seeks them of itself the moment an energetic will does not stop it. Though no longer under any illusion with respect to it, Francis returned to his former life. Was he trying to divert his mind, to forget that day of bitter thought? We might suppose so, seeing the ardor with which he threw himself into his new projects.

An opportunity offered itself for him to realize his dreams of glory. A knight of Assisi, perhaps one of those who had been in captivity with him at Perugia, was preparing to go to Apulia under orders from "the gentle count" of Brienne, who was in the

Apulia is the region of Italy that resembles an index finger pointing east into the Adriatic Sea. During Francis's time, thousands of Crusaders visited Apulia and its many abbeys, churches, and relics before setting sail for the Holy Land from its coastal villages.

A recent biographer explains more about Walter of Brienne: "He had rescued Queen Sibila of Sicily from her imprisonment by the Germans in Alsace. With the King of France's blessing he had then sworn to recover her kingdom, which included Apulia on the mainland, and married her daughter. In approval of the enterprise Innocent III had created Walter Count of Lecce and Prince of Taranto. It was precisely the kind of career that Francis dreamed of for himself" (HOUSE, p. 45).

Innocent III was one of the most powerful of the medieval popes. Elected at the young age of 37, he ruled from 1198 to 1216.

south of Italy fighting on the side of Innocent III. Walter's renown was immense all through the Peninsula; he was held to be one of the most gallant knights of the time. Francis's heart bounded with joy; it seemed to him that at the side of such a hero he would soon cover himself with glory. His departure was decided upon, and he gave himself up, without reserve, to his joy.

He made his preparations with ostentatious prodigality. His equipment, of a princely luxury, soon became the universal subject of conversation. It was all the more talked about because the chief of the expedition, ruined perhaps by the revolution of 1202 or by the expenses of a long captivity, was constrained to order things much more modestly. Francis's companions were doubtless not slow to feel chafed by his ways and to promise themselves to make him cruelly expiate them. As for him, he perceived nothing of the jealousies that he was exciting, and night and day thought only of his future glory.

The day of departure arrived at last. Francis on horseback, the little buckler of a page on his arm, bade adieu to his natal city with joy, and with the little troop took the road to Spoleto which winds around the base of Mount Subasio.

What happened next? The documents do not say. They confine themselves to reporting that that very evening Francis had a vision, after which he decided to return to Assisi. It might not be far from the truth to conjecture that once on the way the young nobles took their revenge on the son of Bernardone for his princely airs. At twenty years old one hardly pardons things such as these.

Arriving at Spoleto, Francis took to his bed. A fever was consuming him; in a few hours he had seen all his dreams crumble away. The very next day he took the road back to Assisi.

So unexpected a return made a great stir in the little city, and was a cruel blow to his parents. As for

There were five primary types of travelers at this time in Europe: knights and royal communicants, religious men and women visiting other towns and provinces, sincere pilgrims, merchants, and a growing number of mischievous wanderers. Francis's enthusiasm might have been somewhat of the latter sort, which was increasingly of trouble for the late medieval Church. "By the beginning of the thirteenth century repeated canons directed against impostors, wandering scholars, and other ribalds . . . showed that restlessness had become the curse of Christendom" (WHICHER, p. 221).

doubled his charities to the poor and sought to keep
om society, but the old companions came flocking about
rom all quarters, hoping to find in him once more the tireless
purveyor of their idle wants. He let them have their way.

Nevertheless a great change had taken place in Francis.
Neither pleasures or work could hold his attention for long. He
spent a portion of his days in long country rambles, often accompanied
by a friend very different from the
ones he had known up until now. The
name of this friend is not known, but
some indications suggest that it may
have been Bombarone da Beviglia, the
future Brother Elias.

Francis now went back to
reflecting as at the time of his recovery, but with less bitterness. His own
heart and his friend agreed that it is
not possible to trust either in pleasure
or in glory and yet still find worthy
causes to which to consecrate one's
life. It is at this moment that religious
thought seems to have awakened in him. From the moment that
Francis saw this new way of life his desire to run in it had all the fiery
impetuosity that he put into all his actions.

In 1221, after their return from Syria, Francis appointed Brother Elias vicar of the Franciscan Order. Elias was present at Francis's death five years later, in October 1226, and it was Elias who, in large part, championed the speedy canonization of Francis and was responsible for the building of the basilica to house the body of the saint. Controversy surrounded Elias's leadership of the Order. (See MOORMAN, *chap. 10.)*

He was continually calling upon his friend and leading
him apart into the most sequestered paths. Often Francis directed
his steps to a grotto in the country near Assisi, which he entered
alone. This rocky cave concealed in the midst of the olive trees
became for faithful Franciscans that which Gethsemane is for all
Christians. Here Francis relieved his overcharged heart by heavy
groans. Sometimes, seized with a real horror for the disorders of his
youth, he would implore mercy, but most of the time his face was
turned toward the future. Feverishly Francis sought for that higher
truth to which he longed to dedicate himself, that pearl of great
price of which the Gospel speaks: "For everyone who asks receives,
and everyone who searches finds, and for everyone who knocks, the
door will be opened" (Mt. 7:8).

When he came out after long hours of seclusion, the pallor of his countenance and the painful tension of his features told plainly enough of the intensity of his asking and the violence of his knocks. The "inward man," to borrow the language of the mystics, was not yet formed in Francis, but it needed only the occasion to bring about the final break with the past. The occasion soon presented itself.

His friends were continually making efforts to induce him to take up old habits again. One day he invited them all to a sumptuous banquet. They thought they had conquered, and as in old times they proclaimed him king of the revels. The feast was prolonged far into the night and at its close the guests rushed out into the streets, which they filled with song and uproar. Suddenly they saw that Francis was no longer with them. After long searching, at last they discovered him far behind them, still holding in his hand his sceptre of king of misrule, but plunged in so profound a reverie that he seemed to be riveted to the ground and unconscious of all that was going on.

"What is the matter with you?" they cried, bustling about him as if to awaken him.

"Don't you see that he is thinking of taking a wife?" said one.

"Yes," answered Francis, arousing himself and looking at them with a smile that they did not recognize. "I am thinking of taking a wife more beautiful, more rich, more pure than you could ever imagine."

This reply marks a decisive stage in his inner life. By it he cut the last links that bound him to trivial pleasures. It remains for us to see through what struggles he was to give himself to God, after having torn himself free from the world. His friends probably understood nothing of all that had taken place, but he had become aware of the abyss that was opening between them and him. They soon accepted the situation.

No longer having any reason for caution, Francis gave up more than

One contemporary spiritual writer portrays the almost-converted Francis this way: "He had not yet attained to that inwardness of spirit that would enable him to make a fundamental decision about himself: that he had no choice but to lead the life of a homeless ascetic, a celestial wanderer. What lay ahead for him was not the cloistered life of a monk, or the privileged preserve of a bishop, but that of a perpetual outsider" (COWAN, p. 37).

ever to a passion for solitude. If he often wept over his past dissipations and wondered how he could have lived so long without tasting the bitterness of the dregs of the enchanted cup, he never allowed himself to be overwhelmed with vain regrets.

The poor had remained faithful to him. They gave him an admiration that he knew himself to be unworthy of, but that nevertheless had an infinite sweetness. The future grew bright to him in the light of their gratitude, of the timid, trembling affection that they dared not utter but that his heart revealed to him. Francis promised himself to do all he could to deserve it.

To understand these feelings one must understand the condition of the poor in a place such as Assisi. In an agricultural country poverty does not, as elsewhere, almost inevitably involve moral destitution, that degeneration of the entire human being that renders charity so difficult. Most of the poor people whom Francis knew were in straits because of war, of bad harvests, or of illness. In such cases material succor is but a small part. Sympathy is the thing needed above all. Francis had treasures of it to lavish on them.

As yet no influence strictly ecclesiastic had been felt by Francis. Doubtless there was in his heart the leaven of Christian faith that enters one's being without awareness, but the interior transformation that was going on in him was as yet the fruit of his own intuition. But this period was drawing to a close.

Francis was becoming calm by degrees, finding in the contemplation of nature joys that up to this time he had sipped only hastily, almost unconsciously, and of which he was now learning to relish the flavor. He drew from them not just soothingly; in his heart he felt

"...the interior transformation that was going on in him was as yet the fruit of his own intuition": A curious phrase from Sabatier, who appears to suggest that this was a period of time when Francis was preparing to be a mystic prior to his thorough "conversion." Bonaventure—who was prone to see God's deliberate hand in every event—says it this way: "Throughout all the time of which we have thus spoken, this great servant of God had neither master nor teacher to guide or instruct him, save only Christ our Lord, who, in addition to the gifts already bestowed upon him, was pleased now to visit him with the sweet consolations of His divine grace." For both Sabatier and Bonaventure, these actions of Francis were a prologue to a greater and more complete conversion soon to come.

new compassions springing to life, and with these the desire to act, to give himself, to cry aloud to these cities perched upon the hilltops, threatening as warriors who eye one another before the fray, that they should be reconciled and love one another.

Certainly, at this time Francis had no glimpse of what he was to become; but these hours are perhaps the most important in the evolution of his thought; it is to them that his life owes that air of liberty, that perfume of the fields that make it as different from the piety of the sacristy as from that of the drawing room.

The Umbrian region of Italy features many cities—like Assisi, Spoleto, Montefalco, and Gubbio—built on hilltops. It can be difficult to travel by train in Umbria, as the stations are often located in the valleys, sometimes two or three miles from the historic center of town; those walks, on hot summer afternoons, are not for the faint of heart.

About this time Francis made a pilgrimage to Rome, whether to ask the counsel of friends, as a penance imposed by a confession, or from a mere impulse, no one knows. Perhaps he thought that in a visit to the Holy Apostles, as people said then, he should find the answers to all the questions that he was asking himself.

This journey was marked by an important incident. Many a time when succoring the poor he had asked himself if he himself would be able to endure poverty. No one knows the weight of a burden until he has carried it, at least for a moment, upon his own shoulders. He desired to know what it is like to have nothing and to depend for bread upon the charity or the caprice of the passerby.

"...a visit to the Holy Apostles": The relics of the Apostles Peter and Paul are held, respectively, in the tombs of the Vatican and the Ostian Way, in the southernmost part of Rome. Even today, Rome is often referred to as "the city of the Apostles Peter and Paul." Visitors to the city today must see the historic Church of Santa Maria del Popolo where hang two great paintings of Caravaggio side-by-side: The Crucifixion of St. Peter and The Fall of Saul (1601–02).

There were swarms of beggars crowding the Piazza before the great basilica. He borrowed the rags of one of them, lending him his garment in exchange, and a whole day he stood there, fasting, with outstretched hand. The act was a great victory, the triumph of compassion over natural pride. Returning to Assisi, he doubled his kindnesses to those of whom he had truly the right to call himself the brother. With such sentiments he could not long escape the influence of the Church.

"... the Piazza": The plaza surrounding St. Peter's Basilica in Rome.

On all the roadsides in the environs of the city there were then, as now, numerous chapels. Very often Francis must have heard mass in these rustic sanctuaries, alone with the celebrant. Recognizing the tendency of simple natures to bring home to themselves everything that they hear, it is easy to understand his emotion and agitation when the priest, turning toward him, would read the Gospel for the day. The Christian ideal was revealed to him, bringing an answer to his secret anxieties. And when, a few moments later, he would plunge into the forest, all his thoughts would be with the poor carpenter of Nazareth, who placed himself in his path, saying, "Follow me."

Nearly two years had passed since the day that he felt the first shock, the first wave of his conversion. A life of renunciation now appeared to Francis as the goal of his efforts, but he felt that his spiritual novitiate was not yet ended. He suddenly experienced a bitter assurance of that fact.

He was riding on horseback one day, his mind more than ever possessed with the desire to lead a life of absolute devotion, when at a turn of the road he found himself face to face with a leper. The frightful malady had always inspired in him an invincible repulsion. He could not control a movement of horror, and by instinct he turned his horse in another direction.

But if the shock had been severe, the defeat was complete. Francis reproached himself bitterly; retracing his steps and springing from his horse he gave to the astounded sufferer all the money that he had, then kissed his hand as he would have done to a priest. This new victory marked a new era in his spiritual life.

It is far indeed from hatred of evil to love of good. They are more numerous than we think who, after some severe experience, have renounced what the ancient liturgies call "the world," with its pomps and lusts. But the greater number of those who have renounced the world have not at the bottom of their hearts the smallest grain of pure love. In vulgar souls disillusion leaves only a frightful egoism.

Francis's "Testament" is the last of his writings, composed just before his death in 1226. It is also our primary source for knowing about the events in Francis's life that he believed to be most formative. How striking, then, that the opening paragraph of his "Testament" reads:

> *The Lord gave me, Brother Francis, the ability to do penance in the following way: When I was in sin, even the sight of lepers was like acid to me. But the Lord himself led me among them. When I left, all that had been so acidic to me was turned into sweetness in my soul and my body. And shortly afterward, I got up and left the world.* (FRANCIS, p. 96).

Francis was certainly not alone in his revulsion toward lepers. The medieval response to the disease was inherited from ancient days going back to the biblical book of Leviticus, chapter 13. In Francis's time, local priests performed a ceremony in which the priest would recite: "I forbid you to enter church, monastery, fair, mill, marketplace or tavern. . . . I forbid you ever to leave your house without your leper's costume . . . to live with any woman other than your own . . . to touch a well, or well cord, without your gloves . . . to touch children, or to give them anything . . . to eat or drink, except with lepers" (DAVIES, pp. 279–80).

CHAPTER THREE
The Church About 1209—Part One

St. Francis was inspired as much as any person may be, but it would be a palpable error to study him apart from his age and from the conditions in which he lived. We know that he desired and believed his life to be an imitation of Jesus, but what we know about the Christ is in fact so little, that St. Francis's life loses none of its strangeness for that. His conviction that he was but an imitator preserved him from all temptation to pride, and enabled him to proclaim his views with incomparable vigor without seeming in the least to be preaching himself.

We must therefore not isolate Francis from external influences or show him too dependent on them. During the period of his life at which we have now arrived, 1205–1206, the religious situation of Italy must more than at any other time influenced his thought and urged him into the path that he finally entered.

The morals of the clergy were as corrupt as ever, rendering any serious reform impossible. If some among the heresies of the time were pure and without reproach, many were trivial and impure. Here and there a few voices were raised in protest, but the prophecies of Joachim of Fiore had no more power than those of St. Hildegard to put a stop to wickedness. The *little poor man*, driven away, cast out of doors by the creatures of Innocent III, saved Christianity.

We cannot here make a thorough study of the state of the Church at the beginning of the thirteenth century; it will suffice to trace some of its most prominent features.

Sabatier does not exaggerate about the abuses in the Church of the twelfth and thirteenth centuries. The secular clergy were a frequent object of reformist derision. St. Anthony of Padua wrote around the time of Francis's death that they "flay the faithful by forced offerings, whereon they fatten their horses, their foals, and the sons of their concubines" (COULTON 2, p. 428).

The first glance at the secular clergy brings into startling prominence the ravages of simony; the traffic in ecclesiastical places was carried on with boundless audacity, and benefices were put up to the highest bidder. The bishops, for their part, found a thousand methods, often most out of keeping with their calling, for extorting money from the simple priests. Violent, quarrelsome, contentious, they were held up to ridicule in popular ballads from one end of Europe to the other. As to the priests, they bent all their powers to accumulate benefices and secure inheritances from the dying, stooping to the most despicable measures for providing for their bastards.

The monastic orders were hardly more reputable. A great number of these had sprung up in the eleventh and twelfth centuries; their reputation for sanctity soon stimulated the liberality of the faithful, and thus fatally brought about their own decadence.

The clergy, though no longer respected, still overawed the people through the superstitious terror of their power. Here and there might have been perceived many a forewarning of direful revolts. The roads to Rome were crowded with monks hastening to claim the protection of the Holy See against the people among whom they lived. The pope would promptly declare an interdict, but it was not to be expected that such a resource would avail forever.

Yet we must not assume that all was corrupt in the bosom of the Church. Then, as always, the evil made more noise than the good, and the voices of those who desired a reformation aroused only passing interest.

At this time, in late medieval Europe, there were thousands of disenchanted youth, and others, who were in many cases university trained, traveling as vagabonds from city to city, writing lewd, humorous, and satirical verses in Latin in reaction to the Church and societal norms. These poets were generally called goliards, referring either to Goliath, the biblical giant slain by David, or to gula, the sin of gluttony. The movement was pervasive enough that St. Bernard of Clairvaux once referred to both Abelard, the controversial young theologian, and Arnold of Brescia (mentioned by Sabatier, below), both accused of heresy, as goliards. (See WHICHER.)

Jacques of Vitry, a thirteenth-century cardinal of the Church, tells an incredible story of a priest who was tired of the miserly habits of one of his flock who attended services each year only on Easter. The priest placed an old penny into the miser's mouth at communion, rather than a host. When the man asked about it afterwards, the priest persuaded him that God had changed the Eucharist into a penny as punishment for the man's lack of generosity. (See COULTON 2, p. 30.)

Among the populace there was superstition unimaginable. The pulpit, which ought to have shed abroad some little light, was as yet open only to the bishops, and the few pastors who did not neglect their duty in this regard accomplished very little, being too much absorbed in other duties. It was the birth of the mendicant orders that obliged the entire body of secular clergy to take up the practice of preaching.

"mendicant orders": Mendicant literally means "a beggar." Three mendicant orders were founded as reform movements in the thirteenth century—Franciscans, Dominicans, and Carmelites—emphasizing a vow to personal poverty and begging alms.

"secular clergy": Those who are ordained but do not follow a religious rule (as monks do). They are similar to what today we most often refer to as parish priests, as opposed to members of religious orders.

Public worship, reduced to liturgical ceremonies, no longer preserved anything that appealed to the intelligence; it was more and more becoming a sort of self-acting magic formula. Once upon this road, the absurd was not far distant. Those who deemed themselves pious told of miracles performed by relics with no need of aid from the moral act of faith.

In one case a parrot, being carried away by a kite, uttered the invocation dear to his mistress, "Sancte Thoma adiuva me," (St. Thomas, help me!) and was miraculously rescued. In another, a merchant of Groningen, having purloined an arm of St. John the Baptist, grew rich as if by enchantment so long as he kept it concealed in his house, but was reduced to begging as soon as, his secret being discovered, the relic was taken away from him and placed in a church.

These stories, we must observe, do not come from ignorant enthusiasts, hidden away in obscure country places; they are given us by one of the most learned monks of his time, who relates them to a novice by way of forming his mind!

"tohu-bohu": This odd anachronism is used to mean something similar to the Genesis account of the early Creation as "formless and void"—chaotic, confused.

The list of the heresies of the thirteenth century is already long, but it is increasing every day, to the great joy of those erudite ones who are making strenuous efforts to classify everything in that tohu-bohu of mysticism and folly.

In that day heresy was very much alive; it was consequently very complex and its powers of transformation infinite. In certain counties of England there are at the present day villages having as many as eight and ten places of worship for only a few hundred inhabitants. Many of these people change their denomination every three or four years, returning to one and then leaving it again, and so on, as long as they live. Their leaders set the example, throwing themselves enthusiastically into each new movement only to leave it before long. They would all find it difficult to give an intelligible reason for these changes. They say that the Spirit guides them, and it would be unfair to disbelieve them, but the historian who should investigate conditions like these would lose his head in the labyrinth unless he made a separate study of each of these Protean movements.

A great part of Christendom was in a somewhat similar condition under Innocent III. But while the sects of which I have just spoken move in a very narrow circle of dogmas and ideas, in the thirteenth century every sort of excess followed in rapid succession. Still, a few general characteristics may be observed.

In the first place, heresies were no longer metaphysical subtleties as in earlier days; Arius and Priscillian, Nestorius and Eutyches were dead indeed. In the second place, they no longer arose in the upper and governing class, but proceeded especially from the inferior clergy and the common people. The blows that actually threatened the Church of the Middle Ages were struck by obscure laboring men, by the poor and the oppressed, who in their wretchedness

Sabatier refers to four leaders of early heretical movements.

"Arius" (256–336): A priest from Alexandria, Egypt, he argued that Christ, the Son of God, was not co-eternal with God, the Father.

"Priscillian": A Spaniard who taught extreme asceticism based on his belief in the basic evil of all matter. He was burned at the stake for suspicion of witchcraft in Avila, 383.

"Nestorius" (c. 381–451): A Patriarch of Constantinople, he argued that Jesus Christ had two distinct natures, human and divine, which were voluntarily, not truly, united.

"Eutyches": The leader, or Archimandrite, of a large monastery near Constantiople, he was sent into exile after the Council of Chalcedon (451), at the age of seventy-three, for teaching that Christ possessed only one nature, not two, after the Incarnation.

"Humiliati": This odd group was an association of lay people who dressed plainly and practiced asceticism of various kinds, devoting themselves to charity. The Humiliati originated in Lombardy in the eleventh or early twelfth century. First approved by Innocent III in 1201, the Order witnessed the supression of its male branch in 1571 by a papal bull after one of its leaders attempted to murder an emissary of Pope Pius V who was charged with reforming it. There are still today some spiritual descendants of the Humiliati in Italy.

"Arnold of Brescia": A fascinating Italian monk who was active as a reformer before Francis's birth (d. 1155). Told to confine himself to a monastery, he refused and spoke out against abuses in the Church of his day. He preached about the sanctity of poverty and even challenged the exclusive right of priests to administer the sacraments and hear confessions. Eventually, Arnold was hanged by the Roman authorities, with the blessing of the Church, and his ashes were scattered over the Tiber River so that his followers would not venerate his bones.

"Waldensians": A reform movement from the twelfth and thirteenth centuries founded by Peter Waldo from the city of Lyons. The Waldensians, also called "the poor of Lyons," claimed to represent a true remnant who, from within, had been resisting the Catholic Church and attempting to reform it since the days of Constantine in the fourth century.

and degradation felt that she had failed in her mission. No sooner was a voice uplifted, preaching austerity and simplicity, than it drew together not only the laity, but members of the clergy as well.

Two great currents are apparent: on one side the Cathars, on the other, innumerable sects revolting from the Church by their very fidelity to Christianity and the desire to return to the primitive Church. Among the sects of the second category the close of the twelfth century saw in Italy the rise of the Poor Men, who without doubt were a part of the movement of Arnold of Brescia. They denied the efficacy of sacraments administered by unworthy hands. A true attempt at reform was made by the Waldensians. Their history, although better known, still remains obscure on certain sides. Their name, Poor Men of Lyons, recalls the former movement, with which they were in close agreement, as also with the Humiliati. All these names involuntarily suggest that by which St. Francis afterward called his Order.

The analogy between the inspiration of Peter Waldo, founder of the Waldensians, and that of St. Francis was so close that one might be tempted to believe the latter a sort of imitation of the former. But this would be a mistake: The same causes produced in all quarters the same effects; ideas of reform, of a return to Gospel poverty, were in the air, and this helps us to understand how it was that before many years the Franciscan preaching reverberated through the entire world. If at the outset the careers of these two men were alike, their later lives were very different. Waldo, driven into heresy almost in spite of himself, was obliged to accept the consequences of the premises that he himself had laid down, while Francis, remaining the obedient son of the Church, bent all his efforts to develop the inner life in himself and his disciples. It is indeed most likely that through his father Francis had become acquainted with the movement of the Poor of Lyons. Hence his oft-repeated counsels to his friars of the duty of submission to the clergy. When he went to seek the approbation of Innocent III, it is evident that the prelates with whom he had relations warned him, by the very example of Waldo, of the dangers inherent in his own movement.

Waldo had gone to Rome in 1179, accompanied by a few followers, to ask at the same time the approbation of their translation of the Scriptures into the venacular and the permission to preach. They were granted both requests on condition of gaining for their preaching the authorization of their local clergy. Walter Map (d. 1210), who was charged with their examination, was constrained, while ridiculing their simplicity, to admire their poverty and zeal for the apostolic life.

> "... while Francis, remaining the obedient son of the Church": It is important to realize that heresy is primarily a charge of insolence and disobedience, more so than a misinterpretation of doctrine. It is a question of challenging established order and authority.

Two or three years later they met a very different reception at Rome, and in 1184 they were anathematized by the Council of Verona. From that day nothing could stop them, even to the forming of a new Church. They multiplied with a rapidity hardly exceeded afterward by the Franciscans. By the end of the twelfth century we find them spread abroad from Hungary to Spain; the first attempts to hunt them down were made in the latter country. Other countries were at first satisfied with treating them as excommunicated persons.

Obliged to hide themselves, reduced to the impossibility of holding their chapters, which ought to have come together once or twice a year, and which, had they done so, might have maintained among them a certain unity of doctrine, the Waldensians rapidly underwent a change according to their environment. Some obstinately insisted upon calling themselves good Catholics; others went so far as to preach the overthrow of the hierarchy and the uselessness of sacraments. The multiplicity of differing and even hostile branches seemed to develop almost hourly. Under pretext of pilgrimages to Rome they were always on the road. The methods of travel of that day were peculiarly favorable to the diffusion of ideas. While retailing news to those whose hospitality they received, they would speak of the unhappy state of the Church and the reforms that were needed.

As a young child, St. Bonaventure was healed through Francis, and later became one of the first to record his legend. After Bonaventure's Life was written and distributed, the Chapter of Paris (1266), an official gathering of Franciscan leaders, ordered that all previous biographies of Francis be destroyed. The earlier lives of Francis written by Thomas of Celano were preserved only in certain Cistercian and Benedictine monastery libraries.

It was Bonaventure's life of Francis that inspired the great painter Giotto with the subject matter for twenty-eight fresco paintings depicting popular scenes from Francis's life. They can still be seen in the upper church of the Basilica di San Francesco in Assisi.

CHAPTER FOUR
The Church About 1209—Part Two

The most powerful and determined enemies of the Church were the Cathars. Sincere, audacious, often learned and keen in argument, having among them some choice spirits and people of great intellectual powers, they were the preeminent heretics of the thirteenth century. Their revolt did not bear upon points of detail and questions of discipline, like that of the early Waldensians; it had a definite doctrinal basis, taking issue with the whole body of Catholic dogma. But, although this heresy flourished in Italy and under the very eyes of St. Francis, there is need to discuss it only briefly. His work may have received many infiltrations from the Waldensian movement, but Catharism was wholly foreign to it.

This is naturally explained by the fact that St. Francis never consented to occupy himself with questions of doctrine. For him faith was not of the intellectual but the moral domain; it is the consecration of the heart. Time spent in dogmatizing appeared to him as time lost. The Cathars, then, had no direct influence upon St. Francis.

Catharist doctrine rested upon the antagonism of two principles, one bad, the other good. The first had created matter; the second, the soul, which, for generation after generation passes from one body to another until it achieves salvation. Matter is the cause and the seat of evil. All contact with it constitutes a blemish; consequently the Cathars renounced marriage and property and advocated suicide. All this was mixed up with the most complicated cosmological myths.

Perhaps the most telling example of the radical Catharist distinction between matter and spirit was in their depiction of the meaning of the cross of Christ. The Cathar cross, often depicted on tombstones in the regions of Languedoc and in the lands of the former Yugoslavia, is a thorough triumph of spirit over matter. An upright and serene Jesus is luminously shown to be as a tree of life, reaching toward heaven, moon, stars, or sunburst—the Land of Light—a triumph over the world of twisted, dark matter.

This dualism of the Cathars stood in stark contrast to Francis's joyful hymn, "The Canticle of the Sun" (also known as "The Canticle of the Creatures"), in which he praises the creation in each of the four basic elements from antiquity: water, air, fire, earth. (See chap. 20.)

With all his energy Innocent III had not been able to check this evil in the states of the Church. The case of Viterbo tells much of the difficulty of repressing it. In March 1199, the pope wrote to the clergy and people of this town to recall to their minds, and at the same time to increase, the penalties pronounced against heresy. For all that, the Patarini (as the Cathars were called in Italy) had the majority in 1205, and succeeded in naming one of themselves consul.

The wrath of the pontiff at this event was unbounded. He fulminated a bull menacing the city with fire and sword, and commanding the neighboring towns to throw themselves upon her if within a fortnight she had not given satisfaction. It was all in vain: the Patarini were dealt with only as a matter of form; it needed the presence of the pope himself to assure the execution of his orders and obtain the demolition of the houses of the heretics and their abettors (autumn of 1207).

Italy may well be grateful to St. Francis. He did not pause to demonstrate by syllogisms or theological theses the vanity of the Catharist doctrines; but he made a new ideal to shine out before the eyes of his contemporaries, an ideal before which all these fantastic sects vanished as birds of the night take flight at the first rays of the sun. A great part of St. Francis's power came to him thus through his systematic avoidance of polemics. The latter is always more or less a form of spiritual pride. It only deepens the chasm that it undertakes to fill up. Truth needs not to be proved; it is its own witness.

The only weapon that he would use against the wicked was the holiness of a life so full of love as to enlighten and revive those

"the Patarini": Sabatier explains in a footnote: *"The most current name in Italy [for the Cathars] was that of the Patarini, given them no doubt from their inhabiting the quarter of second-hand dealers in Milan:* la contrada dei Patari, *found in many cities.* Patari! *is still the cry of the ragpickers in the small towns of Provence. In the thirteenth century Patarino and Catharo were synonyms."* One of Sabatier's contemporaries explains further: *"In the sordid alleys of Milan, to which the degraded trades were consigned as to a ghetto, the booths of the sellers of old iron and rags, the bazaar of the Pataria, there thus sprang up an enthusiastic Christianity"* (GEBHART, p. 55). *Rags were raw material for making paper at this time. For whatever reason, this trade was common among the members of the Cathars.*

about him, and compel them to love. The disappearance of Catharism in Italy, without an upheaval, and above all without the Inquisition, is thus an indirect result of the Franciscan movement, and not the least important among them. At the voice of the Umbrian reformer Italy roused herself, recovered her good sense and fine temper. She cast out those doctrines of pessimism and death, as a robust organism casts out morbid substances.

But Francis was not immune to the influence of all heresy. As we discussed above, Francis's thought ripened in an atmosphere thoroughly saturated with the ideas of the Poor Men of Lyons. Unconsciously to himself they entered into his being. Similarly, the prophecies of one Calabrian abbot exerted upon St. Francis an influence more difficult to appreciate, but no less profound.

Sabatier explains in a footnote: "I do not assert that no trace of Catharism is to be found after the ministry of St. Francis, but it was no longer a force, and no longer endangered the very existence of the Church."

The direct influence of Francis was actually only one part of the struggle against the Cathars, who were prevalent in southern France and central and northern Italy at this time. Innocent III declared the fight against the Cathar heresy to be a true crusade in 1209, equivalent to the crusades to retake the Holy Land. St. Dominic founded the Dominican Order just a few years after the birth of the Franciscans in response to the growth of the Cathars. The Inquisition followed soon thereafter.

Standing on the confines of Italy and as it were at the threshold of Greece, Joachim of Fiore was the last link in a chain of monastic prophets who during nearly four hundred years succeeded one another in the monasteries and hermitages of southern Italy. The most famous among them had been St. Nilo, a sort of untamed John the Baptist living in desert places but suddenly emerging from them when his duties of maintaining the right called him elsewhere. We see him on one occasion appearing in Rome itself, to announce to pope and emperor the unloosing of the divine wrath.

"St. Nilo, a sort of untamed John the Baptist": Nilus of Calabria (c. 910–1005), of Greek descent, inspired by Athanasius's Life of St. Anthony, was remarkable for two things: his attempts to reform corruptions in Western monasteries through asceticism, and his unsuccessful efforts to reconcile Eastern (Byzantine) and Western (Benedictine) monasticism.

Scattered in the Alpine solitudes of the Basilicata region in southern Italy, these Calabrian hermits were continually obliged to retreat higher and higher into the mountains to escape the populace, who, pursued by pirates, were taking refuge there. They thus passed their lives between heaven and earth, with two seas for their horizon. Disquieted by fear of the corsairs and by the war-cries whose echoes reached even to them, they turned their thoughts toward the future. The ages of great terror are also the ages of great hope; it is to the captivity of Babylon that we owe, with the second part of Isaiah, the pictures of the future that have not yet ceased to charm the soul of humanity; Nero's persecutions gave us the Apocalypse of St. John, and the paroxysms of the twelfth century the eternal gospel.

Converted after a life of dissipation, Joachim of Fiore traveled extensively in the Holy Land, Greece, and Constantinople. Returning to Italy he began, though a layman, to preach in the outskirts of Rende and Cosenza. Later on he joined the Cistercians of Cortale, near Catanzaro, and there took vows. Shortly after being elected abbot of the monastery in spite of refusal and even flight, he was seized after a few years with the nostalgia of solitude, and sought from Pope Lucius III a discharge from his functions (1181), that he might consecrate all his time to the works that he had in mind. The pope granted his request and even permitted him to go wherever he might deem best in the interest of his work. Then began for Joachim a life of wandering from monastery to monastery that carried him even as far as Lombardy, to Verona, where we find him with Pope Urban III.

When he returned to the south, a group of disciples gathered around him to hear his explanations of the most obscure passages of the Bible. Whether he desired to or not he was obliged to receive them, to talk with them, to give them a Rule, and, finally, to install them in the very heart of the Sila, the Black Forest of Italy, over against the highest peak, in gorges where the silence is interrupted only by the murmurs of the Arno and the Neto, which have their source not far from there.

This new Athos received the name of Fiore (flower), transparent symbol of the hopes of its founder. It was there that he put the finishing touch to writings that, after fifty years of neglect, were

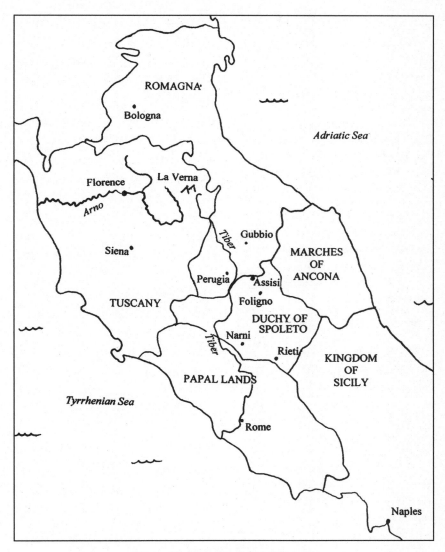

Central Italy in the Days of Francis

Joachim had a similar effect as that of Francis on his followers: "Joachim's one great interest was to study the prophecies; his one great pleasure to celebrate mass. During mass he was in a sort of ecstasy, his face (usually the colour of a dry leaf) became like that of an angel, and sometimes he wept. When he preached, the young monks gazed on his face as if he were an angel presiding over them, and when he knelt in prayer his countenance was aglow as if he looked upon Christ face to face" (SEDGWICK, vol. 1, p. 41).

Sabatier adds this note about "Sila, the Black Forest of Italy": "La Sila is a wooded mountain, situated eastward from Cosenza, which the peasants call Monte Nero. The summits are nearly 2,000 meters above the sea."

The allegorical method was a common and accepted method of biblical interpretation throughout the later Middle Ages. By this method, for instance, Meister Eckhart, a German Dominican mystic who lived a century after Francis, taught that the true meaning of Christmas was the mystical birth of God in human hearts. The allegorical method persists today, perhaps most commonly in interpretations of the Song of Songs as more than a beautiful story of human love; it is also an allegory of the intimacy possible in the Divine-human relationship.

to become the starting-point of all heresies, and the ailment of all souls burdened with the salvation of Christendom. The people of the first half of the thirteenth century, too much occupied with other things, did not perceive that the spiritual streams at which they were drinking descended from the snowy mountaintops of Calabria. It is always thus with mystical influences. There is in them something vague, tenuous, and penetrating that escapes an exact estimation.

He always remained riveted to the text, upon which he commented in the allegorical method, and by this method he brought out the most fantastic improbabilities. A few pages of his books would wear out the most patient reader, but in these fields, burnt over by theological arguments more drying than the winds of the desert, fields where one at first perceives only stones and thistles, one comes at last to the charming oasis, with repose and dreams in its shade.

The exegesis of Joachim of Fiore in fact led up to a sort of philosophy of history; its grand lines were calculated to make a striking appeal to the imagination. The life of humanity is divided into three periods: In the first, under the reign of the Father, humanity lived under the rigor of the law; in the second, reigned over by the Son, people live under the rule of grace; in the third, the Spirit will reign and humanity will live in the plenitude of love. The first is the period of servile obedience; the second, that of filial obedience; the third, that of liberty. In the first, people lived in fear; in the second, they rest in faith; in the third, they shall burn with love. The first saw the shining of the stars; the second sees the whitening of the dawn; the third will behold the glory of the day. The first produced nettles, the second gives roses, the third will be the age of lilies.

If now we consider that in the thought of Joachim the third period, the Age of the Spirit, was about to open, we will understand with what enthusiasm people hailed the words that restored joy to hearts still disturbed with millenarian fears.

It is evident that St. Francis knew these radiant hopes. Who knows even that it was not the Calabrian Seer who awoke his heart to its transports of love? If this be so, Joachim was not merely his precursor; he was his true spiritual father. However this may be, St. Francis found in Joachim's thought many of the elements that, unconsciously to himself, were to become the foundation of his institute.

The noble disdain that Francis shows for all people of learning, and that he sought to inculcate upon his Order, was for Joachim one of the characteristics of the new era. "The truth that remains hidden to the wise," he says, "is revealed to babes. Dialectics closes that which is open, obscures that which is clear; it is the mother of useless talk, of rivalries and blasphemy. Learning does not edify, and it may destroy, as is proved by the scribes of the Church, swollen with pride and arrogance, who by dint of reasoning fall into heresy."

This was the time when Europe's first great universities were first flourishing: in Bologna (Italy), Paris (France), and Oxford (England). Others soon sprouted throughout Europe, including Italy, even before Francis's death: Naples (1224), Padua (1222), Reggie, Siena, and others.

We have seen that the return to Gospel simplicity had become a necessity. All the heretical sects were on this point in accord with pious Catholics, but no one spoke in a manner so Franciscan as Joachim of Fiore. Not only did he make voluntary poverty one of the characteristics of the age of lilies, but he speaks of it in his pages with so profound, so living an emotion,

Why didn't Francis simply become a monk, when he heard God speak to him? That is an obvious question that is rarely asked. Here is an attempt at an answer: "The Legend of the Three Companions—written by friars Angelo, Leo, and Rufino almost twenty years before Bonaventure's official Life—tells us that it was this moment before the cross of San Damiano [see p. 47] that initiated Francis's identification with Christ, and in particular, with his Passion. Could it be that Francis was seeking a connection to the institutional Church when he prayed before icons in churches? Perhaps he wanted God to tell him what to do, how to be a Christian of true commitment, and he expected a different answer. Francis sought a connection, to be sure, but was it spiritual only, or ecclesiastical, as well? When he received his word from God, he did not run off and join a monastic order. That's an important piece of information.

"Joining the Benedictines or the Cistercians would have been the most logical thing for a young man to do in circumstances like Francis's, fresh from a private communication from God. But Francis knew, as did everyone at the time, of the massive corruption in the church. He began his work, instead, in a mendicant, reform tradition (epitomized by Peter Waldo and Joachim of Fiore a few decades earlier), only tangentially related at first to the Catholic Church. Francis left San Damiano with his mission in mind, and he plunged his hands in both pockets and gave every coin to the attendant priest, who happened to be nearby. He was on his first mission: to literally repair the fallen chapel." (SWEENEY, pp. 37–38).

that St. Francis could do little more than repeat his words. The ideal monk whom Joachim describes, whose only property is a lyre, is a true Franciscan before the letter, him of whom the *Poverello* of Assisi always dreamed.

The feeling of nature also bursts forth in him with incomparable vigor. One day he was preaching in a chapel that was plunged in almost total darkness, the sky being quite overcast with clouds. Suddenly the clouds broke away, the sun shone, and the church was flooded with light. Joachim paused, saluted the sun, intoned the *Veni Creator*, and led his congregation out to gaze upon the landscape.

It would be by no means surprising if toward 1205 Francis should have heard of this prophet, toward whom so many hearts were turning, this anchorite who, gazing up into heaven, spoke with Jesus as a friend talks with his friend, yet knew also how to come down to console people and warm the faces of the dying at his own breast.

Meanwhile, at the other end of Europe, in the heart of Germany, the same causes had produced the same effects. From the excess of the people's sufferings and the despair of religious souls was being born a movement of apocalyptic mysticism that seemed to have secret communication with the one that was rousing the Peninsula. They had the same views of the future, the same anxious expectation of new cataclysms, joined with a prospect of a reviving of the Church.

"Cry with a loud voice," said her guardian angel to St. Elizabeth of Schönau (d. 1164), "cry to all nations: Woe! for the whole world has become darkness. The Lord's vine has withered, there is no one to tend it. The Lord has sent laborers, but they have all been found idle. The head of the Church is ill and her members are dead. . . . Shepherds of my Church, you are sleeping, but I shall awaken you! Kings of the earth, the cry of your iniquity has risen even to me."

"Divine justice," said St. Hildegard (d. 1178), "shall have its hour. The last of the seven epochs symbolized by the seven days of creation has arrived, the judgments of God are about to be accomplished; the empire and the papacy, sunk into impiety, shall crumble away together. . . . But upon their ruins shall appear a new nation of God, a nation of prophets illuminated from on high, living in poverty and solitude. Then the divine mysteries shall be revealed, and the saying of Joel shall be fulfilled; the Holy Spirit shall shed abroad upon the people the dew of his prophecies, of his wisdom and holiness."

Dante, the great Florentine poet of The Divine Comedy, *expresses a commonly held view in the century after Francis's death: Joachim was "gifted with the prophetic spirit" (Paradiso, canto xii); he was a John the Baptist for the life, teaching, and reform brought by Francis.*

These hopes were not wholly confounded. In the evening of his days the prophet of Fiore was able, like a new Simeon, to utter his *Nunc dimittis,* and for a few years Christendom could turn in amazement to Assisi as to a new Bethlehem.

CHAPTER FIVE
Struggles and Triumph
(Spring 1206–February 24, 1209)

Since his abrupt return from Spoleto, life in his father's house had daily become more difficult. Bernardone's self-love had received from his son's embarrassment such a wound as with common people is never healed. He might provide, without counting it, money to be swallowed up in dissipation so that his son might stand on an equal footing with the young nobles. But he could never resign himself to see him giving with lavish hands to every beggar in the streets.

Francis, continually plunged in reverie and spending his days in lonely wanderings in the fields, was no longer of the least use to his father. Months passed and the distance between the two men grew ever wider, and the gentle and loving Pica could do nothing to prevent a rupture that from this time appeared to be inevitable. Francis soon came to feel only one desire—to flee from the abode where, in the place of love, he found only reproaches, upbraidings, anguish.

The faithful confidant of his earlier struggles had been obliged to leave him, and this absolute solitude weighed heavily upon Francis's warm and loving heart. He did what he could to escape it, but no one understood him. The ideas that he was beginning timidly to express evoked from those to whom he spoke only mocking smiles or the head-shakings that people sure they are right bestow upon one who is marching straight to madness. He even went to open his mind to the bishop, but the latter understood no more than others his vague, incoherent plans, filled with ideas impossible to realize and possibly subversive.

Among the numerous chapels in the suburbs of Assisi there was one that he particularly loved, that of San Damiano. It was reached by a few minutes walk over a stony path, almost trackless, under olive trees, amid odors of lavender and rosemary. Standing on the top of a hillock, one can see the entire plain through a curtain of cypresses and pines that seem to be trying to hide the humble hermitage and set up an ideal barrier between it and the world.

Served by a poor priest who had scarcely the wherewithal for necessary food, the sanctuary was falling into ruin. There was nothing in the interior but a simple altar of masonry, and on a reredos one of those Byzantine crucifixes still so numerous in Italy, where through the work of the artists of the time has come down to us something of the terrors that agitated the twelfth century. In general, the Crucified One, frightfully lacerated, with bleeding wounds, appears to seek to inspire only grief and compunction; that of San Damiano, on the contrary, has an expression of inexpressible calm and gentleness. Instead of closing the eyelids in eternal surrender to the weight of suffering, it looks down in self-forgetfulness, and its pure, clear gaze says, not "I suffer," but, "Come unto me."

One day Francis was praying before the poor altar: "Great and glorious God, and you, Lord Jesus, I pray you, shed abroad your light in the darkness of my mind. . . . Be found in me, Lord, so that in all things I may act only in accordance with your holy will."

The crucifix of San Damiano, so important in the life of Francis, was taken to the Chapel of San Giorgio by the Sisters of St. Clare after Clare's death. They took it with them when they relocated to San Giorgio, leaving behind the more remote San Damiano. The eyes of the crucifix are specifically mentioned by Sabatier and the earlier biographers. This reminds us of a painter of icons who always leaves the eyes for last, as the eyes are the most important feature—the primary opening into the figure represented.

Thus he prayed in his heart, and behold, little by little it seemed to him that his gaze could not detach itself from that of Jesus. He felt something marvelous taking place in and around him. The sacred victim took on life, and in the outward silence he was aware of a voice that softly stole into the very depths of his heart, speaking to him an ineffable language. Jesus accepted his oblation. Jesus desired his labor, his life, all his being, and the heart of the poor solitary was already bathed in light and strength.

This vision marks the final triumph of Francis. His union with Christ was consummated. From this time he could exclaim with the mystics of every age, "My beloved is mine, and I am his." For the first time, no doubt, Francis had been brought into direct, personal, intimate contact with Jesus Christ.

This look of love cast upon the crucifix, this mysterious colloquy with the compassionate victim, was never to cease. At San Damiano, St. Francis's piety took on its outward appearance and its originality. From that time his way was plain before him. Coming out from the sanctuary, he gave the priest all the money he had about him to keep a lamp always burning, and with ravished heart he returned to Assisi. He had decided to leave his father's house and undertake the restoration of the chapel, after having broken the last ties that bound him to the past. A horse and a few pieces of brightly colored cloths were all that he possessed. Arriving at home he made a packet of the cloths, and mounting his horse he set out for Foligno. This city was then as now the most important commercial town of all the region. Its fairs attracted the whole population of Umbria and the Sabines. Bernardone had often taken his son there, and Francis speedily succeeded in selling all he had brought. He even parted with his horse, and full of joy set out upon the road to Assisi.

This act was to him most important; it marked his final rupture with the past. From this day on his life was to be in all points the opposite of what it had been. The Crucified had given himself to him; he on his side had given himself to the Crucified without reserve or return. To uncertainty, disquietude of soul, anguish, longing for an unknown good, bitter regrets, had succeeded a delicious calm, the ecstasy of the lost child who finds his mother and forgets in a moment the torture of his heart.

From Foligno he returned directly to San Damiano; it was not necessary to pass through the city, and he was in haste to put his projects

---

Historian G. G. Coulton is critical of Sabatier's account of this famous scene. Coulton refers to Francis's as a "pious theft." He writes: "It is very difficult to understand how, in the face of the early biographers, so admirable a writer as M. Sabatier can speak of the Foligno incident as though the horse and cloth had really been the Saint's own" (COULTON 2, p. 31).

This is the story of the prodigal son turned on its head! In the parable, the son wastes his inheritance in dissipation; Francis has taken the first decisive step toward renouncing his worldly goods. In both the parable and in Francis's life, the son leaves his father only to return to him, begging forgiveness and finding grace. The difference of course, in Francis's case, is that he was acting in obedience to his heavenly Father.

---

into execution. The poor priest was surprised enough when Francis handed over to him the whole product of his sale. He doubtless thought that a passing quarrel had occurred between Bernardone and his son, and for greater prudence refused the gift. But Francis so insisted upon remaining with him that he finally gave him leave to do so. As to the money, now become useless, Francis cast it as a worthless object upon a window-seat in the chapel.

Meanwhile Bernardone, disturbed by his son's failure to return, sought for him in all quarters, and was not long in learning of his presence at San Damiano. In a moment he perceived that Francis was lost to him. Resolved to try every means, he collected a few neighbors, and furious with rage hastened to the hermitage to snatch him away, if necessary, by force.

But Francis knew his father's violence. When he heard the shouts of those who were in pursuit of him he felt his courage fail and hurried to a hiding-place that he had prepared for himself for precisely such an emergency. Bernardone ransacked every corner, but was obliged at last to return to Assisi without his son. Francis remained hidden for long days, weeping and groaning, imploring God to show him the path he ought to follow. Notwithstanding his fears he had an infinite joy at heart, and at no price would he have turned back.

This seclusion could not last long. Francis perceived this and told himself that for a newly made knight of Christ he was cutting a very pitiful figure. Arming himself, therefore, with courage, he went one day to the city to present himself before his father and make known to him his resolution. It is easy to imagine the changes wrought in his appearance by these few weeks of seclusion, much of them passed in mental anguish. When he appeared, pale, cadaverous, his clothes in tatters, upon what is now the Piazza Nuova, where hundreds of children play all day long, he was greeted with a great shout, *"Pazzo, Pazzo!"* ("A madman! A madman!") *"Un pazzo ne fa cento"* ("One madman makes a hundred more"), says the proverb, but one must have seen the delirious excitement of the street children of Italy at the sight of a madman to gain an idea how true it is. The moment the magic cry resounds they rush into the street with frightful din, and while their parents look on from the windows, they surround the unhappy sufferer with wild dances mingled with songs, shouts, and savage howls. They throw stones at him, fling mud upon him, blindfold him; if he flies into a rage, they double their insults; if he weeps or begs for pity, they repeat his cries and mimic his sobs and supplications without respite and without mercy.

Francis demonstrated a taste for holy foolishness throughout his life. No doubt his growing spiritual confidence took some measure of pleasure in being ridiculed by the townspeople as he returned to Assisi. Only a few years later, Francis and Brother Rufino preached in Assisi wearing only their underwear. According to another story, when Brother Bernard was sent by Francis to nearby Bologna, Bernard too was set upon by the children of that city. Bernard, probably as Francis had taught him, bore it all with visible joy and even made his way further—to the marketplace—so that the impact of his physical appearance of foolishness would be even greater. Adults joined the children in throwing dust and stones at him, pushing him, and plucking at the hood of his tattered tunic. The story tells that Bernard returned day after day to the marketplace for the same treatment. Finally, someone from the crowd asked him where his great patience and holiness arose from, and Bernard pulled out a copy of Francis's Rule. That is how, according to legend, Bologna and many other towns became the home of early Franciscans.

Bernardone soon heard the clamor that filled the narrow streets and went out to enjoy the show. Suddenly, he thought he heard his own name and that of his son, and bursting with shame and rage he perceived Francis. Throwing himself upon him, as if to throttle him, he dragged him into the house and cast him, half dead, into a dark closet. Everything was brought to bear to change the prisoner's resolve, but all in vain. At last, wearied out and desperate, Bernardone left him in peace, though not without having firmly bound him.

A few days later he was obliged to be absent for a short time. Pica, his wife, understood only too well his grievances against Francis, but feeling that violence would be of no avail she resolved to try gentleness. It was all in vain. Then, no longer able to see him tortured in this way, she set him free. Francis returned straight to San Damiano.

Bernardone, on his return, went so far as to strike Pica in punishment for her weakness. Then, unable to tolerate the thought of seeing his son the jest of the whole city, he tried to procure his expulsion from the territory of Assisi. Going to San Damiano he summoned him to leave the country. This time Francis did not try to hide. Boldly presenting himself, he declared that not only would nothing induce him to abandon his resolutions, but moreover, having become the servant of Christ, he had no longer to receive orders from his father. As Bernardone launched out into invective, reproaching him with the enormous sums that he had cost him, Francis showed him by a gesture the money that he had brought back from the sale at Foligno lying on the window-ledge. The father greedily seized it and went away, resolving to appeal to the magistrates. Bernardone could do no more than disinherit his son, or at least induce him of his own accord to renounce all claim upon his inheritance.

When called upon to appear before the episcopal tribunal Francis experienced a lively joy. His mystical espousals to the Crucified One were now to receive a sort of official consecration. To this Jesus, whom he had so often blasphemed and betrayed by word and conduct, he would now be able with equal publicity to promise obedience and fidelity.

It is easy to imagine the sensation that all this caused in a small town like Assisi, and the crowd that on the appointed day pressed toward the Piazza of Santa Maria Maggiore, where the bishop pronounced sentence. Everyone held Francis to be assuredly mad, but they anticipated with relish the shame and rage of Bernardone, whom everyone detested, and whose pride was so well punished by all of this.

The bishop first set forth the case, and advised Francis to simply give up all his property. To the great surprise of the crowd the latter, instead of replying, retired to a room in the bishop's palace, and immediately reappeared absolutely naked, holding in his hand the packet into which he had rolled his clothes; these he laid down before the bishop with the little money that he still had kept, saying, "Listen, all of you, and understand it well. Until this time I have called Peter Bernardone my father, but now I desire to serve God. This is why I return to him this money, for which he has given himself so much trouble, as well as my clothing, and all that I have had from him, for from henceforth I desire to say nothing else than 'Our Father, who art in heaven.'"

A long murmur arose from the crowd when Bernardone was seen to gather up and carry off the clothing without the least evidence of compassion, while the bishop was obliged to take under his mantle the poor Francis, who was trembling with emotion and cold.

The scene of the judgment hall made an immense impression. The ardor, simplicity, and indignation of Francis had been so profound and sincere that scoffers were disconcerted. On that day he won for himself a secret sympathy in many souls. The incident is simply a new manifestation of Francis's character, with its ingenuousness, its exaggerations, its longing to establish a complete harmony, a literal correspondence, between words and actions.

After emotions such as he had just experienced he felt the need of being alone, of realizing his joy, of singing the liberty he had finally achieved along all the lines where once he had so deeply suffered, so ardently struggled. Leaving the city by the nearest gate, he plunged into the deserted paths that climb the sides of Mount Subasio.

It was the early spring. Here and there were still great drifts of snow, but under the ardor of the March sun winter seemed to own itself vanquished. In the midst of this mysterious and bewildering harmony the heart of Francis felt a delicious thrill; all his being was calmed and uplifted; the soul of things caressed him gently and shed upon him peace. An unaccustomed happiness swept over him and he made the forest resound with his hymns of praise.

So Francis went on his way, deeply inhaling the odors of spring, singing at the top of his voice one of those songs of French chivalry that he had learned in days gone by. The forest in which he was walking was the usual retreat of such people of Assisi and its environs as had reason for hiding. Some ruffians, aroused by his voice, suddenly fell upon him. "Who are you?" they asked. "I am

Other biographers recount that Francis was wearing one garment underneath his father's expensive clothes—significantly—"a hair shirt next to his skin" according to The Legend of the Three Companions, *representing an ascetic's devotion to God* (THREE, p. 80). *On the contrary, Giotto's famous fresco painting on the north wall of the upper church in the Basilica di San Francesco depicts a naked Francis under the bishop's robe. Either way, "Francis was a master of dramatic gestures and visual tableaux, and, unsurprisingly, representations of these played an important part in his cult"* (HOLMES, p. 55). *Chesterton adds, he "was one of the founders of the mediaeval drama"* (CHESTERTON, p. 78).

the herald of the great King," he answered, "but what is that to you?"

His only garment was an old mantle that the bishop's gardener had lent him at his master's request. They stripped it from him, and throwing him into a ditch full of snow they said, "There is your place, poor herald of God."

The robbers gone, he shook off the snow that covered him, and after many efforts succeeded in extricating himself from the ditch. Stiff with cold, with no other covering than a worn-out shirt, he none the less resumed his singing, happy to suffer and thus to accustom himself the better to understand the words of the Crucified One.

"He went out half-naked...a man without a father. He was penniless, he was parentless, he was to all appearances without a trade or a plan or a hope in the world; and as he went under the frosty trees, he burst suddenly into song" (CHESTERTON, p. 66).

He directed his steps toward Gubbio, where he knew that he would find a friend. Perhaps this was he who had been his confidant on his return from Spoleto. Whoever it was, he received from him a tunic, and a few days later set out to return to his dear San Damiano. After having fashioned for himself a hermit's dress, he began to go into the squares and open places of the city. Having sung a few hymns there, he would announce to those who gathered around him his project of restoring the chapel.

Many deemed him mad, but others were deeply moved by the remembrance of the past. As for Francis, deaf to mockery, he spared himself no labor, carrying upon his shoulders, so ill-fitted for severe toil, the stones that were given him. During this time the poor priest of San Damiano felt his heart swelling with love for this companion who had at first caused him such embarrassment, and he strove to prepare for him his favorite dishes. Francis soon perceived it and his delicacy took alarm at the expense that he caused his friend. Thanking him, he resolved to beg his food from door to door.

It was not an easy task. Each hour, so to speak, brought to him a new struggle. One day he was going through the town begging for oil for the lamps of San Damiano, when he arrived at a house where a banquet was going on. A great number of his former companions were there, singing and dancing. At the sound of those well-known voices he felt as if he could not enter; he even turned away, but very soon, filled with confusion by his own cowardice, he returned quickly upon his steps, made his way into the banquet-hall, and after confessing his shame, put so much earnestness and fire into his request that everyone desired to cooperate in this pious work.

His bitterest trial however was his father's anger, which remained as violent as ever. Although he had renounced Francis, Bernardone's pride suffered none the less at seeing his mode of life, and whenever he met his son he overwhelmed him with reproaches. The tender heart of Francis was so wrung with sorrow that he resorted to a sort of stratagem for charming away the spell of the paternal imprecations. "Come with me," he said to a beggar, "be to me as a father, and I will give you a part of the alms that I receive. When you see Bernardone curse me, if I say, 'Bless me, my father,' you must sign me with the cross and bless me in his stead."

In the spring of 1208 he finished the restoration of San Damiano. He had been aided by many people of good will, setting the example of work and above all of joy, cheering everybody by his songs and his projects for the future. He spoke with such enthusiasm and contagious warmth of the transformation of his dear chapel, of the grace that God would accord to those who would come there to pray, that later on it was believed that he had spoken of Clare and her holy maidens who were to retire to this place four years later.

This success soon inspired him with the idea of repairing the other sanctuaries in the suburbs of Assisi. Those that had struck him by their state of decay were St. Peter and St. Mary, of the Portiuncula, also called Santa Maria degli Angeli. The former is not otherwise mentioned in his biographies. As to the second, it was to become the true cradle of the Franciscan movement.

This chapel, still standing at the present day after escaping revolutions and earthquakes, is a true Bethel, one of those rare spots in the world on which rests the mystic ladder that joins heaven to earth. There were dreamed some of the noblest dreams that have soothed the pains of humanity. It is not to Assisi in its marvelous basilica that one must go to divine and comprehend St. Francis; one must turn toward Santa Maria degli Angeli at the hours when the stated prayers cease, at the moment when the evening shadows lengthen, when all the fripperies of worship disappear in the obscurity, when all the countryside seems to collect itself to listen to the chime of the distant church bells. Doubtless it was Francis's plan to settle there as a hermit. He dreamed of passing his life there in meditation and silence, keeping up the little church and from time to time inviting a priest there to say mass. Nothing as yet suggested to him that he was in the end to become a religious founder. One of the most interesting aspects of his life is in fact the continual development revealing itself to him. There is hardly anyone, except St. Paul, in whom is found to the same degree the devouring need of being always something more, always something better, and it is so beautiful in both of them only because it is absolutely instinctive.

When he began to restore the Portiuncula his projects hardly went beyond a very narrow horizon. He was preparing himself for a life of penitence rather than a life of activity. But once these works were finished it was impossible that this somewhat selfish and passive manner of achieving his own salvation should satisfy him long. When the repairs were finished meditation occupied the greater part of his days. A Benedictine of the Abbey of Mont Subasio came from time to time to say mass at Santa Maria; these were the bright hours of St. Francis's life. One can imagine with what pious care he prepared himself and with what faith he listened to the divine teachings.

The Portiuncula (lit. "little portion") included the little chapel and land surrounding it—also known as the Church of Our Lady of the Angels (Santa Maria degli Angeli), or simply the church of Saint Mary, located approximately two miles from Assisi, in the plain below the city, near the road that travelers would take to Foligno in one direction, Perugia in the other. In his final days, Francis insisted that his brothers carry his dying body back to his beloved chapel, Portiuncula. (See one early eighteenth-century artist's rendering of Portiuncula below, on p. 165.)

One day—it was probably February 24, 1209—the festival of St. Matthias mass was being celebrated at the Portiuncula. When the priest turned toward him to read the words of Jesus, Francis felt himself overpowered with a profound agitation. He no longer saw the priest; it was Jesus, the Crucified One of San Damiano, who was speaking: "As you go, proclaim the good news, the kingdom of heaven has come near. Cure the sick, raise the dead, cleanse the lepers, cast out demons. You received without payment; give without payment. Take no gold, or silver, or copper in your belts, no bag for your journey, or two tunics, or sandals, or a staff; for laborers deserve their food." These words burst upon him like a revelation, like the answer of Heaven to his sighs and anxieties.

"This is what I want," he cried, "this is what I was seeking. From this day forth I shall set myself with all my strength to put it in practice." Immediately throwing aside his stick, his scrip, his purse, his shoes, he determined immediately to obey, observing to the letter the precepts of the apostolic life.

As will become clear over the next four chapters, Francis had an almost inexplicable magnetism. Even though he was known to occasionally speak in forbidding language, as Jesus sometimes did in the Gospels, and he asked seemingly impossible things of his followers, as Jesus also did, thousands of people joined Francis in his "new" apostolic work within the first few years. This wasn't strategized or planned. As one recent biographer has put it: "Francis seemed to have none of the qualities usually found in a leader, religious or otherwise.... Francis founded his movement in spite of himself. Whether the brotherhood should grow or not seems never to have crossed his mind." (THOMSON, p. 35). What, then, can explain the explosion of the early Franciscan movement other than that it was Spirit-driven?

CHAPTER SIX

First Year of Apostolate
(Spring 1209–Summer 1210)

The very next morning Francis went up to Assisi and began to preach. His words were simple, but they came so straight from the heart that all who heard him were touched. His person, his example, were themselves a sermon, and he spoke only of that which he had himself experienced, proclaiming repentance, the shortness of life, a future retribution, the necessity of arriving at Gospel perfection.

It is not easy to realize how many waiting souls there are in this world. The greater number of people pass through life with souls asleep. Yet the instinct for love and for the divine is only slumbering. The human heart so naturally yearns to offer itself up, that we have only to meet along our pathway someone who, doubting neither himself nor us, demands it without reserve, and we yield it to him at once. The cause of the miserable failure of all the efforts of natural religion is that its founders have not had the courage to lay hold upon the hearts of people. They have not understood the imperious desire for immolation that lies in the depths of every soul, and souls have taken their revenge in not heeding these too lukewarm lovers.

Francis had given himself up too completely not to claim from others an absolute self-renunciation. In the two years and more since he had left the world, the reality and depth of his conversion had shone out in the sight of all; to the scoffings of the early days had gradually succeeded in the minds of many a feeling closely akin to admiration. This feeling inevitably provokes imitation.

"the imperious desire for immolation that lies in the depths of every soul": Chesterton illuminates this brilliantly: *"[People] will ask what selfish sort of woman it must have been who ruthlessly exacted tribute in the form of flowers, or what an avaricious creature she can have been to demand solid gold in the form of a ring; just as they ask what cruel kind of God can have demanded sacrifice and self-denial. They will have lost the clue to all that lovers have meant by love; and will not understand that it was because the thing was not demanded that it was done"* (CHESTERTON, p. 73).

At Assisi Francis had often enjoyed the hospitality of a rich and prominent man named Bernard of Quintavalle. One day the joy of Francis was very great as he divined Bernard's intentions; he had decided to distribute his goods to the poor and cast in his lot with Francis. The latter desired his friend to pass through a sort of initiation, pointing out to him that what he himself practiced, what he preached, was not his own invention, but that Jesus himself had expressly ordained it in his word.

At early dawn they bent their steps to the St. Nicholas Church, accompanied by another neophyte named Peter, and there, after praying and hearing mass, Francis opened the Gospels that lay on the altar and read to his companions the portion that had decided his own vocation: the words of Jesus sending forth his disciples on their mission.

The early texts actually show Francis less confident and perhaps more spontaneous than is described here by Sabatier. Hearing that Bernard wanted to join him in his life of penitence, Francis told him that it was not easy. His reply then showed a degree of uncertainty as to what should happen next; Francis advised that they go to the bishop's house where there would be a priest, hear mass, and pray until tierce (the third hour after sunrise), at which time they (Francis in his discernment and Bernard after the glow of conversion had naturally dimmed a bit) would open the missal to discover God's will. (See BROWN, *pp. 42–45.)*

"Brothers," he added, "this is our life and our Rule, and that of all who may join us. Go then and do as you have heard."

The persistence with which *The Legend of the Three Companions* relate that Francis consulted the book three times in honor of the Trinity, and that it opened of its own accord at the verses describing the apostolic life, leads to the belief that these passages became the Rule of the new association, if not that very day at least very soon afterward:

> If you wish to be perfect, go, sell your possessions, and give the money to the poor, and you will have treasure in heaven; then come, follow me. (Mt. 19:21)
>
> Then Jesus called the twelve together and gave them power and authority over all demons and to cure diseases, and he sent them out to proclaim the kingdom of God and to heal. He said to them, "Take nothing for your journey, no staff, nor bag, nor bread, nor money—not even an extra

tunic. Whatever house you enter, stay there, and leave from there. Wherever they do not welcome you, as you are leaving that town shake the dust off your feet as a testimony against them." They departed and went through the villages, bringing the good news and curing diseases everywhere. (Lk. 9:1–6)

Then Jesus told his disciples, "If any want to become my followers, let them deny themselves and take up their cross and follow me. For those who want to save their life will lose it, and those who lose their life for my sake will find it. For what will it profit them if they gain the whole world but forfeit their life? Or what will they give in return for their life?" (Mt. 16:24–26)

At first these verses were hardly more than the official Rule of the Order—(the true Rule was Francis himself)—but they had the great merit of being short and absolute, of promising perfection, and of being taken from the Gospel.

Bernard immediately set to work to distribute his fortune among the poor. Full of joy, his friend was looking on at this act, which had drawn together a crowd, when a priest named Sylvester, who had formerly sold him some stones for the repairs of San Damiano, seeing so much money given away to everyone who applied for it, drew near and said:

Translators of the most authoritative edition of The Legend of the Three Companions *summarize: "Two highly disputed texts,* The Legend of the Three Companions *and* The Assisi Compilation, *reflect the contributions of the three friars who identify themselves in the first text as Brothers Leo, Angelo, and Rufino and in the second text as 'we who were with him.' Both texts provide facts about and insights into Francis not found in the earlier lives and, as such, are indispensable in knowing the details of his life and vision"* (ASSISI, p. 62).

"The missal, which had thus played its part in the creation of the Franciscan order, later came into the possession of Bishop Guido; today it can be seen at the Walters Art Gallery in Baltimore, Maryland" (HOUSE, p. 79).

"Brother, you did not pay me very well for the stones that you bought from me."

Francis had too thoroughly killed every germ of avarice in himself not to be moved to indignation by hearing a priest speak this way. "Here," he said, holding out to him a double handful of coins that he took from Bernard's robe. "Here, are you sufficiently paid now?"

"Quite so," replied Sylvester, somewhat abashed by the murmurs of the bystanders. This picture, in which the characters stand out so strongly, must have taken strong hold upon the memory of those who saw it. It taught them, better than all Francis's preachings, what manner of men these new friars would be.

The distribution finished, they went at once to Portiuncula, where Bernard and Peter built for themselves cabins of boughs, and made themselves tunics like that of Francis. They did not differ much from the garment worn by the peasants, and were of that brown, with its infinite variety of shades, that the Italians call beast color. One finds similar garments today among the shepherds of the most remote parts of the Apennines.

The first brothers lived as did the poor people among whom they so willingly moved. Portiuncula was their favorite church, but it would be a mistake to suppose that they sojourned there for any long periods. It was their place of meeting, nothing more. Their life was that of the Umbrian beggars of the present day, going here and there as fancy dictated, sleeping in haylofts, in leper hospitals, or under the porch of some church.

They went up and down the country, joyfully sowing their seed. It was the beginning of summer, the time when everybody in Umbria is out of doors mowing or turning the grass. The customs of the country have changed little. Walking in the end of May in the fields about Florence, Perugia, or Rieti, one still sees, at nightfall, the bagpipers entering the fields as the mowers seat themselves upon the haycocks for their evening meal. They play a few pieces, and when the train of haymakers returns to the village, followed by the harvest-laden carts, it is they who lead the procession, rending the air with their sharpest strains.

The joyous Penitents who loved to call themselves *Joculatores Domini*, God's *jongleurs*, no doubt often

---

Here is one account of an occasion when Francis ate together with a leper: "A bowl was placed between the two of them. The leper was completely covered with sores and ulcerated, and especially the fingers with which he was eating were deformed and bloody, so that whenever he put them in the bowl, blood dripped into it. Brother Peter and the other brothers saw this, grew very sad, but did not dare say anything out of fear of the holy father. The one who wrote this, saw it and bore witness to it" (ASSISI, p. 167).

did the same. They did even better, for not willing to be a charge to anyone, they passed a part of the day in aiding the peasants in their field work. They worked and ate together; field-hands and friars often slept in the same barn; and when at the morrow's dawn the friars went on their way, the hearts of those they left behind had been touched. They were not yet converted, but they knew that not far away, over toward Assisi, were living men who had renounced all worldly goods, and who, consumed with zeal, were going up and down preaching penitence and peace.

We have arrived at the most unique and interesting period in the history of the Franciscans. At the sight of these men—bare-footed, scantily clothed, without money, and yet so happy—people's minds were much divided. Some held them to be mad, others admired them, finding them widely different from the vagrant monks, that plague of Christendom.

When the brothers went up to Assisi to beg from door to door, many refused to give to them, reproaching them with desiring to live on the goods of others after having squandered their own. Many a time they had barely enough not to starve to death. It would even seem that the clergy were not entirely without part in this opposition. The Bishop of Assisi said to Francis one day: "Your way of living without owning anything seems to me very harsh and difficult." "My lord," Francis replied, "if we possessed property we should have need of arms for its defense, for it is the source of quarrels and lawsuits, and the love of God and of one's neighbor usually finds many obstacles in it. This is why we do not desire temporal goods."

The argument was unanswerable, but Guido began to rue the encouragement that he had formerly offered the son of Bernardone. The only counsel that the bishop could give Francis was to come into the ranks of the clergy, or, if asceticism attracted him, to join some already existing monastic order. If the bishop's perplexities were great, those of Francis were hardly less so. He was too acute not to foresee the conflict that threatened to break out between the friars and the clergy. He saw that the enemies of the priests praised him and his companions beyond measure. On the other hand, the families of the Penitents could not forgive them for having distributed their goods among the poor, and attacks came from this direction with all the bitter language and the deep hatred natural to disappointed heirs. From this point of view the brotherhood appeared as a menace to families, and many parents trembled for fear that their sons would join it. As to the clergy, they could not but feel a profound distrust of these lay converters, who, though they aroused the hatred of some interested persons, awakened in more pious souls first astonishment and then admiration. Suddenly to see people without title or diploma succeed brilliantly in the mission that has been officially confided to ourselves, and in which we have made pitiful shipwreck, is cruel torture.

After the death of Francis, some of his followers radicalized his message and actions in their own lives. One of the most colorful of these characters was Angela of Foligno, who cared for lepers with great devotion. Legend has it that she demonstrated her complete trust in God by eating from the sores on the lepers' bodies, saying that she partook of them as if they were the host of the Eucharist itself. Her actions recall the time in Francis's young adult life when he first took to begging alms, forsaking the good food to which he was accustomed in his father's house: "But when he wanted to eat the mixed food offered him, he felt revulsion because he was not accustomed not only to eating such things, but even at looking at them. At last overcoming himself, he began to eat, and it seemed to him that no delicacy had ever tasted so delicious" (THREE, p. 82).

But the more St. Francis was to find himself in contradiction with the clergy of his time, the more he was to believe himself the obedient son of the Church. Confounding the gospel with the teaching of the Church, he was for a good while to border upon heresy, but without ever falling into it. Happy simplicity, thanks to which he had never to take the attitude of revolt!

He resolved, therefore, to undertake a new mission. The *Three Companions* have preserved for us the directions that he gave to his disciples:

"'Let us consider that God in his goodness has not called us merely for our own salvation, but also for that of many people, that we may go through all the world exhorting people, more by our example than by our words, to repent of their sins and bear the commandments in mind. You will find people full of faith, gentleness, and goodness who will receive you and your words with joy, but you will also find others, and in greater numbers—faithless, proud, blasphemers—who will speak evil of you, resisting you and your words. Be resolute to endure everything with patience and humility.'

"Hearing this the brothers began to be agitated. St. Francis said to them: 'Have no fear, for very soon many nobles and learned men will come to you. They will be with you preaching to kings and princes and to a multitude of peoples. Many will be converted to the Lord, all over the world.'"

We know that many high-born men joined Francis in those early days, choosing to live, as Francis had, in voluntary poverty. The decision to join Francis and give away one's property and possessions could have a wide impact on many others — beyond the one who made it for religious reasons. "In a society where the rights of the individual counted less than those of the family, it was not easy for an owner to get rid of his goods, for he had to obtain the agreement of all those having rights and to compensate them before proceeding to their alienation," explains one expert. But, of course, in those days neither wives nor children possessed any such rights. "Thus in almost every case, the entrance into the fraternity of the disciples of Francis created a kind of social upheaval and sparked within public opinion reactions ranging from misgivings to outright hostility toward this little handful of crazies who were disrupting the typical manner of parceling out goods among successors and the strategies of the family clan." (VAUCHEZ, p. 45).

CHAPTER SEVEN
St. Francis and Innocent III
(Summer 1210)

Seeing the number of his friars increasing daily, Francis decided to write the Rule of the Order and go to Rome to procure its approval by the pope.

This resolution was not lightly taken. It would be a mistake in fact to take Francis for one of those inspired ones who rush into action upon the strength of unexpected revelations, and, thanks to their faith in their own infallibility, overawe the multitude. On the contrary, he was filled with a real humility, and if he believed that God is revealed in prayer he never for that excused himself from the duty of reflection or even from reconsidering his decisions. St. Bonaventure does him great wrong in picturing many of his important resolutions as taken in consequence of dreams; this is to rob his life of its profound originality. Francis was one of those who struggle, and, to use one of the noblest expressions of the Bible, of those who *by their perseverance conquer their souls*. Thus we shall see him continually retouching the Rule of his institute, unceasingly revising it down to the last moment.

The first Rule that he submitted to Rome has not come down to us. We only know that it was extremely simple, and was composed especially of passages from the Gospels. It was doubtless only the repetition of the verses that Francis had read to his first companions, with a few precepts about manual labor and the occupations of the new brothers.

Innocent III had now for twelve years occupied the throne of St. Peter. Still young, energetic, resolute, he enjoyed that superfluity of authority given by success. Coming after the feeble Celestine III, he had been able in a few years to reconquer the temporal domain of the Church, and so to improve the papal influence as almost to realize the theocratic dreams of Gregory VII. He had seen King Pedro of Aragon declaring himself his vassal and laying his crown upon the tomb of the apostles. At the other end of Europe, John Lackland had been obliged to receive his crown from a legate after having sworn homage, fealty, and an annual tribute to the Holy See. Preaching union to the cities and republics of Italy, causing the cry "Italia! Italia!" to resound like the shout of a trumpet, he was the natural representative of the national awakening. Finally, by his efforts to purify the Church, by his indomitable firmness in defending morality and law, he was gaining a moral strength that in times so disquieted was all the more powerful for being so rare.

When Innocent III suppressed ecclesiastical disorders it was less for love of good than for hatred of evil. This priest did not comprehend the great movement of his age—the awakening of love, of poetry, of liberty. He never suspected the unsatisfied longings, the dreams, unreasoning perhaps, but beneficent and divine, that were silently stirring in the depths of people's hearts. He was a believer, but he drew his religion rather from the Old Testament than from the New, and if he often thought of Moses, the leader of his people, nothing reminded him of Jesus, the shepherd of souls.

Celestine III (pope from spring 1191 to January 1198) was already 85 years of age when elected. He is most memorable for his loyalty to Abelard, his former teacher in Paris, when Bernard of Clairvaux led the council of Sens against him (1140). Later, Celestine also petitioned for leniency for Thomas Becket. At the time, "Becket judged him one of the only two incorruptible cardinals" (KELLY, p. 185).

Innocent III's power is perhaps best exemplified in his vow to protect every "citizen" of the Roman Church in the same manner that the ancient emperor Trajan had put fear in the hearts of those who would harm any citizen of Rome. He also excommunicated Emperor Otto IV in 1211.

His reception of Francis furnished to Giotto, the friend of Dante, one of his most striking frescos. The pope, seated on his throne, turns abruptly toward Francis. He frowns, for he does not understand, and yet he makes a real but futile effort to comprehend.

What Francis asked for was simple enough. He claimed no privilege of any sort, but only that the pope would approve of his undertaking to lead a life of absolute conformity to the precepts of the gospel. There is a delicate point here that it is quite worthwhile to see clearly. The pope was not called upon to approve the Rule, since that came from Jesus himself. At the very worst all that he could do would be to lay an ecclesiastical censure upon Francis and his companions for having acted without authority, and to enjoin them to leave

*Our image of Francis the saint often
obscures Francis the human being.
Zofia Kossak's little-known historical
novel about the life of Francis and his
early followers offers many intriguing
hypothetical everyday scenes. Here is
a sample glimpse of the debates the
brothers might have had while composing the first Rule while traveling to
Rome to present it to the pope:*

"Elias continued to read:

'And the most important commandment given to the brethren is that
they shall love each other. By that sign
they will know you for the true disciple
of Our Lord, that you shall have love
for each other. And every man who
shall come to the brethren, be he a thief
or a robber, must be welcomed gladly
even as he were one of them.'

Brother Elias once more put the
parchment down:

'And to this, too, the Holy Father
will never agree,' he remarked. 'Why,
'tis pure folly! So if a notorious murderer
came to us we should take him in and
perhaps even offer him hospitality.'

'Aye,' nodded Francis with conviction. 'Because who knows whether
we can't bring him to repent?'

'And he, in the meantime, will rob
the brothers and . . .'

'What will he rob them of? What
can he do to us? None of us fears death.
She is our sister. Only those who
possess aught can be robbed. We have
naught'" (KOSSAK, pp. 39–40).

to the secular and regular clergy the
task of reforming the Church.

Cardinal Giovanni of San
Paulo presented Francis and his companions to Innocent III. Naturally, the
pope was not sparing of expressions
of sympathy, but he also repeated
to them the remarks and counsels
that they had already heard so often.
"My dear children," he said, "your life
appears to me too severe. I see indeed
that your fervor is too great for any
doubt of you to be possible, but I
ought to consider those who shall
come after you, lest your mode of
life should be beyond their strength."
Adding a few kind words, he dismissed
them without coming to any definite
conclusion, promising to consult the
cardinals and advising Francis in
particular to address himself to God.

Francis's anxiety must have
been great. It seemed to him that he
had said all that he had to say. For new
arguments he had only one resource—
prayer. Francis felt his prayer answered
when in his conversation with Jesus
the parable of poverty came to him.
He returned to lay it before the pope:

"There was in the desert a
woman who was very poor, but beautiful. A great king, seeing her beauty,
desired to take her for his wife, for he
thought that by her he should have
beautiful children. When the sons were grown, their mother said to
them: 'My sons, you have no cause to blush, for you are the sons of
the king. Go to his court and he will give you everything you need.'

"When they arrived at the court the king admired their beauty, and finding in them his own likeness he asked: 'Whose sons are you?' And when they replied that they were the sons of a poor woman who lived in the desert the king clasped them to his heart with joy, saying, 'Have no fear, for you are my sons.'"

"Very holy father," added Francis, "I am this poor woman whom God in his love has deigned to make beautiful, and of whom he has been pleased to have lawful sons. The King of Kings has told me that he will provide for all the sons that he may have for me."

So much simplicity, joined with such pious obstinacy, at last conquered Innocent. When Francis heard the words of the supreme pontiff he prostrated himself at his feet, promising the most perfect obedience with all his heart. The pope blessed them, saying: "Go, my brothers, and may God be with you. Preach penitence to everyone according as the Lord may deign to inspire you. Then when the All-Powerful will have made you to multiply and go forward, you will refer again to us. We will concede what you ask, and we may then with greater security accord to you even more than you ask."

Francis and his companions were too little familiar with Roman phraseology to perceive that after all the Holy See had simply consented to suspend judgment in view of the uprightness of their intentions and the purity of their faith. The flowers of clerical rhetoric hid from them the shackles that had been laid upon them. The curia, in fact, was not satisfied with Francis's vow of fidelity; it desired in addition to stamp the Penitents with the seal of the Church. From this time they were all under the spiritual authority of the Roman Church.

The thoroughly lay creation of St. Francis had become in spite of himself an ecclesiastical institution. It would soon degenerate into a clerical institution. All unawares, the Franciscan movement had been unfaithful to its origin. The prophet had abdicated in favor of the priest.

Many scholars argue that Innocent III had two motivations, one noble, the other less so. Innocent had a genuine sympathy with Francis's mind for reform and evangelical poverty. But, he also used Francis and his brothers. By bringing the preaching of the early Franciscans under the shadow and sanction of the Church, Francis helped Innocent defuse the power, and remove the seditiousness, of the Humiliati's and Albigensians' similar ideas.

CHAPTER EIGHT
Rivo-Torto (1210–1211)

Thomas of Celano, very brief as to all that concerns Francis's sojourn in the Eternal City, recounts at full length the lightheartedness of the little band on leaving it. Already it began to be transfigured in their memory—pains, fatigues, fears, disquietude, hesitations were all forgotten. They thought only of the fatherly assurances of the supreme pontiff and promised themselves to make ever new efforts to follow the Rule with fidelity.

Full of these thoughts they set out, without provisions, preaching in such places as they came upon along their route. People hastened from all parts to hear these preachers who were more severe upon themselves than on anyone else. Members of the secular clergy, monks, learned people, rich even, often mingled in the impromptu audiences gathered in the streets and public places. Not all were converted, but it would have been very difficult for any of them to forget this stranger whom they met one day upon their way, and who in a few words had moved them to the very bottom of their hearts with anxiety and fear.

Francis was in truth, as Celano says, the bright morning star. His simple preaching took hold on consciences. "The whole country trembled, the barren land was already covered with a rich harvest, the withered vine began again to blossom."

The greatest crime of our industrial and commercial civilization is that it leaves us a taste only for that which may be bought with money, and makes us overlook the purest and truest joys that are all the time within our reach. "Why," said the God of old Isaiah, "do you spend your money for that which is not bread, and your labor for that which does not satisfy? Listen carefully to me, and eat what is good, and delight yourselves in rich food" (Isa. 55:2). Joys bought with money—noisy, feverish pleasures—are nothing compared with those sweet, quiet, modest but profound, lasting, and peaceful joys, enlarging, not wearying the heart.

In the plain of Assisi, at an hour's walk from the city and near the highway between Perugia and Rome, was a ruinous cottage called Rivo-Torto. A torrent, almost always dry, but capable of becoming terrible in a storm, descends from Mount Subasio and passes beside it. The ruin had no owner; it had served as a leper hospital. Now came Francis and his companions to seek shelter there.

The principal motive for the choice of the place seems to have been the proximity of the Carceri, as the shallow natural grottos are called that are found in the forests, halfway up the side of Mount Subasio. These little hermitages, sufficiently isolated to secure them from disturbance, but near enough to the cities to permit their going there to preach, may be found wherever Francis went. They form, as it were, a series of documents about his life quite as important as the written witnesses. Something of his soul may still be found in these caverns in the Apennine forests. He never separated the contemplative from the active life.

The return of the Brothers to Rivo-Torto was marked by a vast increase in popularity.

Regarding the Carceri, one century-old guide to Assisi writes, "Even to call such shelters huts is giving them too grand a name, for they were but caverns excavated in the rock, scattered here and there in a deep mountain gorge. They can still be seen, unchanged since the days of St. Francis save for the tresses of ivy growing thick, like a curtain, across the entrance, for now there are none to pass in and out to pray there.... [L]ater Franciscan writers...no longer caring to live in caves, only saw Dantesque visions when they thought of these arid, sunburnt rocks, rushing torrents and wild wastes of mountains which even shepherds never reached" (GORDON, p. 84). Visitors to Assisi today may visit Carceri ("the Hermitage"), but it requires a fairly steep hike of about two miles, or a short taxi ride. Francis's own grotto at Carceri is an important place of pilgrimage.

The prejudiced attacks to which they had formerly been subjected were lost in a chorus of praises. But they suffered much; this part of the plain of Assisi is inundated by torrents nearly every autumn, and many times the poor friars, blockaded in the lazaretto, were forced to satisfy their hunger with a few roots from the neighboring fields. The barrack in which they lived was so narrow that, when they were all there at once, they had much difficulty not crowding one another.

When the people of Assisi learned that Francis's Rule had been approved by the pope there was strong excitement. Everyone desired to hear him preach. The clergy were obliged to give way: they offered him the Church of San Giorgio, but this church was manifestly insufficient for the crowds of hearers. It was necessary to open the cathedral to him.

St. Francis rarely said anything especially new. To win hearts he had what is worth more than any arts of oratory—an ardent conviction. He spoke as compelled by the imperious need of kindling others with the flame that burned within himself. When they heard him recall the horrors of war, the crimes of the populace, the laxity of the great, the rapacity that dishonored the Church, the age-long widowhood of Poverty, each person felt taken to task in his or her own conscience.

An attentive or excited crowd is always very impressionable, but this peculiar sensitivity was perhaps stronger in the Middle Ages than at any other time. Nervous disturbances were in the air, and upon people thus prepared the will of the preacher impressed itself in an almost magnetic manner.

To understand what Francis's preaching must have been like we must forget the manners of today and transport ourselves for a moment to the Cathedral of Assisi in the thirteenth century. It is still standing, but the centuries have given to its stones a fine rust of polished bronze that recalls Venice and Titian's tones of ruddy gold. It was new then, and all sparkling with whiteness, with the fine rosy tinge of the stones of Mount Subasio. It had been built by the people of Assisi a few years before; so, when the people thronged into it on their high days, they not only had none of the vague respect for a holy place that, though it has passed into the customs of other countries, still continues to be unknown in Italy, but they felt themselves at home in a palace that they had built for themselves. More than in any other church there they felt themselves at liberty to criticize the preacher, and they had no hesitation in showing him, either by murmurs of dissatisfaction or by applause, just what they thought of his words. These are the conditions under which Francis first entered the pulpit of San Rufino.

His success was startling. The poor felt that they had found a friend, a brother, a champion, almost an avenger. The thoughts that they hardly dared murmur beneath their breath Francis proclaimed at the top of his voice, daring to bid all, without distinction, to repent and love one another. His words were a cry of the heart, an appeal to the consciences of all his fellow citizens, almost recalling the passionate utterances of the prophets of Israel. Like those witnesses for Yahweh the "little poor man" of Assisi had put on sackcloth and ashes to denounce the iniquities of his people, like theirs was his courage and heroism, like theirs the divine tenderness in his heart.

The cathedral of San Rufino dates from around 1000 C.E. It is named for the first bishop of Assisi, who was martyred during one of the Roman persecutions of Christians (238 C.E.). He was drowned in the Chiascio River and his faithful later buried his bones under the high altar. St. Clare was raised in the home directly to the left of the old cathedral, as you stand facing it.

It was St. Francis who set the example of open-air sermons given in the vernacular, at street corners, in public squares, in the fields. To feel the change that he brought about we must read the sermons of his contemporaries; declamatory, scholastic, subtile, they delighted in the minutiae of exegesis or dogma, serving up refined dissertations on the most obscure texts of the Hebrew Bible, to hearers starving for a simple and wholesome diet.

With Francis, on the contrary, all is incisive, clear, practical. He pays no attention to the precepts of the rhetoricians, he forgets himself completely, thinking only of the end desired, the conversion of souls. And conversion was not in his view something vague and indistinct that must take place only between God and the hearer. No, we will have immediate and practical proofs of conversion. We must give up ill-gotten gains, renounce our enmities, be reconciled with our adversaries.

In Assisi, Francis threw himself into the thick of civil dissension. An agreement in 1202 between the parties who divided the city, following the battles with Perugia, had been wholly ephemeral. The common people were continually demanding new freedoms that

"To understand what Francis's preaching must have been like": Father Cuthbert, in his Life of St. Francis of Assisi, adds: "His language was homely, as it was spoken by the people themselves; he borrowed none of the phrases of the schools: oftentimes the homeliness of the speech was elevated only by the sincerity of the speaker, at other times by the dramatic vividness of the thought or a poetic sensibility to nature" (CUTHBERT, p. 115).

In contrast to the vividness of Francis's preaching, one scholar has summarized that of Pope Innocent III: "These sermons, to the modern reader, are dry...barren.... His preaching shows how scholastic influences had turned the Bible from a book of emotional and ethical truth into a book of scientific truth, and how a vast and minute ecclesiastical polity was hardening and drying the living tissue of the great religious organism" (SEDGWICK, Vol. 1, p. 27).

the nobles and burghers would yield to them only under the pressure of fear. Francis took up the cause of the weak, the *minores*, and succeeded in reconciling them with the rich, the *majores*.

His spiritual family as yet, properly speaking, had no name. Unlike those too hasty spirits that baptize their productions before they have come to light, Francis was waiting for the occasion that would reveal the true name he ought to give it.

One day someone was reading the Rule in his presence. When he came to the passage, "Let the brothers, wherever they may find themselves called to labor or to serve, never take an office that will put them over others, but on the contrary, let them always be under (*sint minores*) all those who may be in the house." These words, *sint minores* of the Rule, after the circumstances then existing in the city, suddenly appeared to him as a providential indication. His institution should be called the Order of the Brothers Minor.

We can imagine the effect of this determination. The saint— for already this magic word had burst forth where he appeared—the saint had spoken. It was he who was about to bring peace to the city, acting as arbiter between the two factions that rent it.

We still possess the document of this *pace civile*, exhumed, so to speak, from the communal archives of Assisi by the learned and pious Antonio Cristofani. The opening lines are as follows:

In the name of God!

May the supreme grace of the Holy Spirit assist us! To the honor of our Lord Jesus Christ, the blessed Virgin Mary, the Emperor Otho, and Duke Leopold.

This is the statute and perpetual agreement between the Majori and Minori of Assisi.

Without common consent there shall never be any sort of alliance either with the pope and his nuncios or legates, or with the emperor, or with the king, or with their nuncios or legates, or with any city or town, or with any important person, except with a common accord they shall do all that there may be to do for the honor, safety, and advantage of the commune of Assisi.

What follows is worthy of the beginning. The lords, in consideration of a small periodical payment, should renounce all feudal rights. The inhabitants of the villages subject to Assisi were put on a par with those of the city, foreigners were protected, and the assessment of taxes was fixed. On Wednesday, November 9, 1210, this agreement was signed and sworn to in the public place of Assisi. It was made in such good faith that exiles were able to return in peace, and from this day we find in the city registers the names of those *émigrés* who, in 1202, had betrayed their city and provoked the disastrous war with Perugia. Francis might well be happy. Love had triumphed, and for several years there were at Assisi neither victors nor vanquished.

CHAPTER NINE

Portiuncula, Early Companions, and Their Work (1211)

Now that they were so numerous the brothers could not continue their wandering life in all respects as in the past. They had need of a permanent shelter and above all of a little chapel. Addressing themselves first in vain to the bishop and then to the canons of San Rufino for the loan of what they needed, they were eventually more fortunate with the abbot of the Benedictines of Mount Subasio. He ceded them in perpetuity the use of a chapel already very dear to their hearts—Santa Maria degli Angeli, or, the Portiuncula.

Francis was enchanted. He saw a mysterious harmony, ordained by God, between the name of the humble sanctuary and that of his Order. The brothers quickly built for themselves a few huts; a quickset hedge served as enclosing wall, and thus in three or four days was organized the first Franciscan convent.

For ten years they were satisfied with this. These ten years are the heroic period of the Order. St. Francis, in full possession of his ideal, sought to inculcate it upon his disciples and succeeded sometimes; but already the too rapid multiplication of the brotherhood provoked some symptoms of relaxation.

The remembrance of the beginning of this period drew from the lips of Thomas of Celano a sort of canticle in honor of the monastic life. It is the burning and untranslatable commentary of the psalmist's cry: "Behold how sweet and pleasant it is to be brothers and to dwell together."

Their cloister was the forest that extended on all sides of Portiuncula, occupying a large part of the plain. There they gathered around their master to receive his spiritual counsels, and there they retired to meditate and pray. It would be a great mistake, however, to suppose that contemplation absorbed them completely during the days that were not consecrated to missionary tours: A part of their time was spent in manual labor.

The intentions of St. Francis have been more misapprehended on this point than on any other. It may be said that nowhere is he

74

more clear than when he ordains that his friars should gain their livelihood by the work of their hands. He never dreamed of creating a mendicant order; he created a laboring order. It is true that we often see him begging and urging his disciples to do the same, but these incidents should not mislead us; they are meant to teach that when a friar arrived in a locale and spent his strength for long days dispensing spiritual bread, he ought not to blush to receive material bread in exchange. To work was the rule, to beg the exception, an exception not at all dishonorable. Did not Jesus and the disciples live on bread given to them? Francis—in his poetic language—gave the name of *mensa Domini*, the table of the Lord, to this table of love around which gathered the little poor ones. The bread of charity is the bread of angels, and it is also that of the birds, which do not reap or gather into barns.

With all his gentleness, Francis knew how to show an inflexible severity toward the idle. He even went so far as to dismiss a friar who refused to work. The Brothers, after entering the Order, were to continue to exercise the calling that they had when in the world, and if they had none they were to learn one. For payment they were to accept only the food that was necessary for them, but in case that was insufficient they might beg. In addition they were naturally permitted to own the instruments of their calling. Brother Ginepro, whose acquaintance we shall make further on, had an awl, and gained his bread wherever he went by mending shoes, and we see St. Clare working even on her deathbed.

This obligation to work with the hands merits all the more to be brought into the light because it was hardly destined to survive St. Francis, and because to it is due in part the original character of the first generation of the Order. Yet this was not the real reason for the existence of the Brothers Minor. Their mission consisted above all in being the spouses of Poverty.

Terrified by the ecclesiastical disorders of the time, haunted by

> *Chesterton explains Francis's attitude toward asceticism: "It was not self-denial merely in the sense of self-control. It was as positive as a passion; it had all the air of being as positive as a pleasure.... The whole point of him was that the secret of recovering the natural pleasures lay in regarding them in the light of a supernatural pleasure"* (CHESTERTON, pp. 73, 64).

painful memories of his past life, Francis saw in money the special instrument of the devil. In moments of excitement he went so far as to execrate it, as if there had been in the metal itself a sort of magical power and secret curse. Money was truly for him the sacrament of evil. He felt that in this respect the Rule could not be too absolute, and that if unfortunately the door was opened to various interpretations of it, there would be no stopping point. The course of events and the periodical convulsions that shook his Order show clearly enough how rightly he judged.

St. Francis renounced everything only that he might better possess everything. The lives of the immense majority of our contemporaries are ruled by the fatal error that the more one possesses the more one enjoys. Our exterior, civil liberties continually increase, but at the same time our inward freedom is taking flight. How many are there among us who are literally possessed by what we possess?

Poverty permitted the brothers to mingle with the poor and speak to them with authority. The ever-thickening barriers that modern life, with its sickly search for useless comfort, has set up between us and nature did not exist for these men, so full of youth and life, eager for wide spaces and the outdoor air. This is what gave Francis and his companions that quick susceptibility to nature that made them thrill in mysterious harmony with her. Their communion with nature was so intimate, so ardent, that Umbria, with the harmonious poetry of its skies, the joyful outburst of its springtime, is still the best document from which to study them.

The originality of St. Francis was brilliant; with him Gospel simplicity reappeared upon the earth. Conversions multiplied with an incredible rapidity. Often, as formerly with Jesus, a look, a word

Sabatier foreshadows the unfortunate interior struggles that ripped apart the Order after Francis's death. The "Spirituals" were pitted against leaders of the Order over the subject of faithfulness to Francis's Rule and ideals regarding living a life of poverty. Raphael Brown summarizes the position of the Spirituals, placing Joachim of Fiore in the equation as he describes "the so-called zelanti, or Spirituals, fanatical Joachimist rigorists and contemplatives who considered the Rule and Testament of St. Francis divinely inspired documents that were equal in rank to the Gospels and were destined to effect in an imminent new age the complete regeneration of the Church and society" (BROWN, pp. 19–20).

sufficed Francis to attach to himself people who would follow him until their death. It is impossible to analyze the best of this eloquence, all made of love, intimate apprehension, and fire. The written word can no more give an idea of it than it can give us an idea of a sonata of Beethoven or a painting by Rembrandt.

The class from which Francis recruited his disciples was still about the same. They were nearly all young men of Assisi and its environs, some the sons of agriculturists, and others nobles; the School and the Church were represented very little among them. Men entered the Order without a novitiate of any sort. It sufficed to say to Francis that they wanted to lead with him a life of evangelical perfection, and to prove it by giving all that they possessed to the poor. The more unpretentious were the neophytes the more tenderness he had for them. Like his Master, he had a partiality for those who were lost, for people whom regular society casts out of its limits, but who with all their crimes and scandals are nearer to sainthood than mediocrities and hypocrites.

Benedict of Nursia's foundational Rule for monks, written about 1,500 years ago, contains similar but softer regulations of poverty, compared to Francis's teachings. Francis's aims were to correct the abuses and laxity that had become commonplace since Benedict, and to follow to the letter the injunctions of Jesus to the first apostles.

In one place, Benedict wrote: "For bedding, a mattress, a blanket, a coverlet and a pillow are enough. The beds should be frequently inspected by the Abbot as a precaution against private possessions. If anyone is found to have anything which was not given him by the Abbot, he is to undergo the severest punishment" (PARRY, p. 87).

The life at Portiuncula must have been very different from that of an ordinary monastery. So much youth, simplicity, and love quickly drew the eyes of people toward it. From all sides they were turned to those thatched huts, where dwelt a spiritual family whose members loved one another more than people love on earth, leading a life of labor, mirth, and devotion. The humble chapel seemed a new Zion destined to enlighten the world, and many in their dreams beheld blind humanity coming to kneel there and recover sight.

Among the first disciples who joined themselves to St. Francis we must mention Brother Sylvester, the first priest who entered the Order, the very same whom we have already seen the day that Bernard of Quintavalle distributed his goods among the poor. Since then he had not had a moment's peace, bitterly reproaching himself for his avarice.

By his age and the nature of the memory he has left behind, Sylvester resembles Brother Bernard. He was what is usually understood by a holy priest, but nothing denotes that he had the truly Franciscan love of great enterprises, distant journeys, perilous missions. Withdrawn into one of the grottos of the Carceri, absorbed in the contemplative life, he gave spiritual counsel to his brothers as occasion served.

The typical Franciscan priest is Brother Leo. The date of his entrance into the Order is not exactly known, but we are probably not far from the truth in placing it about 1214. Of a charming simplicity—tender, affectionate, refined—he was, with Brother Elias, the one who played the noblest part during the obscure years in which the new reform was being elaborated.

We still should say a word concerning two disciples who were always closely united with Brother Leo in the Franciscan memorials—Rufino and Masseo.

Rufino, Leo, Angelo (the "three companions" who composed The Legend of the Three Companions)*, and Masseo were four of Francis's closest friends. In both age and spirit, they were like his sons. The four of them were buried near Francis, "at the four corners of his sarcophagus"* (HOUSE, p. 113).

Born of a noble family connected with that of St. Clare, Rufino was soon distinguished in the Order for his visions and ecstasies, but his great timidity checked him as soon as he tried to preach. For this reason he is always to be found in the most isolated hermitages—Carceri, Verna, Greccio.

Masseo of Marignano, a small village in the environs of Assisi, was his very opposite. Handsome, well-made, witty, he attracted attention by his fine presence and his great facility of speech. He occupies a special place in popular Franciscan tradition. He deserves it. St. Francis, to test his humility, made Masseo the porter and cook of the hermitage, but in these functions Masseo showed himself to be so perfectly a *Minor* that from that time the master particularly loved to have him for companion in his missionary journeys.

For several years the Brothers Minor traveled from lazaretto to lazaretto, preaching by day in the towns and villages and retiring at night to these refuges, where they rendered to the lepers, these "patients of God," the most repugnant services. The Crucigeri Order, who took charge of the majority of leper-houses and hospitals, always welcomed these kindly disposed aides, who, far from asking any sort of recompense, were willing to eat whatever the patients might have left. The following narrative shows Francis's love for these unfortunates, and his method with them:

It happened one time that the Brothers were serving the lepers and the sick in a hospital, near to the place where St. Francis was. Among them was a leper who was so impatient, so unendurable, that everyone believed him to be possessed by the devil, and rightly enough, for he heaped insults and blows upon those who waited upon him. The Brothers would willingly have endured the insults and abuse which he lavished upon them, in order to augment the merit of their patience, but their souls could not consent to hear those which he uttered against Christ and his Mother. They therefore resolved to abandon this leper, but not without having told the whole story exactly to St. Francis, who at that time was dwelling not far away.

When they told him, St. Francis went to the leper, saying, "May God give you peace, my most dear brother."

"And what peace," asked the leper, "can I receive from God, who has taken away my peace and every good thing, and has made my body a mass of stinking and corruption?"

St. Francis said to him: "My brother, be patient, for God gives us diseases in this world for the salvation of our souls, and when we endure them patiently they are a fountain of great merit to us."

"How can I endure patiently pains which torture me day and night? And it is not only my disease that I suffer from, but the friars that you gave me to wait upon me are unendurable, and do not take care of me as they ought."

Then St. Francis took to his knees to pray for the man: "My son, since you are not satisfied with the others, I will wait upon you."

"That is all very well, but what can you do for me more than they?"

"I will do whatever you wish."

"Very well. I wish you to wash me from head to foot, for I smell so badly that I disgust myself."

Then St. Francis made haste to heat some water with many sweet-smelling herbs. He took off the leper's clothes and began to bathe him, while another brother poured out the water. And behold, wherever St. Francis touched him with his holy hands the leprosy disappeared and the flesh became perfectly sound. And in proportion as the flesh was healed the soul of the wretched man was also healed, and he began to feel a lively sorrow for his sins, and to weep bitterly.

Being completely healed both in body and soul, the man cried with all his might: "I have deserved hell for the abuses and outrages which I have said and done to the brothers, for my impatience and my blasphemies." (See BROWN, no. 25.)

These details show the Umbrian movement, as it appears to me, to be one of the most humble and at the same time the most sincere and practical attempts to realize the kingdom of God on earth. How far removed we are here from the superstitious vulgarity of mechanical devotion, the deceitful miracle-working of certain Catholics; how far also from the commonplace, complacent, quibbling, theorizing Christianity of certain Protestants!

Francis is a mystic for whom no intermediary comes between God and his soul. But his mysticism is that of Jesus leading his disciples to the Tabor of contemplation. When, overflooded with joy, they long to build tabernacles that they may remain on the heights and satiate themselves with the raptures of ecstasy, he says to them, "Fools, you know not what you ask." And directing their gaze to the crowds wandering like sheep having no shepherd, he leads them back to the plain, to the midst of those who moan, who suffer, who blaspheme.

But the higher the moral stature of Francis the more he was exposed to the danger of being understood only by the very few, and disappointed by those

In Palestine, a few miles southeast of Nazareth, Mount Tabor rises nearly 2,000 feet above the Mediterranean Sea. The Hebrew Bible tells how the prophetess Deborah instructed Barak to go up the mountain and wait for Sisera, general of the army of the Canaanites, to approach from below. Sisera, with all of his chariots, fell into the trap as Barak descended Tabor with ten thousand soldiers and slaughtered the armies of Canaan (Judg. 4:1–16). In contrast to this bit of history, Tabor is known for its beauty and is often referred to poetically as a place of contemplation. Tabor is not mentioned by name in the New Testament, but both Cyril of Jerusalem and Jerome, two of the greatest of the early Church fathers, identify it as the place of Christ's Transfiguration.

who were nearest to him. Brother Rufino, for example, the same who was destined to become one of the intimates of Francis's later days, assumed an attitude of revolt shortly after his entrance into the Order. He thought it foolish in Francis when, instead of leaving the friars to give themselves unceasingly to prayer, he sent them out in all directions to wait upon lepers. His own ideal was the life of the hermits of the Thebaide, as it is related in the then popular legends of St. Anthony, St. Paul, St. Pachomius, and others.

Rufino once passed Lent in one of the grottos of the Carceri. Holy Thursday having arrived, Francis, who was also there, summoned all the brothers who were dispersed about the neighborhood, whether in grottos or huts, to observe with him the memories to which this day was consecrated. Rufino refused to come. "For that matter," he added, "I have decided to follow him no longer. I mean to remain here and live solitary, for in this way I shall be more surely saved than by submitting myself to this man and his nonsense."

Saints Anthony, Paul, and Pachomius were among the first people to become "desert monks" in the third and fourth centuries C.E., leaving cities like Alexandria and Antioch and entering the desert regions of Egypt, Palestine, and Syria to live in caves. The extreme ascetic feats of these people were often compared to those of the athletes of Greece and Rome.

Young and enthusiastic for the most part, the brothers often found it difficult to keep their work in the background. Agreeing with their master as to fundamentals, they would have liked to make more of a stir, attract public attention by more obvious devotion. There were some among them whom it did not satisfy to be saints, but who also wished to appear such.

CHAPTER TEN
Brother Francis and Sister Clare

Popular piety in Umbria never separates the memory of St. Francis from that of St. Clare.

Clare was born at Assisi in 1194 and was consequently about twelve years younger than Francis. She belonged to the noble family of the Offreduccio. At the age when a little girl's imagination awakes and stirs, she heard the follies of the son of Bernardone recounted at length. She was sixteen when the saint preached for the first time in the cathedral, suddenly appearing like an angel of peace in a city torn by intense dissentions.

To her his appeals were like a revelation. It seemed as if Francis was speaking for her, that he divined her secret sorrows, her most personal anxieties, and all that was ardent and enthusiastic in the heart of this young girl rushed like a torrent that suddenly finds an outlet into the channel indicated by him. After the sermons of Francis at San Rufino, Clare's decision was speedily taken; she would break away from the trivialities of an idle and luxurious life and make herself the servant of the poor. She sought Francis out and opened her heart to him.

Now, it is one of the privileges of saints to suffer more than other people, for they feel in their more loving hearts the echo of all the sorrows of the world, but they also know joys and delights of which most of us never taste. What an inexpressible song of joy must have burst forth in Francis's heart when he saw Clare on her knees before him, awaiting, with his blessing, the word that would consecrate her life to the gospel ideal.

Francis was too kind to submit Clare to useless tests, too much an idealist to prudently confine himself to custom or arbitrary decorum; as when he founded the Order of Friars, he took counsel only of himself and God. In this was his strength; if he had hesitated, or even if he had simply submitted himself to ecclesiastical rules, he would have been stopped twenty times before he had done anything. Francis, a simple deacon, arrogated to himself the right to receive Clare's vows and admit her to the Order without the briefest novitiate. Such an act ought to have drawn down upon its author all the censures of the Church, but Francis was already one of those powers to whom much is forgiven.

Francis decided that on the night between Palm Sunday and Holy Monday (March 18–19, 1212) Clare should secretly quit the paternal castle and come with two companions to Portiuncula, where he would await her, and would give her the veil. She arrived just as the friars were singing matins. They went out, the story goes, carrying candles in their hands, to meet the bride, while from the woods around Portiuncula resounded songs of joy. Then mass was begun at that same altar where, three years

Francis's love for Poverty is often characterized in terms of great intimacy. This is especially true in the earliest documents about him. Even Dante writes, in his Paradiso:

> Then day by day more fervently
>   he loved her.
> She, reft of her first husband,
>   scorned, obscure,
> One thousand and one hundred
>   years and more,
> Waited without a suitor till he
>   came. (CANTO XI)

before, Francis had heard the decisive call of Jesus; he was kneeling in the same place, but surrounded now with a whole spiritual family.

It is easy to imagine Clare's emotion. The step that she had just taken was simply heroic, for she knew to what persecutions from her family she was exposing herself, and what she had seen of the life of the Brothers Minor was a sufficient warning of the distresses to which she was exposing herself in espousing poverty. No doubt she interpreted the words of the service in harmony with her own thoughts:

> [The Lord] said, "Surely they are my people, children who will not deal falsely"; and he became their savior in all their distress.
> It was no messenger or angel but his presence that saved them;
> in his love and in his pity he redeemed them." (Isa. 63:8–9a)

Then Francis read again the words of Jesus to his disciples; Clare vowed to conform her life to them; her hair was cut; all was finished. A few moments after, Francis escorted her to a house of Benedictine nuns at an hour's distance where she was to remain provisionally and await the progress of events.

The very next morning Favorino, her father, arrived with a few friends, inveighing, supplicating, abusing everybody. Clare was immovable, showing so much courage that at last they gave up the thought of carrying her off by force.

She was not, however, at the end of her tribulations. A week after Easter, Agnes, her younger sister, joined her, deciding also to serve poverty. Francis received her into the Order. This time the father's fury was horrible. With a band of relatives he invaded the convent, but neither abuse nor blows could subdue this child of fourteen. In spite of Agnes's cries they dragged her away. She fainted, and the little inanimate body suddenly seemed to them so heavy that they abandoned it in the midst of the fields, some laborers looking with pity on the painful scene, until Clare, whose cry God had heard, hastened to succor her sister.

Francis knew that several others were burning to join his two women friends. He set himself to seek out a retreat where they could live under his direction and in all liberty practice the Gospel rule. Francis, who already was their debtor for Portiuncula, once more addressed himself to the Benedictine monks of Mount Subasio. Happy in this new opportunity to render service to one who was the incarnation of popular claims, they gave him the chapel of San Damiano. In this new hermitage, so well adapted for prayer and meditation, Francis installed his spiritual daughters. In this sanctuary, repaired by his own hands, at the feet of the crucifix that had spoken to him, Clare was henceforward to pray. It was the house of God, but it was also in good measure that of Francis.

At this moment Francis no more expected to found a second order than he had desired to found the first one. In installing Clare at San Damiano he was preparing a refuge for those who desired to imitate her and apart from the world practice the gospel rule. But he never thought that the perfection of which he and his disciples were the apostles and missionaries, and which Clare and her companions were to realize in celibacy, was not also practicable in social positions. Whoever was free at heart from all material servitude, whoever decided to live without hoarding, rich people who were willing to labor with their hands and loyally distribute all that they did not consume, poor people who were willing to work and free to resort, in the strict measure of their needs, to the common fund that Francis called "the Lord's table," these were at that time true Franciscans. It was a social revolution.

There was then at that time neither one order nor several. The gospel of the Beatitudes had been found again, and, as twelve centuries before, it could accommodate itself to all situations.

In installing Clare at San Damiano Francis put into her hands the Rule that he had prepared for her, which no doubt resembled that of the brothers save for the precepts with regard to the missionary life. He accompanied it with the plans of himself and his brothers to supply by labor or alms all the needs of Clare and her future companions. In return they also were to work and render to the brothers all the services of which they might be capable. We have seen the zeal that Francis had brought to the task of making the churches worthy of the worship celebrated in them; he could not endure that the linen put to sacred uses should be less than clean. Clare set herself to spinning thread for the altar-cloths and corporals that the brothers undertook to distribute among the poor churches of the district. In addition, during the earlier years, she also nursed the sick whom Francis sent to her, and San Damiano was for some time a sort of hospital.

The Tertiari, or "Third Order," was formally founded by those who came after Francis, although Francis recognized the needs of men and women who, while remaining in the world, nevertheless desired to live in accordance with his strict interpretation of the gospel. The Third Order (still very active today) became the formal organization for Francis's more simple desires that all people—not just those who took solemn vows of celibacy—would follow the true teachings of Jesus. In his simple way, Francis wrote: "Father, all those whom you have given me in the world were yours and you have given them to me. The words that you gave me, I have given to them" (ARMSTRONG, p. 49). Francis "gave" Christ's words to the people most directly through his preaching and, Sabatier argues, did not see it necessary that most people follow him in the sense of joining the Brothers Minor or Sisters of Clare. (See MOORMAN, chap. 5.)

One or two friars, who were called Zealots of the Poor Ladies, were especially charged with the care of the Sisters, making themselves huts beside the chapel, after the model of those of Portiuncula. Francis was also near at hand; a sort of terrace four paces long overlooks the hermitage. Clare made there a tiny garden, and when at twilight she went there to water her flowers she could see Portiuncula standing out against the aureola of the western sky.

But such a situation could not last long. Clare survived Francis nearly twenty-seven years, and thus had time to see the shipwreck of the Franciscan ideal among the brothers, as well as in almost every one of the houses that had at first followed the Rule of San Damiano. Cardinal Ugolini—the future Gregory IX—in particular, took a part in these matters that is very difficult to understand. We see him continually lavishing upon Francis and Clare expressions of affection and admiration that appear to be absolutely sincere. Yet, the Franciscan ideal—regarded as the life of love at which one arrives by freeing him or herself from all servitude to material things—has hardly had a worse adversary.

In the month of May 1228, Gregory IX went to Assisi for the preliminaries of the canonization of St. Francis. Before entering the city he turned out of his way to visit San Damiano and to see Clare, whom he had known for a long time. He represented to her that the state of the times made life impossible to women who possess nothing, and offered her certain properties. As Clare gazed at him in astonishment at this strange proposition, he said, "If it is your vows that prevent you, we will release you from them."

"Holy Father," replied the Franciscan sister, "absolve me of my sins, but I have no desire for a dispensation from following Christ." In these words is mirrored at full length the spiritual daughter of the

The story of Abelard and Heloise was fresh in the minds of late-twelfth-century Europeans. Eighty years before Francis and Clare first met, the scandal of Abelard and Heloise shocked the Western world on many levels: religious, in the academy, and in popular imagination. Their story became the equivalent of today's popular magazine gossip.

Abelard was the most brilliant—and arrogant—philosopher and theologian of the twelfth century. Heloise, his young student, also became his lover, and their amorous encounters even continued after Heloise's admittance to a convent. When word of the relationship reached Heloise's uncle and guardian, he sent thugs to castrate the young scholar. Abelard became a monk himself soon thereafter and was later accused of heresy by the eminent Bernard of Clairvaux.

This story, in all of its tragedy, is similar to that of Francis and Clare only in their affection for each other. But the mutual love between Francis and Clare was entirely filial.

Poverello. She had penetrated to the inmost depths of Francis's heart, and felt herself inflamed with the same passion that burned in him. She remained faithful to him to the end, but we perceive that it was not without difficulty.

San Damiano often echoed with St. Francis's hymns of love and liberty and did not forget him so soon or become an ordinary convent. Clare remained surrounded with the master's early companions: Egidio, Leo, Angelo, and Ginepro never ceased to be assiduous visitors. These true lovers of poverty felt themselves at home there, and took liberties that would elsewhere have given surprise.

One day an English friar, a celebrated theologian, came according to the minister's orders to preach at San Damiano. Suddenly Egidio, though a simple layperson, interrupted him: "Stop, brother, let me speak," he said. And the master of theology, bowing his head, covered himself with his cowl as a sign of obedience, and sat down to listen.

Clare felt great joy in this. It seemed to her that she was once again living in Francis's days. The little coterie was kept up until her death. She expired in the arms of Brothers Leo, Angelo, and Ginepro. In her last sufferings and her dying visions she had the supreme happiness of being surrounded by those who had devoted their lives to the same ideal as she.

After Francis's death, Clare was in some ways a widow. There are hints of loneliness in her few writings, including her Rule for the sisters. She referred to herself as the plantuncula *of St. Francis, or "little plant" of his movement, a reference, no doubt intentional in similarity to the Portiuncula, or "little portion," the beloved place where Francis often resided, and where he chose to die.*

After Clare died in 1253, the sisters moved from the remote San Damiano to the chapel of San Giorgio, the same place where Francis had been schooled as a boy, and where he first preached in 1209. The Basilica di Santa Clara was built around San Giorgio from 1257 to 1265, and the famous crucifix of San Damiano—the one that had communicated so clearly with Francis—was moved to the chapel of San Giorgio in the new basilica.

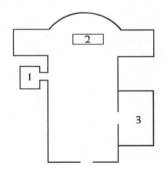

Basic floorplan of Basilica di Santa Clara, as it can be seen today, reproduced after DEAN, p. 9.

1 Chapel of St. Agnes (Clare's younger sister)
2 The high altar
3 Chapel of San Giorgio (also called Chapel of the Crucifix). Clare's tomb is in the crypt below the basilica.

CHAPTER ELEVEN

Francis's Love for All Creatures
(Autumn 1212–Summer 1215)

All eyes were turned toward Syria, where a French knight, Jean of Brienne, had just been declared King of Jerusalem (1210), and toward which were hastening the bands of the Children's Crusade.

The conversion of Francis, radical as it was, giving a new direction to his thoughts and will, had not had power to change the foundation of his character. Francis still remained a knight, and it is perhaps this that won for him in so high a degree the worship of the finest souls of the Middle Ages. There was in him that longing for the unknown, that thirst for adventures and sacrifices, that makes the history of his century so grand and so attractive, in spite of many dark features.

Those who have a genius for religion have generally the privilege of illusion. They never quite see how large the world is. When their faith has moved a mountain they thrill with rapture, like the old Hebrew prophets, and it seems to them that they see the dawning of the day "when the glory of the Lord will appear, when the wolf and the lamb will feed together." We sometimes see that blessed illusion, firing the blood like a generous wine, as these soldiers of righteousness hurl themselves against the most terrific fortresses, believing that these once taken the war will be ended.

The Children's Crusade was one of the most tragic events of the enormously tragic crusading era of the eleventh to fifteenth centuries. Nineteen years after the death of Saladin, the great Muslim leader, and seven years before Francis's visit to the crusading front, a twelve-year-old shepherd boy named Stephen preached a crusade for children in front of the abbey of Saint-Denis, in France. Philip, the French king, saw the boy but sent him away, failing to anticipate the effect that his young witness would have on the families of France and Germany. While young Stephen told the thousands of young followers who eventually amassed at his side that "The seas would dry up before them, and they would pass, like Moses through the Red Sea, safe to the Holy Land," the reality was that nearly every one of the boys and girls died— several thousand in all—either of hunger and fatigue along the way to the Sea, or aboard ship or in the waters somewhere between Marseilles and Palestine (RUNCIMAN, pp. 139–43).

Francis had found such joys in his union with poverty that he believed that one needed only to be human to aspire after the same happiness, and that the Saracens would be converted in crowds to the gospel of Jesus, if only it were announced to them in all its simplicity. He therefore left Portiuncula for this new kind of crusade.

It is not known from what port he embarked; it was probably in the autumn of 1212. A tempest having cast the ship upon the coast of Slavonia, he was obliged to resign himself either to remain several months in those parts or to return to Italy. Francis decided to return, but found much difficulty in securing a passage on a ship that was about to sail for Ancona. When the stock of food fell short Francis shared with the sailors the provisions with which his friends had overloaded him.

No sooner had he landed back in Italy than Francis set out on a preaching tour, in which souls responded to his appeals with more eagerness than ever before. One day, Francis and a companion, perhaps Brother Leo, arrived at the chateau of Montefeltro, between Macerata and San Marino. A grand fete was being given for the reception of a new knight and without hesitation they entered the court where all the nobility of the country was assembled. Taking for his text two lines from a popular poem (*Tanto e il bene ch' aspetto* "The happiness that I expect" / *Ch'ogni pena m e diletto* "is so great that all pain is joyful to me"), Francis preached so touching a sermon that several of those present forgot for a moment the party for which they had come.

It was perhaps also during this Lent (spring 1213) that Francis retired to an island in Lake Trasimeno, making a sojourn there that afterward became famous in his legend. But his aim at this time was not to evangelize Italy. His friars were already scattered over it in great numbers. Francis still desired to gain them access to new countries.

Not having been able to reach the infidels in Syria, he resolved to seek them in Morocco. A short time before (July 1212), the troops of the Almohades had met an irreparable defeat in the plains of Tolosa. Beaten by a coalition of the Kings of Aragon, Navarre, and Castile, Mohammed-el-Naser returned to Morocco to die. Francis felt that this victory of arms would be nothing if it were not followed by a peaceful victory of the gospel spirit.

The early biographers are unfortunately most laconic with regard to this expedition. They merely say that on arriving in Spain he was so seriously ill that a return home was imperative. Beyond a few local legends, not very well attested, we possess no other information on the labors of the saint in this country, or upon the route that he followed either in going or returning. But the mission in Spain must have taken place between the Whitsunday of 1214 and that of 1215.

Now we are approaching one of the most obscure periods of his life. Francis seems to have passed through one of those crises of discouragement so frequent with those who long to realize the ideal in this world. Had he seen in the check of his missions to Syria and Morocco a providential indication that he had to change his method? Had he discovered the warning signs of the misfortunes that were to come upon his family? We do not know. But about this time Francis felt the need of turning to St. Clare and Brother Sylvester for counsel on the subject of his doubts and hesitations. Their replies restored to him peace and joy. God, by their mouths, commanded him to continue his apostolate.

Full of joy received through Clare, going on his way south-west from Assisi toward Bevagna, Francis saw some flocks of birds. He turned aside a little from the road to go to them. Far from taking flight, they flocked around him as if to bid him welcome.

"Brother birds," Francis said, "you ought to praise and love your Creator very much. He has given you feathers for clothing, wings for flying, and all that is needful for you. He has made you the noblest of creatures, permits you to live in the pure air, and you neither have to sow or reap; he takes care of you, watches over you, and guides you." Then the birds began to arch their necks, to spread out their wings, to open their beaks, to look at him as if to thank him, while he went up and down in their midst stroking them with the border of his tunic, sending them away at last with his blessing.

On this same tour, passing through Alviano, Francis spoke a few exhortations to the people, but the swallows so filled the air with their chirping that he could not make himself heard. "It is my turn to speak," he said to them. "Little sister swallows, listen to the word of God. Keep silent and be very quiet until I have finished."

We see how Francis's love extended to all creation, how the diffused life shed abroad on all things inspired and moved him. From the sun to the earthworm that we trample under foot, everything breathed in his ear the ineffable sigh of beings that live and suffer and die, and in their life as in their death have a part in the divine work.

"Praised be you, Lord, with all your creatures, especially for my brother Sun that gives us the day and through him you show your light. He is beautiful and radiant with great splendor. Of you, Most High, he is the symbol."

Bonaventure wrote often on the mystical importance of light. All light emanates from a Platonic form of Light, according to Bonaventure. "Light is the substantial form of bodies; by their greater or lesser participation in light, bodies acquire the truth and dignity of their being" (ECO, p. 50).

Here again, Francis revives the Hebrew inspiration, the simple and grandiose view of the prophets of Israel. "Praise the Lord!" the royal psalmist sang. "Praise the Lord, fire and frost, snow and mists, stormy winds that do his will, mountains and hills, fruit-trees and cedars, beasts and cattle, creeping things and birds with wings!"

The day of the birds of Bevagna remained in his memory as one of the most beautiful of his whole life, and though usually so reserved he always loved to tell of it. He felt that he owed to Clare these pure ardors that brought him into a secret and delicious communion with all beings; it was she who had revived him from sadness and hesitation. In his heart he bore an immense gratitude to her who, just when he needed it, had known how to return to him love for love, inspiration for inspiration.

Francis's sympathy for animals, as we see it shining forth here, has none of the sentimentalism that in the poets of the thirteenth century is so often false and affected. In him it was not only true, but had in it something alive, healthy, robust. It is this vein of poetry that awoke Italy to self-consciousness, made her in a few years forget the nightmare of Catharist ideas, and rescued her from pessimism. By it Francis became the forerunner of the artistic movement that preceded the Renaissance, the inspirer of that group of pre-Raphaelites, awkward, grotesque in drawing though at times they were, to whom we turn today with a sort of piety, finding in their ungraceful saints an inner life, a moral feeling that we seek elsewhere in vain.

If the voice of the Poverello of Assisi was so well understood it was because in this matter, as in all others, it was entirely unconventional. How far we are, with him, from the fierce Pharisaic piety of those monks that forbade even the females of animals to enter their monasteries! Francis's notion of chastity in no sense resembles this excessive prudery. One day in Siena he asked for some turtle-doves, and holding them in the skirt of his tunic, he said: "Little sisters, you are simple, innocent, and chaste. Why did you let yourselves be caught? I shall save you from death and have nests made for you so that you may bring forth young and multiply according to the commandment of our Creator." And he went and made nests for them all, and the turtle-doves began to lay eggs and bring up their broods under the eyes of the brothers.

At Rieti a family of red-breasts were the guests of the monastery, and the young birds made marauding expeditions on the very table where the brothers were eating. Not far from there, at Greccio, they brought to Francis a leveret that had been taken alive in a trap. "Come to me, brother leveret," he said to it. And as the poor creature, being set free, ran to him for refuge, he took it up, caressed it, and finally put it on the ground that it might run away. But it returned to him again and again so that Francis was obliged to send it to the neighboring forest before it would consent to return to freedom.

One day Francis was crossing the Lake of Rieti. The man in whose boat he was making the passage offered Francis a fish of uncommon size. Francis accepted it with joy, but to the great amazement of the fisherman put it back in the water, bidding it bless God.

Francis was, like many of us, one who saw the Creator most clearly through the creation. Never a severe ascetic in his theology (he was no John of the Cross), Francis resembled in some ways his later countryman, Dante, who, even on the threshold of the beatific vision in the Paradiso couldn't for long seem to take his eyes off of Beatrice, his childhood friend and love.

"Francis was not a lover of nature. He never even uses the word. What Francis loved were birds, flowers, fire, water, animals, and people. He was interested in the concrete: he loved [people], not humanity; wolves, not wildlife; Christ, not Christianity." (CUNNINGHAM 2, p. XII).

We would never be done if we related all the incidents of this kind, for the sentiment of nature was innate with him; it was a perpetual communion that made him love the whole creation. He was ravished with the witchery of great forests; he had the terrors of a child when alone at prayer in a deserted chapel, but he tasted ineffable joy merely in inhaling the perfume of a flower, or gazing into the limpid water of a brook.

The perfect lover of poverty permitted one luxury—he even commanded it at Portiuncula—flowers. The brothers were bidden not to only sow vegetables and useful plants, but to reserve one corner of good ground for our sisters, the flowers of the fields. Francis talked with them also, or rather he replied to them, for their mysterious and gentle language crept into the very depth of his heart.

The thirteenth century was prepared to understand the voice of the Umbrian poet. The sermon to the birds closed the reign of Byzantine art and of the thought of which it was the image. It is the end of dogmatism and authority; very uncertain, no doubt, and to be followed by obstinate reactions, but nonetheless marking a date in the history of the human conscience.

Many among the companions of Francis were too much the children of their century, too thoroughly imbued with its theological and metaphysical methods, to quite understand a sentiment so simple and profound as Francis's love for all creatures. But each in degree felt its charm. Here, Thomas of Celano's language rises to an elevation that we find in no other part of his works, closing with a picture of Francis that makes us think of the Song of Songs:

"Of more than middle height, Francis had a delicate and kindly face, black eyes, a soft and sonorous voice. There was in his whole person a delicacy and grace that made him infinitely lovely. All these characteristics are found in the most ancient portraits."

Fresco painting of Francis from *Sacro Speco* ("holy cave"), the grotto in which St. Benedict lived for a time in the fifth century. A Benedictine abbey still surrounds this place today in Subiaco, Italy. (Art reproduced from SEDGWICK, 1:74.)

CHAPTER TWELVE

His Inner Life and Wonder-Working

The missionary journey, undertaken under the encouragement of St. Clare and so poetically inaugurated by the sermon to the birds of Bevagna, appears to have been a continual triumph for Francis. Legend definitely takes possession of him. Whether he will or not, miracles burst forth under his footsteps. Quite unexpectedly the objects of which he had made use produced marvelous effects; folk came out from the villages in procession to meet him.

One day Brother Masseo desired to put his modesty to the test:

"Everybody follows you, everyone desires to see you, hear you, and obey you, and yet for all that you are neither beautiful, nor learned, nor of noble family. Where does it come from, then, that it should be you whom the world desires to follow?"

On hearing these words the blessed Francis, full of joy, raised his eyes to heaven, and after remaining a long time absorbed in contemplation he knelt, praising and blessing God with great fervor. Then turning toward Masseo, he said, "You wish to know why it is me whom people follow? You wish to know? It is because the eyes of the Most High have willed it. He continually watches the good and the wicked, and as his most holy eyes have not found among sinners any smaller person, not any more insufficient and more sinful, therefore

Masseo was the handsome brother mentioned above (chap. 9, p. 78). Despite his physical beauty and personal grace and charm, Masseo's humility was a delight to Francis. The Little Flowers* tells many stories of Masseo and Francis together. One story depicts the two brothers begging their daily bread while on a journey to France. Masseo went through one street, Francis another. And while Masseo received choice food—fresh bread cut from the loaf—Francis received only meager scraps. The discrepancy only added to Francis's joy, we are told, and the two men blessed the gifts received by Divine Providence.

* The Little Flowers is a collection of short tales from the life and legend of Francis compiled by one Brother Ugolino (not to be confused with Cardinal Ugolino, Francis's contemporary, who became Pope Gregory IX) after the saint's death. First written in Latin, the book was titled Actus Beati Francisci et Sociorum Ejus ("The Deeds of St. Francis and His Companions"), and later abridged and translated into Italian as I Fioretti di San Francesco ("The Little Flowers of St. Francis").

he has chosen me to accomplish the marvelous work that God has undertaken. He chose me because he could find no one more worthless, and he wished here to confound the nobility and grandeur, the strength, beauty, and the learning of this world."

This reply throws a ray of light upon St. Francis's heart. The message that he brought to the world is once again the glad tidings announced to the poor; its purpose is the taking up again of that messianic work that the Virgin of Nazareth caught a glimpse of in her *Magnificat*, that song of love and liberty, the sighs of which breathe the vision of a new social state. He comes to remind the world that the welfare of humanity, the peace of our hearts, the joy of our lives, are neither in money, nor in learning, nor in strength, but in an upright and sincere will.

It was in prayer that Francis found the spiritual strength that he needed; he therefore sought for silence and solitude. If he knew how to do battle in the midst of people in order to win them to the faith, he loved, as Celano says, to fly away like a bird going to make its nest upon a mountain.

With people like Francis, the prayer of the lips, the formulated prayer, is hardly more than an inferior form of true prayer. Even when it is sincere and attentive, and not a mechanical repetition, it is only a

The Magnificat, or "Song of Mary," is one of the loveliest prayers in scripture. It is recorded in Luke's Gospel (1:46–55) and used in public prayer in most Protestant and Catholic liturgical churches:

My soul magnifies the Lord,
and my spirit rejoices in God my
Savior,
for he has looked with favor on the
lowliness of his servant.
Surely, from now on all generations
will call me blessed;
for the Mighty One has done great
things for me,
and holy is his name.
His mercy is for those who fear him
from generation to generation.
He has shown strength with his
arm;
he has scattered the proud in the
thoughts of their hearts.
He has brought down the powerful
from their thrones,
and lifted up the lowly;
he has filled the hungry with good
things,
and sent the rich away empty.
He has helped his servant Israel,
in remembrance of his mercy,
according to the promise he made to
our ancestors,
to Abraham and to his descendants
forever.

prelude for souls not dead of religious materialism. Formulas of prayer are as incapable of speaking the emotions of the soul as model love-letters of speaking the transports of an impassioned heart. To pray is to talk with God, to lift ourselves up to God, to converse with God that God may come down to us. It is an act of meditation, of reflection, that presupposes the effort of all that is most personal in us. Looked at in this sense, prayer is the mother of all freedom. Whether or not it be a soliloquy of the soul with itself, the soliloquy would be none less than the very foundation of a strong individuality.

Now we have come to one of the most delicate features of the life of Francis—his relations with diabolical powers. Customs and ideas have so profoundly changed in all that concerns the existence of the devil and his relations with people, that it is almost impossible to picture to oneself the enormous place that the thought of demons occupied at that time in the minds of people.

The best minds of the Middle Ages believed without a doubt in the existence of the perverse spirit, in his perpetual transformations in an endeavor to tempt people and cause them to fall into his snares. Even in the sixteenth century, Luther, who undermined so many beliefs, had no more doubt of the personal existence of Satan than of sorcery, conjurations, or possessions.

Finding in their souls a wide background of grandeur and wretchedness, from where they sometimes heard a burst of distant harmonies calling them to a higher life, soon to be overpowered by the clamors of the brute, our ancestors could not refrain from seeking the explanation of this duel. They found it in the conflict of the demons with God.

This is how St. Francis, with all people of his time, explained the disquietudes, terrors, and anguish with which his heart was at times assailed, as well as the hopes, consolations, and joys in which his soul was most often bathed. Wherever we follow his steps local tradition has preserved the memory of rude assaults of the tempter that he had to undergo.

Francis believed himself to have many a time fought with the devil, but while for his contemporaries and some of his disciples apparitions, prodigies, and possessions were daily phenomena, for Francis they were exceptional, and remained entirely in the background.

In the iconography of St. Benedict, as in that of most of the popular saints, the devil occupies a preponderant place. In that of St. Francis he disappears so completely that in the long series of Giotto's frescos at Assisi the devil is not seen a single time.

In the same way all that is magic and miracle-working occupies in Francis's life an entirely secondary rank. Jesus in the Gospels gave his apostles power to cast out evil spirits, and to heal all sickness and all infirmity. Francis surely took literally these words, which made a part of his Rule. He believed that he could work miracles, and he willed to do so, but his religious thought was too pure to permit him to consider miracles otherwise than as an entirely exceptional means of relieving the sufferings of people. Not once do we see him resorting to miracle to prove his apostolate or to bolster up his ideas. His tact taught him that souls are worthy of being won by better means. This almost complete absence of the marvelous (miracles occupy only ten paragraphs in Celano's first biography of the saint) is all the more remarkable in that it is in absolute contradiction with the tendencies of his time.

Many heretical groups, by contrast, often took advantage of this thirst for the marvelous to dupe the faithful. The Cathars of Moncoul, for example, made a portrait of the Virgin representing her as one-eyed and toothless, saying that in his humility Christ had chosen a very ugly woman for mother. They had no difficulty in healing several cases of disease by its means; the image became famous, was venerated almost everywhere, and accomplished many miracles until the day when the heretics divulged the deception to the great scandal of the faithful.

Open the life of Francis's disciple, St. Anthony of Padua (d. 1231) and it is a tiresome catalog of prodigies, healings, resurrections. One would say it was rather the prospectus of some scientist who had invented a new drug than a call to people to conversion and a higher life. It may interest invalids or devotees, but neither the heart nor the conscience is touched by it. It must be said in fairness to Anthony of Padua that his relations with Francis appear to have been very slight.

Among the earliest disciples who had time to fathom their master's thought to the very depths we find traces of this noble disdain of the marvelous. They knew too well that the perfect joy is not to astound the world with miracles, but that it lives in the love that goes even to self-immolation. *Mihi absit gloriari nisi in cruce Domini.* "May I never boast of anything except the cross of our Lord Jesus Christ . . ." (Gal. 6:14). This is, to this day, the motto of the Brothers Minor.

Thus Brother Egidio asked of God the grace not to perform miracles. He saw in them, as in the passion for learning, a snare in which the proud would be taken, and that would distract the Order from its true mission.

St. Francis's miracles are all acts of love. The greater number of them are found in the healing of nervous maladies, those apparently inexplicable disquietudes that are the cruel afflictions of critical times. His gentle glance, at once so compassionate and so strong, that seemed like a messenger from his heart, often sufficed to make those who met it forget their suffering.

Jesus was right in saying that a look sufficed to make one an adulterer. But there is also a look—that of the contemplative Mary, for example—that is worth all sacrifices because it includes them all, because it gives, consecrates, immolates the one who looks. Civilization dulls this power of the glance. A part of the education the world gives us consists in teaching our eyes to deceive, in making them expressionless, in extinguishing their flames.

Thomas of Celano recounts: "A Brother was suffering unspeakable tortures. Sometimes he would roll on the ground, striking against whatever lay in his way, frothing at the mouth, horrible to see. At other times he would become rigid, and again, after remaining stark outstretched for a moment, would roll about in horrible contortions." Francis came to see him and healed him.

But these are exceptions, and the greater part of the time the saint withdrew himself from the entreaties of his companions when they asked miracles at his hands.

"In one of the frescos of the Upper Church of Assisi, Giotto has represented St. Clare and her companions coming out from San Damiano all in tears, to kiss their spiritual father's corpse as it is being carried to its last home. With an artist's liberty he has made the chapel a rich church built of precious marbles.

"Happily the real San Damiano is still there, nestled under some olive-trees like a lark under the heather. It still has its ill-made walls of irregular stones, like those that bound the neighboring fields. Which is the more beautiful, the ideal temple of the artist's fancy, or the poor chapel of reality? No heart will be in doubt.

"Francis's official historians have done for his biography what Giotto did for his little sanctuary. In general, they have done him ill-service. Their embellishments have hidden the real St. Francis, who was, in fact, infinitely nobler than they have made him to be" (SABATIER, p. XXXIII).

CHAPTER THIRTEEN
The Chapter-General of 1217 and the Influence of Ugolino

The four years that followed the Whitsunday of 1216 form a stage in the evolution of the Umbrian movement when Francis was battling for autonomy. We find here rather delicate shades of distinction that have been misunderstood by Church writers as much as by their adversaries. If Francis was sure not to put himself in an attitude of revolt toward the Church hierarchy, he also would not compromise his independence, and he felt that all the privileges that the court of Rome could heap upon him were worth nothing in comparison with freedom.

A great number of legendary anecdotes put Francis's disdain for privileges in the clearest light. Even his dearest friends did not always understand his scruples.

"Do you not see," they said to him one day, "that often the bishops do not permit us to preach, and make us remain several days without doing anything before we are permitted to proclaim the word of God? It would be better to obtain a privilege from the pope, and it would be for the good of souls."

"I would first convert the prelates by humility and respect," he replied quickly. "For when they have seen us humble and respectful toward them, they will beg us to preach and convert the people. As for me, I ask of God no privilege unless it be that I may have none, to be full of respect for all people, and to convert them, as our Rule ordains, more by our example than by our speech."

The question of whether Francis was right or wrong in his antipathy to the privileges of the curia does not come within the domain of history; it is evident that this attitude could not continue long; the Church knows only the faithful and rebels. But the noblest hearts often make a stand at compromises of this kind; they desire that the future should grow out of the past without convulsion and without a crisis.

The chapter of 1217 was notable for the definitive organization of the Franciscan missions. Italy and the other countries were

Sabatier passes over the death of Pope
Innocent III in silence. We have the following story, passed down to us through
Jacques of Vitry. "On July 11 [1216]
the pope had been struck down by an
embolism. Because it was very hot, the
funeral rites had been rushed; and there
was no one to watch over the body in the
locked cathedral. The next day, in the
early morning, Vitry entered with several
members of the Curia and found Innocent
III lying naked and stinking on the
pavement, all alone in the somber, massive Romanesque church, which still lay
shrouded in night. The pope's crosier,
tiara, and precious vestments had all
been carried off by robbers in the darkness. In a famous letter the French bishop
described the horror he witnessed. 'I have
seen with my own eyes,' he added, 'how
vain, brief, and ephemeral is the glory of
this world'" (GREEN, p. 174).

In his novel Saint Francis, Nikos
Kazantzakis tells his story from the
perspective of Brother Leo, the book's
narrator. Kazantzakis supposes that it
was Leo—not Elias, as Sabatier
believed—who was Francis's confidant
in the early years. In the novel, Leo remi-
nisces to Francis, after the saint's death:
"You told me what you told no one else.
You took me by the hand, we went into
the forests, scrambled up mountains, and
you spoke.... I know things about you,
therefore, that no other person knows.
You committed many more sins than
people imagine; you performed many
more miracles than people believe"
(KAZANTZAKIS, p. 18).

divided off into a certain number of
provinces, each having a provincial
minister.

Immediately on his accession,
Pope Honorius III had sought to revive
the popular zeal for the Crusades. He
preached it continuously, appealing to
prophecies proclaiming that under his
pontificate the Holy Land would be
reconquered. The renewal of fervor
that ensued, and of which the rebound
was felt as far as Germany, had a
profound influence on the Brothers
Minor. This time Francis, perhaps
from humility, did not put himself at
the head of the friars charged with a
mission to Syria. For a leader he gave
them the famous Elias.

This brother, who from this
time appears in the foreground of
this history, came from the most
humble ranks of society. The date
and circumstances of his entrance
into the Order are unknown, and
hence conjecture has come to see in
him that friend of the grotto who
had been Francis's confidant shortly
before his decisive conversion. In
his youth he had earned his living in
Assisi, making mattresses and teaching a few children to read. Then he
spent some time in Bologna, and
then suddenly we find him among
the Brothers Minor charged with the
most difficult missions.

In the inner Franciscan circle,
where Leo, Ginepro, Egidio, and

many others represent the spirit of freedom, the religion of the humble and the simple, Elias represents the scientific and ecclesiastical spirit, prudence and reason.

He had great success in Syria and received into the Order one of the disciples most dear to Francis, Caesar of Speyer. Later, Caesar was to make the conquest of all southern Germany in less than two years (1221–23), and in the end he sealed with his blood faithfulness to the strict observance of the Rule, which he defended against the attacks of Brother Elias himself.

Caesar of Speyer offers a brilliant example of those suffering souls thirsty for the ideal, so numerous in the thirteenth century, who everywhere went up and down, seeking first in learning, then in the religious life, that which should assuage the mysterious thirst that tortured them. Disciple of the scholastic Conrad, he had felt himself overpowered with the

Brother Elias was deposed in 1239 and soon after excommunicated. He repented on his deathbed, but the century of oral tradition that followed, leading up to Brother Ugolino's compiling of The Little Flowers of St. Francis, *portrayed Elias as not only egomaniacal and despotic, but even demonic.*

Some historians view Brother Elias in a more gentle light. One historian explains: "His successors, Albert of Pisa and Aymon of Faversham, obtained from the Papal Curia seven times as many Bulls, dispensations and privileges as Elias in the whole period of his rule. They decreed that official posts should be reserved for priests, which signified the exclusion of laymen from all government of the Order" (GOAD, pp. 149–50).

desire to reform the Church. While still a layperson he had preached his ideas, not without some success, since a certain number of women of Speyer had begun to lead a new life. However, their husbands disapproving, Caesar was obliged to escape their vengeance by taking refuge in Paris, and then he went to the East where in the preaching of the Brothers Minor he found again his hopes and his dreams. This instance shows how general was the waiting condition of souls when the Franciscan gospel blazed forth, and how its way had been prepared everywhere.

The friars who went to Germany under the leadership of Giovanni of Penna were far from having the success of Elias and his companions. They were completely ignorant of the language of the country that they had undertaken to evangelize. Perhaps Francis had not taken into account the fact that, although Italian might suffice in all the countries bathed by the Mediterranean, this could not be the case in central Europe. The lot of the party going to Hungary was not any better, and for the same reasons. We may thank the Franciscan authors for preserving for us the memory of these setbacks, and not attempting to picture the friars as suddenly knowing all languages by divine inspiration, as was so often done later on.

Francis himself made preparations for going to France. When he arrived at Florence he found Cardinal Ugolino there, sent by the pope as legate to Tuscany to preach the crusade and take all necessary measures for assuring its success. Surely, Francis did not expect the reception that the prelate gave him. Instead of offering encouragement, the cardinal urged him to give up his project:

"I am not willing, my brother, that you should cross the mountains. There are many prelates who ask nothing better than to stir up difficulties for you with the court of Rome. But I and the other cardinals who love your Order desire to protect and aid you, on the condition, however, that you do not leave this province."

"But monsignor," Francis responded, "it would be a great disgrace for me to send my brothers far away while I remain idly here, sharing none of the tribulations that they must undergo."

"Why, then, have you sent your brothers so far away, exposing them to starvation and all sorts of perils?" the cardinal asked.

"Do you think," replied Francis warmly, as if moved by prophetic inspiration, "that God raised up the brothers for the sake of this country alone? God has raised them up for the awakening and the salvation of all people, and they shall win souls not only in the countries of those who believe, but also in the very midst of the infidels."

The surprise and admiration that these words awoke in Ugolino were not enough to make him change his mind. He insisted so strongly that Francis turned back to Portiuncula. Souls thirsty with the longing for sacrifice often have scruples such as these and they refuse the most lawful joys that they may offer them to God. Instead, Brother Pacifico and Brother Agnello of Pisa, later destined to head the first mission to England in 1224, led the missionaries sent into France.

Francis passed the following year (1218) in evangelizing tours in Italy. It is naturally impossible to follow him in these travels,

A fresco painting of Pope Gregory IX (formerly Cardinal Ugolino) in *Sacro Speco* ("holy cave"), the grotto in which St. Benedict lived for a time in the fifth century. A Benedictine abbey still surrounds this place today in Subiaco, Italy. (Art reproduced from SEDGWICK, 1:110.)

the itinerary of which was fixed by his daily inspirations. But it is very possible that he paid a visit to Rome during this time.

Francis's communications with Ugolino were much more frequent than is supposed by the early biographers. We must make a larger place for Ugolino in Francis's story than has been made in the past. At this point in the story, the struggle had definitely opened between the Franciscan ideal—chimerical, perhaps, but sublime— and ecclesiastical policy, to go on until the day when, half in humility, half in discouragement, Francis, heartsick, abdicated the direction of his spiritual family.

Ugolino returned to Rome at the end of 1217. During the following winter he devoted his time to the special study of the question of the new religious orders, and summoned Francis before him. Ugolino, who better than anyone else knew Umbria, Tuscany, Emilia, the March of Ancona, all those regions where the Franciscan preaching had been most successful, was able to judge the power of the new movement and the imperious necessity of directing it. He felt that the best way to allay the prejudices that the pope and the sacred college might have against Francis was to present him before the curia.

At first Francis was much abashed at the thought of preaching before the Vicar of Jesus Christ, but upon the entreaties of his protector he consented, and for greater security he learned by heart what he had to say.

Ugolino himself was not entirely at ease. Thomas of Celano pictures him as devoured with anxiety; he was troubled about Francis, whose artless eloquence ran many a risk in the halls of the Lateran Palace. He was also not without some more personal anxieties, for the failure of his protégé might be most damaging to himself.

Ugolino's anxiety only increased when, on arriving at the feet of the pontiff, Francis forgot all he had intended to say. But Francis frankly admitted it, and seeking a new discourse from the inspiration of the moment, spoke with so much warmth and simplicity that the assembly was won.

The Holy See must have been greatly perplexed by this strange man, whose faith and humility were evident, but whom it was impossible to teach ecclesiastical obedience. St. Dominic happened to be in Rome at the same time and was overwhelmed with favors by the pope. Several years earlier, Innocent III had asked Dominic to choose one of the rules already approved by the Church for his own, and Dominic had adopted that of St. Augustine. Honorius therefore was not sparing of privileges for him. Ugolino surely tried to use the influence of Dominic's example with St. Francis.

An English pilgrim of the late Middle Ages described the relics that he was able to see in the Lateran Basilica in Rome at about this time: "the ark of the covenant, the table of the law, the golden urn of manna ... a tunic made by the Virgin, Christ's purple garment, two bottles of blood and water from His side, the remains of His cradle, the five loaves and two fishes, the Lord's table, and the cloth with which He wiped the feet of the apostles; in addition, the blood of John the Baptist and the ashes from his cremation and his hair-shirt ... and the heads of St. Peter and St. Paul" (PARKS, p. 244).

The curia saw clearly that Dominic, whose order barely comprised a few dozen members, was not one of the moral powers of the time, but its sentiments toward him were not as mixed as they were with regard to Francis. To unite the two orders would have been singularly pleasing to Ugolino.

One day Dominic, by dint of pious insistence, induced Francis to give him his cord, and immediately girded himself with it. "Brother," he said, "I earnestly long that your order and mine might unite to form one sole and same institute in the Church." The Brother Minor wished to remain as he was, and declined the proposition. But so truly was Dominic inspired with the needs of his time and of the Church that less than three years after this, at the chapter held at Bologna in 1220, he was led to transform his Order of Canons of St. Augustine into an order of mendicant monks, whose constitutions were outlined on those of the Franciscans.

"There was a striking contrast between Francis and Dominic, manifest even in their physical appearance. Wearing a garment the color of earth and dust, the Poverello reminded the viewer of a sparrow or, as they were called in France, a moineau—a little monk.... Dominic was altogether different. In his handsome habit of yellow wool so pale it looked white, he had an air of somewhat intimidating nobility" (GREEN, p. 170).

A few years later the Dominicans took, so to speak, their revenge, and obliged the Brothers Minor to give learning a large place in their work. Thus, the two religious families rivaled each other, impressed and influenced each other, yet never so much as to lose all traces of their origins—summed up for one in poverty and lay preaching, for the other in learning and the preaching of the clergy.

Rosalind Brooke confirms Sabatier's judgment in the last paragraph of the chapter you have just read, and expands upon it, when she summarizes: "To the disciples of St. Francis it has seemed obvious that Dominic imitated Francis; to students of Dominic the hypothesis has seemed without foundation. The one meeting that is well recorded may have marked a turning point in Dominic's life. It helped him to see his way to converting his order (a tiny group still at the time), from a group of preachers among the heretics in Languedoc into a worldwide order of friars. But if that is so, the compliment was presently returned. Leading Franciscans studied the organization of the Dominicans and grafted some of it on to their own order.... Dominic's order from the first comprised trained, instructed preachers, intended to fulfill the role the parish clergy of the thirteenth century could least effectively perform. And trained, effective preachers is what the Franciscans soon became – so much so that by the late thirteenth century the role of the lay brothers had been forgotten." (BROOKE, p. 11–12).

CHAPTER FOURTEEN
St. Dominic and St. Francis

Art and poetry have done well in inseparably associating St. Dominic and St. Francis. The glory of the first is only a reflection of that of the second, and it is in placing them side by side that we succeed best in understanding the genius of the Poverello.

If Francis is the man of inspiration, Dominic is that of obedience—one may say that his life was passed on the road to Rome, where he continually went to ask for instructions. His legend was therefore very slow to be formed; but neither the zeal of Gregory IX for his memory nor the learning of his disciples was able to do for the *Hammer of heretics* what the love of the people did for the *Father of the poor*.

We have already seen the efforts of Cardinal Ugolino to unite the two orders, and the reasons he had for this course. He went to the chapter-general that met at Portiuncula (June 3, 1218), to which also came St. Dominic with several of his disciples. The Brothers Minor went in procession to meet the cardinal, who immediately dismounted from his horse and lavished affection upon them. An altar was set up in the open air, at which he said mass, Francis performing the functions of deacon.

Dominic was amazed at the absence of material cares. Francis had advised his brothers not to trouble themselves in any respect about food and drink; he knew from experience that they might fearlessly trust all that to the love of the neighboring population. The joy of the Franciscans, the sympathy of the people with them, the poverty of the huts of Portiuncula, all this impressed Dominic deeply. So much was he moved by it that in a burst of enthusiasm he announced his resolution to embrace Gospel poverty.

Ugolino, though also moved, did not forget his former anxieties. The Franciscan Order was too large not to include a group of malcontents; a few friars who before their conversions had studied in the universities began to condemn the extreme simplicity laid upon them as a duty. To men no longer sustained by enthusiasm the short precepts of the Rule appeared a charter all too insufficient for a vast association. They turned with envy toward the monumental abbeys of the Benedictines, the regular Canons, the Cistercians, and toward the ancient monastic legislations. They had no difficulty in perceiving in Ugolino a powerful ally, or in confiding their observations to him.

When Ugolino deemed the propitious moment arrived, he made a few suggestions to Francis in a private conversation. Might he give to his disciples, especially to the educated among them, a greater share of the burdens? Might he consult them, gain inspiration from their views? Was there not room to profit from the experience of the older orders? Though all of this was said casually and with the greatest possible tact, Francis felt himself wounded to the quick, and without answering he drew the cardinal into the very midst of the chapter.

"My brothers," he said with fire, "the Lord has called me into the ways of simplicity and humility. In them he has shown me the truth for myself and for those who desire to believe and follow me. Do not, then, come speaking to me of the Rule of St. Benedict, of St. Augustine, of St. Bernard, or of any other, but solely of that which God in his mercy has seen fit to show to me, and of which he has told me that he would, by its means, make a new covenant with the world."

This warmth in defending and affirming his ideas profoundly astonished Ugolino, who did not add a word. As for Dominic, what he had just seen at Portiuncula was to him a revelation. He felt that his zeal for the Church could not be greater, but he also perceived that he could serve her with more success by certain changes in his weapons.

A few months later, Dominic set out for Spain. The intensity of the crisis through which he passed has not been sufficiently noticed. The religious writers recount at length his sojourn in the grotto of Segovia, but they see only the ascetic practices, the prayers, the genuflections, and do not think of looking

---

"Francis was of the people and the people recognized themselves in him. He had their poetry and their aspirations. He espoused their claims and the very name of his institute had at first a political signification: in Assisi, as in most other Italian towns, there were majores *and* minores, the popolo grasso *and the* popolo minuto. *Francis resolutely placed himself among the latter. This political side of his apostolate needs to be clearly apprehended if we would understand its amazing success and the wholly unique character of the Franciscan movement in its beginning"* (SABATIER, pp. XVI–XVII).

---

for the cause of all this. From this period it might be said that Dominic was unceasingly occupied in copying Francis, if the word did not have such a displeasing sense. When he arrived at Segovia, Dominic followed the example of the Brothers Minor, founding a hermitage in the outskirts of the city, hidden among the rocks that overlook the town, and from there he descended from time to time to preach to the people. The transformation in his mode of life was so evident that several of his companions rebelled and refused to follow him in the new way.

Thus St. Dominic also arrived at the poverty of the gospel. But while Francis had soared to it as on wings, seeing in it the final emancipation from all the anxieties that debase this life, Dominic considered it only as a means; it was for him one more weapon in the arsenal of the host charged with the defense of the Church. But we must not see in this a mere vulgar calculation. Dominic's admiration for him whom he imitated and followed was sincere and profound, but genius is not to be copied. This sacred malady was not his. Dominic has transmitted to his sons a sound and robust blood, thanks to which they have known nothing of those paroxysms of hot fever, those lofty flights, those sudden returns that make the story of the Franciscans the story of the most tempest-tossed society the world has ever known, in which glorious chapters are mingled with pages trivial and grotesque, sometimes even coarse.

Dante's Paradiso *inseparably linked Dominic and Francis. In canto xii, Dante wrote of the changes found in Francis's order after his death: "His family, that had straight forward moved / With feet upon his footprints, are turned around." Then, Dante writes, out of the mouth of the spirit of Bonaventure: "'Twill not be from Casal nor Acquasparta, / From whence come such unto the written word / That one avoids it, and the other narrows'" (lines 115–16, 124–26).*

As general of the order from 1257 until his death in 1274, Bonaventure sought a "middle way" between the two extremes of the "Spirituals," or strict observers of Francis's original Rule, and those, like Ugolino, who sought to bring the order in line with others, under the Holy See in Rome. When Dante has Bonaventure referring to "Casal nor Acquasparta," he is foretelling the future, referring to Dante's contemporaries, Ubertino of Cassale, a leader of the Spirituals, and Matteo d'Acquasparta, who was general of the order beginning in 1287.

(Ubertino of Cassale is a major character in Umberto Eco's fascinating historical novel The Name of the Rose. *The debates of the Spirituals form much of the intellectual background of the book.)*

CHAPTER FIFTEEN

The Egyptian Mission: Preaching to the Sultan (Summer 1218–Autumn 1220)

At the chapter of 1218, Francis heard the malcontented murmurs of the missionaries that he had sent out the year before to Germany and Hungary. They had returned completely discouraged. The account of the sufferings they had endured produced so great an effect that from that time forward many of the friars added to their prayers this formula: "Lord, preserve us from the heresy of the Lombards and the ferocity of the Germans."

This explains how Ugolino at last succeeded in convincing Francis of his duty to no longer expose his friars to heretics. It was decided that at the end of the next chapter the missionaries should be armed with a papal brief that would serve them as ecclesiastical passport:

> Honorius, bishop, servant of the servants of God, to the archbishops, bishops, abbots, deacons, archdeacons, and other ecclesiastical superiors, salutation and the apostolic blessing.
>
> Our dear son, brother Francis, and his companions of the life and the Order of the Brothers Minor, having renounced the vanities of this world to choose a mode of life that has merited the approval of the Roman Church, and to go out after the example of the Apostles to cast in various regions the seed of the word of God, we pray and exhort you by these apostolic letters to receive as good catholics the friars of the above mentioned society, bearers of these presents, warning you to be favorable to them and treat them with kindness for the honor of God and out of consideration for us.
>
> Given (at Rieti) this third day of the ides of June (June 11, 1219), in the third year of our pontificate.

That summer was the time fixed by Honorius III for making a new effort in the East and directing upon Egypt all the forces of the crusaders. For his part, Francis thought the moment had arrived for realizing the project that he had not been able to execute in 1212.

Strangely enough, Ugolino, who two years before had hindered his going to France, now left him in entire freedom to carry out this new expedition. Francis left Portiuncula in the middle of June and went to Ancona, from where the crusaders were to set sail for Egypt on St. John's Day (June 24).

Many friars joined him—a fact not without its inconveniences for a journey by sea, where they were obliged to depend on the charity of the owners of the boats, or of their fellow travelers. We can understand Francis's embarrassment on arriving at Ancona and finding himself obliged to leave behind a number of those who so earnestly longed to go with him.

We do not know what itinerary they followed. Only a single incident of the journey on the way to the continent has come down to us: the story of the disciplining of Brother Barbaro, guilty of speaking evil against another, on the island of Cyprus. Francis was implacable with regard to loose tongues so customary among pious people, and which often made a hell of religious houses that, on the surface, appeared most peaceful. On this occasion, the offense appeared even more grave because it had been uttered in the presence of a stranger, a knight of that district. The latter was stupefied on hearing Francis command the guilty one to eat a lump of donkey's dung that lay there, adding, "The mouth that has distilled the venom of hatred against my brother must eat this excrement."

The Emperor at this time was, by most accounts, an enemy of the Church and a reluctant crusader. One of the most colorful leaders of the time, Frederick II "was a Norman, raised in Umbria and Sicily as a ward of Pope Innocent III (he was baptized in the same church as St. Francis), intelligent, multilingual, much interested in mathematics and philosophy, acquainted with and respectful of the Muslim religion. Like St. Francis, Frederick was always traveling, but he did not travel lightly. His entourage included a harem, elephants, camels, falcons, a guard of Lucera Saracens, Arab, Greek, and Jewish attendants, doctors and scientists, his crown, his jewels, and a good part of his extensive library" (MARTIN, p. 256).

After years of broken promises to the Holy See, and the public urging of the new pope (Gregory IX, formerly Ugolino, who had such influence over Francis), Frederick II finally left for the Holy Land in 1227, only to disembark fifty miles into his journey. Gregory and Frederick exchanged excommunication and condemnation of each other, and nine months later, Frederick sailed again for Syria. When he arrived, it was not to fight; instead, he negotiated a treaty with the sultan to cede most of Jerusalem, Nazareth, and Bethlehem to the Europeans for ten years, and he hastily returned to Italy.

It is probable that the missionaries debarked at St. Jean d'Acre, arriving there about the middle of July. From the moment that he arrived, Francis was heartbroken with the moral condition of the Christian army. Even with the presence of numerous prelates and the apostolic legate, it was disorganized for want of discipline. He was so affected by this that when there was talk of battle he felt it his duty to advise against it, predicting that the Christians would definitely be beaten. No one heeded him, and on August 29 the crusaders, having attacked the Saracens, were terribly routed.

His predictions won him a marvelous success. In this mass of men from every corner of Europe, the troubled, the seers, the enlightened ones, those who thirsted for righteousness and truth, were elbowed by rascals, adventurers, those who were greedy for gold and plunder, capable of much good or much evil. Loosed from the bonds of family, property, and the habits that usually entwine themselves around a person's will, these men were ready for a complete change in their manner of life. Those among them who were sincere and had come there with generous purposes were, so to speak, predestined to enter the peaceful army of the Brothers Minor. Francis was to win in this mission fellow-laborers who would assure the success of his work in the countries of northern Europe.

In a letter to friends, Jacques of Vitry, the French priest recently appointed bishop of Acre, describes the impression produced on him by Francis:

I announce to you that Master Reynier, Prior of St. Michael, has entered the Order of the Brothers Minor, an Order that is multiplying rapidly on all sides because it imitates the primitive Church and follows the life of the Apostles in everything. The master of these brothers is named Brother Francis. He is so lovable that he is venerated by everyone. Having come into our army, he has not been afraid, in his zeal for the faith, to go to our enemies. For many days he announced the word of God to the Saracens, but with little success. Then the sultan, King of Egypt, asked him in secret to ask God to reveal to him, by some miracle, which is the best religion.

Colin, the Englishman, our clerk, has entered the same order, as also two more of our companions, Michael and Dom Matthew, to whom I had given the rectorship of the Sainte Chapelle. Cantor and Henry have done the same, and still others whose names I have forgotten.

For the interviews between Francis and the sultan, it is best to keep to the narratives of Jacques of Vitry and William of Tyre. Although William of Tyre wrote at a comparatively late date (between 1275 and 1295), he wrote as a historian and founded his work on authentic documents. We see that he knows no more than Jacques of Vitry of the proposal said to have been made by Francis to pass through a fire if the priests of Muhammed would do the same, in order to establish the superiority of Christianity.

Sabatier tells us very little of Francis and the sultan. One historian of the Crusades adds: "[Francis] now asked permission of Pelagius [a cardinal of the Church in Spain, sent by Pope Honorius to lead the crusaders] to go to see the Sultan. After some hesitation Pelagius agreed, and sent him under a flag of truce to Fariskur. The Muslim guards were suspicious at first but soon decided that anyone so simple, so gentle and so dirty must be mad, and treated him with the respect due to a man who had been touched by God" (RUNCIMAN, pp. 159–60).

We know how little such an appeal to signs is characteristic of St. Francis. Perhaps the story, which comes from Bonaventure, was born out of a misconception. The sultan, like a new Pharaoh, may have laid it upon the strange preacher to prove his mission by miracles. Either way, Francis and his companions were treated with great consideration, a fact all the more meritorious when you consider that hostilities were then at their height.

Returning to the crusading camp, Francis and his companions remained there until after the taking of Damietta (November 5, 1219). This time the Christians were victorious. Jacques of Vitry relates at length the shocking conditions of the city, where the victors found piled heaps of dead bodies, quarreled over the sharing of booty, and sold the wretched

In Kazantzakis's novel, Brother Leo describes the scene: "Francis ran among the soldiers of Christ and exhorted them with tearful eyes to be merciful, but they drove him away, jeered him, and continued to break down the doors of the houses. How can I ever forget the cries of the women and the groans of the men they slaughtered! The blood ran in rivers; wherever you turned you stumbled over a severed head. The air was thick with moans and wailing" (KAZANTZAKIS, p. 243).

creatures who had not succumbed to pestilence. All these scenes of terror, cruelty, and greed caused Francis profound horror. The human beast was let loose, and the apostle's voice could no more make itself heard in the midst of the savage clamor any more than that of a lifesaver over a raging ocean.

Francis set out for Syria and the holy places. We would gladly follow him in this pilgrimage—through Judea and Galilee, to Bethlehem, Nazareth, and Gethsemane—but the documents here suddenly fail us. What was said to him by the stable where the Son of Mary was born, the workshop where he toiled, the olive tree where he accepted the bitter cup? Setting out from Damietta very shortly after the crusader victory at Damietta he may have easily been at Bethlehem by Christmas 1219. But we know nothing, absolutely nothing, except that his sojourn was longer than had been expected.

Angelo Clareno relates that the Sultan of Egypt, touched by Francis's preaching, gave command that he and all his friars should have free access to the Holy Sepulcher without the payment of any tribute. Bartholomew of Pisa, for his part, says that Francis, having gone to preach in Antioch and its environs, caused all of the Benedictines of the Abbey of the Black Mountain, eight miles from Antioch, to give up their property and join the Brothers Minor. These accounts are meager and isolated, to be accepted only with hesitation. On the other hand, we have detailed information of what went on in Italy during Francis's absence.

A plot was laid against Francis by the very people whom he had commissioned to take his place at Portiuncula, if not with the connivance of Rome and the cardinal protector, at least without their opposition. Here are the facts: On July 25, about one

When Acre (see glossary) fell again into Muslim hands in 1291, the Franciscans fled to Cyprus, where the seat of the province, created in 1217, was located. Officially, Christians were banned from the Holy Land, but the Franciscans remained present, through great persistence, in many ways. In the first half of the fourteenth century, the friars were recognized by the Muslim leaders as "official residents" in the Church of the Holy Sepulcher. At about the same time, Pope Clement VI named the friars as the Church's official custodians of the Holy Land (1342). In 1992, the 650th anniversary of Clement VI's bull, Pope John Paul II reinforced the Franciscans as the Roman Catholic Church's "custodians" of the holy places.

month after Francis's departure for Syria, Ugolino, who was at Perugia, laid upon the Sisters of Clare at Florence, Siena, Perugia, and Lucca that which his friend had so obstinately refused for the friars, the Benedictine Rule.

At the same time, St. Dominic, returning from Spain full of new ardor after his retreat in the grotto of Segovia, and fully decided to adopt for his order the rule of poverty, was strongly encouraged in this purpose and overwhelmed with favors. Honorius III saw in him the providential man of the time, the reformer of the monastic orders; he showed him unusual attentions, going so far, for example, as to transfer to him a group of monks belonging to other orders, whom he appointed to act as Dominic's lieutenants on the preaching tours that he believed it to be his duty to undertake, and to serve, under his direction, an apprenticeship in popular preaching.

At the time of his departure for the East, Francis had left two vicars in his place, the Brothers Matthew of Narni and Gregory of Naples. The former was especially charged to remain at Portiuncula to admit postulants, the latter was to pass through Italy to console the brothers.

The two vicars began at once to overturn everything. It is inexplicable how men still under the influence of their first fervor for a Rule that in their freedom they had promised to obey could have dreamed of such innovations if not urged on and upheld by those in high places. Their efforts were bent toward alleviating the vow of poverty and multiplying observances.

It was a trifling matter in appearance, but in reality it was much more, for it was the first movement of the old spirit against the new. It was the effort of people who unconsciously, I am willing to assume, made religion an affair of rite and observance, instead of seeing it, like St. Francis, as the conquest of freedom that makes us free in all things. This is the free-

A contemporary biographer of Francis explains: "A rumor had reached the Porziuncula that Francis was dead. As a result many of the newer friars, who didn't know him, had urged his vicars, Matthew and Gregory, to bring the brotherhood more into line with the traditional orders" (HOUSE, p. 218).

dom that leads each soul to obey the divine and mysterious power that the flowers of the fields adore, that the birds of the air bless, that the symphony of the stars praises, and that Jesus of Nazareth called *Abba*, or, Father.

The first Rule was excessively simple on the matter of fasts. The friars were to abstain from meat on Wednesdays and Fridays; they might add Mondays and Saturdays, but only on Francis's special authorization. The two vicars and their followers complicated this rule in a surprising manner. At the chapter-general held in Francis's absence (May 17, 1220), they decided, first, that in times of feasting the friars were not to provide meat, but if it were offered to them spontaneously they were to eat it; second, that all should fast on Mondays as well as Wednesdays and Fridays; third, that on Mondays and Saturdays they should abstain from milk products unless by chance the adherents of the Order brought some to them.

These beginnings bear witness to an effort to imitate the ancient orders, with the vague hope that they would be substituted for them. These modifications of the Rule did not pass, however, without arousing the indignation of a part of the chapter. A lay brother made himself their eager messenger and set out for the East to entreat Francis to return without delay.

There were also other causes of disquiet. A certain Brother Giovanni of Conpello had gathered together a great number of lepers of both sexes and written a rule, intending to form with them a new order. He had afterward presented himself before the supreme pontiff with a train of these unfortunates to obtain his approbation. The report of Francis's death had even been spread abroad, so that the whole Order was disturbed, divided, and in the greatest peril. The dark presentiments that Francis seems to have had were exceeded by the reality. The messenger who brought him the sad news found him in Syria, probably at St. Jean d'Acre. Francis embarked at once with Elias, Peter of Catana, Caesar of Speyer, and a few others, and returned to Italy in a vessel bound for Venice.

CHAPTER SIXTEEN
Crisis in the Order (Autumn 1220)

On his arrival in Venice, Francis informed himself more exactly concerning all that had happened, and convoked the chapter-general at Portiuncula for Michaelmas (September 29, 1220). His first care was doubtless to reassure his sister-friend at San Damiano. A short fragment of a letter that has been preserved to us gives indication of the sad anxieties that filled his mind:

> I, little Brother Francis, desire to follow the life and the poverty of Jesus Christ, our most high Lord, and of his most holy Mother, persevering in it until the end. And I beg you all and exhort you to persevere always in this most holy life and poverty, and take good care never to depart from it upon the advice or teachings of any one at all.

A long shout of joy sounded up and down all Italy when the news of his return was heard. Many zealous brothers were already despairing, for persecutions had begun in many provinces. So, when they learned that their spiritual father was alive and coming again to visit them their joy was unbounded.

From Venice, Francis went to Bologna. The journey was marked by an incident that once more shows his acute and wise goodness. Worn out as much by emotion as by fatigue, one day he found himself obliged to give up finishing the journey on foot. Mounted on a donkey, he was going on his way followed by Brother Leonard of Assisi, when a passing glance showed him what was passing in his companion's mind. "My relatives," the friar was thinking, "would have been far from associating with Bernardone, and yet here I am, obliged to follow his son on foot."

Imagine Brother Leonard's astonishment when he heard Francis saying, as he hastily dismounted from his beast: "Here, take my place. You shouldn't follow me on foot, as you are of a noble and powerful lineage." The unhappy Leonard, much confused, threw himself at Francis's feet, begging for pardon.

The Bolognese prepared an enthusiastic reception for Francis, an account of which has come down even to our times:

I was studying at Bologna, I, Thomas of Spalato, archdeacon in the cathedral church of that city, when in the year 1220, the day of the Assumption, I saw St. Francis preaching on the piazza of the Lesser Palace, before almost every person in the city. The theme of the discourse was the following: Angels, people, the demons. He spoke on all these subjects with so much wisdom and eloquence that many learned people who were there were filled with admiration at the words of so plain a man. His ways were those of conversation; the substance of his discourse rested mainly upon the abolition of enmities and the necessity of making peaceful alliances. His apparel was poor, his person in no respect imposing, his face not at all handsome, but God gave such great efficacy to his words that he brought back to peace and harmony many nobles whose savage fury had even led to the shedding of blood. So great a devotion was felt for him that men and women flocked after him, and they esteemed themselves happy who succeeded in touching the hem of his garment.

Francis remained in Bologna only a very short time. An ancient tradition, of which his biographers have not preserved a trace but nevertheless appears to be entirely probable, says that Ugolino took him to pass a month in the Camaldoli. This retreat was formerly inhabited by St. Romuald, in the midst of the Casentino forest, one of the noblest in Europe, and within a few hours walk of the Verna, whose summit rises up gigantic, overlooking the whole country.

St. Dominic's tomb is housed in Bologna in a basilica named for him. On the cornice of the tomb are statues of the eight patron saints of Bologna, among them, St. Francis and St. Dominic, as well as St. Petronius (early fifth-century bishop of Bologna) and St. Procolus (early Christian martyr, martyred in Bologna), the latter two carved by Michelangelo in 1494. The Basilica also contains the beautiful fresco, Apotheosis of St. Dominic, by Guido Reni.

We know how much Francis needed repose. There is no doubt that he also longed for a period of meditation in order to decide carefully in advance on his line of conduct, in the midst of the dark conjectures that had called him home.

The desire to give him a much-needed rest was only a subordinate purpose with Ugolino. We can easily picture his responses to Francis's complaints. The Brothers

Minor were not heretics, but they disturbed the Church as much as the heretics did. How many times had Francis been reminded that a great association, in order to exist, must have precise and detailed regulations? Of course Francis's humility was doubted by no one, but why not manifest it, not only in costume and manner of living, but in all his acts? He thought himself obeying God in defending his own inspiration, but does not the Church speak in the name of God? He desired to be a man of the gospel, but was not the best way of becoming an apostolic man to obey the Roman pontiff, the successor of Peter? Reproaches such as these, mingled with professions of love and admiration on the part of the prelate, must have profoundly disturbed a sensitive heart like that of Francis. His conscience bore him good witness, but with the modesty of a noble mind he was ready enough to think that he might have made many mistakes.

The sojourn at Camaldoli was prolonged until the middle of September and it ended to the cardinal's satisfaction. Francis decided to go directly to the pope, then at Orvieto, with the request that Ugolino should be given him as official protector entrusted with the direction of the Order.

A dream that Francis had once had recurred to his memory: He had seen a little black hen that, in spite of her efforts, was not able to spread her wings over her whole brood. The poor hen was himself, the chickens were the friars. This dream was a providential indication commanding him to seek for them a mother under whose wings they could all find a place, and who could defend them against the birds of prey. At least so he thought.

Does his profound humility, with the feeling of culpability that Ugolino had awakened in him, suffice to explain his attitude with regard to the pope, or might we suppose that he had a vague thought of abdicating? The scene has been preserved for us:

> Not daring to present himself in the apartments of so great a prince, he remained outside before the door, patiently waiting until the pope should come out. When he appeared, St. Francis made a reverence and said: "Father Pope, may God give you peace." "May God bless you, my son," he replied. "My lord," Francis said, "you are great and often absorbed by great affairs. Poor friars cannot come and talk with you as often as they need to

do. You have given me many popes, but give me a single one to whom I may address myself when need arises, and who will listen in your stead, discussing my affairs and those of the Order." "Whom do you wish I should give you, my son?" "The Bishop of Ostia." And he gave him to him.

Conferences with Ugolino began. He immediately accorded Francis some amends: The privilege granted the Sisters of Clare was revoked; Giovanni of Conpello was informed that he had nothing to hope for from the curia; and leave was given to Francis himself to compose the Rule of the Order. At the same time, a bull was issued—not merely for the sake of publishing this ordinance but especially to mark in a solemn manner the commencement of a new era in the relations between the Church and the Franciscans—the fraternity of the Umbrian Penitents became an Order in the strictest sense of the word.

From this time it became impossible for Francis to remain minister general. He felt it himself. Heartbroken, soul-sick, he would have found in the energy of his love those words, those glances that up to this time had taken the place of rule or constitution, giving to his earliest companions the intuition of what they ought to do and the strength to accomplish it. But an administrator was now needed at the head of this family that he suddenly found to be so different from what it had been a few years before.

The recent events had not taken place without in some degree weakening his moral personality;

One of the few writings of Francis to exist in the original is a letter to his dear friend, Brother Leo, with whom he so often traveled the countryside of Umbria, as told in the beautiful stories of The Little Flowers. *It was probably written at about this time, in response to a query from Leo asking whom he should follow, Francis, or the new leaders of the Order. "Brother Leo, brother Francis sends you health and peace. My son, I speak to you now just as a mother would. All the words which we have exchanged in our travels I can sum up in a single word of advice; in this way it will not be necessary for you to search me out for further advice. Here is my advice: Whatever seems right for you to do to better serve the Lord and to follow in his footsteps and in his poverty, do it with God's blessing and my approval. But if it seems necessary for your soul or your consolation to come and see me, and you want to come, then come. Do, I beg you, come"* (CUNNINGHAM 2, p. 162; see also SABATIER, pp. 261–62).

from being continually talked to about obedience, submission, humility, a certain obscurity had come over this luminous soul. Inspiration no longer came to it with the certainty of other days. The prophet had begun to waver, almost to doubt himself and his mission. He pictured to himself the chapter that he was about to open—the attack, the criticisms that would be its object—and labored to convince himself that if he did not endure them with joy he was not a true Brother Minor. He resolved then to put the direction of the Order into the hands of Peter of Catana. It is evident that there was nothing spontaneous in this decision, and the fact that this brother was a doctor of laws and belonged to the nobility squarely argues the transformation of the Franciscan institute.

At the chapter-general that followed, nothing reveals the demoralized state of Francis better than the decision taken to drop out one of the essential passages of the old Rule, one of his three fundamental precepts, beginning with these words: "Carry nothing with you." How did they go to work to obtain from Francis this concession which a little while before he would have looked on as a denial of his call, a refusal to accept in its integrity the message that Jesus had addressed to him?

Something of Francis's pain has passed into the touching narrative of his abdication that the early biographers have given us:

> "From here forward," he said to the friars, "I am dead for you, but here is Brother Peter of Catana, whom you and I will all obey." And prostrating himself before him he promised him obedience and submission. The friars could not restrain their tears when they saw themselves becoming in some sort orphans, but Francis arose, and, clasping his hands, with eyes upraised to heaven, said: "Lord, I return to you this family that you have confided to me. Now, as you know, most sweet Jesus, I have no longer strength or ability to keep on caring for them. I confide them therefore, to the ministers. May they be responsible before you at the day of judgment if any brother, by their negligence or bad example, or by a too severe discipline, should ever wander away."

The functions of Peter of Catana were destined to continue only a very short time. He died on March 10, 1221. During this period of a few months, Francis remained at Portiuncula, and desirous of showing himself submissive, he nevertheless found himself tormented by the desire to shake off his chains and fly away as in former days, to live and breathe in God alone. The following, somewhat lengthy, incident says plenty about Francis and the brothers at this time:

> One day a novice who could read the psalter, though not without difficulty, obtained from the minister general—that is to say, from the vicar of St. Francis—permission to have one. But as he had learned that Francis desired the brothers to be covetous neither of learning or for books, he would not take his psalter without his consent.

"Father," the novice said to St. Francis, "it would be a great consolation to have a psalter. Though the minister general has authorized me to get it, I would not have it unknown to you."

"Look at the Emperor Charles," Francis replied with fire. "Roland and Oliver and all the paladins, valorous heroes and gallant knights who gained their famous victories in fighting infidels, in toiling and laboring even unto death! The holy martyrs also have chosen to die in the midst of battle for the faith of Christ! But now there are many of those who aspire to merit honor and glory simply by relating their feats. Yes, among us also there are many who expect to receive glory and honor by reciting and preaching the works of the saints, as if they had done them themselves!"

A few days later, St. Francis was sitting before the fire when the novice drew near to speak with him again about his psalter. "When you have your psalter," Francis said to him, "you will want a breviary, and when you have a breviary you will seat yourself in a pulpit like a great prelate and will beckon to your companion, 'Bring me my breviary!'"

Francis's love for poverty, and hate of pride, were two reasons for his strong opinion about the brothers not possessing books. But it is also worth noting that books, before paper, were extravagantly expensive. For example, more than two hundred years after the time of Francis, "It had been calculated that each copy of the Gutenberg Bible (641 leaves) printed on parchment required the skins of 300 sheep" (Hugh Kennedy, in Times Literary Supplement, *August 16, 2002).*

In Francis's Rule of 1221, composed soon after the time of his exchange with the young friar over the psalter, after he had relinquished control of his Order, Francis acquiesced: "The clergy may have only such books as are necessary for their office, and the laymen who can read may be allowed to possess a psalter."

St. Francis said this with great vivacity. Then, taking up some ashes he scattered them over the head of the novice, repeating: "There is the breviary! There is the breviary!"

Several days later, Francis was walking up and down along the roadside not far from his cell when the same Brother came again to speak to him about his psalter. "Very well, go on," Francis said, "you have only to do what your minister tells you." At these words, the novice went away, but Francis, reflecting on what he had said, called to the friar, crying, "Wait for me!" When Francis had caught up with him, he said, "Retrace your steps a little way, I beg you. Where was I when I told you to do whatever your minister told you as to the psalter?" Then, falling on his knees on the spot pointed out by the friar, Francis prostrated himself at his feet, crying, "Pardon, my brother, pardon, for he who would be Brother Minor ought to have nothing but his clothing!"

*Augustine Thompson disagrees with Sabatier's interpretation of what it meant for Francis to step down as leader of the order. He finds Sabatier's account too romantic (a common criticism of the French scholar) and tragic. Thompson writes: "In theory, it was a striking role reversal." But, "No one was deceived, much less the pope and the Franciscan leadership. Francis remained the de facto leader. During his lifetime, Francis intervened in the movement's governance, legislated for it, and corrected the order's leaders. He now did so with good conscience because he was no longer 'officially' in charge and so not 'above' the others. Francis's vicars in fact recognized their subordinate role and never used the later title 'minister general' during his lifetime." (*THOMPSON *p. 80) I suspect the historical reality is somewhere in between Sabatier's and Thompson's views.*

CHAPTER SEVENTEEN
Francis's Doubts and Weaknesses

The evolution of the Order hurried on with a rapidity that nothing was strong enough to check. The creation of ministers among the Brothers Minor, done in the chapter of 1221, was an enormous step.

Ministers need residences; those who command must have subordinates within reach; and the Brothers, therefore, could no longer do without friaries. This change naturally brought about many others.

Up to this time they were only itinerant preachers, having no need for churches. They were, as Francis had wished, the friendly auxiliaries of the clergy. With churches it was inevitable that they would first fatally aspire to preach in them and attract a crowd to them, and then in some way erect them into counter parishes (counter to the secular churches, or, those not run by members of monastic orders).

The bull of March 22, 1222, shows us the papacy hastening these transformations with all of its power. The pontiff accords to Brother Francis and the other friars the privilege of celebrating the sacred mysteries in their churches in times of interdict, on the natural condition of not ringing the bells, or closing the door, and previously expelling those who were excommunicated. In 1222, it appears that the Order as yet had no "times of interdict," but it is not difficult to see in the pontiff's actions a pressing invitation to change their way of working, leaving this privilege to be availed later.

Another document of the same time shows a like purpose, though manifested in another direction. By the bull *Ex parte* of March 29, 1222, Honorius III laid upon the Preachers and Minors of Lisbon conjointly a singularly delicate mission. He gave them full powers to proceed against the bishop and clergy of that city, who were exacting from the faithful one-third of their property, to be left to them by will, refusing the Church's burial service to those who disobeyed. The fact that the pope committed to the brothers the care of choosing what measures they should take proves how anxious they were in Rome to forget the object for which the brothers had been created, and to transform them into deputies of the Holy See. We perceive here the influence of Ugolino, who refounded the Brothers Minor after his own heart in the person of Elias.

What was Francis doing all this time? We have no clear evidence, but he had probably left Portiuncula and gone to live in one of those Umbrian hermitages that always had such a strong attachment for him. There is hardly a hill in central Italy that has not preserved some memento of him. It would be hard to walk half a day between Florence and Rome without coming upon some hut on a hillside bearing his name or that of one of his disciples.

There was a time when these huts were inhabited, when in these leafy booths Egidio, Masseo, Bernard, Sylvester, Ginepro, and many others whose names history has forgotten, received visits from their spiritual father. They gave Francis love for love and consolation for consolation. His poor heart had great need of both, for in his long, sleepless nights it had come to him at times to hear strange voices. Weariness and regret were laying hold of him, and looking over the past Francis was almost driven to doubt himself, his Lady Poverty, and everything.

Two and a half months after the untimely death of Peter of Catana, Brother Elias, the new vicar of the Order, presided over the Whitsunday chapter of May 30, 1221. "About three thousand friars were there assembled, but so great was the eagerness of the people of the neighborhood to bring provisions, that after a session of seven days they were obliged to remain two days longer to eat up all that had been brought. The sessions were presided over by Brother Elias, Francis sitting at his feet and pulling at his robe when there was anything that he wished to have put before the brothers" (SABATIER, p. 265).

Between Chiusi and Radicofani—an hour's walk from the village of Sartiano—a few brothers made a shelter that served them as a hermitage, with a little cabin for Francis in a retired spot. There he passed one of the most agonizing nights of his life. The thought that he had exaggerated the virtue of asceticism and not counted enough upon the mercy of God assailed him, and suddenly he came to regret what he had done with his life. A picture of what he might have been, of the tranquil and happy home that might have been his, rose up before him in such living colors that he felt himself giving way. In vain he disciplined himself with his hempen girdle until the blood came, but the vision would not leave.

It was midwinter and a heavy fall of snow covered the ground. He rushed out without his garment and, gathering up great heaps of snow, began to make a row of images. "See," he said, "here is your wife, and behind her are two sons and two daughters, with the servant and the maid carrying all the baggage." With this childlike representation of the tyranny of material cares that he had escaped, Francis finally put away the temptation.

There is nothing to show whether or not we should fix at the same time another incident that legend gives us taking place at Sartiano. One day, a brother whom Francis asked, "From where did you come?" replied, "From your cell." This simple answer was enough to make the vehement lover of Poverty refuse to occupy it again. "Foxes have holes," he loved to repeat, "and the birds of the air have nests, but the Son of Man had nowhere to lay his head. When the Lord spent forty days and forty nights praying and fasting in the desert, he built himself neither cell or house, but made the side of a rock his shelter."

It would be a mistake to think, as some have done, that as time went on Francis changed his point of view. Certain ecclesiastical writers have assumed that since he desired the multiplication of his Order, he for that very reason consented to its transformation. The suggestion is specious, but in this matter we are not left to conjecture; almost everything that was done in the Order after 1221 was done either without Francis's knowledge or against his will. If one were inclined to doubt this, it would only be necessary to read that most solemn and most adequate manifesto of Francis's thought—his will. In it, he is shown freed from all the temptations that had at times made him hesitate in the expression of his primitive ideal, and set it up in opposition to all the concessions that had been wrung from his weakness.

Francis's will may be seen almost as a revocation of the Rule written in 1223. But, it would be a mistake to see in it the first attempt made to return to the early ideal. The last five years of his life were one incessant effort at protest, both by his example and his words.

CHAPTER EIGHTEEN
The Brothers Minor and Learning (1222–1223)

In 1222, Francis addressed a letter filled with sad forebodings to his brothers in Bologna. In that city, where the Dominicans were occupied with making a stronghold for themselves, the Brothers Minor were more than anywhere else tempted to forsake the way of simplicity and poverty. Francis's warnings put on such dark and threatening colors that, after the famous earthquake of December 23, 1222, which spread terror over all of northern Italy, there was no hesitation in believing that he had predicted the catastrophe.

He had indeed predicted a catastrophe that was nonetheless horrible for being entirely moral, and the vision of which forced from him the most bitter imprecations:

> Lord Jesus, you chose your apostles to the number of twelve, and if one of them did betray you, the others, remaining united to you, preached your holy gospel, filled with one and the same inspiration. Behold now, remembering those former days, you have raised up the religion of the brothers in order to uphold faith, and by them the mystery of your gospel may be accomplished. Who will take their place if, instead of fulfilling their mission and being shining examples for all, they are seen to give themselves up

Seismic activity has always been common throughout Italy. Most recently, on September 26, 1997, two friars and two art experts were killed in Assisi when portions of the ceiling of the basilica, including famous frescos by Giotto, Cimabue, and others, crashed to the floor. Scenes of this were seen on television around the world. Tremors continued throughout October of that year, injuring others and leaving thousands homeless. An October 31 letter that year from a Franciscan pilgrimage program leader in Milwaukee, and a visit to Assisi by Pope John Paul II on January 3, 1998, helped to draw thousands of pilgrims to Assisi, many of whom helped in rebuilding efforts throughout the city, most of which was completed by early 2001.

Art historians have warned that the severity of the earthquake damage to the Assisi frescos could have been lessened if it were not for structural changes made to the building a few decades before, when concrete beams were added to the roof in place of ancient wooden ones. This practice has been fairly common in recent years, including in Padua, where the Scrovegni Chapel contains some of Giotto's most beautiful frescos.

to works of darkness? Oh, may they be accursed by you, Lord, and by all the court of heaven, and by me, your unworthy servant, they who by their bad example overturn and destroy all that you did in the beginning and cease not to do by the holy brothers of this order.

This passage from Thomas of Celano, the most moderate of the early biographers, shows to what a pitch of vehemence and indignation the gentle Francis could be worked up. In spite of natural efforts to throw a veil of reserve over the anguish of the founder, we find traces of it at every step. "The time will come," he said one day, "when our order will so have lost all good renown that its members will be ashamed to show themselves by daylight."

Francis believed his sons to be attacked with two maladies: unfaithful at once to poverty and humility. But perhaps he dreaded for them the demon of learning more than the temptation of riches.

He had no difficulty in seeing that there will always be enough students for the universities, and that if scientific effort is a homage to God, there is no risk of a lack of this sort of worshiper. But Francis looked in vain about him for those who would fulfill the mission of love and humility reserved for his order, if the friars were to be unfaithful to it.

So there was more in his anguish than the grief of seeing his hopes confounded. The defeat of an army is nothing compared with the overthrow of an idea, and in him an idea had been incarnated—the idea of peace and happiness restored to humankind by the victory of love over the trammels of material things.

By an ineffable mystery he felt himself to be one by whom humanity yearns to be renewed—to use the language of the Gospel, born again. In this lies his true beauty.

———— ◦◦◦ ————

A generation after Francis's death, under Bonaventure's leadership of the Brothers Minor, "The typical friar was to be no longer the wandering evangelist who worked in the fields, tended the sick, slept in barns and churches, a simple, devout, homely soul content to take the lowest place and be idiota et subditus omnibus, *but a member of a religious house, well educated and well trained, a preacher and director of souls, a man whom the community could respect and whose services would be valued. In bringing about this change S. Bonaventura set the friars on the road which they were henceforth to travel. It is, therefore, not without reason that he has been called 'the second founder of the Order'"* (MOORMAN, p. 154).

———— ◦◦◦ ————

130

By this, far more than by a vain conformity, an exterior imitation, he is a Christ.

The man who would run after ruffians that he might make disciples of them could be pitiless toward his fellow-laborers who by an indiscreet, however well-intentioned, zeal forgot their vocation and would transform their order into a scientific institute. Can you imagine Jesus joining the school of the rabbis under the pretext of learning how to reply to them, weakening his thought by their dialectic subtleties and fantastic exegesis? He might have become a great doctor, but would he have become the Savior of the world? Probably not.

When we hear preachers going into raptures over the marvelous spread of the gospel preached by twelve poor fishermen of Galilee, we should point out to them that the miracle is at once more and less astounding than they say. It is more, for among the twelve, several returned to the shores of their charming lake, and forgetful of the mystic net, thought of the Crucified One, if they thought of him at all, only to lament him and not to raise him from the dead by continuing his work in the four quarters of the world. It is less, for if even now preachers would go forth with love, sacrificing themselves for each and all as in the old days their Master did, the miracle would be repeated again. But no; theology has killed religion.

Never was learning more eagerly coveted than in the thirteenth century. The Empire and the Church were anxiously asking of it the arguments with which they might defend their opposing claims. Innocent III sent the collection of his decretals to the University of Bologna and heaped favor upon it. Frederick II founded the school in Naples and the Patarini themselves sent their sons from Tuscany and Lombardy to study in Paris.

At the time of Francis's successful preaching in Bologna in August, 1220 (see chap. 16, pp. 119–120), he had also strongly reprimanded Peter Staccia, the provincial minister and a doctor of laws, not only for having installed the Brothers in a house that appeared to belong to them, but especially for having organized a sort of college there. It appears that the minister paid no attention to these reproaches. When Francis became aware of his obstinacy he cursed him with frightful vehemence. His indignation was so great that when, later on, Peter Staccia was about to die and his numerous friends came to beg Francis to revoke his malediction, all their efforts were in vain.

It is difficult now to imagine the rivalry that existed at this time between the Dominicans and Franciscans to draw the most illustrious masters into their respective orders. Petty intrigues were organized in which the devotees each had his part, to lead such and such a famous doctor to assume the habit. Perhaps Francis did not at the outset perceive the gravity of the danger, but illusion was no longer possible, and from this time he showed, as we have seen, an implacable firmness.

The Dominicans and the Franciscans were soon at the center of the intellectual renaissance of the thirteenth century. For example, Alexander of Hales was perhaps the most important early recruit of the Franciscans. He "was already a celebrated teacher . . . when he joined the Order of Friars Minor about the year 1236. For the next two years he ruled the newly created Franciscan school and attracted a large number of pupils. Seven years later, in August 1245, he died, leaving his Summa Theologica *. . . the first medieval writer to make use of the whole of the Aristotelian corpus"* (MOORMAN, pp. 240–41).

"Suppose," he would say, "that you had subtlety and learning enough to know all things, that you were acquainted with all languages, the courses of the stars, and all the rest— what is there to be proud of? A single demon knows more on these subjects than all the people in this world put together. But there is one thing that the demon is incapable of and that is the glory of humanity: to be faithful to God."

After the Rule of 1223 was written and approved on November 25 of that year, further demonstrating the struggles of Francis against the ministers for the preservation of his ideal, Francis and many of his companions journeyed to Rome, accepting the hospitality of Cardinal Ugolino. One day, Ugolino, and most of his guests, were surprised to find Francis absent as they were about to sit down at table. Francis soon returned, carrying a quantity of pieces of dry bread that he joyfully distributed to all the noble company. His host, somewhat abashed by this proceeding, reproached Francis a little after the meal. Francis explained that he had no right to forget, for a sumptuous feast, the bread of charity on which he was fed every day, and that he desired to show his brothers that the richest table is not worth so much to the poor in spirit as the table of the Lord.

We have seen that during the earlier years the Brothers Minor had been in the habit of earning their bread by going out as servants. Some of them—a very small number—had continued to do so. But little by little, all had changed in this matter as well. Under pretense of serving, most of the friars entered the families of the highest personages of the pontifical court and became their confidential attendants. Instead of submitting themselves to all, as the Rule of 1221 ordained, they were above everyone. By way of protest, Francis only had one weapon, his example.

It was now mid-December. An ardent desire to observe the life and memories of Christmas had taken possession of Francis. In spite of cold and the north wind he joyfully traveled to the valley of Rieti where he opened his heart to one of his friends, the knight Giovanni of Velita, who undertook the necessary preparations.

In the Middle Ages a religious festival was above all things a representation, more or less faithful, of the event that it recalled. Hence there were the *santons* of Provence, the processions of the *Palmesel*, the Holy Supper of Maundy Thursday, the Road to the Cross of Good Friday, and the drama of the Resurrection of Easter. Francis was too thoroughly Italian not to love these festivals where every visible thing speaks of God and of God's love. The population of Greccio and its environs was, therefore, assembled, as well as the brothers from the neighboring monasteries.

santons: Clay figurines, both secular and religious. Santons likely derive their use from the Provencal word santoun, "little saint," and are often used in manager scenes.

Palmesel: German carved wooden sculptures, often processed on wheels, to commemorate Christ's entry into Jerusalem riding a donkey (Mt. 21:1–11).

Thomas of Celano, in his first life of Francis, tells us that Francis repeatedly used the phrase "bambino from Bethlehem" when referring to Jesus. "Saying the word 'Bethlehem' in the manner of a bleating sheep, he fills his whole mouth with sound but even more with sweet affection. He seems to lick his lips whenever he uses the expressions 'Jesus' or 'babe from Bethlehem,' tasting the word on his happy palate and savoring the sweetness of the word" (ARMSTRONG, p. 256). Also, notably, Thomas, and later Bonaventure, were the first to refer to Francis as a deacon, beginning with this scene of his singing the Gospel. This could suggest that Francis was actually ordained at some point in time.

Jacopone (d. 1306) was not only a poet but something of an early Franciscan holy fool. In public, he was known to crawl on all fours saddled as a donkey, and to appear at solemn gatherings tarred and feathered. Some scholars doubt the attribution of Stabat Mater Dolorosa *to Jacopone—it has been variously ascribed to others, including Popes Innocent III and Gregory XI. It became part of the Roman Catholic breviary in 1727. The* Stabat Mater Speciosa *did not, and there is more consensus on Jacopone as the author of it.*

The complete Stabat Mater Speciosa *has thirteen double stanzas of six lines each. Sabatier quotes stanza one, lines one to three, stanza two, lines four to six, and stanza eight, lines one to three. See opposite page for a rough, English translation of the Latin quoted by Sabatier. As Sabatier mentions, the text of* Stabat Mater Speciosa *stands in contrast to the* Stabat Mater Dolorosa, *also about Mary, which begins:* Stabat Mater dolorosa juxta crucem lacrimosa dum pendebat Filius *("The grieving mother stood weeping at the cross on which her son was hanging").*

On the evening of the vigil of Christmas one might have seen the faithful hastening to the hermitage by every path with torches in their hands, making the forests ring with their joyful hymns.

Everyone was rejoicing—Francis most of all. The knight had prepared a stable with straw and brought an ox and a donkey, whose breath seemed to give warmth to the poor *bambino*, numbed with cold. At the sight the saint felt tears of pity warm his face; he was no longer in Greccio, his heart was in Bethlehem.

Finally they began to chant matins, then the mass was begun, and Francis, as deacon, read the Gospel. Already, hearts were touched by the simple recital of the sacred legend in a voice so gentle and so fervent, but when he preached, his emotion soon overcame the audience. His voice had so unutterable a tenderness that they also forgot everything and were living over again the feeling of the shepherds of Judea, who in those days of old went to adore the God made man, born in a stable.

Toward the close of the thirteenth century, the author of the *Stabat Mater Dolorosa*, Jacopone da Todi, that Franciscan of genius who spent a part of his life in dungeons, inspired by the memory of Greccio, composed another *Stabat*, that of joy, *Stabat Mater Speciosa*. This hymn of Mary beside the manger is not less noble than that of Mary at the foot of the cross. The sentiment is even more tender, and it is hard to explain its neglect except by an unjust caprice of fate.

Stabat Mater speciosa
Juxta foenum gaudiosa
Dum jacebat parvulus

Quae gaudebat et ridebat
Exultabat cum videbat
Nati partum inclyti

Fac me vere congaudere
Jesulino cohaerere
Donec ego vixero

The beautiful mother / stood blissfully at the crib / in which her child lay. / Joyful and laughing / and exultant she watched / the birth of her divine son. / Help me to rejoice with you / and share in the adoration of Jesus / as long as I live.

CHAPTER NINETEEN
The Stigmata (1224)

The upper valley of the Arno forms in the very center of Italy a country apart—the Casentino—which through centuries had its own life, somewhat like an island in the midst of the ocean. The river flows out from it by a narrow defile at the south, and on all other sides the Apennines encircle it with a girdle of inaccessible mountains.

The people are charming and refined; the mountains have sheltered them from wars, and on every side we see the signs of labor, prosperity, a gentle gaiety. The vegetation on the borders of the Arno is thoroughly tropical; the olive and the mulberry marry with the vine. On the lower hill-slopes are wheat fields divided by meadows, and then come the chestnuts and the oaks, higher still the pine, fir, larch, and above all the bare rock.

Among all the peaks there is one that especially attracts the attention. Instead of a rounded and somewhat flattened top, it rises slender, proud, and isolated. It is the Verna.

One might think it to be an immense rock fallen from the sky, a little like a petrified Noah's ark on the summit of Mount Ararat. The basaltic mass, perpendicular on all sides, is crowned with a plateau planted with pines and gigantic beeches, and accessible only by a footpath. Such was the solitude that Orlando, Count of Chiusi, had given to Francis, and to which Francis had already many a time come for quiet and contemplation.

La Verna is located in the Casentine Valley, south of Bologna and east of Florence. Sabatier notes that "The forest has been preserved as a relic. Alexander IV fulminated excommunication against whoever should cut down the firs of Verna" (SABATIER, p. 289). Another historian, echoing Sabatier, writes: "Its summit, covered with fir-trees, straight and close together, appears like a great whale that has rested there since the days of the flood. Below the forest lie huge boulders of rock and yawning chasms, upheaved, says the legend, during the earthquake at the time of the Crucifixion. To this solitary place came Francis in the year 1224 to celebrate by forty days of fasting and prayer the feast of St. Michael the Archangel" (GORDON, p. 72).

A monastery sits today at the top of La Verna, and in the chapel there are the famous terracotta panels (ceramics) of biblical scenes executed by members of the talented della Robbia family in the fifteenth and early sixteenth centuries. It is a popular place of pilgrimage today.

Seated upon the few stones of the Penna, the highest point on the plateau, he heard only the whispering of the wind among the trees, but in the splendor of the sunrise or the sunset he could see nearly all of the districts in which he had sown the seed of the gospel: the Romagna and the March of Ancona, losing themselves on the horizon in the waves of the Adriatic; Umbria; and farther away, Tuscany, vanishing in the waters of the Mediterranean.

Francis desired to return to La Verna after the chapter of 1224. This meeting was the last at which he was present. A new Rule was put into the hands of the ministers there, and a mission to England decided upon.

In the early days of August, Francis made his way toward La Verna. With him were only a few brothers: Masseo, Angelo, and Leo. The first had been charged to direct the little band and to spare Francis all duties except prayer.

"They came to this mountain in high spirits. Francesco had accepted Count Orlando's offer without his usual reservations about the hospitality of the wealthy and powerful. The wise count had not offered them a seat at his table, soft beds, or polished floors; he did not seek, as so many did, to make house pets of the friars. Rather, he offered them a rugged wilderness in which to pray and fast, a place uninhabited because inhospitable. Francesco was convinced the invitation was from God" (MARTIN, pp. 66–67).

They were on the road two days when it became necessary to seek a donkey for Francis, who was too feeble to continue on foot. The brothers, in asking for this gift, failed to conceal the name of their master, and the peasant, to whom they had addressed themselves respectfully, asked permission to join them, guiding the beast himself.

After going on for a time, the peasant said, "Is it true, that you are Brother Francis of Assisi?"

"Very well," he went on, after the answer was in the affirmative, "apply yourself to be as good as folk say you are, that they may not be deceived in their expectations—that is my advice."

Francis immediately got down from the donkey and, prostrating himself before the peasant, thanked him warmly.

Meanwhile, the warmest hour of the day had come on. The peasant, exhausted with fatigue, little by little forgot his surprise and joy. One does not feel the burning of thirst any less when walking beside a saint. He had begun to regret his kindness, and at that moment Francis pointed with his finger to a spring, unknown until then, and which has never been seen since.

At last they arrived at the foot of the last precipice. Before scaling it they paused to rest a little under a great oak, and immediately flocks of birds gathered around them, testifying their joy by songs and flutterings of their wings. Hovering around Francis, they alighted on his head, his shoulders, or his arms. "I see," he said joyfully to his companions, "that it is pleasing to our Lord Jesus that we live in this solitary mount, since our brothers and sisters the birds have shown such great delight at our coming."

Two of the finest paintings in the Assisi cycle of Giotto are inspired by this time on La Verna. "The Stigmata" is one of the most imitated images in the history of art, and the "Miracle of the Spring" portrays Francis in prayer to God for water on behalf of the poor peasant, and as a result, water gushing forth from dry rock. Thus was Francis shown to be a new Moses, to whom Jesus too was often compared in early Christian literature.

This mountain was at once his Tabor and his Calvary. We must not wonder, then, that legends have flourished here even more numerously than at any other period of his life. Many of them have the exquisite charm of the little flowers, rosy and perfumed, that hide themselves modestly at the feet of the fir trees of La Verna.

The summer nights up there are of unparalleled beauty. Nature, stifled by the heat of the sun, seems then to breathe anew. In the trees, behind the rocks, on the turf, a thousand voices rise up, sweetly harmonizing with the murmur of the great woods. But among all these voices there is not one that forces itself upon the attention; it is a melody that you enjoy without listening. You let your eyes wander over the landscape, still for long hours illumined with hieratic tints by the departed star of the day, and the peaks of the Apennines, flooded with rainbow hues, drop down into your soul what the Franciscan poet Thomas of Celano called the nostalgia of the everlasting hills.

More than anyone else, Francis felt it. The very evening of their arrival, seated upon a mound in the midst of his brothers, he gave them his directions for their dwelling-place. He spoke with them of his approaching death with the regret of the laborer overtaken by the shades of evening before the completion of his task, with the sighs of the father who trembles for the future of his children.

For himself during this time he desired to prepare for death by prayer and contemplation, and he begged them to protect him from all intrusion. Orlando, who had already come to bid them welcome and offer his services, had at Francis's request hastily caused a hut of boughs to be made at the foot of a great beech. It was there that Francis desired to dwell, at a stone's throw from the cells inhabited by his companions. Brother Leo was charged to bring him that which he would need each day.

In his brief "Rule for Hermitages," about five years earlier, Francis had written: "Let those who wish to stay in hermitages in a religious way be three brothers or, at the most, four; let two of these be 'the mother' and have two 'sons' or at least one. Let the two who are 'mothers' keep the life of Martha and the two 'sons' the life of Mary and let one have one enclosure in which each one may have his cell in which he may pray and sleep" (ARMSTRONG, p. 61).

He retired to his hut immediately after this memorable conversation, but several days later, embarrassed no doubt by the pious curiosity of the friars who watched all his movements, he went farther into the woods, and on Assumption Day he began there the Lent that he desired to observe.

Genius has its modesty as well as love. The poet, the artist, the saint, need to be alone when the Spirit comes to move them. Every effort of thought, of imagination, or of will is a prayer, and one does not pray in public. Jesus felt it deeply: The raptures of Tabor are brief; they may not be told.

Before these soul mysteries materialists and devotees often demand precision in the things that can the least endure it. The believer asks in what spot on the Verna Francis received the stigmata; whether the seraph that appeared to him was Jesus of a celestial spirit; what words were spoken as he imprinted them upon him; and the believer no more understands that hour when Francis fainted with woe and love than the materialist who asks to see with his eyes and touch with his hands the gaping wound.

Francis was distressed for the future of the Order, and with an infinite desire for new spiritual progress. He was consumed with the fever of saints—that need of immolation that wrung from St. Teresa the passionate cry, "Either to suffer or to die!" He was bitterly reproaching himself for not having been found worthy of martyrdom, not having been able to give himself for him who gave himself for us.

We touch here upon one of the most powerful and mysterious elements of the Christian life. We may very easily not understand it, but we may not deny it. It is the root of true mysticism. The really new thing that Jesus brought into the world was that, feeling himself in perfect union with the heavenly Father, he called all people to unite themselves to him and through him to God: "I am the vine, you are the branches. Those who abide in me and I in them bear much fruit, because apart from me you can do nothing" (Jn. 15:5).

The Christ not only preached this union, he made it felt. On the evening of his last day he instituted its sacrament, and there is probably no sect that denies that communion is at once the symbol, the principle, and the aim and goal of the religious life.

The night before he died he took the bread and broke it and distributed it to them, saying, "Take and eat, for this is my body."

Jesus, while presenting union with himself as the very foundation of the new life, took care to point out to his brethren that this union was before all things a sharing in his work, in his struggles, and his sufferings: "If any want to become my followers, let them deny themselves and take up their cross daily and follow me" (Lk. 9:23).

St. Paul entered so perfectly into the Master's thought in this respect that he uttered a few years later this cry of a mysticism that has never been equalled: "I have been crucified with Christ; and it is no longer I who live, but it is Christ who lives in me" (Gal. 2:19–20). This utterance is not an isolated exclamation with him; it is the very center of his religious consciousness. Paul goes so far as to say—at the risk of scandalizing many Christians—"In my flesh I am completing what is lacking in Christ's afflictions for the sake of his body, that is, the church" (Col. 1:24).

Perhaps it has been useful to enter into these thoughts in order to show to what point Francis is allied to the apostolic tradition during these last years of his life, as he renews in his body the passion of Christ. In the solitudes of the Verna, as formerly at San

Damiano, Jesus presented himself to him as the Crucified One, the man of sorrows.

On the Verna, Francis was even more absorbed than usual in his ardent desire to suffer for Jesus and with him. His days were divided between exercises of piety in the humble sanctuary on the mountain top and meditation in the depths of the forest. He even forgot the services, and remained several days alone in a cave of the rock going over in his heart the memories of Golgotha. At other times he would remain for long hours at the foot of the altar, reading and re-reading the Gospel and entreating God to show him the way in which he ought to walk. The book almost always opened of itself to the story of the Passion, and this simple coincidence—though easy enough to explain—was enough to excite him.

The vision of the Crucified One took fuller possession of his faculties as the day of the Elevation of the Holy Cross drew near (September 14), a festival now relegated to the background, but in the thirteenth century celebrated with a fervor and zeal very natural for a solemnity that might be considered the patronal festival of the Crusades.

Francis doubled his fastings and prayers, "quite transformed into Jesus by love and compassion," says one of the legends. He passed the night before the festival alone in prayer, not far from the hermitage. In the morning he had a vision. In the rays of the rising sun, which after the chill of night came to revive his body, he suddenly perceived a strange form. A seraph, with outspread wings, flew toward him from the edge of the horizon and bathed his soul in raptures unutterable. In the center of the vision appeared a cross, and the seraph was nailed upon it.

When the vision disappeared, he felt sharp sufferings mingling with

The story of the stigmata is told in the tales of The Little Flowers. *One historian writes that, in contrast to it, Thomas of Celano's telling of the events are "suspiciously elaborate." Sabatier follows* The Little Flowers *version more closely than the even more fantastical language of Thomas of Celano and the other early biographers. "By contrast Leo and Angelo were only a few hundred yards away and later the same morning heard from Francis's own lips what he had seen and felt.... Long after Francis died, [Brother Leo] told the full story...to a spiritual lay brother in the next generation, James of Massa. He in turn passed it on to the friars in the Marches from whom* The Little Flowers *emanated in the fourteenth century"* (HOUSE, pp. 257–58).

Francis fascinates us, in part, because he seems to contain opposites. For example, as we read from the chapter just concluded to the one that follows, we see how he is both a sublime mystic and a man whose faith is grounded in the creation itself. It is interesting to imagine these two qualities exhibited in his two hands. At the end of his life, in his personal "Testament," Francis spoke of his hands in a way that encompassed his entire ministry: "God gave me brothers.... We were simple and subject to each other.... I worked with my hands, then, and I still desire to do so." (FRANCIS, pp. 97-98).

the ecstasy of the first moments. Stirred to the very depths of his being, he was anxiously seeking the meaning of it all when he perceived on his body the stigmata of the Crucified One.

CHAPTER TWENTY

The Canticle of the Sun (Autumn 1224–Autumn 1225)

A little more than two weeks later, Francis left La Verna and went to Portiuncula. He was too exhausted to think of making the journey on foot, and Count Orlando put a horse at his disposal.

We can imagine the emotion with which he said goodbye to the mountain on which had been unfolded the drama of love and pain that consummated the union of his entire being with the Crucified One. If we are to believe a recently published document, Brother Masseo, one of those who remained on the Verna, made a written account of the events of this day.

They set out early in the morning. Francis, after having given his directions to the brothers, had a look and a word for everything around—for the rocks, the flowers, the trees, and for brother hawk, a privileged character that was authorized to enter his cell at all times, and that came every morning with the first glimmer of dawn to remind him of the hour of service.

Then the little band set upon the path leading to Monte-Acuto. Arriving at the gap from where one receives the last sight of the Verna, Francis alighted from his horse and, kneeling on the earth with face turned toward the mountain, said, "Adieu, mountain of God, sacred mountain, *mons coagulatus, mons pinguis, mons in quo bene placitum est Deo habitare.* Adieu, Monte-Verna, may God bless you, the Father, the Son, and the Holy Spirit. Abide in peace; we shall never see one another again."

Suddenly the Italian does not suffice and Francis is obliged to resort to the mystical language of the breviary to express his feelings. A few minutes later the rock of the ecstasy had disappeared.

"mons coagulatus, mons pinguis, mons in quo bene placitum est Deo habitare": *Francis is quoting from the Latin psalter, roughly translated into English as: "a fat mountain, a curdled mountain, a mountain in which God is pleased to dwell." Even when we ascend the hill of the Lord, we can never fully penetrate the incomprehensible mysteries there. "Fat" and "curdled" are God's mysteries. (Cross-reference to Psalm 68:15–16 in today's English language psalters.)*

143

The brothers had decided to spend the night at Monte-Casale, the little hermitage above Borgo San-Sepolcro. All of them, even those who were to remain on the Verna, were still following their master. As for Francis, he was so absorbed in thought that he became entirely oblivious to what was going on, and did not even perceive the noisy enthusiasm that his passage aroused in the numerous villages along the Tiber.

At Borgo San-Sepolcro he received a real ovation without even then coming to himself. But when they had left the town he seemed suddenly to awake and asked his companions if they would soon be arriving.

The first evening at Monte-Casale was marked by a miracle. Francis healed a friar who was possessed. The next morning, having decided to spend several days in this hermitage, Francis sent the brothers back to the Verna, and with them Count Orlando's horse.

In one of the villages through which they had passed the day before, a woman had been lying several days between death and life unable to give birth to her child. Those about her had learned of the passage of the saint through their village only when he was too far distant to be overtaken. We can imagine the joy of these poor people when the rumor was spread that he was about to return. They went to meet him and were terribly disappointed to find only the friars. Suddenly an idea occurred to them: Taking the bridle of the horse consecrated by the touch of Francis's hand, they carried it to the sufferer, who, having laid it upon her body, gave birth to her child without the slightest pain.

This miracle, established by entirely authentic narratives, shows the degree of enthusiasm felt by the people for the person of Francis. As for him, after a few days at Monte-Casale, he set out with Brother Leo for Citta of Castello. There, he healed a woman suffering from frightful nervous disorders and remained an entire month preaching in this city and its environs.

Winter was almost closing on the day when Francis and Leo finally set forth. A peasant lent Francis his donkey, but the roads were so bad that they were unable to reach any sort of shelter before nightfall. The unhappy travelers were obliged to spend the night under a rock. The shelter was more than rudimentary; the wind drifted the snow in upon them and nearly froze the unlucky peasant who, with abominable oaths, heaped curses on Francis. But Francis replied with such cheerfulness that he made the peasant at last forget both the cold and his bad humor.

The next day, the saint reached Portiuncula. He stayed only briefly, however, and soon left to evangelize southern Umbria. We know almost nothing of this trip, except that Brother Elias accompanied him, and Francis was so feeble that Elias could not conceal his uneasiness about it. Ever since his return from Syria (August 1220), Francis had been growing continually weaker, but his fervor had increased from day to day. Nothing could check him, neither suffering nor the entreaties of the brothers. Seated on a donkey he would sometimes travel to three or four villages in one day. But now he was losing his sight.

Meanwhile a sedition had forced Honorius III to leave Rome (end of April 1225). After passing a few weeks at Tivoli, he established himself at Rieti, where he remained until the end of 1226. The pope's arrival had drawn to this city, with the entire pontifical court, several physicians of renown. Cardinal Ugolino, who had come in the pope's train, hearing of Francis's malady, summoned him to Rieti for treatment. But despite Brother Elias's urging, Francis hesitated a long time before accepting the invitation. It seemed to him that a sick man has but one thing to do—place himself purely and simply in the hands of the heavenly Father. What is pain to a soul that is fixed in God!

Elias, however, overcame his objections at last and the journey was determined, but first Francis desired to go and see Clare and enjoy a little rest near her. He remained at San Damiano much longer than he had proposed to do, from the end of July to the beginning of September 1225. His arrival at this beloved monastery was marked by a terrible aggravation of his malady. For fifteen days he was so completely blind that he could not even distinguish light. The care lavished on him produced no result, since every day he passed long hours in weeping—tears of penitence, he said, but also of regret. How different they were from those tears of his moments of inspiration and emotion that had flowed over a countenance all illumined with joy! They had seen him, in such moments, take up two bits of wood, and, accompanying himself with this rustic violin, improvise French songs in which he would pour out the abundance of his heart.

But the radiance of genius and hope had now become dimmed. Rachel weeps for her children and will not be comforted because they are not. There are in the tears of Francis this same *quia non sunt* for his spiritual sons.

"Ah, if the brothers knew what I suffer," St. Francis said a few days before the impression of the stigmata, "with what pity and compassion they would be moved!" But they, seeing in him the one who had laid cheerfulness upon them as a duty becoming more and more sad and keeping aloof from them, imagined that he was tortured with temptations of the devil.

Clare divined what could not be uttered. At San Damiano her friend was looking back over all the past. Here, the olive-tree to which, a brilliant cavalier, he had fastened his horse; there, the stone bench where his friend, the priest of the poor chapel, used to sit; over there, the hiding-place in which he had taken refuge from the paternal wrath; and, above all, the sanctuary with the mysterious crucifix of the decisive hour.

In the nave of the Upper Basilica di San Francesco in Assisi are twenty-eight frescos representing the life and legend of Francis. The great painter Giotto is believed to be their creator, although this is hotly debated even today. At this point in our narrative of Francis's life, we have just passed number nineteen in the cycle, that of Francis receiving the stigmata. Other scenes from these paintings are never discussed by Sabatier and most modern biographers, including a vision of some of the brothers at Rivo-Torto of Francis traveling to heaven in a chariot like Elijah (number eight), and a vision of Brother Leo in which the highest throne of heaven, formerly occupied by Satan (before the angels revolted) is reserved for Francis, the most humble (number nine).

In living over these pictures of the radiant past, Francis aggravated his pain, yet they spoke to him of other things than death and regret. Clare was there, as steadfast, as ardent as ever. Long ago transformed by admiration, she was now transfigured by compassion. Seated at the feet of him whom she loved with more than earthly love she felt the soreness of his soul, and the failing of his heart.

She kept him near her, and taking part in the labor, she made him a large cell of reeds in the monastery garden, so that he might be entirely at liberty as to his movements. How could he refuse a hospitality so thoroughly Franciscan? It was indeed, but only too much so: Legions of rats and mice infested this retired spot. At night they ran over Francis's bed with an infernal uproar, such that he could find no rest from his sufferings. But he soon forgot all of that when near his sister-friend. Once again she gave back to him faith and courage. "A single sunbeam," he used to say, "is enough to drive away many shadows."

Little by little the man of the former days began to show himself, and at times the sisters would hear, mingling with the murmur of the olive trees and pines, the echo of unfamiliar songs seeming to come from the cell of reeds. One day he was seated at the monastery table after a long conversation with Clare. The meal had hardly begun when suddenly he seemed to be rapt away in ecstasy. *"Laudato sia lo Signore!"* ("Praise the Lord!") he cried on coming to himself. He had just composed "The Canticle of the Sun."

O most high, almighty, good Lord God,
to you belong praise, glory, honor, and all blessing!
Praised be my Lord God with all Your creatures,
and especially our Brother Sun,
who brings us the day and who brings us the light.
Fair is he and shines with a very great splendor:
O Lord, he signifies You to us!
Praised be my Lord for our Brother Wind,
and for air and cloud, calms and all weather
through which You uphold life in all creatures.
Praised be my Lord for our Sister Water,
who is very useful to us and humble and precious and clean.
Praised be my Lord for our Brother Fire,
through whom You give us light in the darkness;
and he is bright and pleasant and very mighty and strong.
Praised be my Lord for our Mother Earth,
who does sustain us and keep us,
and brings forth many fruits and flowers of many colors, and grass.
Praised be my Lord for all those who pardon one another for Your sake,
and who endure weakness and tribulation;

blessed are they who peaceably endure, for You, O most High,
shall give them a crown.
Praised be my Lord for our Sister Death of the Body,
from whom no one can escape.
Woe to those who die in mortal sin.
Blessed are they who are found walking by Your most holy will,
for the second death shall have no power to do them harm.
Praise and bless the Lord, and give thanks to Him
and serve Him with great humility.

It is fairly easy to imagine how the originality of Francis's ideas was not always appreciated within the established norms of traditional religious life. This story—of Francis teaching his brothers to be God's jugglers—recalls the vehement words of the old monk, Jorge, in Umberto Eco's novel The Name of the Rose. *Jorge poisoned the pages of a hidden book about laughter in the abbey scriptorium, wanting to protect the young and the curious from the greater poison of laughter: a "weakness, corruption, the foolishness of our flesh." At the end of the novel, Jorge says with contempt to his accuser, a Franciscan: "You are a clown, like the saint who gave birth to you all. You are like your Francis, who ... begged in French, and imitated with a piece of wood the movements of a violin player, who disguised himself as a tramp to confound the gluttonous monks, who flung himself naked in the snow, spoke with animals and plants, transformed the very mystery of the Nativity into a village spectacle, called the lamb of Bethlehem by imitating the bleat of a sheep" (ECO 2, pp. 474, 477–78).*

Joy had returned to Francis, joy as deep as ever. For a whole week he put aside his breviary and passed his days in repeating "The Canticle of the Sun."

During a night of sleeplessness he heard a voice saying to him, "If you had faith as a grain of mustard seed, you would say to this mountain, 'Be removed from here,' and it would move away." Was not the mountain his sufferings, the temptation to murmur and despair? "Be it, Lord, according to your word," Francis replied with all his heart, and immediately he felt that he was delivered.

Francis might have perceived that the mountain had not greatly changed its place, but for several days he turned his eyes away from it and had been able to forget its existence.

For a moment he thought of summoning to his side Brother Pacifico, the king of verse, to retouch his canticle. His idea was to attach to him a certain number of friars who would go with him from village to village, preaching. After the sermon they would sing the hymn of the sun, and they were to close by saying to the gathered crowd, "We are God's jugglers. We desire to be paid for our sermon and our song. Our payment will be that you persevere in penitence."

"Is it not in fact true," Francis would add, "that the servants of God are really like jugglers, intended to revive the hearts of men and lead them into spiritual joy?"

The Francis of the old raptures was back—the layman, the poet, the artist.

CHAPTER TWENTY-ONE

His Last Year
(September 1225–End of
September 1226)

Francis's notion of friars being God's jugglers turned on their head the traditional religious attitudes toward spontaneous movement and song. Before Francis, a religious person (in particular, a monk) was supposed to be, like the angels, static in movement and grave in emotion. The Cistercian theologian Bernard of Clairvaux, a century before Francis, disparagingly compared a juggler's gyrating body with a monk's bent body in prayer: "In fact what else do seculars think we are doing but playing when what they desire most on earth, we fly from; and what they fly from we desire? Like acrobats and jugglers who with their heads down and feet up, stand or walk on their heads, and thus draw all eyes to themselves. But this is not a game for children or the theatre where lust is excited by the effeminate and indecent contortions of the actors, it is a joyous game, decent, grave and admirable, delighting the gaze of heavenly onlookers" (CAMILLE, p. 59).

What would Ugolino have thought of Francis's plan to send out his friars, transformed into God's jugglers, singing "The Canticle of Brother Sun" throughout the countryside? Perhaps he never heard of it. But his protégé finally decided to accept his invitation and left San Damiano in September 1225.

The landscape that lies before the eyes of the traveler from Assisi, when suddenly emerging on the plain of Rieti, is one of the most beautiful in Europe. From Terni the road follows the sinuous course of the Velino, passes not far from the famous cascades, whose clouds of mist are visible, and then plunges into the defiles in whose depths the torrent rushes noisily, choked by a vegetation as luxuriant as that of a virgin forest. On all sides are walls of perpendicular rocks, and on their crests, several hundred yards above your head, are feudal fortresses, among others the Castle of Miranda.

After four hours of walking, you see the defile opening out and you find yourself without transition in a broad valley, sparkling with light. The highway goes directly toward Rieti, passing between tiny lakes; here and there roads lead off to little villages, which you see, on the hillsides, between the cultivated fields and the edge of the forests; there are Stroncone, Greccio, Cantalice, Poggio-Buscone, and ten other small towns that have given more saints to the Church than a whole province of France.

Francis had often gone over this district in every direction. Like its neighbor, the hilly March of Ancona, it was peculiarly prepared to receive the new gospel. In these hermitages, with their almost impossible simplicity, perched near the villages on every side without the least care for material comfort, was a school of the Brothers Minor—impassioned, proud, stubborn, almost wild, who did not wholly understand their master, who did not catch his exquisite simplicity, his dreams of social and political renovation, his poetry and delicacy, but who did understand the lover of nature and of poverty. They did more than understand him; they lived his life, and from that Christmas festival observed in the woods of Greccio down to today they have remained the simple and popular represen-tatives of the Strict Observance. From them comes *The Legend of the Three Companions*, the most lifelike and true of all the portraits of the Poverello, and it was there, in a cell three paces long, that Giovanni of Parma had his apocalyptic visions.

The news of Francis's arrival spread quickly, and long before he reached Rieti the population had come out to meet him. To avoid this noisy welcome, he craved the hospitality of the priest of St. Fabian. This little chapel, now known under the name of Our Lady of the Forest, stands somewhat aside from the road on a grassy mound about three miles from the city. He was heartily welcomed there, and as he desired to remain for a little, prelates and devotees began to flock there over the following few days.

It was the time of the early grapes. It is easy to imagine the disquietude of the priest on perceiving the ravages made by these visitors among his vines, his best source of revenue, but he probably exaggerated the damage. One day, Francis heard him venting about his misfortune.

"Father," Francis said, "it is useless for you to disturb yourself for what you cannot control. But, tell me, how much wine do you get on average?"

"Fourteen measures," replied the priest.

"Very well, if you have less than twenty this year, I will make up the difference." This promise reassured the worthy man, and when at the vintage he received twenty measures, he had no hesitation in believing in a miracle.

After Ugolino's pleadings, Francis accepted the hospitality of the bishop's palace in Rieti. Thomas of Celano enlarges with delight on the marks of devotion lavished on Francis by this prince of the Church.

It is important to realize that Francis, in his own lifetime, entered into the condition of a relic. The mania for amulets displayed itself around him in all its excesses. People quarreled not only over his clothing, but even over his hair and the parings of his nails. Did these exterior demonstrations disgust him? Did he sometimes think of the contrast between these honors offered to his body, which he picturesquely called "Brother Ass," and the subversion of his ideal? If he had feelings of this kind, those who surrounded him were not the people to understand them, and it would be idle to expect any expression of them from his pen.

Pilgrims and tourists to the basilica in Assisi may see the tunic worn by St. Francis. He wrote, beautifully, in the first Rule: "Let all the brothers wear poor clothes and, with the blessing of God, they can patch them with sackcloth and other pieces.... [L]et them ... not cease doing good nor seek expensive clothing in this world, so that they may have a garment in the kingdom of heaven" (ARMSTRONG, p. 65). Francis's tunic shows signs of his loving patchwork.

Soon after arriving at the bishop's palace Francis had a relapse and asked to be moved to Monte-Colombo, a hermitage hidden amidst trees and scattered rocks an hour distant from Rieti. He knew this place, having retired there several times before, most notably while preparing the Rule of 1223.

The doctors attending him had exhausted the therapeutic arsenal of the time and decided to resort to cauterization. It was decided to draw a rod of white-hot iron across his forehead.

When the poor patient saw them bringing in the brazier and the instruments, he had a moment of terror, and immediately making the sign of the cross over the glowing iron, said, "Brother fire, you are beautiful above all creatures. Be favorable to me in this hour. You know how much I have always loved you. Be courteous, then, today."

After the crude procedure was over, and his companions who had not had the courage to remain, came back, Francis said, smiling, "Oh, cowardly folk, why did you go away? I felt no pain. Brother doctor, if it is necessary you may do it again."

This experiment was no more successful than the other remedies. In vain they revitalized the wound on the forehead by applying plasters, salves, and even by making incisions in it. The only result was to increase the pains of the sufferer.

One day in Rieti soon thereafter, Francis thought that a little music would relieve his pain. Calling a friar who had formerly been clever at playing the guitar, he begged him to borrow one; but the friar was afraid of the scandal this might cause, and so Francis gave up the idea.

But God took pity on him, and sent the following night an invisible angel to give Francis such a concert as is never heard on Earth. Hearing the music, Francis lost all bodily feeling, according to *The Little Flowers*, and at one moment the melody was so sweet and penetrating that if the angel had given one more stroke of the bow, the sick man's soul would have left his body.

Francis was attended to by papal physicians, presumably the best in the land, but in the end, all medicine before science was fairly much the same. Geoffrey Chaucer (d. 1400), in the Prologue to his Canterbury Tales, *characterizes the physician with tongue-in-cheek humor that would be generally accurate of medicine before science at the time of St. Francis:*

> *With us there was a doctor of physic;*
> *In all this world was none like him*
>   *to pick*
> *For talk of medicine and surgery;*
> *For he was grounded in astronomy.*
> *He often kept a patient from the pall*
> *By horoscopes and magic natural.*
> *Well could he tell the fortune*
>   *ascendant*
> *Within the houses for his sick patient.*
> *He knew the cause of every malady,*
> *Were it of hot or cold, of moist*
>   *or dry,*
> *And where engendered, and of what*
>   *humour;*
> *He was a very good practitioner.*
>   *(SOURCEBOOK, lines 411–22)*

There was some degree of amelioration of his condition when the doctors left him, and we find him throughout the most remote hermitages of Umbria during the winter months of 1225 to 1226. As soon as he had gained a little strength he was determined to begin preaching again.

He went to Poggio-Buscone, a three hours' walk north from Rieti, for the Christmas festival. People flocked there in crowds from all over the country to see and hear him. "You come here," he said, expecting to find a great saint. What will you think when I tell you that I ate meat all through Advent?"

At St. Eleutheria, a few minutes walk from Rieti, at a time of extreme cold that tried Francis very much, he had sewn some pieces of stuff into his tunic, and that of his companion, in order to make their garments a little warmer. One day his companion came home with a fox-skin, with which he proposed to line his master's tunic. Francis rejoiced over this, but would permit this excess consideration for his body only on the condition that the piece of fur be placed on the outside, over his chest. Each of these incidents, almost insignificant at first view, show how he detested hypocrisy even in the smallest detail.

There are many legends about the origin of Portiuncula, the "little portion" of a place where Francis lived, and later, insisted on dying. Legend has it that fourth-century hermits from the Valley of Josaphat first built the Portiuncula chapel to house relics in their possession from the grave of the Blessed Virgin. It is also believed that in the early sixth century the chapel was occupied by St. Benedict, author of the well-known Rule for monks. The chapel, Santa Maria degli Angeli, or "Our Lady of the Angels," most likely gained its name as a reference to the legend of Mary's ascent into heaven in the company of angels. Other local legends attribute the name of Francis's beloved little place to the occasional singing of angels actually heard there.

We will not follow him to his dear Greccio, or to the hermitage of St. Urbano, perched on one of the highest peaks of the Sabine. The accounts that we have of the brief visits he made there at this time tell us nothing new of his character or of the history of his life. They simply show that the imaginations of those who surrounded him were extraordinarily overheated; the smallest incidents immediately took on a miraculous coloring.

The documents also do not say how it came about that Francis decided to go to Siena. Apparently, there was in that city a physician of great fame as an occultist. The treatment he prescribed was no more successful than that of the others, but with the return of spring Francis made a new effort to return to active life. We find him describing the ideal Franciscan monastery, and another day explaining a passage in the Bible to a Dominican.

Did the latter, a doctor of theology, desire to ridicule the

rival order by showing its founder incapable of explaining a somewhat difficult verse? It appears extremely likely.

"My good father," he said, "how do you understand this
saying of the prophet Ezekiel, 'If you do not warn the wicked of
his wickedness, I will require his soul of you'? I am acquainted with
many people whom I know to be in a state of moral sin, and yet I am
not always reproaching them for their vices. Am I, then, responsible
for their souls?"

At first Francis excused himself, alleging his ignorance,
but urged by his interlocutor he said at last: "Yes, the true servant
unceasingly rebukes the wicked, but he does it most of all by his
conduct, by the truth that shines in his words, by the light of his
example, by all the radiance of his life."

He soon suffered a relapse so grave that the brothers thought
his last hour had come. They were especially frightened by the hem-
orrhages, which reduced him to complete prostration. Brother Elias
hurried to his side and at his arrival acquiesced to Francis's desire to
be taken back to Umbria. Toward the middle of April they set out,
going in the direction of Cortona. It is the easiest route, and at the
delightful hermitage of that city Francis remained for a short time.
But Francis was in a hurry to see once more the skies of his native
country, Portiuncula, San Damiano, the Carceri, all those paths and
hamlets that one sees from the terraces of Assisi and that recalled in
him so many sweet memories.

Instead of going by the nearest road, they made a long circuit
by Gubbio and Nocera, to avoid Perugia, fearing some attempt of the
people there to take possession of the saint. Such a relic as the body
of Francis held a value similar to that
of the sacred nails of the true cross or
the sacred lance of Christ's passion.
Battles were fought over less than that.

They made a short stop near
Nocera, about an hour east at the hermitage of Bagnara, on the slopes
of Monte-Pennino. His companions

*"Two years after Francis's death, the
King of France and all his court kissed
and revered the pillow that Francis had
used during his illness"* (SABATIER, p.
315).

were again very worried. The swelling that was showing itself in
Francis's lower limbs was rapidly gaining in the upper part of his

body, as well. The Assisans learned this, and wishing to be prepared for whatever might happen, sent their men-at-arms to protect the saint and to hasten his return.

Bringing Francis back with them, the brothers and soldiers stopped for food at the hamlet of Balciano, about halfway between Nocera and Assisi. In vain they begged the inhabitants to sell them provisions. As the escorts were confiding their disappointment to the friars, Francis, who knew these good peasants, said: "If you had asked for food without offering to pay, you would have found all that you wanted." He was right, for, following his advice, the men received all that they desired, for nothing.

The arrival of the party at Assisi was hailed with frantic joy. This time Francis's fellow-citizens were sure that the saint was not going to die somewhere else. Thomas of Celano, in fact, is even more explicit: "The multitude hoped that he would die very soon, and that was the subject of their joy."

The customs of relics and their importance have changed so much that we cannot thoroughly comprehend the good fortune of possessing the body of a saint. We find here several incidents that we may be tempted to consider shocking or even ignoble, if we do not make an effort to put them all into their proper surroundings.

Francis was installed in the bishop's palace; he would have preferred to be at Portiuncula, but the brothers were obliged to obey the injunctions of the populace, and to

Saints' relics were indeed highly prized in the late Middle Ages. "Although major liturgical manuals of the twelfth and thirteenth centuries insisted that it is logically impossible for one body to be buried in two places, this is exactly what happened. The bodies of the saints were divided up to provide relics. Division of the saints resulted not merely (as it had in antiquity) from the kinds of execution martyrs suffered at the hands of their tormentors. . . . Division was now also deliberately practiced immediately after death. Holy bodies were cut up so that parts could be given to religious communities that wished to share in the saint's power and presence. . . . When monks and canons squabbled over the relics of saints or the entrails of kings and cardinals, they were fighting for possession of more than the revenues associated with masses for the dead. The greater the number of parts and places in which noble or holy figures rested after death, the more far-flung their presence" (BYNUM, pp. 201–2, 205). The relics of saints were housed in containers called reliquaries, beautiful vessels of different shapes and designs often decorated with elaborate jewels and gold plating.

make doubly sure that it was safe, with guards placed at all the entrances to the palace. Francis remained much longer here than anyone had anticipated; it perhaps lasted several months (July to September). This dying man did not want yet to die. His anxieties for the future of the Order, which a little while before had been in the background, now returned, more agonizing and terrible than ever.

"We must begin again," he thought, "and create a new family who will not forget humility, who will go and serve lepers and, as in the old times, put themselves always, not merely in words, but in reality, below all men." To be obliged to look on at the dreaded decomposition of his order, he, the lark, to be spied upon by soldiers watching for his corpse—there was quite enough here to make Francis mortally sad.

Four Brothers had been especially charged to lavish care upon him: Leo, Angelo, Rufino, and Masseo. We already know them; they are of those intimate friends of the first days who had heard in the Franciscan gospel a call to love and liberty.

One day one of them said to the sick man: "Father, you are going away to leave us here. Point out to us, then, if you know him, the one to whom we might in all security confide the burden of the generalship of the Order."

Francis did not know the ideal brother who was capable of assuming such a duty, but he took advantage of the question to sketch the portrait of the perfect minister general We have two versions of this portrait, the one that was retouched by Thomas of Celano, and the original, much shorter and more vague, but showing us Francis desiring that his successors should have but a single weapon, an unalterable love. And so he left his successors, the ministers general of the Order, a letter that they should pass on from one to another, and where they should find, not directions for particular situations, but the very inspiration of their activity.

> To the Reverend Father in Christ, Minister General of the entire Order of the Brothers Minor. May God bless you and keep you in his holy love.
>
> Patience in all things and everywhere, this, my brother, is what I especially recommend. Even if they oppose you, if they strike you, you should be grateful to them and desire that it should be thus and not otherwise.

In this will be manifest your love for God and for me, his servant and yours, that there shall not be a single friar in the world who, having sinned as much as one can sin, and coming before you, shall go away without having received your pardon. And if he does not ask it, you ask it for him, whether he wills it or not.

And if he should return again a thousand times before you, love him more than myself in order to lead him to doing well. Have pity always on these brothers.

These words show plainly how Francis had directed the Order in former days. In his dream the ministers general were to act with pure affection and tender devotion toward those under them. But was this possible for one at the head of a family whose branches extended over the entire world? It would be hazardous to say, for his successors have not been wanting for distinguished minds and noble hearts, but with the exception of Giovanni of Parma and two or three others, this ideal is in sharp contrast with the reality. St. Bonaventure himself would later drag his master and friend, Giovanni of Parma, before an ecclesiastical tribunal, causing him to be condemned to perpetual imprisonment. Only the intervention of a cardinal outside of the Order finally secured the commutation of the sentence.

The agonies of grief endured by the dying Francis over the decadence of the Order would have been less poignant if they had not been mingled with self-reproaches for his own cowardice. Why had he deserted his post, given up the direction of his family, if not from idleness and selfishness? And now it was too late to take back this step; in hours of frightful anguish he asked himself if God would hold him responsible for this subversion of the ideal.

Shattered by fever, Francis would suddenly rise up in his bed, crying with a despairing intensity: "Where are they who have ravished my brothers from me? Where are they who have stolen away my family?"

Alas, the real criminals were nearer to him than he thought. The provincial ministers, of whom he appears to have been thinking when he spoke those words, were only instruments in the hands of the clever Brother Elias, and what else was he doing but putting his intelligence and energy at Cardinal Ugolino's service?

Far from finding any consolation in those around him, Francis was constantly tortured by the confidences of his companions, who, compelled by mistaken zeal, aggravated his pain instead of calming it. Witness this exchange, supposed to have been between Brother Leo and his spiritual father:

"Forgive me, Father," said one of them to him one day, "but many people have already thought what I am going to say to you. You know how, in the early days, by God's grace the Order walked in the path of perfection? All that concerns poverty and love, as well as for all the rest, the brothers were of one heart and one soul. But for some time now that is entirely changed. It is true that people often excuse the brothers by saying that the Order has grown too large to keep up the old observances. They even go so far as to claim that infidelities to the Rule, such as the building of great monasteries, are a means of edification of the people, and so the primitive simplicity and poverty are held for nothing. Evidently, all of these abuses are displeasing to you. But then, people ask, why do you tolerate them?"

"God forgive you, brother," replied Francis. "Why do you lay at my door things I can do nothing about? As long as I had direction of the Order, and the brothers persevered in their vocation, I was able in spite of weakness to do what was needed. But when I saw that, without caring for my example or my teaching, they walked in the ways you have described, I confided them to the Lord and to the ministers. It is true that when I relinquished the direction of the Order, alleging my incapacity as the motive, if they had walked in the way of my wishes I would have desired that until my death they would never have another minister."

Francis's complaints became so sharp and bitter that, to avoid scandal, the greatest prudence was exercised as to who was permitted to see him. Disorder was everywhere, and every day brought with it a new contingent of subjects for sorrow. There was much confusion of how to practice the Rule—the Franciscan ideal was veiled, not only from brothers in faraway places, or those who had recently joined the Order, but even from those who had lived under the influence of the founder. Under these circumstances, Francis dictated a letter to all members of the Order, which he thought would be read at the opening of chapters and perpetuate his spiritual presence among them.

In the letter Francis is perfectly true to himself. As in the past, he desires to influence the brothers not by reproaches but by fixing their eyes on perfect holiness.

> To all the revered and beloved Brothers Minor, to Brother A_____ [here the future copyists were to insert the name of the current minister general], minister general, its Lord, and to the ministers-general who shall come after him, and to all the ministers, custodians, and priests of this fraternity, humble in Christ, and to all the simple and obedient brothers, the oldest and the most recent, Brother Francis, a small and dying man, your little servant, gives you greeting!
>
> Hear, my lords, you who are my sons and my brothers, give ear to my words. Open your hearts and obey the voice of the Son of God. Keep his commandments with all your hearts and perfectly observe his counsels. Praise him for he is good, and glorify him by your works.
>
> God has sent you through all the world that by your words and example you may bear witness of him, and so that you may teach all people that he alone is all powerful. Persevere in discipline and obedience, and with an honest and firm will keep what you have promised.

After this opening, Francis immediately moves to the essential matter of the letter: the love and respect due to the sacrament of the altar. Faith in this mystery of love appeared to Francis to be equivalent with the very salvation of the Order. To Francis, the question of this dogma presented itself quite differently than it does to most of us today for whom faith belongs solely in the intellectual sphere. The thought that there could be any merit in believing never entered his mind; the fact of the real presence of God in the host was for him of almost concrete evidence. Therefore his faith in this mystery was an energy of the heart—that the life of God, mysteriously present upon the altar, might become the soul of all his actions.

To the eucharistic transubstantiation, effected by the words of the priest, Francis added another, that of his own heart:

> God offers himself to us as to his children. This is why I beg you, all of you, my brothers, kissing your feet, and with all the love of which I am capable, to have all possible respect for the body and blood of our Lord Jesus Christ.

Then, addressing himself particularly to the priests:

If the blessed Virgin Mary is justly honored for having carried Jesus in her womb, if John the Baptist trembled because he dared not touch the Lord's head, if the sepulcher in which he lay for a little time is regarded with such adoration, oh, how holy, pure, and worthy should be the priest who touches with his hands, who receives into his mouth and into his heart, and who distributes to others the living, glorified Jesus, the sight of whom makes angels rejoice!

Understand your dignity, brother priests, and be holy, for he is holy. Let each man be struck with amazement, let the whole earth tremble, let the heavens thrill with joy when the Christ, the Son of the living God, descends upon the altar into the hands of the priest. Oh, wonderful profundity! Oh, amazing grace! Oh, triumph of humility! See, the Master of all things, God, and the Son of God, humbles himself for our salvation, even to disguising himself under the appearance of a bit of bread. Contemplate, my brothers, this humility of God and enlarge your hearts before him.

We see what vigor of love Francis's heart held for Holy Communion. He closes this section of his letter with long counsels to the brothers, and after having urged them to keep their promises faithfully, all his mysticism breathes out and is summed up in a prayer of admirable simplicity.

God Almighty, eternal, righteous, and merciful, give to us poor wretches to do for your sake all that we know of your will, and to will always what pleases you, so that inwardly purified, enlightened, and kindled by the fire of the Holy Spirit, we may follow in the footprints of your beloved Son, our Lord Jesus Christ.

Francis's solicitudes reached far beyond the limits of the Franciscan Order. His longest epistle is addressed to all Christians. Its words are so living that you might think you hear a voice speaking behind you, and this voice, almost as serene as the one from the mountain in Galilee that proclaimed the law of the new times, becomes here and there unutterably sweet, like that one that sounded in the upper chamber on the night of the first eucharist.

As Jesus forgot the cross that was standing in the shadows, so Francis forgets his sufferings and, overcome with a divine sadness, thinks of humanity, for whom he would give his life. He thinks of his spiritual sons whom he is about to leave without having been able to make them feel as he would have them feel: "Father, I have given them the words that you have given me.... For them I pray!"

The whole Franciscan gospel is in these words, but to understand the fascination that it exerted we must have gone through the school of the Middle Ages and there listened to the interminable tournaments of dialectics by which minds were dried up. We have already seen the Church of the thirteenth century, honeycombed by simony and luxury, and able, under the pressure of heresy or revolt, only to make a few futile efforts to stop the evil.

> To all Christians, monks, clerics, or laypeople, whether men or women, to all who dwell in the whole world, Brother Francis, their most submissive servant, presents his duty and wishes the true peace of heaven and sincere love in the Lord.
>
> Being the servant of all people, I am bound to serve them and to give to them the wholesome words of my Master. This is why, seeing I am too weak and ill to visit each one of you in particular, I have resolved to send you my message by this letter and to offer you the words of our Lord Jesus Christ, the Word of God, and of the Holy Spirit, which are spirit and life.

He closes by showing the foolishness of those who set their hearts on the possession of earthly goods, and concludes with a very realistic picture of the death of the wicked.

> His money, his title, his learning, all that he believed himself to possess, all are taken from him. The worms will eat his body and the demons will consume his soul, and he will lose both soul and body.
>
> I, Brother Francis, your little servant, beg and ask you by the love that is in God, ready to kiss your feet, to receive with humility and love these and all other words of our Lord Jesus Christ and to conform your conduct to them. Let those who devoutly receive them and understand them pass them on to others. And if they persevere in them unto the end, may they be blessed by the Father, the Son, and the Holy Spirit. Amen.

If Francis ever made a Rule for the Third Order it must have closely resembled this epistle. Everything in these long pages looks toward the development of the mystic religious life in the heart of each Christian. But even when Francis dictated them, this high view had become a utopia, and the Third Order was only one battalion more in the armies of the papacy.

Francis also did not forget his sister-friend at San Damiano. Hearing that she was troubled, knowing him to be so ill, he desired to reassure her. He still deceived himself as to his real condition, writing to Clare promising soon to come and see her. To this assurance he added some affectionate counsels, advising her and her companions not to go to extremes with their penances. In order to set her an example of cheerfulness he added a laud in the vernacular, which he set to music himself.

Meanwhile, the bishop of Assisi, the irritable Guido, always at war with somebody, was at this time quarrelling with the governor of the city. Nothing more was needed to excite in the little town a profound disquiet. Guido had excommunicated the governor, and the latter had issued a prohibition against selling, buying, or making any contract with ecclesiastics. The differences grew more bitter and no one appeared to dream of attempting a reconciliation. We can better understand Francis's grief over this if we remember that his very first effort had been to bring peace to his native city, and that he considered the return of Italy to union and concord to be the essential aim of his apostolate. War in Assisi would be the final dissolution of his dream.

The dregs of this cup were spared him, thanks to an inspiration that broke forth from his imagination. To the Canticle of the Sun he added a new verse:

> Be praised, Lord, for those who forgive for love of you,
> and bear trials and tribulations.
> Happy are they who persevere in peace,
> by you, Most High, shall they be crowned.

Then, calling a friar, he charged him with begging the governor to go, with all of the notable people whom he could assemble, to the paved square in front of the bishop's palace. The governor, to whom legend gives the nobler part in the whole affair, at once yielded to the saint's request. As we hear from eyewitnesses:

> When he arrived and the bishop had come out of the palace, two friars stepped forward and said: "Brother Francis has made, for the praise of God, a hymn which he prays you will listen to." And immediately they began to sing the hymn of Brother Sun with its new verse.
>
> The governor listened, standing in an attitude of profound attention, weeping, for he dearly loved the blessed Francis. When the singing ended, he said, "Know in truth that I desire to forgive the lord bishop, that I wish and ought to look on him as my lord, for if someone were even to assassinate my brother I would be ready to pardon the murderer."
>
> With these words he threw himself at the bishop's feet and said, "I am ready to do whatever you wish, for the love of our Lord Jesus Christ and his servant Francis."
>
> The bishop took him by the hand, lifted him up and said, "In my position it would become me to be humble, but since I am naturally too quick to wrath, you must pardon me."

This unexpected reconciliation was immediately looked on as miraculous, increasing even more the reverence of the Assisans for their fellow-citizen.

The summer was drawing to a close. After a few days of relative improvement, Francis's sufferings became greater than ever. Incapable of movement, he even thought that he ought to give up his ardent desire to see San Damiano and Portiuncula once more, and gave the brothers all his directions about the latter sanctuary: "Never abandon it, for that place is truly sacred. It is the house of God." It seemed to him that if the brothers remained attached to that bit of earth, that chapel ten feet long, those thatched huts, they would find there the living reminder of the poverty of the early days, and could never wander far from it.

After hearing from a doctor that he was not expected to live past the autumn, Francis cried with an expression of joy, "Welcome, Sister Death!" He began to sing and sent for Brothers Angelo and Leo. When they arrived they were made, in spite of their emotion, to sing the Canticle of Brother Sun. They were at the last doxology when Francis, stopping them, improvised the greeting to death:

> Be praised, Lord, for our Sister Death of the body,
> from whom no one may escape.
> Alas for them who die in a state of mortal sin;
> happy they are who are found to have conformed to
> your most holy will,
> for the second death will do them no harm.

From this day the palace rang unceasingly with his songs. Continually, even through the night, he would sing the Canticle of Brother Sun or some others of his favorite compositions. Then, wearied, he would beg Angelo and Leo to go on.

One day Brother Elias thought it his duty to make a few remarks on the subject. He feared that the nurses and the people of the neighborhood would be scandalized; ought not a saint to be absorbed in meditation in the face of death, awaiting it with fear and trembling rather than indulging in gaiety that might be misinterpreted? Perhaps

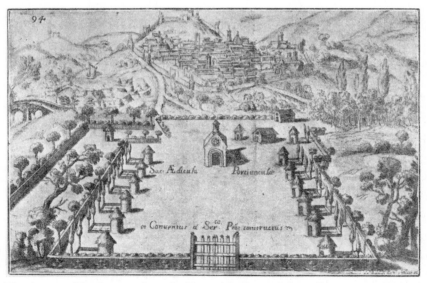

This drawing, "The Portiuncula in the Time of St. Francis," originally appeared in a book published in Montefalco, Italy, in 1704. The proximity of Portiuncula to Assisi in the background is clear, as is the original chapel, and to the right of it, the infirmary where Francis died, now called the "Chapel of St. Francis." Surely, the gate seen in this drawing (and probably quite a bit more) was added later, after Francis's death. (GORDON, p. 107)

Bishop Guido, too, was troubled. It seems likely that he was annoyed at having his palace crowded with Brothers Minor all these long weeks. But Francis would not yield; his union with God was too sweet for him to consent not to sing it.

They decided at last to move Francis to Portiuncula. His desire was to be fulfilled. He was to die beside the humble chapel where he had heard God's voice consecrating him an apostle.

His companions, bearing their precious burden, took the way through the olive-yards across the plain. From time to time the invalid, unable to distinguish anything, asked where they were. When they were halfway there, at the hospital of the Carceri where long ago he had tended the leper, and from where there was a full view of all the houses of the city, he begged them to set him on the ground with his face toward Assisi. Raising his hand he bade adieu to his native place and blessed it.

CHAPTER TWENTY-TWO

Francis's Will and Death
(End of September—October 3, 1226)

The last days of Francis's life were radiant with beauty. He went to meet death singing, says Thomas of Celano, summing up the impression of those who saw him then.

To be once more at Portiuncula after so long at the bishop's palace was not only a real joy to his heart, but the pure air of the forest must have been good for his physical well-being. He took advantage of this time to dictate his will.

In this record, which is of incontestable authenticity, the most solemn manifestation of his thought, the Poverello reveals himself absolutely, with candor, humility, and sincerity. His conscience proclaims here its sovereign authority: "No one showed me what I ought to do, but the Most High himself revealed to me that I ought to live conformed to his holy gospel."

When one speaks this way, submission to the Church is encroached upon. We may love her, hearken to her, venerate her, but we feel ourselves, perhaps without daring to admit it, superior to her. Let a critical hour come, and one finds oneself heretic without knowing it or wishing it. "Ah, yes," said Angelo Clareno, "St. Francis promised to obey the pope and his successors, but they cannot and must not command anything contrary to the conscience or to the Rule." For him, as for all of the spiritual Franciscans, when there is conflict between what the inward voice of God ordains and what the Church wills, he has only to obey the former.

Even today, thinkers, moralists, and mystics may arrive at solutions very different from those of the Umbrian prophet, but the method that they often employ is his. We may acknowledge Francis as the precursor of religious subjectivism. The Church immediately acknowledged as much. Four years after Francis dictated his last will and testament, perhaps to the very day (September 28, 1230), Ugolino, then Pope Gregory IX, solemnly interpreted the Rule—in spite of Francis's forbidding all commentary on it or his will—and declared that the Brothers Minor were not bound to the observation of the will.

Certainly the Church should be mistress in her own house. There would be nothing wrong if Gregory IX had created an order conformed to his views and ideas, but in this case, we can only feel a bitter sadness.

Upheld by the papacy, the Brothers of the Common Observance made the Spirituals sharply expiate their attachment to Francis's last requests. Caesar of Speyer died violently at the hand of the brother placed in charge of him. The first disciple, Bernard of Quintavalle, hunted like a wild beast, passed two years in the forests of Monte-Sefro, hidden by a woodcutter. The other first companions who did not succeed in flight had to undergo the most severe treatment. In the March of Ancona, the home of the Spirituals, the victorious party used terrible violence. Francis's will was confiscated and destroyed; they went so far as to burn it over the head of a friar who persisted in desiring to observe it.

Francis's Will—A Literal Translation

See in what manner God gave to me, Brother Francis, to begin to do penitence: When I lived in sin it was very painful to me to see lepers, but God led me into their midst and I remained there a little while. When I left them, that which had seemed bitter to me had become sweet and easy.

A little while later I left the world, and God gave me such a faith in his churches that I would kneel down with simplicity and say: "We adore you, Lord Jesus Christ, here and in all your churches that are in the world, and we bless you that by your holy cross you have ransomed the world."

The Lord also gave me and still gives me a great faith in priests who live according to the form of the holy Roman Church; because of their sacerdotal character, even if they persecuted me, I would return to them. And even if I had all the wisdom of Solomon, if I should find poor secular priests, I would not preach in their parishes without their consent. I desire to respect them as I do the others, to love them and honor them as my lords. I will not consider their sins, for in them I see the Son of God. I do this because here below I see nothing. I perceive nothing corporally of the most high Son of God except his most holy Body and Blood, which they receive and they alone distribute to others.

I desire above all things to honor and venerate these most holy mysteries and to keep them precious. Whenever I find the sacred names of Jesus or his words in indecent places I desire to take them away. We ought to honor and revere all the theologians and those who preach the most holy word of God, dispensing to us spirit and life.

When the Lord gave me some brothers, no one showed me what I ought to do, but the Most High revealed to me that I ought to live according to the model of the holy gospel. I caused a short and simple formula to be written and the lord pope confirmed it for me.

Those who presented themselves to observe this kind of life distributed all that they had to the poor. They contented themselves with only a tunic, patched within and without, with the cord and breeches, and we desired to have nothing more.

The clerics said the office as other clerics do, and the laymen said the Paternoster.

We loved to live in poor and abandoned churches, and we were ignorant and submissive to all. I worked with my hands and will continue to, and I will that all of the friars work at some honorable trade. Let those who have none learn one, and flee idleness. Let us resort to the table of the Lord, begging our bread from door to door. The Lord revealed to me the salutation that we ought to give: "God give you peace!"

Let the brothers take great care not to receive any gifts of churches, habitations, and all that people will build for them, except as in accordance with the holy poverty that we have vowed to in the Rule, and let them not receive hospitality except as strangers and pilgrims.

I absolutely forbid the brothers, in whatever places they may be found, from asking any bull from the court of Rome, whether directly or indirectly, under pretext of church or convent or preaching, nor even for their personal protection. If they are not received well somewhere let them go elsewhere, doing penance with the benediction of God.

I desire to obey the minister general of this fraternity and the guardian whom he may be pleased to give me. I desire to put myself entirely into his hands, to go nowhere and to do nothing against his will, for he is my lord.

Although I am simple and ill, I will, however, always want a cleric who will perform the daily office, as it is said in the Rule. Let all of the other brothers also be careful to do the office according to the Rule. If it comes to pass that any man does not perform the daily office, or desires to make changes to it, or is not Catholic, let the brothers bind him by obedience and deliver him to the minister. The minister shall guard him as a prisoner day and night until they have placed him in the hands of the Lord Bishop of Ostia, who is the lord, the protector, and the corrector of all the brotherhood.

Let the brothers not say: "This is a new Rule," for this is only a reminder, a warning, an exhortation. It is my will and testament, that I, little Brother Francis, make for you, my blessed brothers, in order that we may observe in a more catholic way the Rule that we promised the Lord to keep.

Let the ministers general, and all of the other ministers, be held by obedience to add nothing to and take nothing from these words. Let them always keep this writing near them, beside the Rule, and in all future chapters when the Rule is read let these words also be read.

I absolutely forbid by obedience all of the brothers from introducing commentaries to the Rule, or to this will, under the pretext of explaining it. Since the Lord has given me to speak and to write the Rule and these words in a clear and simple manner, understand them in the same way, and put them into practice until the end.

Whoever will have observed these things shall be crowned in heaven with the blessings of the heavenly Father, and on earth with those of his well-beloved Son and the Holy Spirit, with the assistance of all the heavenly virtues and all the saints.

And I, little Brother Francis, your servant, confirm to you so far as I am able this most holy benediction. Amen.

After thinking of his brothers, Francis thought of his dear Sisters of San Damiano, and he made a will for them. It has not come down to us, but in the last words that he addressed to the Sisters of St. Clare, after calling on them to persevere in poverty and union, he gave them his benediction. Then he recommended them to the brothers, reminding them never to forget that they are all members of the same religious family. After having done all that he could do for those whom he was about to leave, he was ready; he had finished his work.

Did he then think of the day when, cursed by his father, he renounced all earthly goods and cried to God with an ineffable confidence, "Our Father who art in heaven!"? We cannot say, but he desired to finish his life by a symbolic act that very closely recalls the scene in the bishop's palace.

Francis asked to be stripped of his clothing and laid on the ground. He wished to die in the arms only of his Lady Poverty. With one glance he embraced the twenty years that had glided by since their union: "I have done my duty," he said to the brothers, "may Christ now teach you yours!" This was Thursday, October 1.

They laid him back on his bed, and according to his wishes, they again sang to him the Canticle of the Sun. At times, he added his voice to those of his brothers, and also, he sang Psalm 142, that song of passionate hope:

> With my voice I cry to the Lord; with my voice I make supplication to the
>   Lord.
> I pour out my complaint before him; I tell my trouble before him.
> When my spirit is faint, you know my way.
> In the path where I walk they have hidden a trap for me.
> Look on my right hand and see—there is no one who takes notice of me;
> no refuge remains to me; no one cares for me.
> I cry to you, O Lord; I say, "You are my refuge, my portion in the land of
>   the living."
> Give heed to my cry, for I am brought very low.
> Save me from my persecutors, for they are too strong for me.
> Bring me out of prison, so that I may give thanks to your name.
> The righteous will surround me, for you will deal bountifully with me.

The hours flowed by and the brothers would not leave Francis alone. "Good father," one of them said, unable to contain himself any longer, "your children are going to lose you and be deprived of the true light for their way. Think of the orphans you are leaving behind and forgive all their faults; give to them all, present and absent, the joy of your holy benediction."

"God is calling me," replied the dying Francis. "I forgive all of my brothers their offenses and faults, and I absolve them according to my power. Tell them so, and bless them all in my name."

Then he laid his hands upon those who surrounded him. He did this with particular emotion toward Bernard of Quintavalle, saying, "I desire, and I urge with all of my power, that whoever shall be minister general of the Order will love and honor him as myself. Let the provincial ministers and all the brothers act toward him as toward me."

He had lost the notion of time. Believing that it was still Thursday, Francis desired to take a last meal with his disciples. Some bread was brought, he broke it and gave it to them, and there in the poor cabin of Portiuncula, without altar and without a priest, they celebrated the Lord's Supper.

Saturday, October 3, 1226, at nightfall, without pain and struggle, he breathed the last sigh. The brothers were still gazing on his face, hoping to still catch some signs of life, when larks alighted, singing, on the thatch roof of his cell, as if to salute the soul that had just taken flight. They gave the little poor man the canonization of which he was most worthy—the only one, doubtless, that he would ever have coveted.

The next day at dawn the Assisans came down to take possession of his body and give it a triumphant funeral. By a pious inspiration, instead of going straight to the city, they went around by San Damiano, and thus realized the promise made by Francis to the Sisters a few weeks before, to come and see them once more.

Francis's remains were buried in the new basilica in 1230, but the brothers concealed them extraordinarily well. Almost six hundred years later, in September 1818, Pope Pius VII gave his permission for a search to be undergone below the main altar of the lower church in the basilica.

Francis's tomb was discovered two months later; his remains were exhumed and a new crypt was built to house them. This crypt—directly beneath the lower church, which is directly beneath the upper church—is visited today by millions of pilgrims each year.

The brothers forgot their sadness on seeing the stigmata, and the inhabitants of Assisi showed an indescribable joy on having their relic at last. They deposited it in the Church of San Giorgio. Less than two years later, on Sunday, July 26, 1228, Pope Gregory IX came to Assisi to preside in person over the ceremonies of canonization, and to lay, the next day, the first stone of the new church dedicated to the one who bore the stigmata.

Built under the inspiration of Gregory IX and the direction of Brother Elias, this marvelous basilica is also one of the documents of this history, and perhaps I have been wrong in neglecting it. Go and look at it—proud, rich, powerful—and then go down to Portiuncula, passing over to San Damiano, and hasten to the Carceri. You will understand the abyss that separates the ideal of Francis from that of the pontiff who canonized him.

In telling the story of Francis's life, we also come to understand something about the complicated relationship between Francis and Brother Elias, as well as the troubled story of Elias as minister general of their order both before and after Francis's death. Sabatier first introduces these troubles in chapter thirteen, pages 102-103. See also the note on page 103 about Elias's excommunication and deathbed repentance.

One recent expert has summarized Elias's life and reputation this way: "Elias had been one of Francis's early and close associates. One might have expected him to be a strong spokesman for the apostolic life as Francis conceived it. Yet his generalate was a stormy one, and it ended so badly that of the Franciscan legenda *only [Celano's first* Life of Francis*], which was written before Elias's fall, speaks well of him. Indeed, [Thomas's second* Life of Francis*] and Bonaventure do not speak of him at all." (BURR, P. 12) Indeed, Thomas speaks well of Elias in the* First Life: *he refers to Elias as "the one [Francis] chose for the role of mother to himself and had made a father of the other brothers." (ARMSTRONG, SECTION 98, P. 267)*

Appraisal of Sabatier's impact on our historical understanding of Francis continues today: "Sabatier's great achievement was in moving Franciscanism out of the framework of sclerotic ecclesiastical historiography and making of it an object of research in the broadest sense of the term: an innovation that would make possible, in the twentieth century, the gradual rediscovery of the historical and human dimension of the Poor Man of Assisi." (VAUCHEZ, P. 237) Another of our most important contemporary historians writes, "[Sabatier's] book was received as a revolution in the area of Franciscan studies, and so it has remained." (DALARUN, P. 30)

Drawing of "The Basilica di San Francesco from the Plain," by Nelly Erichsen, reproduced from GORDON, p. 147.

A FEW NOTES ABOUT
THE EDITING OF SABATIER

Sabatier's *Life* of Francis, as presented here, has been edited and slightly abridged from the first English language edition of 1906, copyright renewed in 1938. Several guidelines have been followed such that would have been invisible to the reader unfamiliar with the first English language editions, but nevertheless, may be of interest to some.

First, grammatical choices have been occasionally updated to reflect contemporary English usage. For example, many uses of "shall" have been replaced by "will," "why" for "wherefore," "freedom" for "liberty," "brothers" for "brethren," and so on. Similarly, the spellings of some common names have been updated to reflect more common, Anglicized usage today: Joachim of Fiore to replace Sabatier's Gioacchino of Fiore, Sylvester to replace Silvestro, St. Clare replacing Santa Clara, and so on. On the other hand, a few proper names have been un-Anglicized, also in order to reflect more common usage today—replacing St. Damian with San Damiano, for instance. Sabatier and his English translator, Louise Seymour Houghton, made the semi-colon ubiquitous; many of these instances have been replaced with alternate punctuation.

In some cases, phrases and sentences have been refashioned. These changes are subtle and, hopefully, will serve today's reader in better understanding Sabatier's intent.

Some of Sabatier's exclusive masculine pronouns referring to all people have been quietly changed to a more inclusive alternative. Obvious typographical mistakes and inconsistencies have been corrected wherever possible.

Sabatier's scholarship was groundbreaking, in its time, but is today somewhat dated. Several cases of this have been excluded from the current edition; at least one other instance has been silently corrected: Clare was born of the noble family Offreduccio, not Sciffi, as Sabatier originally noted (BROWN, p. 326).

A substitute translation (the NRSV) has been given for quotes from the Hebrew or Christian Scriptures. Matthew Arnold's translation of "The Canticle of the Sun," quoted in full by Sabatier, has been retained, but with minor word changes consistent with those made to Sabatier's text as a whole. Selections from Dante's *Divine Comedy*, found in the annotations, are from the historic Longfellow translation.

In three instances, one of Sabatier's chapters has been divided into two, for the sake of length and context. The introduction and chapter fifteen of the original edition have been excluded completely, with the exception of a few quotes inserted as annotations within other chapters and in the editor's Introduction.

GLOSSARY OF TERMS

ACRE
St. Jean d'Acre, or Ptolemais, before it became an important, strategic city held by the crusader armies around 1100 C.E. They built a great fortress there, on the coast of the Mediterranean Sea, about fourteen miles north of Haifa. Visitors to Akko, as Acre is known today, may visit the "underground city" of old Acre; when the city finally fell to the Muslims in 1191 it was almost leveled to the ground.

ARNOLD OF BRESCIA
A fascinating Italian monk who was active as a reformer before Francis's birth (d. 1155). Told to confine himself to a monastery, he refused and spoke out against abuses in the Church of his day. He preached about the sanctity of poverty and even challenged the exclusive right of priests to administer the sacraments and hear confessions. Eventually, Arnold was hanged by the Roman authorities, with the blessing of the Church, and his ashes were scattered over the Tiber River so that his followers would not venerate his bones.

ATHOS
The famous Greek peninsula/mountain/monastic republic, often referred to as the "Holy Mountain," home to many communities, or sketes, of Orthodox Christian monks and hermits.

BULL
Official documents from the Holy See in Rome. The name comes from a Latin word which means "to boil." Both papal and royal documents were sealed distinctively with lead; a bull literally refers to the leaden seal on an official document.

CATHARS
Heretical movement that flourished in late medieval Europe, characterized by a distrust of the material world and a denial of Christ's humanity and bodily resurrection.

CHAPTER-GENERAL
A meeting of all members of an Order at which governing decisions are made.

CISTERCIANS

A monastic Order begun as a reform movement in 1098 in France. Its founders were intent on living more faithfully Benedict of Nursia's foundational Rule for monasteries. In the seventeenth century, two versions, or observances, became distinct within the Cistercians: common and strict (also called "Trappists," named for an abbey in France). Bernard of Clairvaux was an important early Cistercian. The popular spiritual writer Thomas Merton, of the 1940s to 1960s in America, was a Trappist.

CURIA

Leaders and other ministers who assist the pope in governing the Catholic Church.

ELIZABETH OF SCHÖNAU

Benedictine superioress at the monastery of Schönau, and friend of Hildegard of Bingen. Her book, Liber viarum Dei, *similar to Hildegard's better known* Scivias, *uses a prophet's fervor to remind readers to be faithful to Christ, to ward off worldliness (pointing out priests and monks for special admonition), and—foretelling the message of Francis—to put on the poverty and self-denial taught by Christ.*

HILDEGARD

Hildegard of Bingen (d. 1179), was a nun, mystic, and founder of convents, including one in Bingen on the Rhine River in Germany. She was the confidante of popes, kings, and theologians, including Bernard of Clairvaux and Pope Eugenius, who granted an imprimatur for her first, and most influential, visionary work, Scivias *("Know the Ways of the Lord").*

HUMILIATI

This odd group was an association of lay people who dressed plainly and practiced asceticism of various kinds, devoting themselves to charity. The Humiliati originated in Lombardy in the eleventh or early twelfth century. First approved by Innocent III in 1201, the Order witnessed the suppression of its male branch in 1571 by a papal bull after one of its leaders attempted to murder an emissary of Pope Pius V who was charged with reforming it.

MICHAELMAS

From a Middle English term literally meaning "Michael's Mass," September 29, the feast of Saint Michael the Archangel.

MISSAL

A book containing all of the texts that are read or sung during the mass throughout the year.

MENDICANT ORDERS

Mendicant literally means "a beggar." Three mendicant orders were founded as reform movements in the thirteenth century—Franciscans, Dominicans, and Carmelites—emphasizing a vow to personal poverty and begging alms.

POVERELLO

A name for Francis, meaning "little poor man."

SECULAR CLERGY

Those who are ordained but do not follow a religious rule (as monks do). They are similar to what today we most often refer to as parish priests, as opposed to members of religious orders.

SIMONY

To sell or buy spiritual things that should only be gained spiritually. The name derives from a character in the New Testament Book of Acts, Simon Magus, who was scolded by Peter for attempting to purchase the right to become an apostle (8:9–24).

WALDENSIANS

A reform movement from the twelfth and thirteenth centuries founded by Peter Waldo from the city of Lyons. The Waldensians, also called "the poor of Lyons," claimed to represent a true remnant who, from within, had been resisting the Catholic Church and attempting to reform it since the days of Constantine in the fourth century.

WHITSUNDAY

The feast of Pentecost, celebrating the "birthday" of the Church, when, according to the New Testament Book of Acts, the Holy Spirit first descended on the followers of Jesus after his Ascension into heaven.

SUMMARIES OF MAJOR CHARACTERS

ANGELO
One of Francis's closest disciples, co-author of The Legend of the Three Companions. *Angelo Tancredi was of noble birth, from Rieti, and the first knight to join the Brothers Minor. He was with Francis for the Sermon to the Birds.*

BERNARD OF QUINTAVALLE
Along with Leo and Masseo, perhaps the brother closest to Francis's heart. As he lay dying, Francis said of him: "I desire, and I urge with all of my power, that whoever shall be minister general of the Order will love and honor him as myself. Let the provincial ministers and all the brothers act toward him as toward me."

BONAVENTURE
The most important of the second generation of Franciscans (d. 1274). He wrote one of the early biographies of the saint and was elected Minister General of the Order in 1257 at the age of thirty-six. He was a rare combination of scholar, mystic, and saint, known for his great humility. Often referred to as "The Seraphic Doctor."

CAESAR OF SPEYER
Franciscan Brother recruited on Elias's mission to Syria. After Francis's death, in the fights between the defenders of the strict observance and Elias and the leaders of the Order, Caesar was imprisoned and beaten to death.

CLARE
The first woman to join Francis's movement after refusing to be married and completely dedicating herself to the ideals of the early Rule. One of Francis's closest friends, she lived beyond him more than twenty-five years. Two of her sisters—Agnes, who eventually became Abbess of a convent near Florence, and Beatrice—followed Clare in joining the Second Order, as did her mother, Ortolana, the year of Francis's death.

EGIDIO
One of Francis's first and closest disciples. Known for his zest for long, adventurous journeys. He is sometimes referred to as one of Francis's "knights of the round table." Co-author of The Legend of the Three Companions.

ELIAS

Early friend and follower of Francis (d. 1253). Francis appointed him Vicar of the Franciscan Order in 1221, and after Francis's death, he played a large part in Francis's rapid canonization and the building of the Basilica di San Francesco in Assisi. The incredible popularity of Assisi as a place of pilgrimage is owed, in large part, to Brother Elias. He was later deposed as a traitor to Francis's ideals and excommunicated, repenting of his arrogance on his deathbed.

GINEPRO

One of Francis's first twelve disciples and friends. A sustainer of the "Spiritual" movement, adhering closely to the original Rule, after Francis's death. His deeds of holy foolishness were appended to The Little Flowers, *and he was said to "delight in his own confusion."*

INNOCENT III

The pope who approved the formation and ministry of Francis's movement. One of the most important, powerful, and influential of late medieval popes. Elected at the age of 37, he ruled from 1198 to 1216.

JOACHIM OF FIORE

Former Cistercian abbot who became a mendicant reformer in the decades before Francis's conversion. His teachings and influence with his followers were similar to those of Francis. Declared a heretic by the Church.

LEO

One of Francis's closest disciples, co-author of The Legend of the Three Companions. *His occasional stubbornness adds humor to some of the stories in* The Little Flowers. *Nicholas Kazantzakis chose Leo as the narrator for his novel* Saint Francis.

MASSEO

One of Francis's closest companions. A tall, handsome, and intelligent man, Francis tested his humility by appointing him gatekeeper, almsgiver, and cook for the other brothers. He lived longer than most of the early companions of Francis, dying in 1280, more than fifty years after Francis's canonization.

PETER BERNARDONE

Francis's father, a merchant of fine linens, widely traveled. He loved luxury, probably because he had worked very hard to obtain it, and is represented in most biographies of Francis as an enemy of his son's best intentions to love Poverty.

PETER OF CATANA

The first Minister General of the Franciscan Order, installed by Francis himself. Peter led the friars for less than a year. His untimely death led to the period of Brother Elias's leadership.

RUFINO

One of Francis's closest disciples, a nobleman from Assisi, who gave up his worldly position and possessions to join the Poverello. Co-author of The Legend of the Three Companions.

SYLVESTER

The first priest to join the Brothers Minor (1210). Recognized in Franciscan tradition as one of the early contemplatives of the Order, living most of his religious life in a grotto at the Carceri.

THOMAS OF CELANO

An early Franciscan and Francis's first biographer. Known as the poet.

UGOLINO

Cardinal, papal legate, special counsel to Francis, and later, Pope Gregory IX, who presided over the canonization of St. Francis in 1228, only two years after the saint's death.

UGOLINO

Ugolino of Monte Santa Maria, from Naples (d. 1348) was a Spiritual Franciscan brother who compiled the collection of short tales from Francis's life and legend known as The Little Flowers of St. Francis (I Fioretti di San Francesco, *in Italian*), first written in Latin sometime between 1330 and 1340 (under the title Actus Beati Francisci et Sociorum Ejus), *approximately 110 years after the saint's death.*

SOURCES/RECOMMENDED READING

ALCORAN: Anonymous. *The Alcoran of the Franciscans, or a Sink of Lyes and Blasphemies*. London: 1679. Copy in the Sabatier Collection, Rare Books & Manuscripts, Boston Public Library.

ARMSTRONG: Armstrong, Regis J., J. A. Wayne Hellmann, and William J. Short, eds. *Francis of Assisi: Early Documents*. Vol. 1, *The Saint*. New York: New City Press, 1999.

ASSISI: "The Assisi Compilation." In *Francis of Assisi: Early Documents*. Vol. 2, *The Founder*. Ed. Regis J. Armstrong, J. A. Hellmann, and William J. Short. New York: New City Press, 2000.

BPL: Haraszti, Zoltan. "A Library about St. Francis." In *More Books: The Bulletin of the Boston Public Library*, Vol. VI, no. 7 (1931).

BROOKE: Brooke, Rosalind B. *The Image of St. Francis: Responses to Sainthood in the Thirteenth Century*. New York: Cambridge University Press, 2006.

BROWN: Brown, Raphael, trans. *The Little Flowers of St. Francis: A Modern English Translation from the Latin and the Italian with Introduction, Notes, and Biographical Sketches*. New York: Image Books, 1958.

BURCKHARDT: Burckhardt, Jacob. *The Civilization of the Renaissance in Italy*. Trans. Middlemore. London: Phaidon Press, 1945.

BURR: Burr, David. *The Spiritual Franciscans: From Protest to Persecution in the Century After Saint Francis*. University Park, PA: The Pennsylvania State University Press, 2001.

BYNUM: Bynum, Caroline Walker. *The Resurrection of the Body in Western Christianity, 200–1336*. New York: Columbia University Press, 1995.

CAMILLE: Camille, Michael. *Image on the Edge: The Margins of Medieval Art*. Cambridge, MA: Harvard University Press, 1992.

CHESTERTON: Chesterton, G. K. *St. Francis of Assisi*. New York: Image/Doubleday, 2001.

COULTON: Coulton, G. G. *Medieval Panorama: The English Scene from Conquest to Reformation*. Cambridge, UK: Cambridge University Press, 1938.

COULTON 2: Coulton, G. G. *From St. Francis to Dante: Translations from the Chronicle of the Franciscan Salimbene, 1221–1288*. Philadelphia: University of Pennsylvania Press, 1972.

COWAN: Cowan, James. *Francis: A Saint's Way*. Liguori, MO: Liguori/Triumph, 2001.

CUNNINGHAM 1: Cunningham, Lawrence, ed. "The Vitality of the Franciscan Spirit: Reflections on the 750th Anniversary of the Death of St. Francis," *Christian Century*, October 13, 1976.

CUNNINGHAM 2: Cunningham, Lawrence, ed. *Brother Francis: An Anthology of Writings by and About St. Francis of Assisi*. New York: Harper & Row, 1972.

CUTHBERT: Cuthbert, Father, OSFC. *Life of St. Francis of Assisi*. New York: Longmans, Green, and Co., 1927.

DALARUN: Dalarun, Jacques. *The Misadventure of Francis of Assisi: Toward a Historical Use of the Franciscan Legends*, trans. Edward Hagman, OFM Cap. St. Bonaventure, NY: Franciscan Institute Publications, 2002.

DANTE: Alighieri, Dante. *The Divine Comedy*. Vol. 3, *Paradiso*. Trans. Henry Wadsworth Longfellow. Various editions.

DAVIES: Davies, Norman. *Europe: A History*. New York: Oxford University Press, 1997.

DEAN: Dean, Judith. *Every Pilgrim's Guide to Assisi and Other Franciscan Pilgrim Places*. Norwich, UK: Canterbury Press, 2002.

ECO: Eco, Umberto. *Art and Beauty in the Middle Ages*. Trans. Hugh Bredin. New Haven: Yale University Press, 2002.

ECO 2: Eco, Umberto. *The Name of the Rose*. Trans. William Weaver. New York: Harcourt Brace Jovanovich, 1983.

ELKINS: Elkins, James. *Pictures and Tears: A History of People Who Have Cried in Front of Paintings*. New York: Routledge, 2001.

FOLIGNO: Steegmann, Mary G., Trans. *The Book of Divine Consolation of the Blessed Angela of Foligno*. New York: Cooper Square Publishers, 1966.

FRANCIS: Sweeney, Jon M., trans. *Francis of Assisi in His Own Words: The Essential Writings*. Brewster, MA: Paraclete Press, 2013.

GALLI: Galli, Mark. *Francis and His World*. Oxford: Lion Publishing, 2002, and Downer's Grove, IL: InterVarsity Press, 2002.

GEBHART: Gebhart, Emile. *Mystics and Heretics in Italy at the End of the Middle Ages*. Trans. Edward Maslin Hulme. London: George Allen & Unwin, 1922.

GOAD: Goad, Harold E. "The Dilemma of St. Francis and the Two Traditions." In *St. Francis of Assisi: 1226–1926: Essays in Commemoration with a Preface by Professor Paul Sabatier*. Ed. Walter Seton. London: University of London Press, 1926; pp. 129–162.

GORDON: Gordon, Lina Duff. *The Story of Assisi*. Illustrated by Nelly Erichsen and M. Helen James. London: J. M. Dent & Co., 1901.

GREEN: Green, Julien. *God's Fool: The Life and Times of Francis of Assisi*. San Francisco: Harper & Row, 1985.

HOLMES: Holmes, George. *The Oxford Illustrated History of Italy*. New York: Oxford University Press, 2001.

HOUSE: House, Adrian. *Francis of Assisi: A Revolutionary Life*. Mahwah, NJ: HiddenSpring/Paulist Press, 2001.

HUIZINGA: Huizinga, Johan. *Men and Ideas*. London: Eyre & Spottiswoode, 1960.

KAZANTZAKIS: Kazantzakis, Nikos. *Saint Francis*. Trans. P. A. Bien. New York: Ballantine Books, 1966.

KELLY: Kelly, J. N. D. *The Oxford Dictionary of Popes*. New York: Oxford University Press, 1988.

KOSSAK: Kossak, Zofia. *Blessed are the Meek: A Novel about St. Francis of Assisi*. Trans. Rulka Langer. New York: Roy Publishers, 1944.

MARTIN: Martin, Valerie. *Salvation: Scenes from the Life of St. Francis*. New York: Alfred A. Knopf, 2001

MOORMAN: Moorman, John. *A History of the Franciscan Order: From its Origins to the Year 1517*. Oxford: Clarendon Press, 1968.

PARKS: Parks, George B., ed. *The English Traveler to Italy*. Stanford, CA.: Stanford University Press, 1954.

PARRY: Parry, Abbot, OSB. Trans. *The Rule of Saint Benedict*. Herefordshire, UK: Gracewing, 1990.

RUNCIMAN: Runciman, Steven. *A History of the Crusades*. Vol. 3, *The Kingdom of Acre and the Later Crusades*. New York: Cambridge University Press, 1999.

SABATIER: Sabatier, Paul. *Life of St. Francis of Assisi*. Trans. Louise Seymour Houghton. New York: Charles Scribner's Sons, 1906, 1938.

SEDGWICK: Sedgwick, Henry Dwight. *Italy in the Thirteenth Century*, Vols. 1–2. Boston: Houghton Mifflin, 1912.

SETON: Seton, Walter, ed. *St. Francis of Assisi: 1226–1926: Essays in Commemoration with a Preface by Professor Paul Sabatier*. London: University of London Press, 1926.

SOURCEBOOK: Chaucer, Geoffrey. *Canterbury Tales*. Public domain modern translation, Internet Medieval Sourcebook; http://www.fordham.edu/halsall/source/CT-prolog-para.html.

SWEENEY: *Francis and Clare: A True Story*. Brewster, MA: Paraclete Press, 2014.

THOMPSON: Thompson, Augustine, OP. *Francis of Assisi: A New Biography*. Ithaca, NY: Cornell University Press, 2012.

THREE: "The Legend of the Three Companions." In *Francis of Assisi: Early Documents*. Vol. 2, *The Founder*. Ed. Regis J. Armstrong, J. A. Hellmann, and William J. Short. New York: New City Press, 2000.

UGOLINO: Ugolino, Brother. *The Little Flowers of Saint Francis*, introduced and arranged by Jon M. Sweeney. Brewster, MA: Paraclete Press, 2011.

VAUCHEZ: Vauchez, Andre. *Francis of Assisi: The Life and Afterlife of a Medieval Saint*, trans. Michael F. Cusato. New Haven: Yale University Press, 2012.

VORAGINE: de Voragine, Jacobus. *The Golden Legend: Readings on the Saints, Vol. II*. Trans. William Granger Ryan. Princeton: Princeton University Press, 1995.

WHICHER: Whicher, George F. *The Goliard Poets: Medieval Latin Songs and Satires*. New York: New Directions, 1949.

INDEX TO BOOK ONE

BOOK TWO

Francis of Assisi
In His Own Words
the ESSENTIAL WRITINGS

Translated, Introduced, and Annotated
by Jon M. Sweeney

INTRODUCTION

I WILL ALWAYS REMEMBER THE OCCASION IN HIGH school when I first encountered a massive red book about Francis of Assisi in my public library. According to the copyright page it was titled *St. Francis of Assisi: Writings and Early Biographies: English Omnibus of the Sources for the Life of St. Francis*. A mouthful! But the spine—thick as a brick—read simply, "St. Francis of Assisi Omnibus of Sources." *Omnibus*. I had to investigate to find out just exactly what that meant.

The volume weighed at least a few pounds, with nearly 2,000 pages. I'd never seen a book so large. But having recently read my first biography of St. Francis and immediately fallen in love with the life and charism of such an unusual follower of Christ, I grabbed the *Omnibus* from the shelf. Opening the front cover, I saw that it was published by Franciscan Herald Press—what a perfect name for a publisher of such a book—and on reading the foreword, I was enthralled. Everything that anyone would ever want to know about Francis was apparently inside. Even the strawberry red cover, a design detail perfectly suiting the early 1970s when it was first published, appealed. Checking the *Omnibus* out with my library card, I took it home and read studiously for two weeks the first few hundred pages. I have no memory of whether I actually finished reading the book (I seriously doubt it, in fact), but I'm certain that I made a dent, and the enthusiasm for studying the early Franciscan movement was born in me.

Despite the unlikelihood of reading the 2,000-page *Omnibus* all the way through, it is a challenge to find a copy of that classic work in any of its early editions in which the binding is not seriously cracked. In other words, people really read the book and, in publishing terms, it was a "hit." Since that time, there has been no shortage of new books on Francis. Still the world's most popular saint, the stories of his life inspire more people than one can imagine. Since the *Omnibus*, there have been numerous other scholarly renditions of the early biographical writings about him, most notably the now essential three-volume *Francis of Assisi: Early Documents*, published in 1999–2001.[1] And yet I find that as scholars and serious students have more resources than ever at their disposal, we also live in a time when fewer and fewer everyday, non-specialist, spiritually attuned people interested in Francis actually turn to his own words in order to discover him. Most people with an interest in the little poor man (*il poverello*) from Umbria have little firsthand knowledge of his own writings. Sometimes, in fact, they do not realize that he wrote anything at all.

There are many great biographies of St. Francis and those are usually read instead. I have always been most partial to Paul Sabatier's, which I reedited and published more than a decade ago under the title *The Road to Assisi: The Essential Biography of St. Francis* (2003). There are several other excellent ones, too. For instance, I recommend Julien Green's beautifully written *God's Fool: The Life and Times of Francis of Assisi*, translated from the French (1985), and *Francis of Assisi: A Revolutionary Life* by Adrian House (2001) is also very good. For a more scholarly treatment, you might turn to the slim, recent, and authoritative Francis of Assisi: A New Biography, by the medieval historian Augustine Thompson, OP (2012), and the highly acclaimed *Francis of Assisi: The Life and Afterlife of a Medieval Saint* by French scholar Andre Vauchez, recently translated into English (2012). And on the hagiographical side of things, for the most charming collection of tales about the life of St. Francis, you can't do better than Brother Ugolino's *The Little Flowers of Saint Francis* (various editions).

Despite all of these great lives of the Poverello, I still wish that people would turn to Francis's own words first, or at least more often. Even his first biographers—the thirteenth-century writers Thomas of Celano, St. Bonaventure, and the first editors of *The Little Flowers*—rarely quoted from his writings. So it surprises many people to discover that Francis wrote numerous letters, religious poems and songs (*laude*), and a few very important treatises and "rules" for religious life.

Nevertheless, Francis was not a man of many words. He was not a scholarly saint like Augustine or Thomas Aquinas. He was never a famous orator-saint like John Chrysostom. In fact, it is impossible to imagine Francis sitting in a library or with a pen in his hand. Francis wasn't even what you

---

[1] Please refer to "For Further Reading" for full bibliographical information on every book mentioned here in the text and cited in the footnotes.

might call intellectually curious, like the saints Ignatius of Loyola and Teresa of Ávila, both of whom wrote a great deal, studied and pondered ideas, and, as a result of their writings, left us with many biographical details about their lives. Some have even accused Francis of being anti-intellectual, and for good reasons: he often warned his brothers against owning books and excessive reading. He counseled his brothers again and again to study *only if* they could do so without it ruining their spiritual lives. And yet he wrote.

For such a person—focused more on the active than the contemplative or intellectual life—Francis wrote only when a good occasion called for it. One scholar has recently explained this well:

> The Poor Man of Assisi, who was lacking in literary skill, did not behave like an author, nor did he give himself over to it with any confidence. He was writing only to deliver a message, but he attached to it the highest importance, inspired as he was by the certitude that the words he was writing or dictating were not from him, or not only from him, to the extent that it was God himself who had inspired them in him.[2]

This new collection of Francis's writings was created in order to fill a gap. *Francis of Assisi in His Own Words* is intended to be a nonthreatening entry into Francis's thought and spirit, by presenting his own words clearly and succinctly. As a result, the book you have in your hands contains only a fraction of what my old Omnibus contained, only the most essential writings of Francis himself. It also contains only those texts that we know with a good amount of certainty were written by the saint.[3]

THE REAL BROTHER FRANCIS

He began life as Giovanni Francesco di Bernardone and his biography is so familiar that to recount it here seems almost unnecessary. Very briefly, Francis was born in Assisi in 1181, raised in what we would today call an upper-middle-class home. His father, Pietro di Bernardone, traveled back and forth to northern France foar his business as a successful cloth merchant.

---

[2] Vauchez, *Francis of Assisi*, 250.

[3] Even so, there are only two extant manuscripts with Francis's own handwriting, and the earliest copy of some of the writings included in this volume are only as old as the sixteenth century.

Francis helped in his father's shop and may have also seen some of the world, traveling with Pietro abroad as a boy.

As a young man of twenty-one, Francis went off to war against Perugia, as all of the young men were supposed to do to defend their city, only to end up a prisoner. Two years later, he set off to battle once more, but he returned the following day, making it only as far as Spoleto and having seen a vision. Francis proved either to be inept at soldiering or he deserted, or both.

He was a merry young man and loved a good party. But in his young twenties, as his conversion began to take hold, Francis repented of sins of pride, luxury, and selfishness in very public fashion, which only served to embarrass his respectable father further. Francis then stole from his father to give to the poor and Pietro imprisoned him in the basement of their home, hoping that his son would snap out of it. When his father had to go away on business, Francis's mother (about whom we know precious little) freed him, and Francis quickly returned to San Damiano, the somewhat remote church in Assisi that he had grown to love.

He first heard the voice of God at San Damiano in 1206, telling him to "Go and rebuild my Church." Soon thereafter, Francis became a mendicant, a deliberately poor wandering preacher of salvation, and slowly but surely gathered followers, almost by accident. He focused on preaching the good news to people, explaining to them how they could find more joy in their lives, and he helped the sick, caring even for lepers, who in those days were literally cast out of the community and forbidden to come in contact with other people. Francis would wash their bodies and spend time with them.

In the spring of 1209, Francis and eleven companions walked to Rome, Francis with a copy of his new Rule in hand (see pages 17–41 below), to ask Pope Innocent III for a blessing. Over the next fifteen years, Francis traveled to Dalmatia, Spain, France, the ancient city of Acre in the northern Galilee region, and Damietta, Egypt, where he later famously met with the Sultan. Probably in the year 1220 or 1221, Francis resigned as spiritual leader of his own order and another friar was appointed vicar. By the end of his life he watched with a measure of sadness as the order grew beyond the boundaries of his original, most simple intentions (see "The Testament" on pages 95–101 below).

He was considered a saint throughout Europe even before his death on October 3, 1226. As he was dying, we know that people were trying to grab pieces of his clothing, because in their worldview—where proximity to a saint meant a little more holiness in one's life—they literally wanted a piece of him. To this day, he is the world's most popular saint in churches, books, paintings, and every other imaginable representation.

Curiously, we never see Francis smile in paintings, which is unfortunate because according to his biographers he was one of the most joyous of men. He was the leader of a band of brethren who called themselves "God's jugglers" as they worked, played, sweated, and laughed with men in the fields and towns before they ever preached to them. This sunny disposition also showed itself in the ways Francis located God in some startlingly "new" places according to the thirteenth-century worldview: not just in church, or in men and women who were trying to be faithful, but in lepers and outcasts, ravenous wolves, fish and birds, the sun and the moon, even bodily pain and death. This is a man who rolled in the snow, who stripped naked in order to demonstrate to his father how joyfully he had renounced ownership of things, and who preached in his underwear to show humility. Still, we never see him smile and that's a shame. Blame it on the iconographers—the artists and painters who have rendered St. Francis's image since his death in 1226.

There are thousands of paintings of Francis but you might say there is a "top three" list in the history of art. First would have to be the fresco on the wall of the chapel of St. Gregory in the Sacro Speco ("sacred grotto") in Subiaco, a city in the province of Rome. The Subiaco grotto was made famous centuries earlier by St. Benedict of Nursia, who retreated there and founded the Benedictine order within its walls. St. Francis's fresco can be seen just to the right of the entrance to the cave and is inscribed as painted during the second year of the pontificate of Pope Gregory IX. That dates the painting to late 1228 or early 1229, making it the earliest surviving image we have of Francis. Many scholars assume that the man you see in that fresco should be as close a depiction as we will ever have of the real Francis. He is wearing the rough habit of his order, a knotted cord about his waist, his hands are pre-stigmata, and he's barefoot. You will meet that Francis, most of all, in the letters included in this volume.

Second would be Cimabue's famous portrait that hangs in the right transept of the Lower Basilica of San Francesco in Assisi. The Francis you see there appears shorter, swarthier, than the man we see at Sacro Speco. He is showing his stigmatized hands to the painter with downcast, humble eyes. Some biographers prefer this image as the most faithful of the early ones precisely because it seems to show a less idealized man. This feels like the Francis we know from his praises—in this volume, from his "Praises to the Blessed Virgin Mary" and "Praises of the Christian Virtues" (see pages 49–53 below).

And third among the most important paintings of Francis is the one that is most often reproduced: Giotto's famous fresco, also from San Francesco in Assisi, depicting *The Preaching to the Birds*. This is scene fifteen in the narrative cycle located around the nave of the Upper Basilica. You've probably seen it on postcards, coffee mugs, holy medals, in books, films, and on your hotel and tour brochure if you ever visited any town in Umbria. Each of the images from the famous fresco cycles at San Francesco—just like similar cycles in other Franciscan basilicas throughout Italy—depict the notable scenes from the biographies of Francis. Like any good storytelling of a saint, they show Francis on his way of conversion toward heaven. We never find Francis writing about this scene, or almost any other from his life, in these writings. The one exception is "The Testament," on pages 95–101 below.

There are many other popular images of Francis hanging in museums all over the world. Francisco de Zurbarán's famous *Saint Francis in Meditation* in the National Gallery in London is one example. The severe ascetic of the saint that you see there comes through often in these writings. The seventeenth-century Spanish Catholic painter shows a kneeling friar in closet-like solitude, well cowled, his mouth agape speaking to God, holding a skull in contemplation of death. This is a dark, stark, arresting image, far removed from the juggling and joyous side of Francis—but it too is true to who he was. Zurbarán's countryman El Greco painted similar scenes.

When you actually read Francis's writings, you will meet the sometimes severe saint of El Greco, the joyous friend of all creatures seen in the frescos of the Basilica in Assisi, as well as the solitary man of prayer we meet in the image on the wall of Sacro Speco. All of these are "the real Brother Francis."

About This Book

You will find nineteen different texts in this collection of Francis's writings. Each is most likely from the mind or pen of the saint. Often Francis dictated his words to others, but in some instances, such as short letters, he wrote them himself.

These selections were all written over a period of twenty years, from 1206 to 1226, the year in which Francis died. They are arranged here in approximate chronological order, and each is prefaced with an editorial explanation of its setting, purpose, and place in the canon. The translations are my own; I aimed for smooth readability while remaining faithful to the tone and spirit of the originals, and compared my work against that of several others. Francis's quotations from Scripture are rendered using the New Revised Standard Version of the Bible, unless otherwise indicated. I furnish citations for Scripture quotations in the margins.

Prayer Before the Icon Crucifix
of San Damiano
(1206)

This is the prayer that Francis is said to have prayed on that eventful day when God first spoke to him. He was kneeling in the ruined church of San Damiano wanting desperately to hear a word from God when God said in such a way that Francis could understand: "Go and rebuild my Church." Francis responded in his usual, literal way: by gathering bricks in town and reconstructing that very church. This prayer later became Francis's prayer for himself, as well as the spirit of the Franciscan movement. It is textual tradition for it to be laid out as verse, since Francis is widely recognized as one of the first authors of poetry in the Italian vernacular.[4]

    The crucifix before which Francis prayed is actually an icon; it is the image of the crucifix painted onto a twelve-centimeters-thick block of wood in the shape of a cross. It hangs in the Basilica of Santa Clara in Assisi to this day.

Most High,
Most glorious God,
Enlighten the darkness of my heart.
Grant me a right and true faith,
A certain hope, and
A perfect charity, feeling, and understanding
Of You,
So that I may be able to accomplish
Your holy and just commands.
Amen.

---

[4] See for instance, *Italian Poetry: A Selection from St. Francis of Assisi to Salvatore Quasimodo: In Italian with English Translation*, selected and translated by Luciano Rebay (New York: Dover, 1969), 7.

The First Rule

(1209)

Francis founded three religious orders: the Friars Minor (for religiously vowed men), the Poor Clares (for religiously vowed women), and what is usually called simply the Third Order, or Brothers and Sisters of Penance (men and women living "secular" lives but vowed to Franciscan principles and asceticism).

The text that follows is the first version of the Rule Francis wrote for the Friars Minor, of which he was the founding member. In this long document, he lays out most clearly what is expected of a friar. There were later versions of this Rule, but most notable is this one, which Francis wrote in his original fervor and inspiration and personally carried to Rome to seek the approval of Pope Innocent III. Changes were made later in the versions dated 1221 and 1223, and the 1223 version of the Rule is the one still kept by Franciscans today. However, the spirit of Francis comes through most clearly in this earliest edition. That is why it is the one included in this volume.

Headings and chapters—and even sometimes numbered "verses"—were a later editorial addition, used for purposes of organization, clarity, and a sometimes excessive reverence for Francis that is not in keeping with Francis's own intentions. Only headings and chapters are used here. Also, I have added occasional footnotes to highlight or clarify particular points of interest.

In the Name of the Father and of the Son and of the Holy Ghost. Amen. This is the way of life that I, Brother Francis, offered to Pope Innocent, asking that it be granted as mine to live and confirmed by his Holiness. The Pope has so confirmed it, giving this way to me and my brothers now and for always. Brother Francis, and whoever may in the future be in leadership of this way of life, promises obedience and reverence to our Pope Innocent and to all of his successors. All of the brothers shall be bound to obey Brother Francis and his successors in leadership.

1. Obedience, Poverty, Chastity

The rule and life of these brothers is simple: Live in obedience and chastity, without property, and follow the doctrine and footsteps of our Lord Jesus Christ. It is he who said:

"If you wish to be perfect, go, sell your possessions, and give the money to the poor, and you will have treasure in heaven; then come, follow me."

Mt. 19:21

"If any want to become my followers, let them deny themselves and take up their cross daily and follow me."

Lk. 9:23

"Whoever comes to me and does not hate father and mother, wife and children, brothers and sisters, yes, and even life itself, cannot be my disciple."

Lk. 14:26

"And everyone who has left houses or brothers or sisters or father or mother or children or fields, for my name's sake, will receive a hundredfold, and will inherit eternal life."

Mt. 19:29

2. Receiving New Members

If anyone is inspired by God to embrace this way of life, let him come to the brothers and be received by them with kindness. If he is determined to undertake our life, the brothers should be careful not to meddle much in his personal affairs; instead, they should present him to their minister as soon as possible. The minister should then receive the candidate with kindness and encouragement while still diligently explaining the nature of our life.

When this is done, if the man is both willing and able, in good conscience and without compunction, he should go and sell all of his worldly goods and begin distributing them to the poor. The brothers and the ministers of the brothers should be careful not to interfere in any of this; they should not receive any of the money, either themselves or through anyone else. If, however, there is something that they really need, the brothers may accept it, as one who is poor, but not ever money. And when the candidate has returned, the minister should give him the habit of probation for one year. This is two tunics without hood, a cord, pants, and a simple chaperon reaching down to the cord.[5]

When the year of probation has finished, the candidate should be received into obedience. From that point on, it will be unlawful for him to leave for another order, or to "wander beyond obedience," according to the command of the pope and the Gospel, for

Lk. 9:62 "No one who puts a hand to the plow and looks back is fit for the kingdom of God." However, if anyone presents himself who cannot give away his goods without difficulty but has the spiritual will to let them go, that will suffice.

No one may be received in a way that is contrary to the form and practices of the holy Church.

The other brothers who have already promised their obedience may have one tunic with a hood, and, if necessary, another without hood and a cord and pants. The brothers should always be clothed in poor, simple garments, and they may then mend them, lovingly patching them with sackcloth and other pieces, for the Lord says in the Gospel: "Someone dressed in soft robes? Look, those who put on fine clothing and live in

Lk. 7:25 luxury are in royal palaces." Even if they are called hypocrites, let them never stop doing good and let them never desire rich clothes in this world, so that instead they may have a garment in the kingdom of heaven.

---

[5] This "chaperon" needs explanation. Some translators have rendered this as "cape" or "hood," which is confusing since, earlier in the sentence, Francis prescribes that the new friars' tunics are to be *without* hoods. A chaperon (not *chaperone*, the word for an adult who accompanies a minor) was a distinctive piece of medieval headgear, used most often in colder weather. They are pictured in Jan van Eyck paintings as a sort of fancy hat, and that is the wrong impression for early Franciscan use. Instead, one might imagine medieval manuscript illuminations of pilgrims along their way with chaperons, or capes/hoods, pulled back off the head, bunched around the neck, for warmth. Charles Perrault's original French edition of the fairy tale *Little Red Riding Hood* was titled *Le Petit Chaperon rouge*.

3. Praying the Divine Office and Fasting

Our Lord says that a certain kind of devil cannot be expunged without fasting and prayer; however, "whenever you fast, do not look dismal, like the hypocrites."

Mt. 6:16

[6][So, may all of the brothers, clergy and lay, say the divine office, the praises and prayers, as is required of all. Clergy should say the office for both the living and the dead, according to custom. Also, in case there is a deficiency or negligence among the other brothers, the clergy should also say each day the *Miserere mei* and the *Paternoster*. And let them say the *De profundis* with the *Paternoster* for the deceased brothers.[7] They may have only the books necessary to fulfill their office. The lay brothers, if they know how to read the Psalter, may also have one; but those who do not, may not. Lay brothers should say the creed and twenty-four *Paternosters* with the *Gloria Patri* for matins. For Lauds, they may say five. For Prime, Terce, Sext, and None, they should say seven each. For Vespers, twelve. For Compline, the creed and seven *Paternosters* with the *Gloria Patri*. For the dead, seven *Paternosters* with *Requiem aeternam*; and for the deficiency and negligence of the other brothers, three *Paternosters* every day.]

All of the brothers also should fast from the Feast of All Saints until the Nativity of Our Lord, and then from Epiphany, when our Lord Jesus Christ began to fast, until Easter. At all other times, they should not be bound to fast according to this life, except on Fridays. They may eat all foods that are placed before them, according to the Gospel.

---

[6] This long paragraph is placed in brackets because some scholars contend that it was not present in this form in the earliest version of this Rule. Much of this language was most likely added at the general chapter meeting (gathering of all friars to discuss issues and business of the entire Order) of 1221, by a hand other than Francis's, by which time there were divisions such as those described between lay and ordained friars. See Armstrong, *Francis of Assisi*, 65, n. b.

[7] *Miserere mei* means "Have mercy on me, O God" (Ps. 51:1). *Paternoster* means "Our Father" (Mt. 6:9–13). *De profundis* means "Out of the depths" (Ps. 130:1).

4. Ministers Within Our Order

In the name of the Lord, all the brothers who are appointed as ministers are servants of the other brothers. They are to place their brothers in the provinces or places where they should be located, and to visit them and spiritually encourage them. All of my blessed brothers who are not ministers should diligently obey their ministers in these things, as they look to the salvation of their souls, and when they are not contrary to our life.[8] Let them all observe what the Lord says: "In everything do to others as you would have them do to you; for this is the law and the prophets" and "Whatever you do not wish to be done to you, do not do that to others." Also, the ministers are servants and must remember that the Lord says that he "came not to be served but to serve, and to give his life a ransom for many." To them is committed the care of the souls of their brothers, and if any should be lost through their fault or bad example, the ministers will have to give an account before the Lord Jesus Christ on the Day of Judgment.

Mt. 7:12 and
St. Benedict's
Rule

Mt. 20:28

5. How to Correct Brothers
Who Offend

Take care of your souls and those of your brothers, for "it is a fearful thing to fall into the hands of the living God."

If, although, any of the ministers and servants[9] ever commands one of the other brothers to do something contrary to our life or against his soul, that brother is not bound to obey him, because it is not obedience at work when faults or sins are committed. Also, all the brothers who are subject to the ministers and servants should carefully consider the deeds of the same. If they see one of them walking according to the flesh and not according to the spirit, and this continues even after the third admonition, he should be reported

[8] An interesting inclusion by Francis, suggesting that a friar is entitled to disobey an order from his superior if that order is believed to be contrary to the spirit of the Order. See n. 6, below, as well.

[9] Note that Francis uses the phrase "minister and servant" to denote those in leadership. To Francis, a minister is always, by definition, also a servant. This passage is also noteworthy for the way in which Francis builds in the possibility to disobey an order that is deemed unfaithful or unholy.

to the minister and servant of the whole fraternity at the Chapter of Pentecost, regardless of any obstacle that may stand in the way. Heb. 10:31

If, also, among the brothers, there should be someone who desires to live according to the flesh and not according the spirit, the other brothers should admonish, instruct, and correct him humbly and diligently. If he will not amend his ways after the third admonition, they should, without delay, make the matter known to his minister and servant and let the minister and servant do with him whatever seems best before God.

All of the brothers, the ministers and servants as well as the others, should take care not to be troubled or angered because of someone else's sin, for the devil loves to corrupt us through the sin of someone else. Instead, all should come to the spiritual aid of one who has sinned, as best they can, for "those who are well do not need a physician, but the sick do." Mt. 9:12 (NAB)

Moreover, not all of the brothers should have power and authority in these instances, for as the Lord says in the Gospel: "You know that the rulers of the Gentiles lord it over them, and their great ones are tyrants over them. It will not be so among you; but whoever wishes to be great among you must be your servant, and whoever wishes to be first among you must be your slave." No brother should Mt. 20:25–27 do evil or speak evil against another. Each one should rather, in the spirit of charity, willingly serve and obey the other. This is the true and holy obedience of our Lord Jesus Christ.

If any brother has turned away from the commandments of God and wandered from obedience, the other brothers know, as the prophet says, that they are cursed out of disobedience as long as they continue to consciously live in sin. Similarly, when brothers persevere in the commandments of the Lord, which they have promised by the holy Gospel and their lives, they should know that they live in true obedience and are blessed by God.

6. PROVIDING FOR BROTHERS
WHO CANNOT LIVE THE LIFE

If any brother, no matter where he may be, realizes that he cannot observe our life, he should go as soon as possible to his minister and make this known to him. The minister should then try to treat the brother as he himself would wish to be treated if the situation were reversed. And let no one among us ever be called "Prior"—instead, everyone should be called a lesser brother, a Friar Minor. Each one of us should wash the feet of the others.

7. MORE ABOUT SERVANTHOOD AND WORK

None of the brothers, in any of our places, should be treasurers or managers in the houses of those whom they serve or where they work. They should never accept employment that could cause scandal, or that would ever be harmful to their souls. Instead, they should always be the lesser ones, subject to all who live together in the same house.

All of the brothers who know how to work should do so, and work in whatever trade they understand, as long as it is not contrary to the salvation of their souls and can be done with honesty. As the prophet says: "You shall eat the fruit of the labor of your hands; you shall be happy, and it shall go well with you." And so says the apostle: "Anyone unwilling to work should not eat," and "In whatever condition you were called, brothers and sisters, there remain with God."

For their work the brothers may receive whatever is necessary, except for money. Whenever necessary, they should seek for alms like other poor people. They may also have tools and implements necessary for their work. And they should apply themselves diligently in doing good works, as it is said, "Always be busy in some sort of good work so that the devil will find you busy," and again, "Idleness is the soul's enemy."[10] As such, servants of God should always be involved in some sort of good work.

Ps. 128:2
2 Thess. 3:10
1 Cor. 7:24

---

[10] Neither of these quotations is from Scripture. The first is a maxim variously attributed to St. Jerome and St. Gregory the Great. The second is a familiar line from St. Benedict's Rule (Terrence G. Kardong, OSB, *Benedict's Rule: A Translation and Commentary* [Collegeville, MN: Liturgical Press, 1996], 48.1, 382).

The brothers should always be careful that, no matter where they are, whether in a hermitage or any other place, not to appropriate any place as their own, or even to possess it instead of another. And whoever may come to them, either friend or foe, even thief or robber, they should receive all with kindness. And no matter where they are, they should spiritually and diligently show reverence and honor toward one another without complaints. And they should always be careful not to appear sad and gloomy on the outside, like hypocrites do, but show themselves to be joyful, cheerful, and gracious to others, in the name of the Lord.

Cf. Mt. 6:1–6;
Phil. 4:4

8. Do Not Handle Money

Our Lord teaches in the Gospel: "Take care! Be on your guard against all kinds of greed; for one's life does not consist in the abundance of possessions." Therefore, none of the brothers, wherever he may be or go, should ever carry or receive, or cause to be carried or received, money or coin—not even for clothing, books, or in payment for some kind of labor, or indeed for any reason— except for the absolute necessity of caring for a sick brother. For we should not consider money or coin to have any more use than stones. The devil, though, wants to blind those who desire or value it more than stones. So let us be careful not to lose the kingdom of heaven for such a trifle.

Lk. 12:15

If a brother even chances across money somewhere, he should give it no more regard than if it were dust trod underfoot, for it is "vanity of vanities! All is vanity." And then, if by chance, and God forbid, it should ever happen that a brother is found to have actually kept and saved money or coin, except for the previously mentioned purpose of needing to care for the sick, all of the other brothers should consider him an apostate, thief, robber, like the one who held the purse, unless he becomes truly penitent.[11]

Eccles. 1:2

Under no circumstances should the brothers receive money when they go out begging, cause it to be received by others, seek it or cause

---

[11] This reference—"like the one who held the purse"—is to Judas Iscariot. See John 12:4–6.

it to be sought, for any house or place. Likewise, they should never go out with any person seeking money or coin for such places. Still, the brothers may perform all other services that are not contrary to our way of life for these needy places, with the blessing of God. They may beg alms specifically for the lepers—but they should always remain wary of money. Every brother heed this: don't go throughout the world seeking filthy gain.

9. BEGGING ALMS

The brothers should all strive to follow the humility and poverty of our Lord Jesus Christ, and remember that we deserve nothing else in the whole world except what the apostle says: "if we have food 1 Tim. 6:8 and clothing, we will be content with these." Similarly, they should rejoice when they have an opportunity to talk with people who are easily despised, with the poor and the weak, with the sick and lepers, and with anyone who begs in the streets.

Whenever it is necessary, the brothers should go out begging for alms. They shouldn't be ashamed of doing so, but ought to remember that our Lord Jesus Christ, the Son of the living and all-powerful Isa. 50:7 God, once set his face "like flint" and was not ashamed. He was poor and a stranger and lived on alms, both he and the Blessed Virgin, and his disciples. So, if people treat the brothers with contempt and refuse to give them alms, they should still give thanks to God because it is by this sort of shame that they will receive great honor before the mercy seat of our Lord Jesus Christ. And, they should know that the real injury is not to those who suffer insult, but to those who offer it. Alms is an inheritance and a right due to the poor, which our Lord Jesus Christ purchased for us, and the brothers who work hard to seek it will have a great reward. For all that men leave in this world will soon perish, but the charity and good deeds they have done will receive them a reward from God.

A brother should always make his needs known clearly to others, so that other brothers will know and then have the opportunity to minister to him. The brothers should love and nourish each other as a mother loves and nourishes her son, as God gives them the grace.

And "the one who abstains must not pass judgment on the one who eats." Whenever necessary, it is permissible for all of the brothers, wherever they are, to eat of all food that people can eat, as our Lord said of David, who "ate the bread of the Presence, which it was not lawful for him or his companions to eat, but only for the priests." But they should remember what the Lord says: "Be on guard so that your hearts are not weighed down with dissipation and drunkenness and the worries of this life, and that day catch you unexpectedly, like a trap. For it will come upon all who live on the face of the whole earth." But in times of anxious need, the brothers may do as our Lord has given them grace, because necessity has no law.

Rom. 14:3
(NAB)

Mt. 12:4

Lk. 21:34–35

10. When Brothers Are Ill

If any of the brothers falls ill, wherever he may be, the others shouldn't leave his side, unless one of the brothers, or more if necessary, is chosen to serve him as they would wish to be served themselves. In the most urgent circumstances, they may also bring the sick brother to someone who will do what is needed to treat him.

I[12] ask the sick brother to give thanks to the Creator for all things and to desire to be as God wills him to be, whether sick or well, because everyone whom the Lord has predestined to eternal life is disciplined by torments and afflictions and sicknesses and the spirit of sorrow. As the Lord says: "I reprove and discipline those whom I love." If, though, he is upset or angry with God or any of his brothers, or if he is overeager for medicine, with a desire to comfort a body that is soon to die and is also an enemy to his soul, all of this comes to him from evil motivations and is of the flesh. At such a moment, he no longer seems to be like one of the brothers, because he loves his body more than his soul.

Rev. 3:19

---

[12] This is the first moment in this long document where Francis's teaching becomes personal advice, using the first person, as from his own direct experience caring for other brothers.

11. ALWAYS LOVE EACH OTHER

The brothers should always be careful not to slander or argue. Instead, they should aim to maintain silence as long as God gives them the grace. They shouldn't argue among themselves or with others, but instead, should always be ready to humbly say, "We are worthless slaves!" And they shouldn't be angry, for "if you are angry with a brother or sister, you will be liable to judgment; and if you insult a brother or sister, you will be liable to the council; and if you say, 'You fool,' you will be liable to the hell of fire."

Love each other, as the Lord says: "This is my commandment, that you love one another as I have loved you." They should show their love through deeds that they do for each other, as the apostle says, "let us love, not in word or speech, but in truth and action."

"Speak evil of no one." Don't let them grumble or slander others, for it is written that grumblers and slanderers hate God. They should instead "be gentle, and . . . show every courtesy to everyone." They shouldn't judge or condemn, and as the Lord says, they shouldn't pay attention to the small sins of others, but instead, remember their own in the bitterness of their souls. In all, they should strive to "enter through the narrow gate," as the Lord says, "for the gate is narrow and the road is hard that leads to life, and there are few who find it."

Lk. 17:10

Mt. 5:22

Jn. 15:12

1 Jn. 3:18

Titus 3:2a

Rom. 1:29-30

Titus 3:2b

Isa. 38:15

Mt. 7:13-14

12. AVOID THE COMPANY OF WOMEN[13]

The brothers should always, wherever they are or wherever they may go, carefully avoid looking at and being in the company of women. They should not ever share conversation or food, or travel with them alone. Priests who speak with women should do so honestly, giving them penance or appropriate spiritual counsel. A woman should never be received into obedience by any brother; if spiritual counsel has to be given to her, she may then go and do penance wherever she desires. We should all carefully watch over ourselves and hold each other accountable, for the Lord says: "Everyone who looks at a woman with lust has already committed adultery with her in his

---

[13] A curious chapter for the simple reason that, at times, it does not seem to match the spirit in which Francis accepted Clare as the first female Franciscan in March 1212.

heart." And the apostle says: "Do you not know that your body is a Mt. 5:28
temple of the Holy Spirit within you, which you have from God, and
that you are not your own?" 1 Cor. 6:19

[13. FORNICATORS WILL BE PUNISHED[14]

If, at the devil's urging, a brother ever commits fornication, he should
be deprived of his habit and know that he has lost it because of his
own sin; he should put the habit aside completely and be expelled
from our order. After this is done, he should do penance for his sins.]

14. HOW THE BROTHERS SHOULD GO ABOUT THE WORLD

When the brothers travel about the world, they should, "Take
nothing for your journey, no staff, nor bag, nor bread, nor money." Lk. 9:3
Then, "Whatever house you enter, first say, "Peace to this house!"
And, "Remain in the same house, eating and drinking whatever they
provide." Lk. 10:5, 7

"Do not resist an evildoer. But if anyone strikes you on the right Mt. 5:39
cheek, turn the other also." And "from anyone who takes away your
coat do not withhold even your shirt. Give to everyone who begs
from you; and if anyone takes away your goods, do not ask for them
again." Lk. 6:29–30

15. ANIMALS AND RIDING

I[15] command all of the brothers, both clergy and laity, when they
travel about the world, or reside in various places, that they never
have animals with them, or entrust an animal to the care of others, or
in any other way keep one. They should also never ride on horseback
unless they absolutely must do so for reasons of sickness or some
other great necessity.

---

[14] Some scholars suggest that this chapter was added later, for example, sometime after
November 1220. See Armstrong, *Francis of Assisi*, 1:73, n. a.

[15] For only the second time in this long document, Francis uses the first personal singular
pronoun "I" to emphasize his point.

[16. GOING AMONG THE MUSLIMS[16]

The Lord says: "See, I am sending you out like sheep into the midst
of wolves; so be wise as serpents and innocent as doves." If any of the
brothers wish, by divine inspiration, to go among the Muslims and
other unbelievers, they should go with the permission of their minister and servant. If the minister gives him permission to go, and sees
that he is fit for the journey, he will be held accountable to the Lord
if he has not exercised due discernment in this and other decisions.

Mt. 10:16

The brother who goes, then, should conduct himself among
unbelievers in these two ways. First, do not create arguments or
contentiousness, but instead, "For the Lord's sake accept the authority of every human institution," while still confessing yourself to be
Christian. Second, when you see that it is pleasing to God, announce
God's Word, so that they might come to believe in almighty God:
the Father, and Son, and Holy Ghost, the creator of all, our Lord the
redeemer and savior, and so that they might be baptized and become
Christians because "Very truly, I tell you, no one can enter the kingdom of God without being born of water and Spirit."

1 Pet. 2:13

Jn. 3:5

These and other things they should say, pleasing God, for the
Lord says in the Gospel: "Everyone therefore who acknowledges me
before others, I also will acknowledge before my Father in heaven,"
and "Those who are ashamed of me and of my words, of them the
Son of Man will be ashamed when he comes in his glory and the
glory of the Father and of the holy angels."

Mt. 10:32

Lk. 9:26

All the brothers, wherever they may be, should remember that
they have given themselves, forgoing their own personal safety, to
our Lord Jesus Christ. For his love they should be willing to stand
before enemies both visible and invisible, for the Lord says: "Those
who want to save their life will lose it, and those who lose their life
for my sake will save it." "Blessed are those who are persecuted for

Lk. 9:24

[16] This is another chapter that was surely added after 1209. It was not until 1219 that Francis
traveled to Egypt and met with the Sultan, al-Kamil (1180–1238), although he first attempted
to reach Muslim-controlled lands as early as 1212.

Notice the progression in the first paragraph of the chapter: Francis didn't want ministers
sending friars into harm's way upon the old monastic principle of unquestioning obedience
to one's superior. The impulse had to start with God, then the friar, then be confirmed by a
minister/servant.

righteousness' sake, for theirs is the kingdom of heaven." "If they   Mt. 5:10
persecuted me, they will persecute you; if they kept my word, they
will keep yours also." "When they persecute you in one town, flee to   Jn. 15:20
the next." "Blessed are you when people revile you and persecute you   Mt. 10:23
and utter all kinds of evil against you falsely on my account. Rejoice
and be glad, for your reward is great in heaven, for in the same way
they persecuted the prophets who were before you." "I tell you, my   Mt. 5:11–12
friends, do not fear those who kill the body, and after that can do   Lk. 12:4
nothing more." "See that you are not alarmed," for "by your endur-   Mt. 24:6
ance you will gain your souls," and "anyone who endures to the end   Lk. 21:19
will be saved."]   Mt. 24:13

17. PREACHING

None of the brothers should preach contrary to the rites and institu-
tions of the Church or without the permission of his minister servant.
And his minister should always take care to be sure that he doesn't
grant this permission easily or to everyone. Every brother, however,
should preach by his deeds.

Neither minister nor brother should ever make a ministry of the
office of preaching such that cannot be easily given up when necessary, or when it is asked of him. I ask all of my brothers, in the love of
God, whether they preach, or pray, or labor, whether they are clergy
or lay, to study and humble themselves in all things, never to boast or
rejoice or inwardly exalt themselves on account of their good words
and deeds, or even due to any good that God may sometimes say or
do and operate in or through them, as the Lord says: "Nevertheless,
do not rejoice at this, that the spirits submit to you, but rejoice that
your names are written in heaven." We can know with certainty that   Lk. 10:20
nothing truly belongs to us except for our vice and sin. We should
have joy, instead, when we encounter various temptations and when
we are asked to carry afflictions or distresses of the soul or body in
this world, for the sake of eternal life.

All of us, then, brothers, should avoid pride and boastfulness. Let's
steer clear from the wisdom of this world and the thinking of the
flesh, for the spirit of the world tends to be all talk and no action; it

cares little about spirituality and interior holiness, and desires only a spirituality and holiness that shows off to other people. These are the people of whom the Lord says: "Truly I tell you, they have received

Mt. 6:2 their reward."

The spirit of the Lord desires for our flesh to be humiliated, lower, denied, considered by us as less worthy. The spirit of the Lord desires humility and patience, pure simplicity and peace of mind. It desires, above all, righteous fear, holy wisdom, and the divine love of the Father, Son, and Holy Ghost.

We should all refer every good thing to the almighty Lord God most high, acknowledging that all good belongs to him, and thanking him from whom all good comes. May God, the most high and supreme only true God, possess, and be given, and receive all honor and reverence, all praise and blessing, all thanks and glory. It is to God whom all good belongs, and who alone is all good. And when we see or hear evil, or God blasphemed, we should respond by blessing and thanking and praising the Lord God who is indeed blessed forever. Amen.[17]

---

[17] In some manuscripts and in some editions of "The First Rule," there are seven additional chapters, but it seems most likely that this is where Francis concluded the earliest version of this document. For that reason, the additional chapters are not included here.

The First Rule of the Third Order
(1210)

Scholars more often than not have questioned the authenticity of "The First Rule of the Third Order," believing that it was composed by a hand other than Francis's. The editors of the *Omnibus* wrote: "Undoubtedly, Francis very early drew up some kind of short Rule of life for these people who could not leave the world yet wanted to strive after perfection as he was striving after perfection. Quite likely, he did this as early as 1209 or 1210, but certainly before 1221. In 1221, however, Cardinal Ugolino, the Protector of the Franciscan Order and Francis' close friend, took Francis' original short Rule and set it up in more legal form. This Rule, then, was approved orally in that year by Pope Honorius III."[18] For this reason, what follows is a simplified reconstruction of the principles of this important text, without the late medieval legalese. I hope that readers will not make too much of the originality of this particular version; it is not intended to be a scholarly reconstruction of a missing original document. My aim has been simply to highlight what were likely the founding principles Francis had in mind for all lay disciples. As a result, no headings are used in what follows, in contrast to "The First Rule" for the friars, above.

Brother Bernard and Brother Peter Catani were the first men to follow Francis, in the spring of 1209, and become friars. Within a year, so many people throughout Italy wanted to join him in his work that it became problematic as to how to encourage them without disrupting too many families (depriving mothers of more than one son or daughter, leaving spouses without support or care). Francis needed to encourage the people's desire for virtue, repentance, and holy living, to offer them clear ways to respond positively to the preaching of the new friars, and to show them how it was possible to follow Christ with passion and intention while remaining in marital relationships, jobs, and in the towns where they lived. For that purpose, he wrote these basic guidelines for a Christian Franciscan life.

[18] As a result, the *Omnibus* editors place the longer, Ugolino-inspired version of the text in the appendix following their collection of the most authentic writings by Francis. This quote appears on page 167 of the *Omnibus*.

In the name of the Father and the Son and the Holy Spirit. Amen.

AS TO CLOTHING: The men and women belonging to this brother-hood should dress humbly, wearing simple clothing.

AS TO EATING: All should abstain from eating meat except on Sundays, Tuesdays, and Thursdays, on account of illness or weakness, and on special feast days. When there is no fasting, they may eat cheese and eggs. And when they are with religious in their convent homes, they may eat whatever is served to them. Let all be temperate whenever they eat and drink.

AS TO PRAYER BEFORE MEALS: Before lunch and dinner all should say the Lord's Prayer. Likewise after the meal.

AS TO THE DAILY OFFICE: All should daily say the seven hours of the daily office, that is: Matins, Prime, Terce, Sext, None, Vespers, and Compline. If they are sick, they do not have to say the hours, unless they wish.

AS TO THE SACRAMENTS: All should make a confession of their sins three times a year and receive Communion at Christmas, Easter, and Pentecost. They should be reconciled with their neighbors and restore what belongs to others.

AS TO NONVIOLENCE: All should refrain from taking up lethal weapons or bearing them against anybody.

AS TO OATHS: All should refrain from taking formal oaths unless necessity compels it. In ordinary conversation be careful to avoid oaths, swearing thoughtlessly, and slips of the tongue. This happens when there is too much talking. If it does happen, one should, before evening that same day, think carefully over what he has done and say three Our Fathers as penance.

AS TO MASS TOGETHER: All the brothers and sisters of every city and place are to gather every month and participate in Mass. There, every member should give the treasurer one simple coin; this collection being for the poorest brothers and sisters, especially the sick.

AS TO AID TO THE SICK AND THE DYING: Whenever a brother or sister falls ill, the ministers will visit him or her once a week, remind him or her of penance, and perhaps offer financial help from the treasury.

IF ANYONE SHOULD DIE: Let this news be published to the other brothers and sisters so that they may come for the funeral. And after the body is buried, within eight days, let each of us say for the soul of the deceased a Mass (if a priest), fifty psalms (if one knows the Psalter), or fifty Our Fathers with the *Requiem aeternam* at the end of each.[19]

---

[19] *Requiem aeternam* means "eternal rest" and comes from the ancient, familiar introit ("entrance," or beginning) of what is usually called the Requiem Mass, or Mass for the Dead. So, following Francis's instruction, the most common prayer for a friend who has died would be the Our Father followed by *Requiem aeternam dona eis, Domine*—"Grant them eternal rest, O Lord"—fifty times over.

Praises to the Blessed Virgin Mary

(1210–1220)

Francis's devotion to the Blessed Virgin was legendary. In this respect, he followed in the august tradition of the saints who looked to Mary as the prime exemplar of what it means to be a follower of Christ.

In this brief litany, Francis offers accolades that summarize the way in which the Blessed Virgin was set apart by God for a unique role in the history of salvation as the Mother of God.

Long ago, there were tunes that the early Franciscans used to sing these verses—tunes that probably originated with Francis himself. This is the first of three such songs included in this collection of Francis's writings. See also the ones to follow: "Praises of the Christian Virtues," as well as the most popular, "Canticle of the Creatures." There are some Franciscans, and others today, who are composing new tunes with which to sing these *laude*.

Praise the holy Lady,
The most holy Queen,
Mary, only Mother of God.

She is forever Virgin,
Heavenly chosen of the Father,
And consecrated by the beloved Son with
        the Holy Ghost the Paraclete.

They three descended in you,
And remaining there still,
For grace's fullness and every goodness.

Praise God's Palace
Praise God's Tabernacle
Praise God's Robe
Praise God's Servant
Praise God's Mother!

Praises of the Christian Virtues
(1210–1220)

In most manuscripts, a few lines are added to the end of the previous writing, "Praises to the Virgin Mary," also praising the holy virtues that are "poured into the hearts of the faithful" who desire to be the servants of God. This is surely because "Praises to the Virgin Mary" was indelibly linked to "Praises of the Christian Virtues" in the early manuscript tradition, and also then presumably in the mind and heart of Francis himself.

Francis begins his "Praises of the Christian Virtues" by addressing again, at the start, the Blessed Virgin Mary ("Queen Wisdom"). The reason for this is simple: Mary is the exemplar of all virtue and was the first follower of Christ. And then Francis shows his passion for—even love of—the virtues, as he personifies them.

P raise, Queen Wisdom!
May "the Lord bless you and
   keep you" with your sister holy pure simplicity.   Num. 6:24
Lady holy poverty, may the Lord keep
   you with your sister holy humility.
Lady holy charity, may the Lord keep
   you with your sister holy obedience.
All of the most holy virtues, may the Lord,
   from whom you proceed and come,
   save you!

There is absolutely no one in the world
   who can truly possess one of you before death.
Whoever possesses one virtue without offending the
   others, possesses them all.
But whoever offends just one, possesses none of them, and offends
   all of them.
Every virtue confounds vices and sins.

Holy wisdom confounds Satan and all of his wickedness.

Pure holy simplicity confounds all the "wisdom of this
1 Cor. 2:6 age" and the wisdom of the flesh.

Holy poverty confounds the cares of the world and the
desire for riches.

Holy humility confounds pride and all the people of this
world, and all that is in it.

Holy charity confounds all evil and carnal temptations,
and all carnal fears.

Holy obedience confounds all bodily and fleshly desires,
keeping the body mortified to the obedience of the
Spirit, and one's brother.

That way, each person is subject to every creature in this
world, not only to people,
but to every beast and animal too,
so all may do whatever they will,
as if "it had been given you from above"
Jn. 19:11 by the Lord.

My First Recommendation
to the Faithful
(1213)

The writings of Francis are usually assigned titles by the editor of a volume such as this one. It can be tricky to appropriately title each piece of writing that was most likely originally composed without thought for such things; who, after all, titles one's letters or prayers? It is in that context that I have deliberately titled this occasional piece with a self-referential, personal pronoun—because that is the nature of the message being delivered.

"My First Recommendation to the Faithful" was most likely written early in Francis's movement, when men and women were coming to join in his gospel work, asking of him, "What should I do?" Francis's answer is quite clear and was based upon his understanding of Jesus's call to the disciples. The final five paragraphs are a good example of how Francis is far more complex than the nature-loving saint he is usually understood to be today. He feared for people's souls and understood hell and its dangers to be both real and imminent.

As for the dating of the letter, we are following the wise recommendation of Augustine Thompson, OP, in his biography of Francis, setting its composition later than was once assumed, "because [the way it is written] implies that Francis had already gained some reputation as a spiritual guide."[20]

Today, this text often appears as the prologue to editions of the Rule for Secular Franciscans

In the name of Our Lord.

To those who do penance, "love the Lord your God with all your heart, and with all your soul, and with all your mind," and "love your neighbor as yourself." Despise the sin and vice of your body, especially when you are to receive the Body and Blood of our Lord, and always strive to be fruitful as a result of your penance.

Mt. 22:37, 39

[20] Thompson, *Francis of Assisi*, 34.

Cf. Isa. 11:2;
Jn. 14:23
How happy and blessed people are when they do these things, and keep doing them! The Spirit of God will rest on them and make its home among them. They are children of our Father in heaven, whose work they do, and they are spouses, brothers, and mothers of our Lord Jesus. We are spouses to Christ when our souls are joined in faith to him. We are brothers to Christ when
Cf. Mt. 12:50
we do the will of our Father in heaven. We are mothers when we carry Christ in our hearts and bodies with a love that is godly and a conscience that is earnest, and when we give birth to Christ through our spiritual practice, as a shining example before all people.

How marvelous it is to have our holy Father in heaven! How holy and comforting it is to have such a beautiful spouse! How humbling, loving, and gratifying it is to have a brother and Son, our Lord Jesus, the one who offered his life for the lives of his sheep. He prayed to the Father, saying:

"I have made your name known to those whom you gave me from the world. They were yours, and you gave them to me, and they have kept your word. Now they know that everything you have given me is from you; for the words that you gave to me I have given to them, and they have received them and know in truth that I came from you;
Jn. 17:6–8
and they have believed that you sent me."

Jn. 17:9a
"I am asking on their behalf; I am not asking on behalf of the world."

"Sanctify them in the truth; your word is truth. As you have sent me into the world, so I have sent them into the world. And for their sakes I sanctify myself, so that they also may be sanctified in truth. I ask not only on behalf of these, but also on behalf of those who will believe in me through their word, that they may all be one. As you, Father, are in me and I am in you, may they also be in us, so that the world may believe that you have sent me. The glory that you have given me I have given them, so that they may be one, as we are one, I in them and you in me, that they may become completely one, so that the world may know that you have sent me and have loved them even as you have loved me. Father, I desire that those also, whom you have given me, may be with me where I am, to see my glory, which you have given me because you loved me before the foundation of the world." Jn. 17:17–24

Amen.

To those who do not do penance, who don't receive the Body and Blood of our Lord, who allow themselves to sin and walk after their evil desires and concupiscence, who don't practice what they have promised to Christ, and who serve the concerns of the world and are most interested in the cares of this life, they are in the devil's grip. It is the devil's work that they do.

They are blind. They are unable to see the true light, our Lord Jesus. They live without any spiritual wisdom because they don't have the Son of God or the true wisdom that comes only from the Father. It is said of such people that their wisdom has been swallowed up, "accursed [are the] ones, who wander from your commandments." They see and recognize, they understand and do wrong, and Ps. 119:21 they knowingly lose their souls.

See, you are blind and deceived, your enemies are the flesh, the world, and the devil, because the body sins and feels sweet doing so, and it can feel bitter to serve God, but "it is from within, from the human heart, that evil intentions come," as our Lord says in the Gospel. You have nothing in this world and nothing in the next. Mk. 7:21 You believe that you will gain this world's vain prizes, but you are deceived because the day will come when death comes, and even though you may not give this a moment's thought, you will die a death most bitter-tasting. Wherever, whenever, and however a person dies in the guilt of sin without penance, the devil snatches his soul from his body, and the anguish you feel cannot be described except by one to whom it has happened.

Every talent and skill and knowledge that they think they have will be taken from them. They leave their wealth behind to friends and family, who take it only to say, "His soul should be cursed because he could have given me more." Their bodies are devoured by worms, and so nothing remains of it—or the soul—as they die from this world, heading to hell where they will only find eternal torment.

We beg all of you, with the love that comes only from God, to hear these words, offered by Jesus Christ in the Gospel, and allow

them to reach you with their love and gentleness. If someone cannot read for himself, may someone else read this to him often. "The
Jn. 6:63 words that I have spoken to you are spirit and life." Keep and observe
them,[21] together with active spiritual practice, to the end. Whoever
has not done these things will be accountable before Jesus Christ, for
Mt. 12:36 "I tell you, on the day of judgment you will have to give an account."

[21] Francis understood "keep and observe them" a bit differently than we might today. As will be
seen later, in other writings, Francis held a reverence for sacred writing, particularly the words
of Scripture, that extended to every piece of parchment or paper upon which such writing
might be found. Some scholars have surmised, probably correctly, that this was because of the
corporeality of these words—they are physical expressions of the eternal Word, similar to how
the Eucharistic host is Christ himself. (See Thompson, *Francis of Assisi*, 228–29.)

A Rule for Hermitages
(1217)

This simple writing demonstrates the essence of early Franciscan spirituality and liturgical practice, with careful specificity as to how to foster both.

Any among us who desire to stay in religious hermitages should do so in numbers of three or, at the most, four. Two of these brothers should be "the mother" and two, or at least one, "the sons." The two who are mothers should follow the life of Martha, and the sons should follow the life of Mary.[22] Each has his own cell where he can pray in solitude and go to sleep.

Lk. 10:39–42

They should all recite Compline each day right after sunset and then, diligently remaining silent, recite their hours, rise for Matins, and "seek first the kingdom of God and his righteousness." They should also recite Prime at the proper hour and then end their silence after Terce, when the sons can once again go to their mothers.

Mt. 6:33 (NAB)

Then, if necessary, beg alms as poor little ones who desire nothing but the love of God. And be sure to recite Sext, None, and at the right hour, Vespers.

Hermitage brothers may not allow anyone to enter or eat within their enclosures. The brothers who are mothers should aim to stay far away from others and to protect their sons from all, so that they are never spoken to. And the brothers who are sons should not talk with anyone but their mothers, and with the minister or custodian of our order, whom they may visit whenever they need to.

Now, "sons" may occasionally take on the role of "mothers," as brothers take turns in these spiritual roles by mutual agreement. And at all times, everyone should aim to eagerly follow the details mentioned here.

---

[22] In the Gospel account, Martha busied herself to prepare their home for Jesus's visit, while Mary "sat at the Lord's feet" (Lk. 10:39).

Letter to Those Who Rule over People
(1220)

Francis most often preached with his actions, rather than his words. He famously wrote in the seventeenth and final chapter of "The First Rule," above, that not every friar is meant to preach, and that preaching is never supposed to become full-time or all-consuming work; however, "Every brother . . . should preach by his deeds."

Still, there were many times when Francis saw fit to exhort others through preaching, and he was known to speak eloquently, spontaneously, and often frankly with the powerful. This letter is one of those moments, and a pivotal document in the early history of the Franciscan order, which has for more than eight hundred years played a prophetic role in the Church and the world.

I am Brother Francis, your small, humble servant of God. I wish you good health and peace, all of you who are mayors, councilmen, magistrates, and governors throughout the world—and any others who also may somehow come to hear these words of mine in the future.

We should all reflect and understand that our day of death is coming soon. I plead with you: do not ever forget the Lord our God, even though the cares of the world and its many concerns preoccupy your attention. We should never turn from God's commandments. For if anyone leaves him, and turns from his commandments, he will be cursed and "in the iniquity that they have committed they shall die." When that day of death comes, all that you believe is yours will be taken away from you. The punishments of hell are greater for those who were the most powerful and world-wise in this life.

Therefore, I desperately plead with you, my worldly superiors, take time to set aside the cares and preoccupations that consume your attention, and receive the holy Body and Blood of our Lord Jesus Christ with passion, remembering him and his holiness. Then, may you foster this same honor to the Lord among the people who

Ezek. 33:13;
cf. Ps. 119:21

are entrusted to your care. Every night you could announce, via messenger or some other simple sign, that your subjects might take time to offer their prayers and thanksgivings to the one, all-powerful God.

If you fail to do this, please know that "on the day of judgment you will have to give an account" before your Lord God Jesus Christ. Mt. 12:36

All of those who keep this letter with them, and observe what is says, will surely be blessed by the Lord God. Cf. Deut. 17:18–19

Letter to a Minister

(1221)

Scholars have attempted unsuccessfully for centuries to identify the recipient of this letter, which is most often labeled in the oldest manuscripts "A letter of St. Francis to an unknown minister." Other early manuscript copies make it "To Brother Elias, a minister"—a minister, indeed, with whom Francis had many dealings and not all of them pleasant; however, that seems both convenient and unlikely. We know from other sources how forthrightly Francis often spoke to his old friend Elias, and there would have been no need for secrecy or subtlety were Elias the recipient. No, rather, the addressee of this letter must have been a person who was not in Francis's normal circle of acquaintances and yet, clearly, a leader of other Franciscans, perhaps in a new outlying province. I believe that Francis never intended for the recipient's name to be known. And, of course, Francis never intended that his writings would be preserved in a book such as this.

Num. 6:24   To my brother, a minister, may "the Lord bless you and keep you."

I communicate this to you, to the best of my ability, out of concern for the state of your soul. You should realize that anything that keeps you from loving the Lord God, and anyone who has personally kept you from the same, whether it be a brother or someone else, even if they have laid hands upon you, all of this happens to you as grace. And, may you desire it to be so and not otherwise. For this will be your true obedience to the Lord God and to myself, because I know for sure that it is right and true.

Love those who do these things to you. And don't wish for something else from them, unless it is a desire that the Lord has given to you. Love them, and don't even wish that they would be better Christians. This will be more than a hermitage to you.[23]

[23] How helpful it would be if we possessed the letter that Francis received from this unknown minister, to which Francis is responding, here. From this unusual, abrupt line, we can surmise that the minister may have been asking Francis for permission to take himself back to a remote hermitage where he might simply pray—and no longer have to deal with the people mentioned in this letter. Francis is saying no, you cannot, for your obedience to God and to others in these ways will be of far more spiritual good to you than will silence and prayer.

If you do this and show your love for the Lord as well as myself, for I am his servant and yours, you will show by your love that there is no friar in the world who has sinned—regardless of how much he has, in reality, sinned—because once he has looked into your eyes he will see only mercy—that is, if he is seeking mercy. And if he is not seeking mercy, you would ask him if he wants mercy. He could sin a thousand times before your eyes and yet you would love him more than me, so that you might draw him to the Lord.

You are always to show mercy to such ones. And you should explain all of this to the guardians, when you can, so that they will understand why you are acting in this way.

At the Chapter at Pentecost, with God's help and after consulting with all of the friars, we will make a new chapter such as this, summarizing the work of our Rule:

> If one of the friars at the instigation of the enemy has committed a mortal sin, he is bound by obedience to his guardian for aid and support. All of the other friars who know that he has sinned may not bring shame upon him or utter any slander about him; they must show great mercy and keep private the sin of their brother because "those who are well have no need of a physician, but those who are sick" do. Similarly, they are bound by obedience to send him to his guardian with a companion. And the guardian should care for him mercifully, just as he himself would want to be cared for, if he were in the same place. Then, if that brother falls into any venial sin, he should confess to his priest, and if there is no priest there, he should simply confess to another brother until a priest is available, to canonically absolve him, as it has been said. And let it be said that none of the friars should have the power to ask any more penance than this: "Go and . . . do not sin anymore."[24]

Mt. 9:12

Jn. 8:11 (NAB)

Now, please keep this document with you until Pentecost, when you will be there with the other friars, and we review it. I hope that you, with the help of our Lord God, help us to care for this issue and every other that is not yet clear in our Rule.

---

[24] There have been historians, such as Paul Sabatier (see *The Road to Assisi*), who have pointed to Francis as a forerunner of what became the Protestant Reformation due to the subtle—and sometimes not so subtle—ways that Francis taught a return to the words of Jesus over the teachings of the Church. This is an instance of that principle at work.

Letter to Brother Anthony of Padua
(1224)

This short and simple message from Francis to one of his most beloved and famous followers is instructive both in terms of what it says and what it doesn't say. Notice that Francis does not trouble himself with any details or subtleties of theology or the methods of teaching it. And notice the one most important instruction that he emphasizes to his young, more brilliant brother.

It was in Bologna where the Franciscans first opened a house for theological study, and this occurred after Francis resigned as the spiritual leader of the Order. Refer back to the words of the original document of Franciscan principles, "The First Rule" of 1209, and you will be reminded of Francis's concerns about book learning. It seems that the occasion for this letter from Francis to Anthony was that the latter was asked to be the instructor of this new theological institute, and despite Francis's diminished official status within the Order, Anthony nevertheless wanted the founder's permission.

I, Brother Francis, send greetings to you, Brother Anthony, my theological superior.

I am pleased that you are now teaching sacred theology to our brothers providing one thing:

As it says in our Rule, please see that you do not squelch the spirit of prayer and devotion in them as they undertake studies of this kind.

Praises to God and
The Blessing of Brother Leo
(1224–1225)

The three closest friends to Brother Francis were Rufino, Angelo, and Leo. They are known as the "Three Companions." All three were buried under the high altar of the Basilica of San Francesco in Assisi, beside their brother, the saint. We know more about Leo than the other two. Leo was perhaps Francis's closest friend, his confidant, companion, secretary, and confessor.

These two writings are presented together because they physically exist together on the same piece of parchment. That parchment is, in fact, one of only two extant writings we possess with the handwriting of Francis himself.

On one side is the no longer legible handwriting of Francis praising God after receiving the stigmata (according to the testimony of Brother Leo). Francis composed these "Praises to God" while descending Mount La Verna, returning from the famous forty-day Lenten fast when he received the world's first stigmata. Some have compared this simple text of Francis to the ancient liturgical hymn of the Church known as *Te Deum*, saying, "It is typical of that wholeheartedness and exuberance which characterize his writings."[25]

The *Te Deum* is commonly prayed each day at the end of Matins, or morning prayer. It begins, *Te Deum laudamus* ("Thee, O God, we praise"). As a testimony to Francis's simple approach to prayer and theology, notice the beauty of his occasional repetitions in these praises to God.

Francis's first biographer, Thomas of Celano, tells the story of the writing of these two texts in chapter 49 of his *Second Life* of Francis. Briefly, Brother Leo was facing some sort of serious temptation in his life and desired from Francis a word of encouragement. Yet, for whatever reason, Leo was hesitant to ask his friend—perhaps because of the solemnity of the moment upon La Verna. Nevertheless, Francis intuits Leo's need and asks Leo to bring him some paper and ink, and he writes these praises of God, followed by a special encouragement to Leo himself.

---

[25] Habig, *St. Francis of Assisi: Omnibus*, 1914.

Praises to God (1224)

You are holy, Lord, the only God.
You do wondrous things.
You are strong.
You are great.
You are the most high.
You are the almighty king, holy Father, king of heaven and earth.
You are three and you are one, the Lord God of gods.
You are good, every good, the highest good, Lord
   God, living and true.
You are love.
You are wisdom.
You are humility.
You are patience.
You are beauty.
You are meekness.
You are a stronghold.
You are rest.
You are joy.
You are hope.
You are justice.
You are all one needs.
You are all the riches we require.
You are beauty.
You are meekness.
You are strength.
You are refreshment.
You are hope.
You are our faith.
You are our only love.
You are all our sweetness.
You are our eternal life.
Great and wonderful Lord,
God almighty, merciful Savior.

On the other side of this rough piece of parchment, preserved today in Assisi, is the utterly simple, also handwritten note from Francis known to us as "The Blessing of Brother Leo." It appears certain that Francis wrote his good friend this blessing while they were together upon La Verna, and to do so, Francis simply repeated the beautiful priestly blessing from the Hebrew Scriptures, adding his friend's name at the end.

THE BLESSING OF BROTHER LEO (1225)

The Lord bless you and keep you;
the Lord make his face to shine upon you, and be gracious to you;
the Lord lift up his countenance upon you, and give you peace. Num. 6:24–26
May God bless you, Brother Leo.

Letter to All the Friars
(1225)

As the early Franciscan scholar Paschal Robinson prefaced this text more than a century ago: "It was at the end of his days when he was ill, that St. Francis wrote this letter to the Minister General and to all the Friars. In it he confesses all his sins to God, to the Saints and to the Friars, and in weighty words urges once again what was ever uppermost in his mind and heart: reverence toward the Blessed Sacrament, observance of the Rule and the Divine Office. The same desires and counsels contained in this letter may also be found in the *Testament*, and there is little doubt that both works were composed about the same time."[26]

The "Letter to All the Friars" is indeed a most personal document. In fact, it is important to keep in mind the sadness in Francis's mind at the time he wrote this letter: he was no longer the minster-general by this time, and many of his friends were straying from the original principles of personal poverty and evangelical witness that Francis had first established. It is in this context that we understand plaintive words such as these: "Listen to me, my brothers and sons, 'listen to what I say.' 'Incline your ear' and your heart and obey the voice of the Son of God."

In the name of the holy Unity and highest Trinity, the Father, the Son, and Holy Spirit.

To all of my devout and much beloved brothers, to Brother Elias,[27] the minister-general of the Order of Friars Minor, its superior, and all of the ministers-general who will come after him, and to all of the ministers, guardians, and priests of this same brotherhood, humble in Christ, simple and obedient brothers, the first and the last:

---

[26] *The Writings of St. Francis of Assisi*, trans. Paschal Robinson (Philadelphia: The Dolphin Press, 1905), 109.

[27] Brother Peter Catani, the first minister-general of the Franciscans, had died in March 1221, after serving for less than a year. Brother Elias was elected to replace him and was the controversial minister-general until more than a decade after Francis's death.

I, Brother Francis, a worthless and sinful man, your little servant, bring you greetings in the name of him who has redeemed and washed us in his precious blood. When you hear his name, adore it with fear and reverence, prostrate on the ground, for he is the Lord Jesus Christ, "Son of the Most High," blessed forever! Lk. 1:32

Listen to me, my brothers and sons, "listen to what I say." "Incline your ear" and your heart and obey the voice of the Son of Acts 2:14
God. Keep his commandments with your whole heart and fulfill Isa. 55:3
his counsels with a perfect mind. Praise him for he is good and exalt him in your good works; for it is to do good works that he has sent you into the world—may you bear witness to the Word by your words and deeds and make known to everyone that there is no other who is almighty and powerful, other than him. Stand strong in your discipline and obedience, with good and firm purpose, fulfilling what you have promised to him. The Lord God offers himself to all of us as his very children. Cf. Gal. 3:26

With all the love I am able to offer, kissing your very feet, I therefore beg you: please show every reverence and honor to the most holy Body and Blood of our Lord Jesus Christ, in whom everything that is in heaven and that is on earth are given peace and harmony in almighty God.

I also beg all of my brothers who are priests, or will one day be priests, or desire to be priests of the Most High, in the name of the Lord, whenever they desire to celebrate Mass, they should offer the true sacrifice of the Body and Blood of our Lord Jesus Christ with purity and reverence, with a holy and blameless intention, never for any earthly reason, or from fear or love of any human being, as if to please someone. Instead, each of them should, as far as the grace of the almighty assists them, be directed to God alone, desiring to please the Most High Lord himself, because he alone does that work as he pleases, as he says: "Do this in remembrance of me." If Lk. 22:19
anyone acts otherwise, he becomes like Judas the traitor and "will be answerable for the body and blood of the Lord"! 1 Cor. 11:27

My priestly brothers, remember what is written in the Law of Moses about how those who sin against the material elements died without mercy, at God's command. "How much worse punishment do you think will be deserved by those who have spurned the Son of God, profaned the blood of the covenant by which they were sanctified, and outraged the Spirit of grace?" For, as the apostle says, a man despises, defiles, and tramples on the Lamb of God when, not discerning and distinguishing the holy bread of Christ from other foods or doings, he eats it unworthily or, even if he is worthy, he eats it disrespectfully, since the Lord says through the prophet: "Accursed is the one who is slack in doing the work of the Lord." Our Lord condemns priests who show little desire to take this to heart, saying: "I will curse your blessings."

Listen,[28] my brothers: If the Blessed Virgin Mary is honored to the degree to which is right, as the one who bore God in her most holy womb; if the blessed Baptist trembled and did not dare to touch the holy forehead of God;[29] if the tomb in which Christ lay for a time is venerated, how holy, just, and worthy should a man be who is to touch with his hands, receive with his heart and his mouth, and offer to others to be received the One who cannot die, but will triumph in glory for eternity—"things into which angels long to look!"

You should understand, my brothers, that you are dignified as priests only because God is holy. The Lord God has honored you above all others through his mystery, but even so, you should show love, reverence, and honor to him to the utmost. It is a terribly miserable thing, and a deplorable weakness, if you ever have God present before you while you are caring for anything else in the whole world!

We should all be seized with fear, the whole world should tremble, all the heavens exult, when Christ, the Son of the living God, is on the altar in the hands of a priest! How lofty and exalted, what sublime humility! What humble sublimity that the Lord of the universe, God and the Son of God, so humbles himself for our salvation that he hides himself within a simple piece of bread! Look at the humility of our God, brothers, and "pour out your hearts before him." Be humbled so that you are then able to be raised up by

Cf. Heb. 10:28–29

Jer. 48:10

Mal. 2:2

1 Pet. 1:12

Ps. 62:8

---

[28] In some respects, this letter has more characteristics of a speech than of an actual written letter. It probably had its origins in talks that Francis gave at general chapter meetings of the Order.

[29] This was an occasional theme in medieval monastic writings, building upon John's statement in Luke 3:16 that John developed such reverence for Jesus that by the time of his baptism he would not touch Jesus, as he touched others who came to him, in baptizing him.

God. Don't keep anything back for yourselves from the One who gives everything to you. He, then, will be able to receive all of you!

I urge and encourage you in the Lord, therefore, wherever you dwell, brothers, to celebrate one Mass per day and no more, according to the rite of the holy Church. If there happens to be more than one priest in a place, the other one should be content, through the love of charity, to hear the celebration of his brother priest, for our Lord Jesus Christ replenishes all who are worthy and are present and absent. Christ is present simultaneously everywhere, but nevertheless, he remains undivided and without change; and, being One everywhere, he works as it pleases him, with the Lord God the Father and the Holy Ghost the Paraclete forever and eternity. Amen.

Since "whoever is from God hears the words of God," we who   Jn. 8:47 have been given the special responsibility for divine tasks should not only hear and do what God says, but also, in order to impress upon ourselves the greatness of our creator and our subjection to him, take great care of the vessels and other objects that contain his holy words. Because of this, I warn all of my brothers, and I lift them up in Christ, that they should always and everywhere revere the divinely written words, so far as they are able, wherever they find them.[30] If they are not preserved well, or if they are carelessly scattered around, the brothers should collect and preserve them, honoring in those words the Lord who has spoken them, because this should concern them. Many things are made holy by the words of God, and it is by the power of the words of Christ that the sacrament of the altar is celebrated.

In addition, I confess[31] all my sins to God the Father and to the Son and to the Holy Ghost, and to the Blessed Virgin Mary and all the saints in heaven and on earth, and to Brother Elias, the minister-general of our order, as to my venerable lord, and to all the priests of our order and to all my other blessed brothers. I have offended God

---

[30] Francis is talking here about the importance of taking care of liturgical books, but also, any instance where the Lord's words appeared on a page. In those days, neither laity nor friars owned personal Bibles; if they possessed any religious books it would have been prayer books for saying the divine office, or copies of the Gospels, and other writings that contained the words of Christ. These various books were, according to Francis, to be safe-housed with deliberate care. He must have felt the need to say these things based upon some experiences with friars or other priests who paid less than respect to the written word.

[31] What a beautiful, honest confession this paragraph is—an example of Francis's simplicity and holy example.

in many ways through my serious faults, especially when I have not observed the Rule that I promised to the Lord, and when I have not said the divine office as the Rule prescribes, either because I was lazy or from some other weakness, or because I am just ignorant and simple.

Therefore, I beg you, Brother Elias, my superior, the minister-general, by all means possible, to have the Rule observed without fail by all of us and ensure that the priests among us say the divine office with devotion before God—not focusing on the beauty of their voices but on the harmony of their intentions, so that the voice may be in harmony with the intention, and in true harmony with God—so that in their purity of heart they will please God and not simply please the ears of the people.

As for me, I promise to keep these rules carefully, as the Lord gives me grace to do so, and I leave them to the brothers who are with me to be observed in the divine office and in the other appointed principles of the Rule. Whoever does not observe these rules, I consider neither a Catholic nor my brother, and I don't wish to see them or speak with them until they have done penance. I say this also about those who have set aside the discipline of the Rule and are wandering about, for our Lord Jesus Christ gave his life so that he would not be disobedient to his most holy Father.[32]

I, Brother Francis, a useless man and an unworthy creature of God, speak by our Lord Jesus Christ to Brother Elias, the minister-general of our entire order, and to all the ministers-general who will come after him, to other custodians and guardians of the brothers, whoever they are or shall be, so that they will have this writing before them, carefully preserving it, and put it into practice. I beg them to guard this writing jealously and to see that these things are carefully observed according to the good pleasure of almighty God now and forever, until the end of this world.

You are blessed by the Lord if you do these things and may he be with you forever. Amen.

---

[32] In this last sentence, Francis is picking up a theme from the Benedictine Rule, in which St. Benedict vilifies "gyrovagues," a pejorative name given to early medieval spiritual itinerants who were unwilling to be settled within a monastery or under the authority of an abbot or rule. The Council of Chalcedon also condemned this practice, in 451.

Almighty, eternal, just, and merciful God, give us scoundrels your grace to do for you what we know you want from us, and always to do that which is pleasing to you. May we be inwardly purified, interiorly illumined, and kindled by the fire of the Holy Ghost, so that we are able to follow in the footsteps of your Son, our Lord Jesus Christ, and by your grace alone make our way to you, the Most High, who live and reign in perfect Trinity and simple unity and glory, God almighty forever and ever. Amen.

Canticle of the Creatures
(1225)

This is undoubtedly Francis's most recognized writing, keeping in mind that the popular prayer repeated and reprinted every day all over the world as "The Prayer of Saint Francis," beginning with the line, "Lord, make me an instrument of your peace," wasn't written by Francis but originated from an anonymous hand about a century ago.

Francis composed the "Canticle of the Creatures" in the Umbrian dialect of vernacular Italian when he was nearly blind, one year before his death. The circumstances are so similar to those in the Bible surrounding the "Song of Moses" in Deuteronomy 31–32 that it seems that Francis must have been inspired by the life of Moses and this earlier poem.[33] However, the content and tone of the two poems couldn't be more different.

He was living in a small hut outside the walls of San Damiano in a place that Clare had prepared for him among the gardens. There, she cared for him. He grew blinder by the day. After sixty days at San Damiano, he was unable to see at all. But in this song, he expresses his wonder and belief in the wildness and expectancies of nature as part of God's plan for human life. This marked the true dividing point—the first real signpost—for what has become the modern understanding of how earth and heaven join together. This text is why St. Francis has long been the patron saint of environmentalists, of any and all who care about creatures and creation.

It is important to clarify that Francis did not "love nature" in any abstract sense. He never lived, spoke, or wrote in that manner. Instead, Francis loved creatures—one by one, easily and often. As one contemporary author has put it: "The *Canticle* signifies that the whole creation is a cosmic Incarnation—earth, air, water, sun, moon, stars—all are related to Brother Sun who is the splendor and radiance of the Most High. We might read Francis' *Canticle* as foreshadowing the new creation, when we will find ourselves related to all things in the spirit of reconciliation and peace."[34]

---

[33] See Deut. 31:14–22, which begins with God telling Moses, "Your time to die is near," and ends with: "That very day Moses wrote this song and taught it to the Israelites." Then, the Song of Moses itself appears in Deut. 32:1–43.

[34] Delio, *Franciscan Prayer*, 136.

Francis begins by integrating the natural and the spiritual in a way that deliberately honored those creatures and aspects of creation that we normally either forget or despise.

Most high, almighty, good Lord God,
    to you belong all praise, glory, honor, and blessing!
Praised be you, O my Lord and God, with all your creatures,
    and especially our Brother Sun,
    who brings us the day and who brings us the light.
He is fair and shines with a very great splendor:
    O Lord, he signifies you to us!
Praised be you, Most High, for Sister Moon and the Stars,
    you set them in the heavens, making them so
    bright, luminous, and fine.
Praised be you, O my Lord, for our Brother Wind,
    and for air and cloud, calms and all weather
    by whom you uphold life in all creatures.
Praise the Lord for our Sister Water,
    who is very useful to us and humble
    and precious and clean.
Praise the Lord for our Brother Fire,
    through whom you give us light in the darkness.
He is bright and pleasant and very mighty and strong.
Praise the Lord for our Mother Earth,
    who sustains us and keeps us,
    and brings forth the grass and all
    of the fruits and flowers of many colors.

This was the beginning of the Canticle, which Francis then taught to his companions, asking them to sing it. Then, he needed to add another verse when the bishop of Assisi was arguing with a local governor so fiercely that the bishop excommunicated the governor and the governor forbade any citizen to enter into any contract with the bishop.

The Mirror of Perfection tells us that Francis was grieved when he heard of their bickering, but "most of all he was grieved that no one had gotten between them to try and make peace."[35] So Francis wrote this additional verse for his song, speaking to the need for mediating justice and peace among the powers of the world.

Praised be you, O my Lord, for all who show forgiveness and
    pardon one another for your sake,
    and who endure weakness and tribulation.
Blessed are they who peaceably endure,
For you, Most High, shall give them a crown.

Last, at the very end of his life, Francis made room for death in his hymn. He could hardly open his eyes, and any sunlight was painful to him. "Brother Ass" he had once called his own body, comparing it to the beast of burden that never does all that its master requires of it. But Francis transformed his discomfort into praise for those parts of earthly existence that most challenged him. Once he was told by his doctors and companions that his infirmities were beyond healing, the time had come to look forward to death, and he did. He asked for Leo and Angelo to come to his side and sing to him of Sister Death. Francis had written the last verse.

Praise to you, O my Lord, for our Sister Death
    and the death of the body from whom no one may escape.
Woe to those who die in mortal sin,
    but blessed are they who are found walking by your most
    holy will,
For the second death
    shall have no power to do them any harm.
Praise to you, O my Lord, and all blessing.
We give you thanks and serve you with great humility.

---

[35] *The Mirror of Perfection* was written anonymously in about 1318, and first published in 1898 in a French edition by Paul Sabatier. Today it is available in many English language editions including in the third volume of Armstrong, *Francis of Assisi*, and in Habig, *St. Francis of Assisi: Omnibus*. The short translation quoted above is from tale 101 in *The Mirror*, in my own translation.

Canticle for the
Women of San Damiano
(1225)

As the twelfth century turned into the thirteenth and the conversion of Francis was beginning to ferment, San Damiano was falling into ruins. It was a nearly abandoned church in Assisi where Francis first heard God speaking to him.

According to Francis's biography, rebuilding that lonely church was his first act of divine obedience. It was later given to him by the Benedictines for his growing movement and became the home of the first community of the second order of Franciscans: the Order of Poor Ladies, or Poor Clares.

A decade later, while Francis was at the convent of San Damiano recuperating, composing his famous "Canticle of the Creatures," he was being nursed daily by Clare and some of the other sisters. With this simpler song (he was still in the singing mode, writing in Umbrian), he wanted to encourage them and ask them not to worry about his fate.

Listen, all little poor ones who are called by God,
    who have come to this place from many other places far and
    wide:
Live truthfully;
    die in holy obedience.
Look away from the life outside,
    for the life of the Spirit is so much better.
Please, in love, I ask,
    use prayerfully what God has given to you.
And if you are ever weighed down by illness,
    or the sickness of another,
    give and take care peacefully.
That weariness and weight will soon be expensively sold
And you all will be crowned as queen in heaven
    with the blessed Virgin Mary.

The Testament
(1226)

This is the last text to come from Francis's mind, if not from his pen. It was surely dictated by him while on his deathbed, most likely at the Portiuncula chapel near Assisi, and to more than one of the friars who were there with him constantly. The word *testament* can mean many things, including a will, a tribute, and an expression of conviction. But in this case, Francis surely had the biblical meaning of the word in mind, as well: testament as covenant—the covenant between God and the Franciscans. He wrote this document while he was dying.

As many scholars have noted over the centuries, this is the only one of his writings to tell us anything at all about his life.[36] We can surmise from some of the others, based on what we know of the saint's biography, but in "The Testament" Francis offers some direct details himself. For that reason alone, it is probably the most valuable writing we possess.

T he Lord gave me, Brother Francis, the ability to do penance in the following way: When I was in sin,[37] even the sight of lepers was like acid to me. But the Lord himself led me among them, and I worked mercy with them, and helped them. When I left, all that had been so acidic to me was turned into sweetness in my soul and my body. And shortly afterward, I got up and left the world.

The Lord gave me a faith in churches so that I would pray simply, saying, "I adore you, Lord Jesus Christ, with all your churches throughout the world. We bless you because you have redeemed the world through your holy cross." Then, the Lord gave me and still gives me such a faith in priests who live according to the Roman Church rite that, even if they were to persecute me,

---

[36] Most recently, Vauchez, *Francis of Assisi*, 250.

[37] As usual, Francis writes most beautifully when he is the most literal. This phrase "when I was in sin" evokes the Prodigal Son wallowing in the pigsty; it literally refers to that time before his conversion had begun, when his entire self/soul/life was plunked down in everything that wasn't God. At the end of the paragraph, he explains simply, "shortly afterward, I got up and left the world," as if he left that sty to return to his Father.

I would still run back to them.[38] Also, if I had all the wisdom of Solomon and came upon some poor priests in other parts of the world, I would preach in their parishes only if they invited me. I want to respect, love, and honor all of them as my superiors. I don't even want to think about there being any sin in them, because I see the Son of God in them and they are my superiors. I do this because I can plainly see, here in this world, the Son of God only in his most holy Body and Blood, which the priests alone receive and administer to others. I want this holy mystery to be honored and venerated above all other things, kept in secure, reserved containers. And whenever I find his holy names or written words in improper places I pick them up and ask that they be collected and stored somewhere more becoming. We should also honor all of our theologians, as well as those who minister the holy divine word, respecting them as ones who administer to us "spirit and life." Jn. 6:63

Then God gave me brothers. No one else showed me what I was supposed to do; but the Most High revealed to me that I should live according to the ways of the Gospel.[39] I had this summarized simply, with some few words, and then the pope confirmed it for me. Those who came to receive life gave all that they had to the poor and were content with one tunic, patched inside and out, with a cord and some trousers. We were simple and didn't wish for more. Those of us who were clerics said the divine office, and the lay brothers said the Our Father. We were happy to stay in churches. We were simple and subject to each other.

I worked with my hands, then, and I still desire to do so. I desperately want every one of my brothers to work at some honest job. Those who don't know how to work should learn, not because they want to receive wages but as an example and to avoid laziness. In fact, when we are not paid for our work, we should return to the Lord's table,

---

[38] The Roman Church was the only option that Francis knew from firsthand experience. But he would have known of Eastern rite churches, as well, and is apparently expressing unfamiliarity with them.

[39] In this late text, Francis provides important spiritually autobiographic, chronological detail about his life, as he marks the progression of his conversion from (a) doing penance/touching lepers, to (b) renewed faith in churches, to (c) renewed faith in priests and sacraments, to (d) patterning his life after the teachings in the Gospel. In the next paragraph comes his discovery that he was to work with his hands.

begging alms from door to door. The Lord revealed to me a greeting that we should use: "May the Lord of peace himself give you peace."

2 Thess. 3:16

The brothers should always be careful not to accept any churches, poor dwellings, or anything else constructed for them unless those buildings reflect the holy poverty that we have promised to live by in the Rule. We should always live in such places as strangers and pilgrims. I strictly command all of the brothers, in obedience to me, that wherever they are, they should never presume to ask, either directly or indirectly through an intermediary, for any letter or grant from the Roman court to secure a church or any other place, whether it be for the sake of their preaching, or for safety, to prevent persecution of their bodies. Instead, wherever they are not received, they should flee elsewhere to another land and do penance with the blessing of God.

Cf. Mt. 10:23

I always want to obey the minister-general of this brotherhood and any other guardian that the minister should want to give me. I want to be such a captive in his hands that I cannot go anywhere or do anything without his desire and permission, because he is my superior. Although I am simple and sick, I always want to have a member of the clergy who can perform the divine office for me, as the Rule states. All the other brothers should also be bound to obey their guardians and perform the office according to the Rule. If someone is ever found who does not wish to perform the divine office according to the Rule, or wants to change it, or who is not Catholic in his beliefs, then the other brothers wherever they may be are bound by obedience to turn such people over to the custodian nearest the place where they found them. The custodian in turn is bound by obedience to guard him strongly, day and night, like a man in chains, so that he cannot possibly escape until he personally places him in the hands of his minister. The minister is then bound by obedience to place him in the care of brothers who will guard him night and day like a man in chains until they turn him over to the Bishop of Ostia, who is the lord, protector, and corrector of this whole brotherhood.

And the brothers must not say, "This is another rule." This is a remembrance, admonition, exhortation, and my personal testament which I, your little Brother Francis, make for you, my brothers, so that we may all observe the Rule we have promised to God in a more Catholic way. The minister-general and all other ministers and custodians are bound by obedience not to add or subtract from these words. They must always have this writing with them in addition to the Rule. And in all chapter meetings held by them, when they read the Rule, they should also read these words.

I firmly command[40] my brothers, both clergy and lay, never to place glosses over the Rule or to say, "This should be seen like this." But just as the Lord gave me the power to compose and write both the Rule and these words simply and purely, you should understand them simply and without any gloss, observing them by holy action until the end.[41]

Whoever observes all of these things will be blessed in heaven with the blessing of the Most High Father and on earth he will be filled with the blessing of his Beloved Son, with the Holy Ghost the Comforter and all the powers of heaven and all the saints. And I, Brother Francis, your servant both in soul and body, confirm this for you with a holy blessing.

Cf. Mt. 5:3

[40] Notice that Francis alternates between using the language of simplicity and obedience to him as the founder of a large religious order.

[41] At the end of Francis's life, he had already watched as leaders of his order began to interpret "The First Rule" and then deviate from Francis's original intentions in it. Knowing this, these final words of his take on a special poignancy. One biographer summarized this a century ago: "Francis had now taken care of the future as well as he could. In the Middle Ages even a Papal bull was not always certain of obedience, and Francis perhaps had not any great confidence in the obedience which the Brethren would give to his last will. But his conscience was quiet—he could do no more." See Johannes Jorgensen, *St. Francis of Assisi: A Biography*, trans. T. O'Conor Sloane (New York: Longmans, Green and Co., 1913), 328.

Letter to Brother Leo
(1226)

This letter has a mysterious provenance. After the death of both Francis and Leo, it somehow ended up in the safekeeping of the Poor Clares in Assisi, who apparently shared it with no one until the year 1604. That is when its existence was first recorded. Then it disappeared from sight for almost three more centuries, until 1895, when we see it in the hands of Pope Leo XIII and manuscript experts who were called in to determine whether or not it was truly from the hand of St. Francis. This debate is ongoing.[42]

The letter was written in Latin, and crudely, showing Francis's poor education.

There is an instance in this document that demonstrates the close friendship between Brother Leo and Francis—so close that it's likely that here we witness the only textual example of the use of Francis's nickname. In the opening line of the Latin original, he refers to himself as *Francissco*, a misspelling of his name in any language. Francis in Italian is *Francesco*. In Latin it is *Franciscus*, meaning "French." It seems that Francis is offering himself to Leo, using his name playfully, combining Latin with perhaps his own nickname, "Sco"![43]

Brother Leo, peace and good health from your Brother Francis-Sco!

I am speaking to you, now, as a mother would, because all of the words we passed between us on the road together I am summarizing in this message and bit of advice. If you ever feel the need for my counsel, I suggest that you turn to this letter.

My advice is this: In whatever way you feel called to serve the Lord, and to make him happy, to follow his footprint and his poverty, do that, and do that with my blessing and with the blessing of the Lord God.

And if you ever want to come and see me, Leo, for the sake of your soul or for any other reason, come, by all means, come back to me.

---

[42] See Armstrong, *Francis of Assisi*, 1:122–23.
[43] Armstrong, *Francis of Assisi*, 1:122, n. c.

Prayer for the
Conclusion of the Offices
(DATE UNKNOWN)

This little prayer was used by the earliest Franciscans every day as they concluded praying each hour of the daily office. For that reason, we may assume that it began as a teaching of Francis.

It was usually prefaced by a series of Bible verses, most of them from the Book of Revelation, which seem to have been used as inspiration before praying the hours. These included "Praise our God, all you his servants, and all who fear him, small and great" (Rev. 19:5); "Holy, holy, holy, the Lord God the Almighty, who was and is and is to come" (Rev. 4:8); and "Worthy is the Lamb that was slaughtered to receive power and wealth and wisdom and might and honor and glory and blessing!" (Rev. 5:12). Then came this prayer, immediately following each hour.

I have organized the prayer as a "concrete poem" (not a term in use in Francis's day), arranging the words so as to convey and reinforce the message conveyed by the words themselves.

Most powerful,
holy, lofty,
supreme God:
You are good, most good, the supreme good!
You alone we give praise, glory,
Thanks, honor, and all good!
Amen.
Amen!
So be it.
So be it!

The Lord's Prayer:
Francis's Extended Version
(DATE UNKNOWN)

In recent decades, some experts have called the authenticity of this teaching prayer into question, saying that we do not have enough direct evidence that it comes from Francis himself. However, we know from the early biographical sources that Francis often prescribed saying the Our Father to combat idleness and gossip and to keep the mind and soul busy during physical work. We also know that the Lord's Prayer was precious to him and that Francis often sought to teach his friars how to pray and how to pray more effectively. It seems likely that this formulation began as an oral teaching, part of Francis's catechetical instruction for his followers, and may have been written down for the first time in the generations after his death.

Our Father,
Most Holy, our Creator and Redeemer, our Savior and our Comforter.

Who art in heaven,
Together with the angels and the saints, giving them light so that they may have knowledge of you, because you, Lord, are Light; inflaming them so that they may love, because you, Lord, are Love; living continually in them and filling them so that they may be happy, because you, Lord, are the supreme good, the eternal good, and it is from you that all good comes, and without you there is no good.

Hallowed be thy name.
May our knowledge of you become ever clearer, so that we may realize the width and breadth of your blessings, the steadfastness of your promises, the sublimity of your majesty, and the depth of your judgments.

Thy kingdom come,
So that you may reign in us by your grace and bring us to your kingdom, where we will see you clearly, love you perfectly, be blessed in your presence, and enjoy you forever.

Thy will be done on earth as it is in heaven:
So that we may love you with our whole heart by always thinking of you; directing our whole intention with our whole mind toward you and seeking your glory in everything; spending all our powers and affections of soul and body with all our strength in the service of your love alone. May we also love our neighbors as ourselves, encouraging them to love you as best we can, rejoicing at the good fortune of others, just as if it were our own, and sympathizing with their misfortunes, giving offense to no one.

Give us this day our daily bread,
Your own beloved Son, our Lord Jesus Christ, so to remind us of the love he showed for us and to help us understand and appreciate it and everything that he did or said or suffered.

And forgive us our trespasses,
In your infinite mercy, and by the power of the passion of your Son, our Lord Jesus Christ, together with the merits and the intercession of the Blessed Virgin Mary and all your saints.

As we forgive those who trespass against us,
And if we do not forgive perfectly, Lord, make us do so, so that we may indeed love our enemies out of our love for you, and pray fervently to you for them, never returning evil for evil, anxious only to serve everybody in you.

And lead us not into temptation.
Neither hidden or obvious, sudden or unforeseen.

But deliver us from evil—
Present, past, or to come. Amen.

Armstrong, Regis J., and Ignatius C. Brady, trans. *Francis and Clare: The Complete Works*. Mahwah, NJ: Paulist Press, 1982.

Armstrong, Regis J., J. Wayne Hellmann, and William J. Short, eds. *Francis of Assisi: Early Documents*. 3 vols. New York: New City Press, 1999–2001.

Burr, David. *The Spiritual Franciscans: From Protest to Persecution in the Century after Saint Francis*. University Park, PA: Pennsylvania State University Press, 2001.

Delio, Ilia, OSF. *Franciscan Prayer*. Cincinnati: St. Anthony Messenger Press, 2004.

Esser, Catejan, OFM. *The Origins of the Franciscan Order*. Chicago: Franciscan Herald Press, 1970. Translated from the German edition.

Franciscan Archive. *The Writings of St. Francis of Assisi*, translated from the critical Latin edition of Kajetan Esser, OFM (1976); a publication of the Franciscan Archive, 1999; available online at http://www.saintsworks.net/books/St.%20Francis%20of%20Assisi%20-%20Writings.pdf.

Green, Julien. *God's Fool: The Life and Times of Francis of Assisi*. New York: Harper & Row, 1985. Translated from the French edition. Published in paperback in 1993.

Habig, Marion A., ed. *St. Francis of Assisi: Writings and Early Biographies: English Omnibus of the Sources for the Life of St. Francis,* 4th rev. ed., translations by Raphael Brown, Benen Fahy, Placid Hermann, Paul Oligny, Nesta de Robeck, Leo Sherley-Price, with a research bibliography by Raphael Brown. Chicago: Franciscan Herald Press, 1983. A two-volume paperback edition was published in 1991.

House, Adrian. *Francis of Assisi: A Revolutionary Life*. Mahwah, NJ: Paulist Press, 2001. Published in paperback in 2003.

Manselli, Raoul. *Saint Francis of Assisi*. Chicago: Franciscan Herald Press, 1984.

Sabatier, Paul. *The Road to Assisi: The Essential Biography of St. Francis*, edited by Jon M. Sweeney. Brewster, MA: Paraclete Press, 2003. Published in paperback in 2004. Sabatier's influential biography was first published in 1894.

Thompson, Augustine, OP. *Francis of Assisi: A New Biography*. Ithaca, NY: Cornell University Press, 2012.

Ugolino, Brother. *The Little Flowers of Saint Francis*, introduced, annotated, and rendered into contemporary English by Jon M. Sweeney. Brewster, MA: Paraclete Press, 2011.

Vauchez, Andre. *Francis of Assisi: The Life and Afterlife of a Medieval Saint*, translated by Michael F. Cusato. New Haven: Yale University Press, 2012.

BOOK
THREE

*The Little Flowers
of St. Francis*

BROTHER UGOLINO

Introduced, annotated, arranged chronologically,
and rendered into contemporary English
by Jon M. Sweeney

O NE OF THE MOST REMARKABLE SPIRITUAL BOOKS ever written, *The Little Flowers of Saint Francis* was originally penned in the mountains of rural Italy by friends of a deceased saint. Since first committed to paper, these stories of St. Francis have been told in order to inspire. For centuries, people have read *The Little Flowers* to become better followers of Jesus.

The book was originally written in Latin—the lingua franca of all serious Christian work in those days—and given the title *Actus Beati Francisci et Sociorum Eius*, which translates as "The Deeds of Blessed Francis and His Companions." From that came a translation into Italian—a budding vernacular in the late thirteenth and early fourteenth centuries—as *Fioretti di Santo Francesco d' Ascesi*, or "The Little Flowers of Saint Francis of Assisi."* Today we usually call it simply *The Little Flowers*.

Many of the stories in *The Little Flowers* are known to us from other biographical sources written at about the same time. In some cases, the stories here are expanded or made more florid; in other cases, stories here appear for the first time.

Amazingly, this collection wasn't translated and published in English until 1864, more than four centuries after they were first published in Latin and then Italian. Those first decades after it appeared were a time of flowery Victorian and Edwardian writing, and sentimental rhapsodizing on the beauty of *The Little Flowers* was commonplace in spiritual literature. I have a fondness for this sort of literature because of its earnestness, as when one such writer describes the issue of authorship of these tales with these sentences:

> The *Fioretti*, if you must needs break a butterfly on your dissecting-board, was written, as I judge, by a bare-foot Minorite of forty; compiled, that is, from the wonderings,

---

* These are sometimes called *Actus* and *Fioretti*, for short.

the pretty adjustments and naïve disquisitions of any such weather-worn brown men as you may see to-day toiling up the Calvary to their Convent.[1]

Similar to the rhapsody just quoted, I've long been convinced that the title of this work stands in the way of its becoming more generally popular today. *The Little Flowers*—the title given to it by the editors of the first Italian edition—reeks with sentiment. It is a title that probably only speaks to the already converted. In English, a metaphorical "flower" still feels somewhat one-dimensional, but *fioretti* could just as easily be translated "blossoms," a word that connotes more of a sense of becoming. It might also help to explain that *fioretti* was also common in early Italian to colloquially connote a collection—somewhat akin to how we might use the adjective "bunch," (another botanical word) today. The negative reaction that the metaphor "little flowers" sometimes inspires made me more than once consider changing the title for the purposes of this new, contemporary English edition of these stories. But that idea was just as quickly discarded; it would be an injustice to so great a classic. Regardless, I recognize how true it is that *The Little Flowers* is perhaps a title that feels irrelevant to many people today who might otherwise benefit from these examples of basic humanity borne in faithfulness to the vision of Christ.

THE QUESTION OF AUTHORSHIP

St. Francis died in 1226, and it was not until a century later—during the 1320s—that these tales were first collected in a serious fashion. Together, the stories represent the singular vision of Francis of Assisi for his time. Brother Leo, Francis's closest friend, was surely one of their early authors, but he was not their final editor. Leo mostly passed them on orally to the other friars who were anxious to preserve the original vision of the early Franciscan movement.

It was an anonymous Italian translator—working during the 1370s—who added some additional stories about St. Francis receiving the stigmata, and these are included in some editions.

But for reasons of space as well as an intention to present only the original collection, those stories are excluded here.

The influential seventeenth-century Irish Franciscan scholar Luke Wadding ascribes the original edition of the *Actus* to Friar Ugolino of Monte Santa Maria, whose name occurs three times in the work. Still, most scholars who have studied the text have concluded that it is likely the work of many hands. The first modern biographer of St. Francis, Paul Sabatier, declared the *Fioretti* to be so widely diverse in authorship that it will always remain anonymous. Some of the friars mentioned in the text are probably also among its authors.

ABOUT THE BOOK

The Little Flowers tells the story of St. Francis and his earliest companions—the men and women of the early Franciscan movement. They are teaching tales, intended to motivate the reader toward holiness. There is never a question as to the sanctity of the subject of these tales; they are not the subject of objective history. They fit historically into the period of writings about Francis that began with St. Bonaventure's "Major Legend," or "Life of St. Francis" (finished in 1263), telling the details of Francis's life while explaining the many-faceted ways of his unusual sanctity. For example, it was in Bonaventure that we first heard a story, probably of dubious foundation in actual fact, that a simple Assisan man used to lay down his coat in the road for Francis Bernardone to walk on as he passed by, when he was still a young boy. Today's modern reader cannot help sensing some mythmaking in tales such as these, whether they appear in Bonaventure's "Life of Francis," or in *The Little Flowers*. One of the great Franciscan scholars of a century ago, Father Cuthbert, explains this best of all: "Now the writer of the *Fioretti* has no thought of driving anybody; he sets the brethren before us as one who would say, 'Look and see the beauty of their lives and withhold your admiration, if you can!'"[2] (More on this, below.)

The characters in these stories are the closest of friends, working together as comrades, living together as family. The

Italian words *frate* and *fratello* are close cousins. Both can mean "brother," although *frate* is a religious brother (or friar) and *fratello* generally indicates a biological brother. The nature of these tales is that the two meanings of *brother* tend to conflate.

There are 53 chapters, most of them quite short. In the earliest manuscripts, the chapters are usually prefaced with a short summary from an editor's hand. I have provided these summaries as well, but only in the form of short chapter titles.

Stories 42–53 are grouped separately from the first 41. This is because while the first 41 are clearly about St. Francis and his earliest companions, the latter group is about friars who were part of the "Spirituals" faction at the time when the *Fioretti* was being composed. These were men of a later generation. The fact that these later stories are presented together with the earlier 41 is part of the slight polemic surrounding the *Fioretti*, as follows: Within a few years of Francis's death, his followers became deeply divided between a smaller group of those who wanted to remain absolutely faithful to the founder's teachings and a larger group of those who viewed his teachings as more temporary. The latter were the leaders of the order. They revered Francis as much as their traditional counterparts, but viewed his role as founder in a different light. Known as the "Conventuals," these leaders believed that Francis's Rule and Testament were important foundational documents but were also open to interpretation by subsequent generations of friars according to needs of a new day. In contrast, the traditionalists or "Spirituals" felt that Francis's teachings were immovable, almost akin to Scripture, in their most conservative moments.

As often happens in such cases, the two sides tended to move to the ideological extreme edges of their positions. The battle was pitted and fierce between the Spirituals, who were probably named derisively, and the Conventuals, who were in authority. In the midst of this, the *Fioretti* was a text produced by the Spirituals, telling stories mostly about friars who were living in friaries in the Marches, the remote part of Italy where they were sometimes quite literally hiding from their brethren, and was intended to aid their cause.

There are other differences between the tales in part 1 and those in part 2. For instance, in contrast to the brief episodes of part 1, part 2 focuses on lengthy profiles of specific friars—almost mini-Lives of them. And then, theologically, there are some small differences. For example, in part 2 there is a preoccupation with the late medieval doctrine of purgatory (a place where souls must be purified before possibly going on to heaven), which was not made formal in the Roman Catholic Church until 1274 at the Second Council of Lyon, nearly a half century after St. Francis's death.

THE CHRONOLOGICAL PROBLEM

The Little Flowers never claims to be a work of history. For example, we meet St. Clare in the fifteenth story, after she has already become a sister, and we are never treated to the dramatic story of Clare's first coming to join St. Francis and the early friars—traditionally assigned to March 20, 1212. That comes from other sources. Instead, the first time we meet Clare is when she comes to eat a meal with Francis and his brothers at St. Mary of the Angels in the valley below Assisi. Similarly, in the second story—the one about Brother Bernard's becoming the first follower of Francis—we hear reference to Francis using stones to build churches, and we are introduced to the term *Friar Minor*, both of these things without any additional information or context. A reader has to turn to the early biographies of Francis for these things. Similarly, the stories in this book do not follow a narrative of any kind. In this respect, they bear all of the marks of a compiled work. Had they been written by one author, that author would surely have striven to link them together more clearly and chronologically.

I believe that today's reader is sometimes prevented from the full benefit of *The Little Flowers* by what I call their chronological problem. They simply don't fit a narrative as they have been traditionally arranged. Today's readers would benefit from having these tales put into an approximate order of their happening.

For example, in the traditional order, the transition from chapter 2 to chapter 3 can be alarming. Chapter 2 is the story of Brother

Bernard's conversion, while Francis was still very young in his own religious life; but suddenly, chapter 3 begins with: "The devout servant of Christ crucified, Francis, had lost his sight. Nearly blind from all of his severe penances and tears. . . ." This tale is told, not from the 1209 of chapter 2, but from a time at least a decade later. In the present edition, this has become chapter 25. Similarly, chapter 20 in the original ordering is a story of Francis appearing from heavenly glory (after his death) to a young friar; but after this tale come many others where Francis is still alive. All of this is understandably confusing.

This edition of *The Little Flowers* is different. I have arranged the stories in what seems to be the most likely chronological ordering according to what we know of the life of St. Francis and the lives of his early followers. (Some of the stories take place, in fact, *after* Francis's death.) In addition to including at the end of each story, in brackets—like these: [ ]—the traditional numbering of that story in every other edition of *The Little Flowers*, I have also added in brackets at the beginning of the stories the approximate or traditionally understood date or dates for the events taking place.

Each of the tales is dated according to the general consensus of scholars. My sources are listed at the back of the book in a section entitled "For Further Reading." Most often these dates are approximate; occasionally they are precise; and sometimes they are a combination of both. For example, in the thirty-fourth story, "How St. Francis knew that Brother Elias would leave the Order," we can only approximate the beginning, but then we know precisely the end, since it is the occasion of Brother Elias's deathbed conversion (April 22, 1253).

CONTROVERSIES BEHIND THE SURFACE OF THESE STORIES

Are they true? In many places, one has the feeling in these stories of reading legends more than facts. Some people refer to them in words similar to those of Professor Rosalind Brooke of Cambridge University, who calls them a "remarkable work of historical fiction."³ Another recent scholar calls them "typically metaphorical, mythological."⁴ It is true that much of what is in here does not appear in other historical sources. However, others take a more sanguine view, as for instance when Raphael Brown offers an explanation for why so much of what is in *The Little Flowers* doesn't appear elsewhere in the historical record:

> How then can we explain the puzzling fact that many of its most interesting stories were not recorded in the first official biographies of the Saint, which were based on the testimony of a number of his companions, including Leo, Angelo, and Rufino? The answer is quite simple. It is really a matter of psychology. The Poverello's best friends would naturally hesitate to mention—and an official biographer would hesitate to describe—a recently canonized Saint of the Church shaking hands with a wolf or eating nothing for forty days or telling his companion to twirl around in a public crossroad or go into a church and preach a sermon while wearing only his breeches.⁵

Still other scholars value these later tellings of early Franciscan events due to the same fact that it was the friends closest to Francis who are doing the telling. What is perceived weakness for some is strength in the opinion of others. One such scholar is Michael F. Cusato: "Even though a very late source, [the *Fioretti*] bears the traces of a long and cherished oral tradition among the friars who were present with [Francis] on La Verna [for the most important moment of his life, the receiving of the stigmata]."⁶

There's no question that these stories are the result of more than a century of brewing in the hearts and spirits of the early Franciscan movement. For that reason they are simultaneously mistrusted as historical fact and venerated for their ability to communicate something at least as important. Nevertheless, for the casual observer or reader, or the one drawn to spiritual literature for its more literary values, this little book is often the only introduction they receive as to who St. Francis was. For the past 150 years, scholars and readers of all kinds have looked to these stories for hints as to Francis's personality, as much as for confirmation of some of the actual happenings of his eventful life. On this subject Hilaire Belloc once wrote this:

> If there is one thing that people . . . have gone wrong upon more than another in the intellectual things of life, it is the conception of a Personality. . . . The hundred-and-one errors which this main error leads to include a bad error on the nature of history. Your modern non-Catholic or anti-Catholic historian is always misunderstanding, underestimating, or muddling the role played in the affairs of men by great and individual Personalities. That is why he is so lamentably weak upon the function of legend; that is why he makes a fetish of documentary evidence and has no grip upon the value of tradition. For traditions spring from some personality invariably, and the function of legend, whether it be a rigidly true legend or one tinged with make-believe, is to interpret Personality. Legends have vitality and continue, because in their origin they so exactly serve to explain or illustrate some personal character in a man which no cold statement could give.[7]

There is no document or collection of documents that has had as much impact on our collective and cultural understanding of Francis of Assisi and the personality of the early Franciscan movement as *The Little Flowers*.[8]

As an example of this, the stories here, unlike those in the first biographies of St. Francis written by Thomas of Celano, often take on a deliberate pedagogy. For example, "Three murderous robbers become Franciscan friars" (chapter 29) has the structure in its second half of an analogical journey that was never intended to be factual, but rather a teaching tale. Does that make it any less valuable as evidence of what Francis and his early companions were like? I don't think so.

What makes these stories relevant today is the power with which they grab hold of the reader, sometimes by the fantastic claims they make for the life of St. Francis and his first followers, to change one's life before God. Hyperbole—if that's what it's called—has always been a rhetorical device and a symptom of deep belief; and it can be a tool of transformation. It all reminds me of the story from the tradition of the Desert Fathers and Mothers of the young monk who says in frustration to the elder monk, "What more can I do? I've done all of the spiritual practices. I've said all of the prayers!" And the elder monk holds out his arms, fingers spread dramatically, and replies, "You can become all flame!" Tradition has it that the elder's fingers appeared to be bursting with fire at that moment.

A further word needs to be said about the controversies brewing in the late thirteenth and then fourteenth centuries between the "Spirituals" and the "Conventuals"—those two groups within the Franciscan Order that were in great tension at the time the *Fioretti* was first written down. The serious rift between these two factions comes through clearly in chapter 33, for example, which reads like a polemic for the Spirituals' cause. And then nowhere in this book is the tension more clear than in the story from part 2, "When God showed Brother James of Massa true secrets" (chapter 48). The vision recounted there is one that graphically depicts the tension between the Spirituals, represented by minister-general Brother John of Parma (1247–57), and the Conventuals, represented by Brother Bonaventure, who replaced Brother John in the role of minister-general of the Order. *The Little Flowers* represents the Spirituals' perspective on the life of St. Francis, and when we encounter the themes of evangelical poverty, faithfulness to the original Rule of Francis, the bad character of Brother Elias, and Francis's likeness to Christ, we are receiving a particular perspective. The Spirituals so identified their founder with Jesus Christ that they were thought to have gone to heretical extremes by others. When in the story "St. Francis keeps Lent on an island in Perugia" (chapter 17) the anonymous Spirituals authors write, "It is believed that Francis only ate the half in reverence to the fasting of our Lord, who for forty days and forty nights took nothing at all; so Francis took half a loaf in order to avoid the sin of pride, that he might not follow too closely the example of Jesus Christ," they are comparing their revered founder to Jesus in ways that understandably made more mainstream Franciscans (as well as a few popes) uncomfortable.

Another theme bubbling beneath the surface of these stories is the demonizing of Brother Elias—the second appointed minister-general of the Friars Minor (in 1221). Elias was an early companion of St. Francis and traveled often with him, and became Francis's vicar before the saint's death. However, after Francis's death Elias ruled the order in controversial ways, marginalizing some of Francis's closest friends (the Spirituals), supervising the building of the inappropriately ornate Basilica of San Francesco in Assisi, and then aligning himself with Emperor Frederick II, an action that led to his excommunication. For these reasons, we see a reinterpretation of Elias's earlier days with his close friend Francis in many of the stories in *The Little Flowers*. Elias becomes almost a devil lurking, waiting to pounce, even though other sources tell us that Francis and Elias were the closest of friends for most of their time together.

Above all, the most persistent theme of the Spirituals was the importance of absolute poverty on the part of a true follower of St. Francis of Assisi. Soon after Francis's death, many of his followers began to interpret the call to poverty to mean something other than, or "less than" owning literally nothing, storing nothing, preparing not at all for what might be needed tomorrow. In this way, the Spirituals felt that they were being faithful not only to Francis but to the teachings of Jesus in the Gospels. One can see the authors of these tales pounding away on that theme, for example, in the agenda-filled tale "St. Francis interprets a vision of Brother Leo" (chapter 33).

OTHER THEMES

St. Francis's love for poverty comes through loud and clear in *The Little Flowers*. Slightly beneath the surface in this love is his hand-in-hand championing of local workers, his desire to dispose of extraneous "things," a life of full simplicity, and the rights of ordinary people versus the powerful. He was remarkably ahead of his time in these respects. See "St. Francis praises holy poverty, and lifts Brother Masseo into the air" (chapter 6) for an example of some of this.

There are also moments in these stories where the reader might be surprised by the language used by St. Francis and his friars. Francis was an earthy man just as he was a man of great holiness. He was frank and forthright. And occasionally he was even crass. In "Brother Rufino is severely tempted by the devil" (chapter 9), you'll see that he was just "common" enough to use one scatological word to forcefully get his very important point across!

In addition to occasional earthly language, there are also sometimes frank discussions of sin and temptation that are unique in late medieval religious literature. For instance, the presence of sexual temptation—even what we today would call sex addiction—is unmistakable in the long tale "The remarkable life of young Brother Simon" (chapter 15). One of the features of the early Franciscans—and surely one of the reasons for the enduring qualities of this classic work—was the way they refused to sugarcoat the troubles that face anyone attempting to live an authentic Christian life.

Another theme that comes through in *The Little Flowers* is St. Francis's unique relationship to religious authority. Many scholars believe that this is a side effect of the Spirituals who compiled and edited the stories rather than an accurate and factual telling of how it truly was. For whatever reason, Francis often seems to "go out on his own" religiously in these stories. Again, see "St. Francis praises holy poverty, and lifts Brother Masseo into the air" (chapter 6) for an example.

A few of the tales are almost genres unto themselves. The most obvious examples of this are "The remarkable life of young Brother Simon" (chapter 15) and "The holy life of Brother John of Penna" (chapter 46), both of which read like short hagiographies, or Lives, of saints. These two narratives match closely the otherworldly, more fantastic, hagiographical style and substance of those saint stories that were collected in Jacobus of Voragine's famous book, *The Golden Legend*. Jacobus did his work in the century before Brother Ugolino pulled together the first Italian edition of *The Little Flowers*. After the Bible and perhaps the *Imitation of Christ*, *The Golden Legend* was the most-read book of the late Middle Ages.

ABOUT THIS EDITION

The 53 tales of this edition of *The Little Flowers* form the traditional core text of the work found in any complete edition. Following the 53 stories are brief biographical sketches of the friars and other notables mentioned in the tales.

In these contemporary English renderings, I have been faithful to the spirit of the stories, and I have compared translations among several excellent editions from the last century. I have attempted on rare occasions to remove the occasional repetition in the original stories. In a few instances I have condensed a paragraph into a sentence or two, but only when it would result in no loss of content, context, or meaning.

NOTES FROM THE INTRODUCTION

1 Maurice Hewlett, *Earthwork Out of Tuscany—Being Impressions and Translations of Maurice Hewlett with Illustrations by James Kerr Lawson* (New York: Macmillan Company, 1902), 38.

2 Father Cuthbert, OSFC, "The Teaching of the *Fioretti*," *The Catholic World*, 89 (1909): 190.

3 Rosalind B. Brooke, *The Image of St. Francis: Responses to Sainthood in the Thirteenth Century* (New York: Cambridge University Press, 2006), 246.

4 Alessandro Vettori, *Poets of Divine Love: Franciscan Mystical Poetry of the Thirteenth Century* (New York: Fordham University Press, 2004), 49.

5 Raphael Brown, ed., *The Little Flowers of St. Francis: First Complete Edition* (New York: Image Books, 1958), 27–8.

6 Michael F. Cusato, *The Early Franciscan Movement (1205–1239): History, Sources, and Hermeneutics* (Spoleto, Italy: Fondazione Centro Italiano di Studi Sull'alto Medioevo, 2009), 212.

7 Hilaire Belloc, *Selected Essays*, ed. J. B. Morton (Baltimore: Penguin Books, 1958), 141.

8 For this reason I find it astonishing that neither the *Fioretti* nor its author merit an entry in the 1,290-page, two-volume reference work *Medieval Italy: An Encyclopedia*, ed. Christopher Kleinhenz (New York: Routledge, 2004).

PART I
STORIES OF ST. FRANCIS OF ASSISI
AND HIS EARLY COMPANIONS

CHAPTER I

How St. Francis came to have twelve companions

[FEBRUARY 24, 1209]

THE FIRST THING YOU MUST KNOW IS THAT ST. FRANCIS was beautifully conformed to Christ in all of the acts of his life. Just as Jesus began preaching and chose twelve disciples to turn away from the world and follow him in poverty and virtue, so too did Francis have twelve companions who followed him when he began to found his Order.

Just as one of Christ's disciples would be a disappointment to God and eventually hanged himself by the neck, so did Francis have a companion such as this, Brother John of Capella, who left the Order and, in the end, hanged himself. To the chosen this remains a lesson for the need of humility and fear. For none can be certain of their own righteousness or their ability to persevere to the end.

Just as the apostles of Christ were renowned for their holiness and example, filled with the Holy Spirit, so too were the first companions of Francis. From the original apostles until now, we have not seen such holy and humble men. One of them, Brother Giles, would be raptured like St. Paul up to the third heaven.* Another, Brother Philip, would be touched on the lips by an angel with a coal of fire, just as the Prophet Isaiah once was.† Another, Brother Sylvester, spoke with God like a friend, as Moses himself had done. Yet another, by the pure clarity of his mind, soared like an eagle to the light of divine wisdom, just like

---

* "The third heaven" is an uncommon term, but is an allusion to 2 Corinthians 12:2–4 where Paul speaks of himself and his experience on the road to Damascus: "I know a person in Christ who fourteen years ago was caught up to the third heaven—whether in the body or out of the body I do not know; God knows. And I know that such a person . . . was caught up into Paradise and heard things that are not to be told, that no mortal is permitted to repeat" (cf. Acts 9:1–9, 22:6–11). The "first" heaven was the atmosphere of earth; the "second" heaven was where the sun, moon, and stars do their work; and the "third" was regarded as the abode of God.

† "Then one of the seraphs flew to me, holding a live coal that had been taken from the altar with a pair of tongs. The seraph touched my mouth with it and said, 'Now that this has touched your lips, your guilt has departed and your sin is blotted out'" (Isa. 6:6–7).

John the Evangelist. That was Brother Bernard, the most humble of men and yet the most profound of explicators of the meaning of Holy Scripture. And yet one more—Brother Rufino, nobleman of Assisi—was canonized in heaven while he still lived in this world. In these ways, the first companions were each marked with a singular holiness. About these marks, there is much more to tell.

[#1 of 53]

CHAPTER 2

The conversion of the first, Brother Bernard

[ca. APRIL 1, 1209–APRIL 16, 1209]

T HE FIRST COMPANION TO JOIN ST. FRANCIS WAS
Brother Bernard of Assisi. His conversion happened like this.

It was in the days when Francis was still wearing his secular clothing, even though he had begun to renounce the things of the world. He had been going around Assisi looking mortified and unkempt, wearing his penance in his appearance in such a way that people thought he had become a fool. He was mocked and laughed at, and pelted with stones and mud by both those who knew him and those who did not. But Francis endured these things with patience and joy, as if he did not hear the taunts at all and had no means of responding to them.

The noble Bernard of Assisi noticed all of this. For two years, he watched Francis as he was scorned by the townspeople—the same people who respected Bernard as one of the wisest and wealthiest men around. Despite the torment, Francis always seemed patient and serene. Bernard pondered these things in his heart. He said to himself, *This man must have grace that comes from God alone.*

But Bernard decided to put the younger man's saintliness to a test. He asked Francis to join him one night for dinner, and they ate together at Bernard's table.

Then, Bernard invited Francis simply to spend the night; he had prepared a room for Francis in his home, in fact, in his very own chamber. This was a part of the test as well.

In that room a lamp burned low all night long. Francis entered the chamber first, and quickly flung himself into bed, pretending that he was eager to drop off to sleep. Then, Bernard came into the chamber prepared for bed, and he too lay down. Before long, Bernard was pretending to be asleep, even going so far as to let out loud sounds of snoring. Hearing such noises coming from the other end of the chamber, Francis got out of his bed and threw himself to the floor to pray.

Francis turned his face toward heaven and raised his hands fervently to God. "My God, my God!" he cried out.

He began to weep, and he prayed in this way all night long until the morning light.

Why did Francis pray these words, "My God, my God!"? Like a prophet, he could see the great things that God would accomplish through him and through the movement that he would begin—and Francis was considering his inadequacy to do what needed to be done. This was his call to God for help.

Bernard of Assisi saw all of this from the other end of the chamber. The words and spirit of Francis touched him deeply, and in that moment, Bernard felt inspired to change his own life also. By the light of morning, Bernard said, "Friar Francis, I have decided to follow you in your work, to live with you your life, and to leave behind the things of this world."

Francis was elated. He said, "Lord Bernard, what you propose doing is of such importance, and will be so difficult, that I think we should seek together from our Lord Christ how we are to do it. Let's go together to the house of the bishop and hear Mass, and remain in prayer until the time of Tierce, asking God to show us his will three times in the reading of the missal."* And so they went together to the bishop's house and they heard Mass, and they stayed at prayer until the hour of Tierce, and then they asked the priest to take up the missal three times for them.

The priest made the sign of the cross over the book, and opening it the first time he read, "If you wish to be perfect, go, sell your possessions, and give the money to the poor, and you will have treasure in heaven; then come, follow me" (Matt. 19:21). Then the priest opened the book for a second time. There occurred these words: "Take nothing for your journey, no staff, nor bag, nor bread, nor money" (Lk. 9:3). And last, the

---

* Tierce is one of the appointed canonical "hours" of monastic daily prayer, usually at 9 AM. A missal was the book a priest used for celebrating the Mass. In the thirteenth century, this would have included much of the text of the New Testament (what is now usually included in a separate book called a Lectionary).

third opening of the book revealed: "If any want to become my followers, let them deny themselves and take up their cross and follow me" (Mk. 8:34).

When they had heard all of these words, Francis said to Bernard, "This is the wisdom that Jesus Christ has given to us. You should go and do exactly what you have heard. And thanks to God for showing us the true way of life!"

Bernard left immediately to gather all of his possessions. He owned many things, and some he distributed to the poor. Some he sold. And with the money that he earned, he gave liberally to widows and orphans, prisoners and pilgrims. In all of this, Francis was by his side.

While they were distributing money to the poor in Assisi, a man named Sylvester saw and said to Francis: "You never paid me for all of those stones that I gave you to repair churches." Francis was amazed at the man's greed at such a moment as this. He thrust his hand into Bernard's pocket, which was filled with money, and then thrust a handful of money into Sylvester's pocket, saying, "If you ask for more, I will give that, too." Sylvester turned and went home.

Later than evening, Sylvester thought about what he had done, and reproached himself. For three nights, then, he had a dream from God. He saw a cross of gold coming from the mouth of Francis; its arms reached from east to west, and the top of the cross went all the way to heaven. Sylvester knew that the Lord was touching him, and for God's glory he too gave away all that he had to the poor and became a Friar Minor. In some of the stories to come, you will see how Sylvester became a holy man and spoke as an intimate friend with God.

In the same way, Bernard received much grace from God once he'd given everything away. He became a friar with the gift of contemplation. Francis used to say that Brother Bernard should be held in reverence by the others because he was the first to live according to the poverty of the Gospel, holding back nothing, offering himself naked into the arms of the Crucified, glory be to him forever and ever. Amen.

[#2 of 53]

CHAPTER 3

———

Brother Masseo tests St. Francis's humility

[ca. 1210–1215]

S T. FRANCIS WAS LIVING AT THE PORTIUNCULA* with
Brother Masseo of Marignano, a man of holiness and discernment with many graceful ways of speaking about divine things, for
which Francis adored him much. One day, Francis was coming back
from the woods where he'd been praying, when Brother Masseo met
him alone on the path. Masseo had gone to find Francis and to test
his humility. He said to Francis, partly in jest, "Why you? Why you?"

"What do you mean, Brother Masseo?" St. Francis replied.

"I mean, why does the world all seem to run after you, to want
you, to listen to and obey you? You aren't good-looking. You
don't know very much. You aren't of noble birth. So . . . why *you*?"

Francis heard all of this and felt joy in his heart. He raised his
face toward heaven, feeling caught up in the spirit of God. He
then came back to the present moment, bowed, and gave praise
to God. In a spirited way he turned back to Brother Masseo and
said, "You want to know 'why me'? Do you really want to know? I
have seen this by the holy eyes of God.

"Those holy eyes have never seen a sinner viler than I am. He
chose me, the worst of them all, for he says that he chooses the
fools of the world to shame the wise, the low things to reduce
the noble and great to nothing—all so that great virtue will be
accredited to God alone and never to one of God's creatures."

At this, Brother Masseo was moved and humbled by St. Francis's
most humble response. To the glory of God in Christ. Amen.

[#10 of 53]

———

* This was St. Francis's most beloved place in the valley of Spoleto below Assisi. The
structure of the Portiuncula—which was known at that time by its religious name, *Santa
Maria degli Angeli* (St. Mary of the Angels)—was built in the early Middle Ages, and there
is a legend that it was originally intended to surround relics of the Virgin brought to
Umbria from the Holy Land. The chapel was owned by the Benedictine monks of Monte
Subasio. In 1211, the abbot gave Francis permanent use of it, and Francis gathered the
friars together in small and temporary dwellings around it.

CHAPTER 4

How St. Francis made Brother Masseo turn around and around

[ca. 1210–1215]

S T. FRANCIS WAS TRAVELING IN TUSCANY WITH Brother Masseo, one of his favorite traveling companions. Brother Masseo knew how to talk with the saint, showed great discretion, and helped Francis to duck the eyes and ears of others when he desired to do so.

On this day, as they were walking on the road together, Masseo a little bit ahead of Francis, they came to a crossroads. It was a spot where they could go to Siena, Florence, or Arezzo. Brother Masseo said, "Father, what road should we take?"

Francis replied, "The road that God desires us to take."

"How will we know that?" Masseo asked.

"By a sign that I will show you. Now, spin yourself around right here and now, twirling in a circle like children who play, and don't stop until I tell you to stop."

Masseo did this, as he was told. He kept turning around in circles until he fell down over and over again, as usually happens when one twirls and gets dizzy in the head. Each time that he stumbled, he got back up and twirled again, not thinking to stop until Francis told him to stop.

After a while, Francis finally said, "Okay, stop!"

Masseo stopped.

Francis asked him, "Now, in which direction do you face?"

"Siena."

"That is the road God wants us to take."

So they traveled on the road to Siena, and Brother Masseo thought about how St. Francis had made him do such a childish thing, and in front of so many other passersby! As they came close to Siena, the people there heard that Francis was coming, and they came out to the road to meet them. They gathered so closely around them that it seemed that the feet of Francis and Masseo hardly touched the ground.

There was a fight going on in Siena at this time, and two people had just been killed. So Francis first went to that place, stood there, and preached to the fighting men. He spoke so beautifully and with such holiness that their fighting ceased. When the bishop heard of this, he invited Francis to his house, welcoming him to stay the night there. But in the morning, Francis and Masseo woke early and left the bishop's house before daybreak.

Brother Masseo wasn't happy about this. He felt that Francis had acted wrongly. He muttered under his breath, "What has the saint done? First he makes me twirl around like a girl, and today he dishonors the bishop?" But then Masseo came to his senses, and felt sorry for his thoughts. He thought to himself, *Brother, you are too proud, passing judgment on what you don't understand. What happened yesterday was clearly God's will.*

Now all of these things going on in Masseo's heart were revealed to Francis by the Holy Spirit. He came up beside Masseo and said, "Hold fast to those thoughts you are having now, for they are the ones inspired by God." Masseo was astounded by this. He could see that Francis knew the secrets of his heart and that divine grace and wisdom surrounded all that he did.

[#11 of 53]

CHAPTER 5

St. Francis tests Brother Masseo's humility

[ca. 1210 – 1215]

ST. FRANCIS WANTED TO HUMBLE BROTHER MASSEO, since Masseo's gifts were so great that he might otherwise get carried away with himself. So one day, while living with those saintly men who were his first companions (including Brother Masseo), Francis said to Masseo before all: "Brother, all of these companions of yours have the gift of contemplation, but you have the gift of preaching. In order that your brothers may have more time and space for prayer and contemplation, I would like you to care for opening the gate to our visitors, giving alms to those who ask for them, and cooking all of our meals. And when we are eating, you are to go outside to eat so that you can be among our visitors and share with them some spiritual words."

Brother Masseo bowed his head and humbly accepted this order from St. Francis. And for the next several days, Masseo was the gatekeeper, the almsgiver, and cook, while his companions spent their time in prayer and contemplation.

After a while, the companions began to feel bad for Masseo, knowing that he was gifted with contemplation probably more so than any of them, and they agreed to ask Francis to redistribute the various duties among them all. Francis heard them, and he agreed. He called Brother Masseo and said to him, "Brother, your companions want to share in the duties that I gave to you."

"Whatever you ask of me, I will do as if I do it for God," Masseo replied.

At this, Francis saw clearly Masseo's humility, and the love of the other companions, and he preached for them a beautiful sermon on these subjects, saying the more graces and gifts that we are given by God, the more that is expected of us.

[#12 of 53]

CHAPTER 6

St. Francis praises holy poverty, and lifts Brother Masseo into the air

[ca. 1210–1215]

ST. FRANCIS WANTED TO BE LIKE JESUS IN ALL things, and this even included the way in which he sent his companions out into the world; so he sent them two-by-two. And in order to show them by example, Francis himself went first, and took with him to France, Brother Masseo.

One day as they came to a village and were feeling hungry, for the love of God they went begging for food, according to the teaching of the Rule. Francis took one road through the village, and Masseo, the other. Since Francis was small and insignificant in appearance, he was considered a pauper by all who saw him. Fools see only what's on the outside, and Francis received almost nothing for his effort. But Masseo, since he was tall and handsome, received plenty.

When they finished begging, they came back together to eat just outside of town. With effort, they found a spring that had a bread stone beside it, and on the stone they placed the food that they received. Right away, Francis saw that there was more bread from Masseo's begging, and the pieces were larger too. He was filled at the sight with joy because of his love for poverty. Francis said: "Brother, we don't deserve these great treasures!" He repeated this several times.

"Father, how can this be a *treasure?*" Masseo asked.

"This is exactly what I consider a treasure," Francis replied. "Nothing we have here required the work of others. Everything here has been provided for us by God. I think we should ask God to help our hearts to see the treasures of this—examples of holy poverty at work."

After this, they got up and continued along, singing, on their way to France.

They came to a church, at which Francis said to Masseo, "Let's go inside and hear Mass and pray." But when they went inside, they saw that the priest was not there, and so Francis immediately went behind the altar to pray. While there, he received a vision from God that set his soul on fire. It was as if love flames were coming out of his eyes and mouth. Francis approached Masseo in this state and cried out, "Brother, give yourself to me!" He said it three times, and by the third time Masseo ran to Francis and hugged him. Then Francis was saying, "Ahhhhhh," in the power of the Spirit, and with this holy breath he lifted Masseo up into the air. Masseo was stunned. He later told the companions that it was the most consoled and loved that he ever felt in his life.

After this, the two began to travel toward Rome, because Francis said, "Let us go to St. Peter and St. Paul and ask them to show us how to possess even more the treasures of holy poverty." Then he added, "Poverty is a heavenly virtue, and by it, everything of the earth loses its value. By poverty, a soul may unite with God. Poverty makes the soul, even while earthbound, talk with angels."

In Rome, while talking about such things, they walked into St. Peter's Basilica. Francis and Masseo each went to a corner of the church to pray to God and the holy apostles for the possession of poverty and its treasures. While Francis was in prayer and in tears, the holy apostles appeared before him. They kissed and hugged him and they said, "Brother, because you have requested and desired to do as Christ himself did, and as we the apostles did, our Lord has sent us to tell you that your prayers have been answered. You and your followers will be given the blessings of true poverty." After this, St. Peter and St. Paul disappeared.

Francis rose and went to find Masseo. He asked him if he had received any special revelations in the church. "No," Masseo replied. And then Francis told him of what had happened to him. They were filled with joy and, as it happened, forgot completely about needing to go to France.

[#13 of 53]

CHAPTER 7

Christ appears among them

[c a . 1 2 1 0 – 1 2 1 5]

ST. FRANCIS DROVE ALL OF HIS THOUGHTS TOWARD Christ, and directed all of his desires to be like Jesus, in all things. On one early occasion, when he was together with his companions, who were still only a few, he began talking about God with his blessed spiritual sons. With fervor, he asked one of them to quickly open his mouth and say something—whatever the Holy Spirit gave to him—to say at that moment. The friar did so, saying something marvelous by the Holy Spirit. Then Francis asked him to be quiet.

Francis then asked another brother to speak similarly. He did, and then Francis asked for his silence.

He then asked a third friar to speak without premeditation, to say something about Our Lord. Like the first two, it was clear that this one spoke with the power of the Holy Spirit. Francis and everyone else there knew so.

One after another that evening, the friars spoke of God and spread beautiful sounds of God's grace all around. Our Lord even appeared among them as a young man. He gave them his blessing—which filled Francis and all of the others with such sweet feelings of holiness that they fainted on the spot. Later, when they came to, Francis said to the gathering: "Brothers, give thanks to Our Lord, who has decided to give some wisdom into the mouths of little children. It is God who opens our mouths and makes our dumb tongues sing."

[#14 of 53]

CHAPTER 8

St. Francis cares for a man with leprosy

[c a .   1 2 1 0 – 1 2 1 5]

WHILE HE WAS LIVING IN THIS WORLD, ST. FRANCIS
always tried to follow in the footsteps of Jesus, doing as
the master had done. As Christ became a man and a pilgrim, so
Francis became a pilgrim, even writing in his Rule how all of his
followers are pilgrims and strangers in this world.

More important, as Christ was a servant to those who were
sick, unclean, and lepers, wishing even to die for them, so Francis,
who longed to be like Christ, served those afflicted with leprosy,
bringing them food, washing their sores, cleaning their clothes,
and even giving them passionate kisses. On many occasions, God
healed the soul of such a one, just as Francis healed his body. And
so it was that Francis willingly went to those with leprosy, and
ordered his friars to do likewise.

It happened on one such occasion that the friars were caring
for lepers and other people with illnesses in a hospital. There
was a certain man there who was seriously ill and also extremely
disagreeable—so much so that people began to wonder if he might
be possessed. Not only did this man verbally attack the friars
who tried to help him, but he would also strike and hurt them in
various ways. Worst of all, he would blaspheme Jesus Christ, the
Blessed Virgin, and other saints, so that after a while no one would
any longer even attempt to care for him. The friars' consciences
demanded that they not tolerate his blasphemy. Still, they brought
the issue to St. Francis, telling him the story of this leprous man.
After hearing the whole story, Francis went to see him.

"God's peace be with you, my brother," he said, greeting the
man.

The man looked angrily at Francis. "What peace do I have? God
has taken everything from me that is good and replaced it with
all that stinks!"

"Be patient, my son," Francis began, "for the weaknesses of the body are given to us so that our souls may be saved. They are a great blessing, if you can endure them with more patience."

"How am I supposed to be patient amid constant pain, every day and all night long? And not only am I crucified with this illness, but your friars cannot care for me. Not one knows how to serve me the way he should!"

At this, Francis listened to the Holy Spirit, who told him of the man's troubled spirit, and he went away to pray to God on his behalf. After a while, he returned to him and said, "I want to care for you myself, since you are not happy with any of the others."

"Okay," the man replied, "but what can *you* do for me?"

"I will do whatever you ask."

"I want you to wash me all over my body. I smell so foul that I cannot stand it myself," the leper said.

Francis did as he asked of him. He boiled water and added sweet herbs. He removed the man's clothes and washed his body with his own hands, while one other friar helped by pouring the water.

While Francis did this, touching the man with his own holy hands, the leprosy began to disappear. The leper saw what began to happen and as it did, he grew remorseful for his sins. As the man's flesh was healing, he began to weep, his conscience being baptized by tears as his body was washed with water.

"Oh my soul," he said finally. "I deserve hell for my sins, my impatience and blaspheming." This continued for fifteen days, as the healed leper plumbed the depths of his soul and sought God's mercy through tears, prayer, and confession. Francis observed all of this and knew that it was a miracle that God made happen through his own hands. So before the people of that place could find out what had happened, Francis fled to a distant place, so that he would not be recognized or glorified. Soon thereafter, the healed leper fell ill with another sickness and, enjoying the sacraments of the Church, he died in holiness and peace.

At the very moment that the leper's soul was in the sky, shining like the sun, flying toward heaven, it spoke to Francis, who was at that moment praying. "Do you know me?" the man's soul said.

"Who are you?" Francis replied.

"I'm the leper who was healed by Christ through your good work. Now, I am heading to paradise. I thank you and God for you. And know that every day the angels and saints give thanks to God for the fruit you have produced in the world through your holy Order," he said. And then he disappeared.

[#25 of 53]

CHAPTER 9

―――

Brother Rufino is severely tempted by the devil

[1210 – 1215]

BROTHER RUFINO WAS ONE OF THE NOBLEMEN OF Assisi who became an early companion of St. Francis. He was a saintly man, but was attacked and tempted by the devil while Francis was still alive.

On this occasion, the devil attacked Rufino regarding predestination; he told the friar that he was eternally damned, predestined to that fate, and no matter what he might do was of no use. Rufino listened to this and became very depressed; then he became ashamed to tell Francis what was happening. He simply stopped praying and fasting.

Then the devil took the opportunity to attack him even further. He went after Rufino on the outside, appearing before the friar in the guise of the crucified Christ. The devil said to Rufino, "Brother, why do you pray and fast so much, when you know that you're not even destined for eternal life? You should listen to me, since I know whom I have chosen. Don't believe the son of Peter Bernardone even if he tells you otherwise.* In fact, don't even ask him about this, for no one but me knows this information. Even St. Francis is damned. Everyone who follows him is going to hell."

Rufino went completely dark with this news from the devil. He lost his faith completely, and his love for Francis vanished.

But Francis knew what was happening, for the Holy Spirit showed it all to him. He called Brother Masseo and asked him to send Brother Rufino to him. "I will have nothing to do with Brother Francis," Rufino told Masseo.

Masseo could even sense what was happening. He could see the

―――――――――

* Peter Bernardone was Francis of Assisi's father. There are occasions in the stories of St. Francis when he accuses himself of arrogance or some other sin by reminding himself that he's simply the son of Bernardone. (See chapter 10.)

evil enemy at work. "Rufino, Francis is like an angel. He has filled people's souls with the light of God. Come with me to see him, for I can see that you are being deceived," he replied.

And so Rufino followed Masseo to go and see Francis. Seeing him coming from afar, Francis cried out, "Brother! You mischievous one! What is that which you are believing?" And he explained to him what had happened, and how that devil was not at all Christ.

"The next time that the devil tells you how you're damned, you tell him, 'Open up, and I'll crap in your mouth!'" Francis told Rufino. "When you tell him that, he will go. He's doing his job, trying to harden your heart toward what is good; but Christ will give you a soft heart of faith. As Christ says through his prophet: 'A new heart I will give you, and a new spirit I will put within you; and I will remove from your body the heart of stone and give you a heart of flesh.'"*

Rufino began to weep. He was at once comforted by Francis's words and convicted at the same time. "Go to confession, my son," Francis told him. "And get back to your prayers, for temptation will always come again."

So it did, and when Brother Rufino was once back in the woods praying, the enemy returned before him looking like Christ.

"Didn't I tell you, brother, not to believe Bernardone and not to bother praying, because your soul is already damned?" the devil said.

"Open your mouth and I will crap in it!" Rufino shouted at him.

And the devil went away so quickly that it caused an avalanche of rocks from Mount Subasio. The ruckus was so great that Francis and other companions came out of Portiuncula to see what had happened.

The next time that Rufino was devoutly praying, the true Christ appeared before him and Rufino's soul burned with love. "You did well, my son," Christ said, blessing Rufino. "The devil depressed you, but I am your Christ, and from this day forward I will never allow you to be depressed like that." Then he left,

---

* Ezekiel 36:26.

and Brother Rufino was left in joy and peace of mind that lasted both day and night. He was like a new man. And so Brother Francis came to say of Rufino that Christ made him a saint even before he died.*

[#29 of 53]

_____

* See two chapters later: "How St. Francis discerned secrets in the hearts of his companions."

CHAPTER 10

___

Why Brother Rufino has to preach in Assisi in his underwear

[1210 – 1215]

BROTHER RUFINO HAD BECOME SUCH A CONTEMPLATIVE, so constantly absorbed in God, that he never spoke and rarely considered the world outside. He had never had the ability or gift of public speaking. Regardless, St. Francis instructed him one day to go into Assisi and preach to the people with the inspiration of God.

"But father, please excuse me. Don't ask me to do this. As you know, I don't have the gift for preaching," Rufino pleaded with Francis.

"You should have obeyed at once, and since you did not, now I tell you: Go into Assisi wearing only your underwear. Find a church and preach to the people naked!"

And so Rufino did as he was told; he undressed and went in his underwear to find a church in Assisi. First, he knelt before the altar and then he ascended to the pulpit and began to speak.

The people who were there began to twitter with laughter. "They are a bunch of crazy penitents!" someone said.

Now, after Rufino had gone, Francis began to recount in his mind how Rufino had obeyed him. He remembered that Rufino had once been a gentleman of Assisi, and he considered what a difficult thing he had asked him to do. Considering all of this, Francis grew deeply sorry for what he had done. He accused himself, saying, "You are the son of Peter Bernardone. You little wretch! Who are you to order the noble Brother Rufino to go naked and preach like a crazy man?

"You should do to yourself what you make others do," he muttered. And so he did.

Immediately, Francis removed his habit and began to make his way fervently into Assisi. Brother Leo quietly carried the habit, as well as Brother Rufino's, and followed behind. Francis found the church where Rufino was preaching. He heard Rufino saying these words, "Leave the world behind, my friends, and give what belongs to others back to them. Keep God's commandments and love your neighbor. Do penance. Do all of these things for the love of heaven, because God's kingdom is coming soon."

Then Francis climbed into the pulpit. The people began to call him crazy too. But then he began to preach such that the men and women who were there soon began to weep. Before long, with devotion in their hearts, the people began to ask God for mercy, and nearly every listener that day was converted to Christ and turned away from the world. Throughout the town people honored Christ's Passion and it was said that never before had such weeping been heard in Assisi in a single day.

When they were all done, St. Francis put Brother Rufino's habit back on him. Only then did he also get dressed. Wearing their clothes once again, they returned to the Portiuncula thanking God for allowing them to forget themselves long enough to be an example for Christ of how the world is to be left behind.

It was on that day that they first saw people reach to touch the hem of their garments in order to receive a blessing.

[#30 of 53]

CHAPTER 11

How St. Francis discerned secrets in the hearts of his companions

[1210 – 1215]

Jesus Christ says in the Gospel, "I am the good shepherd. I know my own and my own know me."* Similarly, our
Father Francis was like a good shepherd and knew by divine telling what were the qualities, moral decisions, and failings of his
companions. With this gift Francis knew how to heal the members
of his spiritual family, sometimes recommending a humbling of
the proud, and for others, raising up the humble.

On one occasion, St. Francis was sitting at the Portiuncula with
his friends talking about God when they noticed that Brother
Rufino was not with them. He was still in the woods talking with
God alone. But while Francis was talking, that virtuous servant of
God, Rufino, returned to the friary. Francis saw him walking by.

"So, brothers," he paused and said to the gathering, "who do you
think is the holiest soul in all the world?"

"You," they all responded to Francis.

"No, I am the most unworthy of all men," Francis quickly
replied. "Don't you see blessed Brother Rufino emerging from
those woods? God has shown me how he is one of the three holiest souls living. I would even call him Saint Rufino right now,
while he is yet alive."

He said these things to the companions when Rufino was
clearly out of range to hear.

But Francis also knew how to be a shepherd who sometimes
shows his sheep where they have failed, as he did with Brother Elias
when he often accused him of pride, and Brother John of Capella,
whose hatred he foresaw would lead him to hang himself. Deeper
still, Francis knew the sheep in whom grace overflowed, such as
Brother Bernard and Brother Rufino, and many others whose moral
failings and virtues he knew by revelation from Jesus Christ. Amen.

[#31 of 53]

---

* John 10:14.

CHAPTER 12

———

Brother Masseo craves the virtue of humility

[1210 – 1215]

FATHER FRANCIS'S EARLIEST COMPANIONS WERE men who were materially poor but wealthy in God. They did not try to obtain things like gold and silver, but instead, with virtues and strength, to persevere toward heaven.

In this spirit, Brother Masseo one day was chatting with St. Francis about God when Francis told him this story:

"There once was a nobleman who was also an intimate friend of God. He had both an active and a contemplative life, and his humility was great to the point that he clearly understood his own sinfulness. He was sanctified and grew by God's grace in all virtue. God looked out for this man and he never fell into sin. . . ."

Now, as Brother Masseo listened to these praiseworthy things, he began to realize that humility itself was the ultimate treasure and that eternal life itself depended upon it. There and then, he vowed never to seek joy in the things of this world, but to pursue the utmost humility in his soul. He made this vow, and then he went to his cell, where he remained the rest of the day, and then for many days on end, fasting, staying awake all night, praying, and weeping to God asking that God might send him to hell for his sins.

This went on until one day when Masseo, in this same spirit of sadness, wandered into the forest. As he cried and sighed to himself and to God, contritely begging God for humility and virtue, a voice from heaven called out.

"Brother Masseo! Brother Masseo!"

"My Lord!" replied Masseo, for he knew that it was Christ who was calling him.

"What will you give me in exchange for all that you desire?" Christ said.

"My very eyes!" Masseo replied.

"But I don't want your eyes," Christ said. "Keep them, and have my grace as well." And with that, the voice was gone.

Masseo was full of joy from that moment forward. He became the humblest of men and took to praying with such joy that he would coo like a pigeon. He always remained in joy-filled contemplation and happiness filled his heart. There was a brother named James of Falerone who once asked Brother Masseo why he was so joyful all the time. "Because when you've found joy and goodness, you never need anything else," he said.

[#32 of 53]

CHAPTER 13

―――

Preaching to the birds

[c a . 1 2 1 0 – 1 2 2 2]

IN THE EARLY DAYS, SOON AFTER HIS HUMBLE CONVERSION and the founding of the movement, St. Francis had great doubts about his vocation. He questioned whether he was called to constant prayer or to preaching—a contemplative or an active life. He wanted to know what would please God the most. So he humbly went to others in order to ask for their help in discerning God's will.

He called Brother Masseo and said, "Go and find Sister Clare and Brother Sylvester and ask them to pray on my behalf to God, and to ask God if I should preach or devote myself entirely to prayer." Masseo did as he was told.

Now Sylvester very often received immediate answers to his prayers, and he did this time as well. He quickly said to Masseo, "Tell Brother Francis this. God has brought him this far so that a harvest of souls will come about as a result. Many people will be saved through him."

Then Masseo went back to Clare, to see if she had received an answer as well. She had. She told Masseo that God told her exactly what he had told Sylvester. At this, Masseo rushed back to Francis. The saint received him with love, washing his feet, preparing food for him to eat after his long walking. And once Masseo had finished eating, Francis asked him to sit with him in the forest outside. He knelt down beside his brother Masseo and said, "What does Jesus want me to do?"

"He wants you to preach wherever you are, for God did not bring you this far for yourself alone, but for the saving of many others."

"All right then, let's go!" Francis replied, leaping to his feet. He grabbed Brother Angelo, and the three ran down the nearest path with a spiritual passion that they didn't even quite understand.

Soon they arrived at Cannara and there, Francis began to preach. Now there were a multitude of swallows in that place who were twittering so loudly that Francis's voice could barely be heard. He asked them to be quiet and they did. The people of Cannara then heard Francis's voice, and saw what the birds did at his command, and many of them wanted to follow him from that moment on.

"Don't hurry away with me now," Francis said. "I will advise you on what to do soon," he said. (From that moment he began to plan for the Third Order.)

Leaving the people of Cannara behind him, he rushed on to Bevagna and there began to preach again until he realized that once again a flock of birds—many kinds—were gathering like an audience to hear him. Francis paused and looked on the birds. He thought of them as his sisters. "Wait for me a moment," he said to his companions. "I am going to preach to *them*." And he walked into the field where the flocks were all gathered in trees above. Upon hearing his voice, and his coming near, they slowly came down to the ground and gathered all around Francis. As he spoke to them, he deliberately touched them, when he could, with the fabric of his habit. Not one of them moved when he did this.

His sermon to the birds was basically this, as recorded by Brother Masseo:

"My little bird sisters, you should praise your Creator because he has given you the gift of flight and freedom, colorful clothing, food and water that you never need to sow, and such beautiful voices. The air is all yours! The mountains and crags and trees are yours! God gives you all that you need. Your Creator loves you. Therefore, always be grateful and praise him."

At these words, the birds stretched their wings, opened their beaks, and moved their heads as if they were making slow bows. It was clear that they heard Francis and appreciated what he had to say. Finally, Francis made the sign of the cross over these creatures and told them that they could leave. At this, they all ascended into the air, in song, forming quickly into four different flocks, flying off to the east, west, south, and north. This signifies that the birds were just like Francis and his first companions. Under the sign of the cross, they flew to the corners of the world, preaching of Christ, possessing nothing of this world, committed entirely to God's will. All of this to the praise of Jesus Christ. Amen. [#16 of 53]

CHAPTER 14

Brother Bernard soars high in contemplation

[1 2 1 0 – 1 2 2 5]

ONCE HE TOOK UP THE FRANCISCAN HABIT, Brother
Bernard of Quintavalle became known for his soaring contemplation. On one occasion while he was at Mass, he became so
absorbed in contemplating divine things that he failed to kneel when
the Body of Christ was elevated. He also did not pull his cowl back
as the others all did, and he sat completely still, without expression,
unaware of anything around him from morning until midafternoon.

After None was over, he returned to his senses.* He then walked
all over the friary, shouting to the others, "Brothers! Brothers!
There is no man anywhere, no matter how great, no matter how
much he was promised in riches, who wouldn't happily carry a bag
of dung to win this amazing treasure!"

For fifteen years Bernard went everywhere with his mind and
countenance turned like this toward heaven. He never ate until he
was satisfied at meals, but would consume as little as was necessary and nothing that tasted good. He also became a man whom
the scholars consulted for help in answering confusing questions
and untying the notes of understanding that sometimes come with
passages of Scripture.

Because Bernard's mind was free, he soared like a swallow. On
occasion, for twenty or thirty days at a time, he would remain on
a mountaintop in divine contemplation. For this reason, Brother
Giles would sometimes say of Brother Bernard that his gift was so
unusual that perhaps he should take his food while flying in the air.

It was because of these graces given to Bernard that St. Francis
would often talk with his brother both day and night. They were
known to spend an entire evening in contemplation together in
the woods, where they had gone to talk about our Lord.

[#28 of 53]

---

* The liturgical hour known as "None," the ninth hour of prayer (nine hours from the time
of dawn), traditionally at about 3 PM.

CHAPTER 15

The remarkable life of young Brother Simon

[1 2 1 0 – 1 2 4 4]

IN THE EARLY DAYS OF OUR ORDER, WHILE ST. FRANCIS was still alive, the young Brother Simon joined the movement. God gave him a great amount of grace and peace, raising him to such a level of contemplation that his whole life was like a mirror of all that's holy. People who knew him for many years have told me of all the things that follow.*

Rarely was he seen away from his cell, and if he occasionally went out with other friars, he was always yearning to talk exclusively about God. He had no schooling whatsoever. He loved the woods. He spoke with such depth, so ethereally, that his words were believed to come from some divine place.

On one occasion Brother Simon went into the woods to talk about God with Brother James of Massa.† They spent the entire evening in devout conversation about the love of Christ, and when morning came, they were surprised to realize how long they had been there. I was told of this by one who was present.

Brother Simon used to receive visits from the Holy Spirit and such divine illuminations that he had to lie down as God's love poured over him. That sweet peace of the Spirit made him seem like he was sleeping on his bed. But he was actually caught up in God, resting mentally as well as physically, visited by the divine presence, ignoring any and all material and sensible things.

On one of these occasions, while he was caught up in God and unaware of what was going on around him, one of the other friars desired to test him. The friar took a hot coal from the fireplace and placed it on Simon's uncovered foot. Brother Simon didn't

---

* This is the first instance where Brother Ugolino refers to himself in the first person, as the narrator of these tales.

† There is a later story devoted to this friar, who some of the prominent friars, such as Brother Giles, believed to be the most holy of them all. See chapter 48, "When God showed Brother James of Massa true secrets."

feel anything, showed no pain or suffering or even a wound to the flesh, even though the coal remained on his foot until it had completely burned itself out.

When he would come to take his meals with the other friars, Brother Simon would first give some spiritual food to his companions through divine conversation, before he began to eat what would sustain his own body. So it happened one day that while he was speaking of God with some of the friars, a young man from San Severino* came to the Lord. He'd been a noble and extremely sensual man in the world, but Simon received him into the Order and gave him the holy habit to replace his secular clothes. This young man remained with Simon to be instructed by him in how to live a religious life.

But the devil hurried in on that young man like a roaring lion, anxious to stop any good work. With every evil breath—the sort of breath that makes coals burn—the devil kindled a burning in the young man's flesh, so much so that he soon gave up hope of resisting temptation.

"Give me my secular clothes back," he said to Brother Simon. "I am under temptations of the flesh that I can no longer resist!"

But Brother Simon looked on him with compassion. "Sit down, son," he said to him, and he proceeded to pour such beautiful words of God into the youth's ears that the flames of temptation and lust melted away in him. Later, when the temptations would return, Simon would always make those desires go away.

But eventually one night the temptations became more than anyone in the world might resist. The young man who was being attacked went to Brother Simon and said, "Give me my clothes back now! I cannot stay any longer!"

"Come and sit down," Brother Simon replied to the troubled youth, and he came and sat beside him. The youth rested his weary, melancholy head on Simon's chest while Simon talked

---

* Probably the San Severino that is a municipality in the Marche region of Italy, where many of the Franciscan Spirituals were living in the generations after St. Francis's death. Could this young man be the same person later identified as Brother Masseo of San Severino in chapter 43?

about God. In his pity for the boy, Brother Simon began to lift his eyes to heaven, praying to God with great devotion. Soon he was caught up in God, and then his prayers were answered. By the time Simon returned to his senses, the youth sensed he was completely free of the temptation. It was as if he had never known it, and the damage of those powerful feelings was transformed into a burning of the Holy Spirit. The burning coal of Brother Simon had lit the youth on fire with a love for God and his neighbor.

It was this young man who later went with compassion and courage to the governor to beg mercy on behalf of a criminal who had been captured and sentenced to lose both of his eyes. With tears and prayer he pleaded that his own eye might be plucked out so that the criminal would only have to lose one of his. The governor and his council, seeing charity truly on fire, saw fit to pardon the criminal completely.*

One more story: There was a day when Brother Simon was out praying in the woods, feeling deep consolation from the Lord in his soul, when a flock of rooks began to caw and clamor, disturbing him with their crying. Simon ordered the birds, in the name of Jesus, to go away and never come back. It's beautiful to remember, now, that for the last fifty years those birds have never again been seen in that place, or throughout the entire region. I, Brother Ugolino, born in Monte Santa Maria,† stayed myself there for three years and saw that wonder firsthand. It was also well-known among the friars and laypeople of the whole area. Amen.

[#41 of 53]

---

* Brother Ugolino might have in mind the remarkable story from the Gospel of Mark 2:1–12 when Jesus heals the paralytic because of the faith of the man's friends (rather than, it seems, from the faith of the paralytic himself).

† Monte Santa Maria is now called Montegiorgio. It is south of Ancona in the Marches region.

CHAPTER 16

Brother Bernard goes as a holy fool to Bologna

[1211]

ST. FRANCIS AND HIS EARLY COMPANIONS WERE CALLED by God to bear the cross of Christ in their hearts and actions. They were called to preach it with words, and to be before others—in manner of appearance, austerity of life, actions, and deeds—as men crucified. For this reason, they took joy in receiving shame and insults for God rather than the honors and praise of the world that other men enjoy.

So they walked the world as pilgrims and foreigners, taking nothing with them but Christ crucified. Because they were living branches of the "true vine," which is Christ, they bore "much fruit" in the souls of all those they won to God.[*]

It came to pass in the beginning days of the Order that St. Francis sent Brother Bernard to Bologna to produce this fruit for God. Taking only holy obedience as his companion, Bernard made the sign of the cross and left.

In order to be truly conformed to Christ, Bernard went directly to the public square of that city and sat down where as many people as possible would see him. He looked the outcast. He knew that he was reproachable in their eyes. And the children were the first to see his unusualness; they began to mock him and make faces as if at a lunatic.

While Bernard sat there in the square, many people gathered around him. Some pulled on his hair. Others threw dirt in his face, and stones. At all of these insults, Bernard remained joyful and persisted there with an expression of contentment. Each day he returned there, and each day he received the same sort of treatment.

After several days, a wise doctor of laws, who had watched what was happening to Brother Bernard and marveled at the virtue of

------

[*] In this paragraph, for "foreigners" see Exodus 2:22; for "taking nothing" Luke 9:3; and for the "true vine . . . much fruit" see John 15:1, 5.

his patience, thought to himself, *Surely this man is some sort of saint.* Finally, he approached Bernard and asked him, "Who are you and where have you come from?"

At this, Bernard simply put his hand in his pocket and pulled out the Rule of St. Francis. He handed it to the learned man. The wise man sat and read it all the way through.* He was amazed at its perfection and impressed by its intelligence. Turning to those that had gathered around him, this doctor of laws said with admiration, "This is the highest form of religious life I have ever encountered! This man and his companions are among the holiest in all the world! Anyone who insults him is committing a sin. This man is a friend of God." And he turned to Brother Bernard and said, "My man, may I give you a place here for prayer, for the sake of my own soul?"

"I think that our Lord himself has inspired you to do so," Bernard answered him. And so the professor led Bernard to his home and then also showed him the place that he had promised to the friars for their work. He furnished it and completed it, all at his expense. And from that day forward, this learned man became a protector in Bologna for the work of Brother Bernard and the Franciscans.

Because of these developments, Brother Bernard quickly became a man of honor in that city, and soon the people there sought to simply see or touch him in order to be blessed. After a while of this, Bernard remembered his lowliness as a follower of the poor man St. Francis, and he departed from there and returned to where Francis was. He said to Francis, "Our place has been founded in Bologna, so you should send friars to maintain and grow it. I am no longer good for that place, myself, for I'm afraid of losing more than I would gain being there."

St. Francis heard all of this, and more of how it had happened, and he rejoiced and gave praise to God.

[#5 of 53]

---

* The original manuscript of the 1209 Rule has long been lost to history, but it would have been about twenty book pages long.

CHAPTER 17

St. Francis keeps Lent on an island in Perugia

[ca. 1211 – 1215]

I N MANY WAYS, AS A TRUE SERVANT OF JESUS CHRIST, St.
Francis was given to the world as Christ himself had been: for
its salvation. God's will was accomplished through Francis, as we
saw in the lives of the twelve companions, the mysteries of the
stigmata, and in the continuous fasting of holy Lent that Francis
kept in the following manner.

He was living near the Perugia Lake on Carnival Day, in the
home of a friend, when he was inspired to spend Lent on an island
in that lake. So he asked his friend to take him in his small craft
out into the lake to that island that no one inhabited. He asked
the friend to do this quietly on Ash Wednesday, so that no one
would notice.

That good friend and follower followed Francis's wish and
prepared his little boat in the middle of the night for the short
journey. Francis took along only two small loaves of bread.

When the friend was dropping Francis off at the island, Francis
begged of him not to mention this to anyone. And he asked him
not to return for him until Holy Thursday had come. And so the
friend left, and Francis remained.

There were no buildings of any kind on this uninhabited island,
and so Francis made a shelter in the midst of some thickets and
bushes. There, he began to pray and contemplate divine things.
There, he stayed for all of Lent, eating only from those loaves of
bread, and drinking nothing at all.

On Holy Thursday, St. Francis's friend returned. The friend
found one of the loaves still whole and the other only half-eaten.
It is believed that Francis only ate the half in reverence to the fasting of our Lord, who for forty days and forty nights took nothing
at all; so Francis took half a loaf in order to avoid the sin of pride,
that he might not follow too closely the example of Jesus Christ.

God would later perform many miracles in that place where Francis endured such beautiful abstinence. From that Lent forward, people began to live on that island, and before very long a small town was there. A friary is there now too, and all of the men and women who live in that place know the story of the reverence and devotion of Francis that Lent.

[#7 of 53]

CHAPTER 18

St. Francis teaches the wolf and people of Gubbio

[ca. 1213 – 1216]

A FAMOUS INCIDENT OCCURRED WHILE ST. FRANCIS was living in the town of Gubbio. A fearsome wolf, made crazy with severe hunger, was devouring both animals and human beings.* The people of Gubbio were terrified and took to carrying weapons with them wherever they went. But even weapons did not keep them safe from this wolf. Before long, they stopped going outside the city gates altogether. But God wanted Francis to show the people of Gubbio a better way.

Francis was already there in Gubbio, and so he decided to walk out to meet this wolf. The people said, "Don't do it, Brother Francis! The wolf will kill you, just as it has others before you!"

But Francis put his entire hope in Christ, the ruler of all creatures, and he walked out to meet the wolf armed with nothing but the sign of the cross. A few local people accompanied him for part of the way, but then they said, "This is where we stop."

"You stay here," Francis replied to them, "but I will go on."

A little further on, where the people could still see clearly what was happening, the wolf bounded toward Francis with his mouth gaping. The saint met the wolf making the sign of the cross, and the creature slowed down. It closed its mouth.

"Come here, Brother Wolf," Francis said to it. "In Christ's name, you must not hurt me or anyone else." The wolf came and lay down at the saint's feet.

Francis continued: "Brother Wolf, you have harmed many people and creatures in this place, cruelly destroying and killing. You

---

* As with many of the tales in this book, people have contested the factuality of this one. In this case, I find the suggestion fascinating that this wolf may have originally been a man. The Italian word for wolf is *lupo*, and there are local legends that St. Francis converted a criminal in this same region who then became Friar Lupo. We know that a certain Friar Lupo traveled with Francis to Spain. See Raphael Brown, *The Little Flowers of Saint Francis* (New York: Image Books, 1958), 321.

deserve to be put to death like a murderer would be; but Brother Wolf, I want to make peace between you and the people of Gubbio. You must not harm them, and they will forgive you for your past sins."

The wolf moved its tail and ears and nodded its head.

"Since you agree, I further promise that the people of Gubbio will feed you every day for as long as you live. You will never again go hungry, leading you to commit these crimes of yours. But again—to be sure—I want you to promise that you will never hurt any creature. Will you?" Francis asked.

The wolf nodded in clear assent.

"Give me a pledge of your agreement to this," Francis said. And the wolf held out its paw, putting it in Francis's outstretched hand.

"So then come with me now, to seal this pact with the people themselves," Francis said. And the wolf walked beside Francis like a lamb into the town of Gubbio until they reached the market square where all of the people had assembled. There, Francis preached a sermon. He said that God allows awful things to happen sometimes because of our sins, and that the fire of hell is far worse than the dangers posed by a hungry wolf. A wolf may be able to kill our bodies, but hell is something truly frightful. And one simple animal shouldn't be able to keep a people in a constant state of fear and trembling. "So come back to God," he said, "and do penance for these sins of yours, and God will bring freedom to both you and this wolf now and in the next world."

Then Francis announced: "Brother Wolf has promised to be peaceful with you. He will no longer harm you. And I have told him that you will provide him with food every day. I stand between you today as we all make this pact." And then the people in one voice agreed to what they had heard.

And Francis turned and said to Brother Wolf, "Do you agree?" The wolf bowed his head and wagged his tail so that everyone there could see. He raised his paw once again and placed it in the hand of Francis. The crowd from Gubbio was amazed at all of this and they shouted praises to God for bringing Francis to their part of the world. From that day forward, the people of Gubbio and the wolf of Gubbio lived together in peace. For two years, Brother Wolf was fed by each house in the town. He harmed no one. Not a single dog ever barked at his comings and goings. Then the wolf died of old age and the people of Gubbio were actually sorry to see their symbol of peace and kindness go.

[#21 of 53]

CHAPTER 19

The haughtiness of Brother Elias

[c a .   1 2 1 3   A N D   c a .   1 2 1 9]*

I N THE BEGINNING DAYS OF THE ORDER, when there were few friars and their houses had not yet been established, St. Francis took a pilgrimage with some of his companions, including Brother Bernard. They traveled on the road to St. James of Compostela.†

Along the Way of St. James, they came across a sick young man in one of the villages. Francis felt compassion for him and said to Brother Bernard, "My son, I'd like you to stay behind and care for him." Bernard quickly agreed and kneeled before Francis in humility, showing that he would obey in obedience to his father. He stayed behind while the others continued on to Compostela.

Arriving at the Church of St. James, they spent the night in prayer. While there, Francis received a revelation showing him that he needed to found many places where Franciscans would reside throughout the world. The Order he'd founded was intended to spread into a great multitude. And then they left St. James and returned the way that they had come. They came eventually back to the place where Brother Bernard had stayed behind with the sick man. The man had recovered fully from his illness, and Francis invited Bernard to travel the Way of St. James the following year.

Meanwhile, Francis returned to the valley of Spoleto,‡ and he and Brother Masseo and Brother Elias and some others went into the woods to pray. Now Francis's companions usually left him alone at

---

* This story contains two sets of approximate dates because the trip of St. Francis to Spain (at the outset) took place in 1213, but the lesson of the latter portion of the tale, where a rule is imposed on the friars not to eat meat, didn't take place until 1219 or later.

† Tradition has it that St. James the Great, one of Jesus' twelve apostles, is buried in northwestern Spain, and the pilgrimage to that place, known as Santiago de Compostela, was one of the most popular destinations throughout the Middle Ages.

‡ A geographical phrase used to mean the place where the Portiuncula is located. See also chapter 23.

these times, as they were afraid to disturb what God might have to say to their father in moments of quiet. But one day, while Francis was at prayer, a handsome young man came to the door of where they were all staying and knocked loudly and rapidly. The friars were surprised by the intrusion. Brother Masseo finally went to the door and opened it, saying, "Where are you from, boy? You've obviously never been here before, or you wouldn't knock so rudely!"

"How is one supposed to knock, then?" the young man said.

"Knock three times," Masseo replied, "and slowly. In fact, then wait for as long as it might take a friar to say an Our Father. And even then, if a friar hasn't yet come, knock quietly once again."

"Well, I'm in a hurry," the man responded, "and I knocked that way because I need to see Brother Francis. He's in the woods praying and I don't want to disturb him—so perhaps you could send Brother Elias to help me, for I have a question and I have heard that he is wise."

Brother Masseo left the doorway and went to Brother Elias, asking him if he would speak with the young man. But Elias was proud and angry and he refused to go.

Masseo didn't then know what to do or what to say to the young man. If he said, *Brother Elias can't come just now*, he'd be lying, but if he told the man the truth, the man would see a bad example. While Masseo pondered these options, the young man knocked again, and just as he had the first time. At that, Masseo returned to the gate and said, "You didn't knock the way I told you to!"

The man replied to Masseo: "Brother Elias will not come, so go and tell Brother Francis that I have come, but since I don't want to interrupt his prayers, ask him to send Elias to me." Masseo did as he was told by this man, who he now realized was an angel.

Masseo went to the woods and found Francis with his face lifted up toward heaven. Without moving, Francis said, "Go tell Brother Elias to go to the young man immediately, as an act of obedience."

When Elias heard Francis's order for him, he was furious. He stomped to the gate and flung open the door, exclaiming, "What do you want!?" The man answered him, "Be careful of anger, brother, because it can darken the soul and cloud the mind."

"What do you want from me!?" Elias demanded again.

"I have come to ask you a question. Is it lawful for followers of the holy Gospel to eat whatever is set before them, as Christ taught? Similarly, is it lawful for any person to impose on followers of the holy Gospel anything that is contrary to its freedoms?"

Brother Elias answered haughtily. "I know these answers very well, but I won't tell you. Go away." He threw the gate closed and left.

But after he'd left the man's presence, Brother Elias began to ponder the questions. He realized that he was unsure of the answers—for he himself had made a rule for the friars, when he was vicar of the Order, that no one was allowed to eat meat. Perhaps that question had been aimed directly at him? Unable to make sense of it all, and recalling how humble the man at the gate had been, Elias returned there and looked for him again. The man wasn't there. Elias searched all around the friary and he was nowhere to be found. The angel had left, for Brother Elias was unfit to speak with the angels.

Once all of this had occurred, St. Francis (who knew of it all) returned from the woods. He found Brother Elias and scolded him, saying, "Only a too-proud friar would drive away a holy angel, who only wanted to teach us something, from this place. I fear that your haughtiness will lead you to end your days outside of this Order." It would later happen just as Francis had predicted.

Meanwhile, on the same day and hour as the angel had left the gate before Brother Elias, he appeared to Brother Bernard, who was returning from the Way of St. James. Bernard was standing on the bank of a river, unable to cross it. The angel greeted Bernard in words that he could easily understand, saying, "Peace be with you, brother."

Brother Bernard was amazed at the handsomeness of the man and his eloquence and peacefulness. He said to him, "Where are you from, young man?"

The angel replied, "I have come from where St. Francis is living, and I went to see him, but was unable to, because he is in the woods with God. Brothers Masseo, Giles, and Elias were there, too, and Masseo taught me the proper way to knock at the gate, the way good friars do. And Elias—not wanting to answer the question that I put to him—then had regret and wanted to see me again, but couldn't.

"Why won't you cross the river?" the angel concluded.

"I am afraid of how deep it is here," Bernard answered him.

"Let's pass over together," the angel said. "There's no need for fear." And he took Bernard's hand. In a flash of a moment, they were standing together on the other side. At this, Brother Bernard knew he was in the presence of an angel. With joy and reverence he shouted out, "O blessed angel of God, tell me, what is your name?"

"It is wonderful," the man said, "but tell me, why do you need to know?" And at that, he disappeared.

Brother Bernard was left in happiness and joyfully continued his journey all the way home to St. Francis and the other brothers. He told them of what had happened, including the very hour when the angel came to him, and they all knew that it was the same angel who had come to the brothers and to Bernard on that very same day. They gave thanks to God.

[#4 of 53]

CHAPTER 20

St. Francis shows special care for some wild birds

[ca. 1215 – 1220]

ONE DAY A BOY IN SIENA CAUGHT SOME TURTLEDOVES and carried them, still fluttering about, to the market. St. Francis, who was always compassionate to creatures, and especially to animals and birds, saw these turtledoves and his heart was moved.

"Will you give these birds to me?" he asked the young boy. "They are innocent creatures that the Bible says are pure and faithful souls. Give them to me so that they don't go to anyone who will kill them."

The boy was inspired by God and Francis's words and he agreed. So Francis gathered up the turtledoves and began talking with them in gentle tones.

"My sisters," he said, "why did you allow yourselves to be captured like this? You are innocent. You need nests where you can lay eggs and multiply as your Creator has instructed you."

With this, Francis took the birds to a place where he then made nests for each of them. And the doves settled down into those nests and began to lay eggs in that place, where the friars also lived. Over time, they became so tame with the men that they were almost like chickens that had been raised from chicks by the brothers. They would even come and go when Francis would bless them.

Back at the market, St. Francis had said to that boy, "You will surely serve our Lord Jesus Christ and become a Friar Minor someday." And so it happened that the youth soon entered the Order. The actions of Francis led to life and joy for some turtledoves, but also to the joy of eternal life for the boy who gave them to him. Christ be praised. Amen.

[#22 of 53]

CHAPTER 21

When St. Francis saw the Portiuncula surrounded by devils

[ca. 1215 – 1220]

ONCE AT PORTIUNCULA, WHILE ST. FRANCIS WAS fervently praying, a vision showed him that the entire place was surrounded by an army of devils. At the same time, he saw that none of the devils could enter the friary on its own; it needed a holy friar to allow it inside. And so—as he watched—they waited.

The next moment, one of the friars in the Portiuncula became stirred up with anger against one of the others. He began to contemplate how to get revenge against his brother. As a result, the gate of virtue briefly fell and a door to evil was opened; a devil found his way inside that place.

Seeing all of this, Francis then watched as that devil crouched itself upon that friar's neck. It was as if a wolf were devouring one of his sheep. Francis called out for the friar, and the man came running to Francis, who instructed him to reveal what was going on between him and his neighbor. The friar, seeing that his spiritual father had "read" his very thoughts, revealed everything to Francis that he had been hiding darkly in his heart, asking humbly for forgiveness. Francis listened to him, and gave him a penance, absolving the man of his sin.

At that moment, the father watched as his son's devil flew away. Christ be praised.

[#23 of 53]

CHAPTER 22

A rich and noble knight becomes a Franciscan friar

[1 2 1 5 – 1 2 2 0]

ST. FRANCIS AND HIS COMPANIONS ARRIVED very late one evening at the house of a venerable gentleman. They were treated with courtesy, reverently given a resting place for the night—so much so that they were made to feel like angels arriving from heaven. The nobleman embraced Francis with a kiss of peace and washed his feet, kissing them too. He lighted a warm fire and set a table of many foods, serving the friars by his own hand, and with joy. These extraordinary kindnesses warmed Francis's heart.

"Father," the nobleman asked Francis, when the meal was done, "I offer you all that I have. And if you need to purchase anything—habits or clothing or anything else—buy it and I will repay you. I want to provide for your needs out of my abundance."

And so, later, when Francis was leaving this man's house with his companions, he remarked to them, "That nobleman would make an excellent member of our Order. Someday, I would like to return here and find that God has touched him further, making him want to join us in serving God. Let's pray that God might further spark his heart by that grace."

A few days later, St. Francis said to one of his companions, "Let's go back to the noble gentleman's house because I feel that God has worked in his heart." And so they took to the road that led to the man's house, but before they could arrive at his door, Francis said to his brother, "Wait here for me. I want to ask God to make our journey a success. I want to ask Christ to give those of us who are weak the ability to snatch strong prey away from the world!" Saying this, he went off in private to pray—but not so privately that he couldn't be seen clearly by the gentleman himself.

The gentleman saw Francis devoutly praying to Christ; and he saw Christ himself standing with Francis beautifully enwrapped in a bright light. Francis was even rising off the ground—both spiritually and physically.

The hand of God came upon the gentleman as he viewed these happenings, touching his heart and inspiring him to leave the world completely behind. He left his mansion and ran to St. Francis. There he found Francis still standing in prayer, and so he too began to pray, and then he knelt before Francis and pleaded with him to show him the way to penance and to join him permanently.

"What should I do, father?" the man said to Francis. "I am ready to give everything to those in need and to run with you after Christ."

This is how it happened that such a nobleman became a Friar Minor and gave all that he had to the poor.

[#37 of 53]

CHAPTER 23

A general chapter is held at St. Mary of the Angels

[1216 or 1218]

CHRIST'S FAITHFUL SERVANT ST. FRANCIS OF ASSISI once
held a general chapter of the early Franciscans in the valley
below Assisi at St. Mary of the Angels.* More than 5,000 friars
were there. While traveling from Bologna to Rome, St. Dominic,
the founder of the Order of Friars Preachers, along with seven of
his friars, heard of this gathering and they went to see what was
happening.

Also there was Lord Ugolino, the cardinal bishop of Ostia,
who was always devoted to Francis and his brothers. Francis once
prophesied that the cardinal bishop would be pope one day, and
so it happened, when he became Pope Gregory IX. But during
this general chapter, Lord Ugolino's court was in Perugia and he
came often to Assisi, sometimes every day, singing the Mass, and
sometimes delivering sermons for the friars.

The cardinal was inspired by the sight of this holy assembly of
brothers sitting in the plain below Assisi. They were in groups of
sixty or one hundred, or more, just talking about God, praying
with one another, crying with each other, and doing acts of
charity. This was a quiet and humble army of men, making no
unnecessary noise, telling no stories, making no jokes, but only
praying the Divine Office and talking about the salvation of
human souls. They slept on the ground or on a pile of straw, and
their pillows were stones or logs.

---

* James of Vitry, a theologian, cardinal, and historian who lived at the time of St. Francis,
wrote in a letter dated 1216, after traveling to see the Franciscans firsthand in Italy: "The
men of this religious order gather once a year in a chosen place, to their great benefit,
that they might dine together and rejoice in the Lord. They get the advice of worthy men
and they decide on and then promote and get papal approval for holy projects. After this
they disperse for the whole year. . . . I am convinced that the Lord . . . wishes before this
world comes to an end to save many souls through these simple and poor men." (Quoted
in *Religious Poverty and the Profit Economy in Medieval Europe*, by Lester K. Little [Ithaca, NY:
Cornell University Press, 1978], 151.)

"This is certainly a camp of the knights of God!" the cardinal exclaimed.

Everyone who saw this gathering of men was impressed by their devotion and holiness. Throughout the valley of Spoleto, people came to witness what was happening, including many of the cardinal's court, barons and other noblemen, bishops and abbots. They came to see St. Francis, the one who had brought together such a gathering—who had plucked these men from out of the world and started such a movement of those who followed the true shepherd, Christ. People said that this was unlike any gathering of men ever before assembled.

When they were all assembled, Francis stood before them as minister-general and preached God's Word as the Holy Spirit directed him. His sermon centered on this theme: "My sons, we have received many good things, but greater things are promised to us by God. Let us use the good things all around us, but even more, let's confidently pursue the promises of God. Our life here on earth is short, and the punishment of eternity is real; suffering here and now is nothing, and the glory of heaven is forever."* He counseled and inspired the friars, encouraging them to live faithfully in the life to which they were committed—pursuing humility, patience, contempt for the values of the world, voluntary poverty, care, attentiveness, prayer, and praise. He asked them to put their faith entirely in the Good Shepherd who cares for all of our needs, body and soul. He went on to say: "In order to learn these lessons here and now I say that none of us shall worry about what we will eat or drink or anything else necessary for our bodies, while we are here in this place together. Let's focus only on praying and praising our Lord. Leave all bodily worries to Christ, who cares for us."

They cheered at this, and with joy. And when he had finished speaking, they rushed back to praying together.

Now St. Dominic was there, and expressed his surprise at this command of St. Francis. It might work for one friar, but for a huge

---

* Perhaps his text was Romans 8:14–18.

group? But before long, the people of the surrounding towns—Perugia, Spoleto, Foligno, Spello, Assisi, and beyond—began delivering food and drink, bread and wine, beans and cheese, to the huge and holy congregation of men. On mules and horses they arrived with pitchers and glasses, tablecloths and other utensils, whatever was needed. Then the knights and noblemen began serving the friars. The clergymen were running here and there like servants, for the sake of the brothers. When Dominic saw all of this, he realized that God was at work and he took back what he had previously said. Dominic knelt before the saint himself and said, "God is the one caring for this holy assembly. I didn't see it at first. I now promise to observe holy poverty myself, and all of the men in my Order will do the same!"

It was during that same general chapter that Francis discovered that many of the friars were wearing metal cilices on their torsos and iron rings on their arms, and as a result were becoming ill or even dying. These objects actually hindered rather than helped prayer. So Francis, the wise father, commanded all the brothers to remove these things. They did, and more than five hundred pieces were thrown into a large pile.

When the chapter was ending, Francis asked the brothers to do good in the world and to escape evil, and he sent them back to the many places from which they'd come. May Christ be blessed! Amen.

[#18 of 53]

CHAPTER 24

St. Francis takes a ship to see the Sultan

[1219]

S T. FRANCIS WAS ZEALOUS IN HIS FAITH TO THE POINT of desiring a martyr's death. One day he took with him twelve of his companions and traveled across the seas to the place of the Sultan* of Babylonia. When they arrived, the Saracen men who protected the roads so that Christians could not travel freely, took them as prisoners, bound and beat them, and then brought them before the Sultan.

There in the Sultan's presence Francis preached by the power of the Holy Spirit. He spoke beautifully of the Catholic religion and even offered to step into a fire to demonstrate his faith. The Sultan admired both his fervor and his distaste for the things of this world—for in his poverty Francis would not accept gifts from the hands of the Sultan. The Sultan also respected Francis's desire for martyrdom. He listened carefully to Francis's words, and asked him to return several times to see him and talk some more. He also gave Francis permission to preach wherever and whatever he chose, giving him and his holy companions a token of himself so that no one would ever do them any harm.

And so, with permission, Francis sent his companions out in pairs throughout the Saracen lands to preach the faith of Jesus. He himself left with a brother and traveled to a region where they found an inn in which to stay overnight. There Francis found a beautiful woman, who was nevertheless undesirable of soul. She asked Francis to go to bed with her.

"If you will do what I want, I will do what you want," Francis replied.

---

* Famously, St. Francis met with Malik al-Kamil (1180–1238), the Sultan of Egypt, at a time when Christian crusaders were preparing an attack on the Nile Delta region that he ruled. Entire books have been written about this episode. See "For Further Reading."

"Okay," she said, "then let's go and prepare a bed." And she led Francis to a bedroom.

But then Francis said, "Come with me. I will show you a most beautiful bed." And he showed her into a room with a large fire roaring in a fireplace. Stripping himself naked, Francis rushed to climb into the fire as if he was leaping into bed. He called to the woman and said, "Undress yourself. Come and enjoy this wonderful bed! You must come here in order to do what I wanted." And he lay there for a long while without the fire burning him at all. The woman was terrified and felt sorry for her sins and intentions. At that moment, she was converted to faith in Christ.

After a while, however, Francis saw that he and his friars would be unable to gather much fruit in this faraway land, and God told him to go home. He returned to the Sultan and told him of their intention to leave.

"Brother, I myself would gladly convert to your faith, but I am afraid," the Sultan said. "If I were to do so, these Saracens would kill both of us, plus your companions. And since you still have much good to do, and I too have things to do for my own soul, I don't want to cause our deaths too soon. Show me what I might do for salvation, and I will obey."

Francis replied, "My lord, I leave you now to return to my country. But when the time for my death has come, and I am gone to heaven, I will send two of my friars back to you and they will bring you the baptism of Jesus Christ, and you will be saved. In the meantime, do not let anything hinder your desires for faith, and when grace comes, God will find you with faith."

The Sultan promised to do as Francis suggested, and the saint left.

After some years, Francis's body died. And then, when the Sultan became ill, he remembered the saint's promise to him, and he stationed guards at all gates with instructions to inform him if any of Francis's friars were ever seen. It was at this time that Francis appeared to two of his friars and told them what to do.

When the Sultan glimpsed them from afar, he was filled with joy. "I now know that God has saved me, just as Saint Francis had promised," he said. And after receiving some instruction in the faith of Christ, those friars baptized the Sultan, and his soul was saved.

[#24 of 53]

CHAPTER 25

Brother Bernard's humility

[ca. 1220]

THE DEVOUT SERVANT OF CHRIST CRUCIFIED, St. Francis, had lost his sight. Nearly blind from all of his severe penances and tears, he set out one day to find Brother Bernard, to speak with his friend. Brother Bernard was adept with words, and Francis loved to talk with him about spiritual things.

When Francis approached the place where Bernard was staying,* he found that Bernard was off in the woods, completely absorbed in prayer and contemplation, united with the Holy One. Francis called his friend, saying, "Come and talk with this blind man!"

Bernard did not answer him or even stir, for his soul was completely lifted up to God at that moment. So Francis called out in the same manner for a second time. And then a third time: "Come and talk with this blind man!"

But Brother Bernard could not hear him at all. So Francis went away with disappointment in his heart, complaining to himself that his brother must not want to speak with him.

While Francis was on his way, returning from where he'd come, he said to the companion at his side, "Wait here for a short minute!" And he dashed over to a quiet and solitary place to pray, begging God to reveal to him why Bernard had ignored his calling out to him.

A voice came to Francis that said, *Why are you troubled, poor little man? Should a man leave me for one of my creatures? When you were calling, Brother Bernard was united with me. Don't fret that he didn't respond to you. He didn't even hear you.*

At this, Francis dashed back to the place where Bernard was, to humbly accuse himself of what he had been thinking about Bernard and his motives.

---

* This may have been the Carceri hermitages, caves where early Franciscans, including Francis on occasion, lived on the slopes of Mount Subasio just outside of Assisi.

Bernard saw Francis coming toward him and ran to greet him, throwing himself down at his feet. Francis quickly made him get up, and he told him what had happened, and ended by saying, "In holy obedience, I ask you to do what I now command of you."

Brother Bernard was wary of this, for Francis was known to be excessive at such moments. So Bernard replied, "I am ready, father, but only if you also promise to also do what I say."

"I agree," Francis said.

"Then say what you want of me, father," Bernard offered.

Francis began: "To punish the presumptions of my heart, I ask you to step on my mouth and my throat three times, while I lie on the ground. And while stepping on me, you should mock me, saying, 'You just lie there, you simple peasant, you son of Peter Bernardone!' And then you must insult me even further, and say, 'Where did you get such pride, since you are worth nothing at all!'"

Now when Brother Bernard heard this, he swallowed hard. But because of holy obedience, he sort of did what was asked of him. But he did it all rather courteously. When Bernard was done, Francis said, "Now, Brother Bernard, order me as you will, because I too have made a promise to obey."

"By like obedience, I ask that you correct me of my faults whenever we are together," Bernard replied.

But Francis marveled at this, for it was difficult for Francis to see many faults in his friend. As a result, from this moment forward, Francis was careful to avoid spending too much time with Brother Bernard, he so wanted to avoid having to point out any faults at all to him. Whenever he desired to speak with Bernard about spiritual things, he was quick to arrive and quick to leave him.

It was always inspiring to watch the affection and love that Francis had for this firstborn son of his. To the praise and glory of Jesus. Amen.

[#3 of 53]

CHAPTER 26

St. Clare joins St. Francis for a meal, and the sisters are relieved!

[c a .   1 2 1 0 – 1 2 2 5]*

S T. FRANCIS OFTEN VISITED ST. CLARE WHEN HE WAS in
Assisi, stopping to talk with her for a while. But after some
time, Clare asked Francis for more than these brief encounters.
She wanted the consolation of joining her friend for a meal.
Several times she asked him if they could eat together, and several
times Francis refused.

After some time, Francis's brothers took note of Clare's desire
and disappointment and said to him, "It seems to us that this
strictness of yours is running counter to divine love. Sister Clare,
who has done so much for the sake of Christ, as a response to
your preaching, asks a simple favor. You should grant it, and then
some!"

"If it seems so to you," Francis replied, "then I will do it.

"But let's have this meal at St. Mary of the Angels, for Clare
has been cloistered at San Damiano for a very long time. She will
like seeing the place where her hair was cut and she was made a
spouse of Christ!"

On the appointed day, Clare arrived at St. Mary of the Angels.
She reverently greeted the Blessed Virgin at the altar, remembering that very place where long before she had taken her vows.
The brothers chatted with her. Francis prepared the table—upon
the floor—which was his custom. And then it was time to eat.

Francis and Clare sat together, and during that first course,
Francis began to speak about God with sensitive holiness and
reverence. It seemed to everyone present—Francis, Clare, Clare's
companion, the brothers—that a rapturous grace surrounded them.

---

* Clare formally joined the Franciscan movement as its first woman on March 18, 1212.
Soon afterward, Francis arranged for San Damiano to become a convent, and Clare lived
there for the rest of her four-plus decades, leaving the grounds rarely and only for a few
hours at a time.

Outside the Portiuncula, it appeared to the people of Assisi and Bettona* that St. Mary's and the entire forest that then surrounded the chapel were aflame. The men of those towns rushed to the place where they thought a fire was blazing, but when they arrived they saw nothing on the outside, no evidence of fire at all. So they went inside, where they found Francis and Clare and the others in deep contemplation. It was at that moment that they knew this had been a heavenly thing.

Later that evening, when everyone inside returned to themselves, they realized how refreshed and nourished they felt beyond all measure. They looked at the table before them and realized that they'd barely touched the food. Clare returned to San Damiano, thankful.

Meanwhile, her sisters were overjoyed to see her. For they had been afraid that Francis might decide to send her to be abbess in some far-off place, as he'd done earlier with their Sister Agnes.

[#15 of 53]

---

* This ancient Umbrian commune is seven miles southwest of Assisi.

CHAPTER 27

The boy who faints when he sees St. Francis talking with Christ

[ca. 1220–1225]

ACERTAIN PURE AND SIMPLE BOY WAS RECEIVED INTO the Order while St. Francis was still alive, and the boy lived among the brothers when because of voluntary poverty they slept on the ground.

One day, Francis arrived in the evening after saying Compline, and wanted to rest before the others so that he could rise to pray again while they slept. He often did this.

The simple boy decided to observe what Francis did and where he went that night, to spy on his holiness. So to insure that he didn't sleep past when Francis awoke, the boy lay down beside Francis, after he fell asleep, and tied the cord of his tunic to that of Francis.

During the night, when the other brothers were fast asleep, Francis woke up and quickly realized that his cord was tied to the lad's. He gently untied it in a way that the boy could not feel his presence. Then, the saint went outside to the forest where he began to pray alone in a small hut. Before too long, the boy woke up on his own and realized what had happened. Francis was gone. So he too quickly rose, in order to go and find the holy father. The boy went out and discovered that the gate toward the forest lay open—so he went in that direction. Soon he found the saint.

The boy approached Francis very slowly. He stood back at a certain distance. But soon, he heard a multitude of voices. He crept slowly closer, and soon he thought he saw a beautiful light surrounding Francis. Within that light the boy saw Jesus Christ, the Blessed Virgin Mary, John the Baptist, the evangelist known as John, and a company of angels, all of them in conversation with Francis. Seeing all of this, the boy trembled and then he fainted, out cold right there on the path from the monastery to the forest.

A little while later, once the mystery and holy conversation was over, while the boy still lay in the middle of the path, Francis nearly stumbled on top of him while walking back to where the brothers were sleeping. He looked on the lad with compassion and took him up in his arms, carrying him back to that place. In the morning, the boy told Francis what he thought he'd seen and Francis said, "Do not tell anyone, at least as long as I live." The boy did as he was told and kept this secret until after the saint's death.

[#17 of 53]

CHAPTER 28

The problem in the vineyard of the parish priest of Rieti

[ca. 1220 – 1225]

O N ONE OF THE OCCASIONS WHEN ST. FRANCIS was suffering because of his eyes, the protector of his order, Cardinal Ugolino, wrote to Francis out of love, telling him to come to Rieti to see a physician. Francis received the letter and went first to San Damiano to see St. Clare, the devout bride of Christ; he wanted to see her before he left for Rieti.

At San Damiano, his eyes became worse. The first night he spent there, he could not see a thing. And so Clare had a cell prepared for him, using reeds and straw, a place where he could be alone and rest. Francis ended up staying there for fifty days in great pain. He was also disturbed by the mice that infested the place. Soon he came to realize that the Lord was punishing him for his past sins. He reached out to God in thankfulness and praise, saying, "I deserve this, Lord, and then some. Good Shepherd, you have shown your mercy in the past; now, help your little lamb have the strength to remain by your side no matter what comes!"

A voice came to Francis from heaven, saying, "Answer me this: If the earth were entirely golden, and the oceans of the earth were balsam, and the mountains were all precious gems, would you still be able to conceive of a treasure more valuable than these? And if that most valuable treasure were given to you as an illness, would you be happy about it?"

"I am not worthy of such a thing," Francis replied.

The voice continued: "Then rejoice, brother, because I am keeping this treasure—it is eternal life—as yours, and your current illness is but a pledge of that gift."

At this word, Francis jumped for joy and called for his companion. "Let's get going to Rieti, to see the cardinal!"

When they were approaching Rieti, a crowd of people wanting to meet him began to gather. They were so numerous that Francis wanted to avoid the city, and so they stopped at a church about two miles outside of town. But soon, the people knew what they had done, and they came there to see the saint camping out in a vineyard nearby that was owned by the priest of the little church. It was grape-harvesting time, and all of the grapes were sure to be ruined under the feet, or eaten by the hands, of those throngs of people. When the priest viewed the damage, he regretted ever allowing Francis to enter his church. These thoughts were revealed to Francis by the Spirit of God.

So Francis asked the priest to come and see him. "Father," he said, "how much wine does your vineyard produce in a good year?"

"Twelve measures," he answered.

"Then please," Francis said, "be patient with these people and allow them to stay. Allow them to take whatever they need. And I promise, for the love of God, that your vineyard will produce twenty measures this year."

The priest listened to this promise of Francis and allowed the people to eat whatever they chose. It was a wonderful sight—the vineyard being stripped and ruined by the throngs, for Francis saw that God was doing great things in the souls of the people. Many of them were going away drunken with love for God, turning away from the things of the world, and discovering more heavenly desires.

When all was done, only a few bunches of grapes were left on the vines. But still, the priest ordered that the remaining grapes be gathered and pressed and, as Francis had said, twenty measures resulted that year.

[#19 of 53]

CHAPTER 29

Three murderous robbers become Franciscan friars

[ca. 1220–1225]

THE BLESSED FRANCIS WAS ALWAYS TRAVELING, seeking to tell men and women of the way to salvation. Everywhere he traveled he was guided by the Holy Spirit, and made new family members. He spread God's grace to Slavonia, the Marches of Trevisi and Ancona, Apulia, the land of the Saracens, and other provinces, making followers of Christ wherever he went.

On one occasion, while he was traveling through Monte Casale,* a young nobleman of great refinement stopped St. Francis in order to speak with him. "Father," he said, "I would like to become one of your followers."

"My son, you are too young, and too noble, for us. Would you truly be able to endure a life of poverty and difficulty?" Francis replied.

"You are men just like me," the noble young man said. "What you can endure, I can endure."

Francis liked this answer very much, and named him Brother Angelo, and within a short amount of time Angelo was made guardian† of the region of Monte Casale by St. Francis.

Now in this time there were three infamous robbers roaming the countryside, and one day they came to where the friars of Monte Casale were residing. They asked Brother Angelo to feed them, and Angelo answered angrily, "You not only rob and murder, but you want to take what has been donated for feeding God's servants! You don't even deserve to be alive! Go somewhere else to insult the God who created you! Don't come back here!"

They went away, but they were furious.

---

* A mountainous region in Sicily.

† Franciscans have always used the name "guardian" to refer to what other orders refer to as abbots or superiors.

Later that same day, Francis returned to Monte Casale, carrying bread and wine that he had begged along the way. When he arrived, Angelo told him what had happened and how he had successfully driven away the three infamous men. But Francis scolded Angelo.

"You acted cruelly. Sinners will come back to their God by humility, not by scolding. Christ tells us that those who are well do not need a physician, but those who are sick do.

"You acted uncharitably," he continued. "For that, I command you to take this bread and wine and find those three men somewhere in these mountains. Offer it to them. Kneel before them and ask their forgiveness. Then ask them—using my name—to stop doing what they have been doing, to fear the Lord, and no longer harm their neighbors. If they will do this, promise them that we will give them the food and drink that they need, always. Then come back here to me."

Angelo went out to do what he had been commanded by Francis. And Francis prayed earnestly that it would succeed and that God would soften those robbers' hearts.

Before too long, Angelo found the men, gave them the provisions, and told them all that Francis had instructed him to say. The men accepted the gifts and while they were eating, began to talk to one another.

"You know, terrible things await us in hell," one said. "We don't fear men or God and probably have no conscience left at all. And look at this holy friar," he continued, "who brought us food and wine, a promise from his holy father, and all because of a few words that he said to us about our wickedness."

"You're right," the other two said, "but so what?"

The first man spoke again. "Let's go and see St. Francis. If he gives us hope and tells us that God's mercy is possible even for us, than let's do what he says and free our souls from certain hell." The others agreed, and they all left hastily.

When they arrived, they said to Francis, "Father, we don't believe that we can ever receive God's mercy, but if you think it's possible, we're ready to do penance and obey you in whatever you command."

Francis welcomed them with open arms and love. He told them the truth: that God would show his mercy to them, and that Jesus Christ came into the world in order to redeem sinners just like them. As a result, these three robbers renounced their evil and the world and he opened the Franciscan Order to them. For their part, the men began their great penance.

Before long, two of the robbers died and went to heaven, while the third man lived for fifteen more years, doing penance all the while. He kept the usual forty-day fasts that the other friars did, plus he ate only bread and water three days every week. He never owned more than one habit, he walked about barefoot, and he never went to bed after Matins.* During those fifteen years, St. Francis also transitioned from this world to the next.

Then one night, temptation came to the friar who remained. He was tempted to fall asleep after the Matins prayers had ended. He resisted and resisted until finally he could no longer and yielded to temptation. The friar lay down to sleep. That moment—as his head touched the pillow—he began to dream.

He was led up to a mountaintop that looked down on a deep valley. There were jagged rocks on both sides, and he was frightened as he glanced downward. The angel that accompanied him to the mountain suddenly then pushed him over the edge, and he fell headlong into the ravine, his body ricocheting off the rocks and ledges until he struck the bottom floor. As he lay there, he was certain that his bones and limbs were shattered to pieces. At that moment, the angel called down to him, "Get up! You still have a long journey!"

"You are cruel," the friar responded, "for can't you see that I am in pieces?"

So the angel came down to him and touched him. At that moment, the friar was healed. He was one piece again.

Then the angel pointed the direction where the friar must continue on his journey—through a field of thorns, briars, and swamp. He told the friar that he must walk barefoot until he

---

* Matins is the name for the first prayer time of the day. It was usually scheduled for the hour before the sun's rising.

reached a fiery furnace, and then, he must climb in. The friar soon reached the furnace, and there, the angel reminded him that he must climb in. Surrounding that furnace were devils with threatening pitchforks if he didn't. So he jumped in.

Once inside the furnace, the friar saw before him his old godfather. "How did you get in here?" he asked.

"Go a little farther inside and you will also see your godmother," the man replied. The friar went in farther, and he saw his godmother, also all aflame.

"Why are you undergoing such cruel torment?" he pleaded with her.

She answered him, "It happened when St. Francis foretold that famine was coming, and my husband and I lied about the measure of the grain that we sold. As a result, we're burning, here and now." The angel listened to all of this and then thrust the friar out of the furnace.

"Move on," he said. "You still have perils to experience."

"You are cruel," the friar repeated to the angel. But at that, the angel touched him once more and made him feel strong and well all over again.

Next, the angel led the friar to a narrow, slippery bridge without handrails that crossed a treacherous river. The roaring waters below were filled with scorpions and dragons, and the angel said, "Get going. You must cross."

"How can I?" the friar cried.

"Follow me, and you will," the angel replied. At this, the friar followed the angel onto the bridge and into the middle of it. But at that moment, the angel flew away and the friar remained alone on the bridge, looking down at the frightening beasts below. He was so frightened that he couldn't move. The friar cried out to Jesus for help, weeping, asking to be saved from this.

At that moment, the friar felt wings growing upon his body. He paused a few moments to wait until they were sufficient for him to fly as the angel had done. But he couldn't wait long enough and his fear overtook him; the friar tried taking to the air with his stubble wings but then fell back down, striking the bridge, clinging to it for his very life.

Again the wings seemed to grow, but slowly, and again he tried to fly, but his wings were insufficient, and he fell back onto the bridge. "If these wings begin to grow again, I will wait for them," the friar said.

Then a third time the wings grew. It seemed to the friar that 150 years went by while he waited there upon that bridge waiting for those wings to come in fully. And when they did, he was finally able to fly up to the palace where the angel had first gone. He reached the palace gate and the keeper asked of him, "Who are you and why are you here?"

"I am a Friar Minor."

"Well, wait here for a moment," the gatekeeper said, "and I will bring St. Francis to see if he recognizes you." And as the keeper went away, the friar looked around him at the beauty of the place. He saw whole choirs of angels, and saints besides. While he looked around, there appeared not only Francis, adorned with five star-like wounds of the stigmata, but also Brother Bernard, wearing a crown of stars, and Brother Giles, shining with light, and many other men and women.

"Let him come," Francis said to the gatekeeper, "for he is a friar." And he led the friar into the palace and the friar suddenly felt all sweetness and forgot all of his tribulations. Once he'd seen all of the beauties of that place, Francis said to him, "Now, my son, you have to return to the world for another seven days. While you are there, prepare yourself, and soon I will come for you again." The last thing he remembered was how disappointed he felt at having to leave the presence of those blessed ones.

Then, the friar woke up. He recovered his consciousness just at the moment that the bell was ringing for Prime.* It seemed that years had gone by during his dream, but it turned out that it was only the time from Matins until dawn.

The friar told his guardian all about his dream, and about the seven-day period that St. Francis had told him about. Then the friar came down with a fever. And seven days later, Francis came to get him with a throng of saints. To the praise and glory of God. Amen. [#26 of 53]

---

* Prime is known as the first liturgical "hour" of daily prayer, usually beginning at 6 AM, or dawn.

CHAPTER 30

The source of joy, or, St. Francis and Brother Leo

walking in the freezing rain

[ca. 1221–AUGUST 1224][*]

S T. FRANCIS WAS OUT WALKING ONE WINTER'S DAY with Brother Leo, from Perugia to St. Mary of the Angels. The air was bitterly cold.

Francis called out to Leo, who was walking a distance ahead of him, "Brother, even if the Friars Minor in every country are an example of holiness and integrity to the world, there is no real joy in that." Leo said nothing, but only kept walking.

They went on a bit farther and then Francis called out to Leo again, saying, "Brother, if a Friar Minor can help the blind to see, the paralyzed to walk, the possessed to drive out their devils, the deaf to hear, the lame to walk, the dumb to speak—even the dead to rise again after four days; you should write this down: the source of joy isn't in any of that, either."

They walked on further. Leo said nothing.

Francis called out to him yet again, saying, "Brother, if a friar knows all the languages and sciences and scriptures in the world, and if he knows how to prophesy, as well as the consciences of others—write this down: there's no joy in that!"

Leo kept going. They kept walking along as they were, with Leo ahead of Francis. Francis had to call out even louder than before: "Brother! God's little sheep! If a friar can speak with the tongues of angels, and knows the courses of the stars, and the power of herbs to cure, and every treasure of knowledge in the world including about birds and fish and animals and humans and roots and stones and waters—write it down, brother: the source of joy isn't there!"

---

* St. Francis and Brother Leo were frequent companions in Francis's last half-decade. Leo was even Francis's confessor. The events of this story likely happened before August 1224, because after that the narrative of Francis's life is dominated by the stigmata and his failing health.

Still they kept walking and one more time Francis called out: "Brother, if a friar preaches in a way that converts all of the infidels to faith in Christ, even that is not the source of joy."

That was enough. After two miles of this, Brother Leo spun around in frustration.

"In God's name, father, please, tell me, where then is the source of joy to be found?!"

"When we arrive at St. Mary's," Francis began, "and we're soaked by the rain and chilled to the bone, completely drenched with mud and so very hungry, and we ring at the gate and the brother on duty comes to the gate and says, 'Who are you?' We will say, 'We are your brothers.' But if he argues with us and says, 'You aren't telling me the truth. I don't trust you. You might steal from us. Go away!' then he won't open the gate and we'll have to stand outside in the freezing snow and cold until night falls.

"Then, if we have to endure more insults there, and show patience and humility and charity to that brother porter—whom God has made to say what he might say, just to test us—write it down, brother: that's the source of our joy!"

Francis continued. "We may then continue to knock on the gate, and that brother will be angry now, and send us away with curses as well as blows. He might say, 'Get away from here! Who do you think you are, trying to come in here?!' If we bear all of this with patience and receive his insults with joy and charity in our hearts—write this down too, brother: that is the source of joy!

"For we bear all of this inasmuch as we bear the sufferings of Jesus Christ. We bear it all because we love him."

[#8 of 53]

CHAPTER 31

St. Francis and Brother Leo have trouble praying together

[ca. 1221–AUGUST 1224]

S T. FRANCIS WAS OUT WALKING ONE DAY WITH Brother Leo, his closest friend and companion, when it came time to pray the Divine Office. It was in the earliest days of Francis's new movement, when the brothers lived in the utmost simplicity; for this reason, and given their remote location, Francis and Leo had no books at hand when the hour for morning prayer had come.

Francis said to Leo: "Since we do not have a prayer book with us, but it is still important that we spend time praising God, let us create something new.

"I will speak and you will answer, as I teach you.

"I will say 'O Brother Francis, you have done so many sins and evils in this world. You are deserving of hell.'

"And you, Leo, will respond, 'So it is, Francis, you deserve the lowest depths of hell.'"

Brother Leo nodded that he understood and gave Francis assurances of his perfect obedience. "Let us begin, father," he agreed.

And so Francis began the new liturgy. He said, "You have done so many sins and evils in this world, Brother Francis, that you are deserving of hell."

"But God will work through you so much good," Leo replied earnestly, "that surely you will go to paradise."

"No, no, no," Francis said, "that is not right. When I say my part, you must say as I have instructed you, repeating, 'You are worthy only to be set among the cursed in the depths of hell.'"

Again, in obedience, Brother Leo replied, "Willingly, father. I will do it."

This time, Francis paused and painfully considered his words. After a few moments, with tears in his eyes and while pounding his heart, Francis said in a much louder voice: "O Lord of heaven and earth, I have done so much evil and so many sins in this world that I am worthy only to be cursed by you!"

And Leo quickly replied in turn: "O Brother Francis, God will do great things for you and you will be blessed above all others!"

Francis was perplexed and more than a little bit angry.

"Why do you disobey me, Brother Leo? You are to repeat as I have instructed you!"

"God knows, father," Leo answered, "that each time I set my mind to do as you say, God then makes me say what pleases him."

How could Francis argue with this? He marveled at Leo's words, searching them for the divine purpose. Nevertheless, after some time, Francis quietly said, "I pray most lovingly that you will answer me this time as I have asked you to do." Leo agreed to try, but try as he might, again and again, he could not do as Francis wished.

Time after time, into the night, past Compline and throughout the early hours of the morning, the entreaties of Francis grew ever more passionate as Leo's joy grew ever larger. Their prayers never did match, and they never did agree, praying responsively as Francis had hoped.

[#9 of 53]

CHAPTER 32

———

Two scholars in Bologna become Franciscan friars

[c a . 1 2 2 3 – 1 2 3 2]*

O NE DAY, ST. FRANCIS ARRIVED IN THE CITY OF Bologna, and when people began to hear of his arrival, they hurried to catch a glimpse of him. Soon there was a large crowd—so large, in fact, that Francis could hardly get through it to the city square.

In the square, which was filled with men, women, and students, Francis stood up on a high spot and began to preach as the Holy Spirit told him what to say. His words were so marvelous that people thought he might be an angel. Those words were like arrows piercing the hearts of those who heard them, and Francis converted many people from sin to penitence that day.

Among those that day who were inspired by God through Francis's sermon were two highborn students that had come from the Marches of Ancona. One was named Pellegrino, from Falerone, and the other went by the name Riccieri, from Muccia. Francis knew them already, for the Holy Spirit had revealed it to him, so Francis welcomed them joyfully. "Pellegrino, you will remain in a humble position in our order. And Riccieri, you will serve the other friars," Francis told them.

And so it was that Brother Pellegrino remained a lay brother, even though he'd already been a scholar, but he said that he didn't wish to become a priest. This humility served him well and Pellegrino grew in perfection and virtue and by God's grace in love for Jesus Christ.

So on fire was Pellegrino for Christ that he soon traveled to Jerusalem so that he could see firsthand the places where the Savior had walked. He took with him a book of the Gospels and read about the holy places as he traced where the God-man

---

* Pellegrino's death is mentioned in this story, and he didn't die until March 1232. Riccieri died two years later, so it is likely that this story was first written down in 1233.

had walked, touching them with his own feet, embracing those holy steps with his arms, kissing them with his lips, and wetting them with his tears.* Pellegrino inspired devotion in anyone who watched him. Then, by God's will, he returned to Italy.

As a pilgrim for God and a citizen of heaven, Pellegrino rarely visited his wealthy family anymore. Instead he encouraged them to love God and despise the things of the world. Brother Bernard—the one who had been Father Francis's firstborn spiritual son—would say that Brother Pellegrino was one of the most ideal friars in all the world. Above all, he was a pilgrim, and he never allowed himself to find peace or comfort in creaturely or temporal things. Instead he was always looking toward heavenly things and pursuing virtue and love. When he passed from this life to Christ, he was full of virtue, and miracles followed him.

Meanwhile, Brother Pellegrino's companion Brother Riccieri led an active life of service, humility, and holiness. He became a close friend of St. Francis and learned many things from him. And just as Francis had foreseen, he served the other friars, becoming minister of the province of the Marches of Ancona. There he governed with wisdom for many years, following the example of Jesus Christ, who always wanted to see action more than teaching.

On one occasion, God's will allowed a temptation to surround him. Riccieri was soon consumed with this trouble and tried to overcome it with severe spiritual disciplines and prayers and weeping all night long. He couldn't shake free from the temptation. He felt that he had been abandoned by God, since relief did not come easily. He said quietly to himself, "I will go and see Father Francis, and if he welcomes me as he usually does, then I will know that God still loves me. If he does not, I am lost."

At this time, Francis was lying ill in the bishop's residence in Assisi. There, before Riccieri came to see him, God revealed to him what was happening. Francis called for his friends, Brothers Masseo and Leo.

---

* This is likely referring to the path of Christ known as the *Via Dolorosa* (Latin for "Way of Suffering") that has been established since the days of the Emperor Hadrian, tracing the steps that Jesus walked through Old Jerusalem on his way to Calvary.

"Go quickly and find Brother Riccieri. Hug him and tell him that I have a special affection for him that is different from what I feel for any other friar in the world," Francis said. And obediently, Masseo and Leo did as Francis requested. Upon receiving such a loving greeting, Riccieri's soul welled up with joy, and his heart overflowed with happiness. He proceeded to the bishop's residence and found Francis there.

Despite his serious illness, Francis got up upon seeing Brother Riccieri, and hugged him. "My dear son, I have a special affection for you that is different from what I feel for any other friar in the world," Francis told him. And he made the sign of the cross on Riccieri's forehead, and then kissed him there as well. Then he said, "God gave you that temptation, but God can also take it from you." And as he said those words, the temptation dropped off that friar as though it had never meant a thing. All that was left was the complete love of God.

[#27 of 53]

CHAPTER 33

———

St. Francis interprets a vision of Brother Leo

[1 2 2 4 – 1 2 2 6]

WHEN ST. FRANCIS WAS QUITE ILL, BROTHER LEO would take care of him with beautiful devotion. On one such occasion, when Leo was near Francis but engaged himself deeply in prayer, he became caught up in ecstasy of the Spirit and he saw a vision of a wide, teeming river.

Leo was watching people cross this river. He saw many friars go by, each carrying a load on his back. Some of the friars walked across the river one third of the way; others walked halfway; and others made it almost all the way to the other side—but then Leo watched as a strong current of water pulled all of them underwater and carried them rapidly away. All of them died a violent death in the river, crushed by the waters because they were burdened by the loads they carried on their backs into the river. Brother Leo felt deeply saddened as he saw this tragedy unfold in his vision.

But then suddenly, he saw more friars, and they had no loads to burden them. He saw that they had only poverty, and it made them shine. These friars crossed the river without any problem at all, and once Leo watched this, he woke up from his dream.

St. Francis could sense that Leo had seen a vision, and he asked him, "Describe to me what you've seen." Leo did, telling him everything.

"It was a true vision," Francis replied, "for the world is that river, and the friars who were consumed by it are the ones who no longer desire to follow the Gospel in perfect poverty. But the friars who crossed the river without harm are those who want to possess nothing of this world, nothing but Christ naked on the cross. They take the joyful burden of that cross, and that cross alone, into the world, and in obedience to Christ they pass sweetly and easily."

[#36 of 53]

CHAPTER 34

How St. Francis knew that Brother Elias would leave the Order

[ca. 1225–APRIL 22, 1253]

ST. FRANCIS AND BROTHER ELIAS WERE STAYING together in Portiuncula when it was revealed to Francis that Elias would soon be damned, leave the Franciscan Order, and die alone. This caused Francis to pull away from the friar, to avoid speaking or eating with him, and to turn away when he saw Elias coming his way. Soon, Elias began to notice that Francis would do these things and he desired to know why. Approaching Francis one day, Francis turned aside, and Elias grabbed him to stop him from pulling away, pleading with him to say why he was avoiding him.

"It's been shown to me," Francis replied, "that you will leave our Order because of your sins and that you will die alone."

Brother Elias began to weep and threw himself on the ground at Francis's feet. "Dearest father, please, by the love of Christ, do not avoid me on account of this, but help me like a good shepherd helps his sheep!" Elias pleaded. "I beg you to pray to God on my account, so that God will remember me when I come to my end, and have mercy upon me!" Elias said this with devotion and tearfulness, and Francis was deeply moved.

So Francis prayed to God, and while he was in prayer, he was given an answer that his request had been granted and that the sentence upon Elias would be revoked in his last days. Elias wouldn't suffer damnation after all, even though he would surely leave the Order and die outside of it. That is indeed what occurred.

When King Frederick of Sicily* rebelled against the Church, the pope excommunicated him and all who were aiding him, which

---

* When Pope Gregory IX excommunicated Emperor Frederick II (1194–1250), he called him the antichrist. Pope Innocent IV, following Gregory IX, also battled with and freshly excommunicated Frederick, calling him a heretic and a "friend of Babylon," among other things.

included Brother Elias. Elias was known then as one of the world's wisest souls, and had rebelled against both Church and his Order by going over to the other side. He too was excommunicated by the pope and stripped of his Franciscan habit.

At about that same time, Elias became very ill. When his biological brother (who was also in the Order, and remained there, in good standing) heard of Elias's sickness, he went to see him. "Brother, I am so sorry that you have been excommunicated and could die outside of the Order. Can you see a way that I might help you?" his brother asked him.

"I don't know what you could do other than go to the pope on my behalf," Elias responded. "Ask him if, for the love of Christ and of St. Francis, whom I was once devoted to, to consider lifting my excommunication and restoring me to good standing."

"For your sake, I will do whatever I can for your salvation," his brother said. And leaving his side, the brother traveled to the pope and humbly asked for mercy for his brother.

So it happened that, by the assistance of the prayers of St. Francis, when his brother asked, the pope granted this request, telling the brother that if when he returned to Elias's side, Elias was still alive, he may absolve the excommunication and restore to Elias his habit.

Elias's brother hurried from the papal court back to Elias to bring him this news. When he arrived, he found Elias very near death, but still breathing, and he absolved him. Thus it was that Brother Elias put his habit back on, received the final sacrament of the Church, and died in peace.* He had placed faith in the prayers of St. Francis, and it is believed that those prayers were what brought him his final graces.

[#38 of 53]

---

* Many of the tales show marks of multiple authorship over a period of time, such as this one, which begins by declaring that Elias would die outside of the Order but then concludes by saying that his habit was restored to him.

CHAPTER 35

When St. Anthony preaches to the fish in the sea

[1 2 2 5 – 1 2 3 0]

OUR LORD JESUS CHRIST USED THE MOST FOOLISH of all creatures—fish—to rebuke the world for its foolish ignorance, just as he had once used the ass of Balaam in the Old Testament.* In the process, Christ showed people that they should listen to St. Anthony's beautiful preaching and teaching.

St. Anthony was in Rimini, a place with many heretics, desiring to show them the way back to true faith, and he preached Christ and Holy Scripture to them for several days in a row. But the people were hard of heart and refused to listen. Then one day, by God's inspiration, Anthony traveled to the mouth of the river at Rimini and stood on the bank overlooking the sea.† He started calling to the fish in God's name, preaching to them, "You, fish of the waters, listen to God's word—for the heretics refuse!" And when he said this, a huge gathering of fish rose up before his eyes and near the bank where he stood. They stuck their heads out of the water and looked carefully toward Anthony. In a field of color and like an army readying for battle, schools of fish, large and small, situated themselves to see Anthony's face and to listen to his sermon. They were a packed crowd, looking like a horde of pilgrims heading for an indulgence, before the holy father. There, they listened with humility to what Anthony had to say.

"My fish brothers," St. Anthony said, "give thanks to God your creator, the one who gave you all that you need, whether fresh or salt water. He also gives you refuge from storms, an easy mode of travel, and the food that you need to live. When God first created you, he said, be fruitful and multiply, and he blessed you. During the Flood, as other animals died, you were saved by God completely.

---

* See Numbers chapter 22.

† Rimini is located on the eastern shore of Italy near where two major rivers, the Marecchia and the Ausa, empty into the Adriatic Sea.

"You are able to go wherever you please with your powerful fins. It was you who kept the prophet Jonah alive, and then threw him up onto dry land three days later. It was you who helped Our Lord Jesus to pay the tax when he was poor and had nothing.* It was you whom our King Jesus selected for food both before his resurrection and in a mysterious way, following it.† Because of all of this, you should praise God, who has blessed you more abundantly than other creatures."

Hearing all of this, the fish all nodded their heads, and some opened their mouths, praising God as best they could.

"Blessed be God! Fish in the water give God more glory than heretical people! So-called irrational creatures listen more intently to God's word than people without faith!" Anthony cried.

People began to hear of this miracle, as it was happening, and they soon came running to see. When they saw the actions of the fish, even the heretics felt sorry. They sat there and listened, too, to the words of St. Anthony, who kept on preaching. His words about the Catholic faith were beautiful that day, and by them all of the heretics came back to true belief in Christ and those who were already faithful were blessed and filled with joyfulness.

When it was all over, Anthony blessed the fish before they swam away. And when they left, they were expressing their own joy with games in the sea.

[#40 of 53]

---

* This reference is from Matthew 17:24–27. Collectors of the temple tax ask Peter why his teacher (Jesus) does not pay. Jesus instructs Peter, saying, "Go to the lake and cast a hook; take the first fish that comes up; and when you open its mouth, you will find a coin; take that and give it to them for you and me."

† For "and in a mysterious way, following it," see John 21:1–14.

CHAPTER 36

St. Anthony of Padua preaches a sermon
that every language can understand

[1 2 2 8 – 1 2 3 0]

S T. ANTHONY OF PADUA WAS THE CHOSEN COMPANION of
St. Francis whom Francis sometimes called his "bishop."

On one occasion this vessel of the Holy Spirit was preaching
before the pope and his cardinals, who represented many different lands speaking many different tongues: Greek, Latin, French,
German, Slavic, and English. On fire with God's Holy Spirit like
one of the first apostles, Anthony preached so effectively and
clearly that every man present understood his words as if they'd
been spoken in his own language. They were all amazed. It seemed
that the original miracle of the Pentecost had just been repeated
before their eyes and ears.

"Isn't he a Spaniard?" one of them asked another.

"How can we possibly hear him in our own Greek, Latin,
French, German, Slavic, and English? We are from so many different lands!"

Even the pope was amazed at this, as well as at Anthony's deep
knowledge of Holy Scripture. "He is the Ark of the Covenant—a
treasury of Holy Scripture!" the pope said.

Such was the nature of those companions of St. Francis who
were like soldiers with heavenly weapons, bringing sustenance
with the essence of the Holy Spirit, protecting Christ's flock
against traps set by the enemy.* Even the Vicar of Christ was one
such as these, to the glory of our Lord, Jesus. Amen.

[#39 of 53]

---

* Another instance of multiple authors/editors: three metaphors in one sentence! In the
sentence that follows, the reference is to Pope Gregory IX, a friend and follower of St.
Francis. Gregory IX became supreme pontiff less than six months after St. Francis's death.
He was pope from 1227 to 1241.

CHAPTER 37

_____

The beautiful death of St. Francis and Brother Bernard

[SEPTEMBER 1226 and ca. 1242]

BROTHER BERNARD WAS A MAN OF TRUE HOLINESS, so much so that St. Francis praised him often. One day while Francis was devoutly at prayer, God revealed to him that Bernard was going to endure many attacks by the devil. This troubled Francis like a father who worries for his son, and Francis prayed to God for days, with many tears, asking Christ Jesus for victory over the devil in this thing.

One day, while Francis was praying fervently thus to God, God said to him, *Don't be afraid, Francis, for these temptations will not happen without my permission, and will be an exercise in virtue for Bernard. In the end, he will be victorious over them all, for Bernard is already a great one in my kingdom.*

This gave Francis great joy, and he gave thanks to Jesus for it. From that moment forward, Francis held no more reservations about the trials to come for his friend, and he held his friend in even greater esteem and love.

Francis showed this love for Bernard during his lifetime, but also on his deathbed. When Francis was dying, in the way that the patriarch Jacob had died—with his sons all around him, grieving for their departing father—he asked, "Where is my firstborn? Come to me, son, so that I may bless you before I go."

At Francis's words, Brother Bernard whispered in Brother Elias's ear (for Elias was his vicar), "Father, please go to the saint's right hand. He wants to bless you." Now, Francis had lost most of his sight by this time. Elias came close to Francis, who put his right hand on Elias's head and said, "This is not the head of my firstborn, Bernard."

Then Bernard moved to Francis's other side, to where his left hand lay. Francis crossed his arms, so as to place his right hand on the head of Bernard and his left on Elias, and said, "God the

Father and our Lord Jesus Christ bless you in every way. You are the firstborn, chosen in this Order to be a holy example and to follow Jesus in Gospel poverty. Not only did you give away all that you had, but you offered yourself completely and sweetly to God. You are blessed by our Lord and by me, his poor little one. Bless your walking, your standing still, your watching, your resting, your living, and your dying.

"Anyone who blesses you will himself be blessed, and any who curse you will not go unpunished. You are now to be the head of all the brothers. Let them follow your instructions. You have the power to admit and to release any and all from the ranks. No other friar is to lord over you, and you are free to reside wherever you may wish."

Then Francis died. And after his death, the brothers revered Brother Bernard as their father. When Bernard himself was close to death, a multitude of friars came from all over the world, including the holy one, Brother Giles. When Giles beheld Bernard, he cried out with joy, "*Sursum corda*, Brother Bernard, *sursum corda!*"*

(Bernard had quietly told one of the other brothers to prepare a special place where Brother Giles might go to be in contemplation. This had been done.) Then, when Bernard came to the last hour, he raised himself up and said to his brothers, "Most dear friends, I won't say too much. But please, consider yourselves as you see me, now. This I know in my soul: not for even a thousand worlds would I have turned away from the service of our Lord Jesus Christ.

"Here and now, I confess all my sins—to Jesus my Savior, and to you. I beg you all: love each other." And after he said this, Bernard lay back in his bed and his face shown with joyfulness. The friars marveled at him again; and in that joy Bernard departed this life and left to join with the angels.

[#6 of 53]

---

* *Sursum corda* is Latin for "Lift up your hearts." Since ancient days, it has been part of the preface to the Eucharistic prayer.

CHAPTER 38

How St. Clare blesses bread to be broken at table with the pope

[1228 OR 1235]

ST. CLARE WAS ST. FRANCIS'S *PIANTICELLA*, HIS "little plant," and was such a fervent follower of Christ and his cross that bishops and cardinals and even the pope wanted to see and talk with her. They all visited her, and often, in person.

On one occasion, the pope himself—knowing that Clare was a vessel of the Holy Spirit—traveled to her monastery in order to talk and listen with her about heavenly matters. They talked for a long time about salvation and praising God, and while they were talking, Clare ordered some loaves of bread. She asked that they be brought and set out on the table so that Christ's vicar might bless them.

When Clare and the pope were done talking, Clare knelt before the Holy Pontiff and asked him if he would bless the loaves. The pope said, "Faithful sister Clare, you will please bless them and make the sign of the cross over them, in honor of the one to whom you have dedicated your whole life."

"Holy Father, I cannot," she replied, "for I am a small and sinful woman who would never presume to do such a thing in the presence of Christ's own vicar."

"Don't think of it as presumption," he said, "but obedience, for I command you to bless these loaves in this way." And so, obediently, Clare devoutly made the sign of the cross over the bread, blessing them. At that moment something amazing occurred: a clearly visible cross appeared marked on the surface of each of the loaves. When the pope saw this miracle, he thanked God, and then after blessing St. Clare, he took some of the bread with him as he left.

From that moment on, St. Francis would send people with illnesses to Clare and her sisters, for it was clear that their prayers and blessings, by virtue of the cross, would restore health to God's glory. Amen.

[#33 of 53]

---

* Pope Gregory IX (1227–1241).

CHAPTER 39

*St. Francis appears in a vision to a friar
thinking of leaving the Order*

[1231]

A DELICATE, NOBLE YOUTH ONCE ENTERED THE ORDER of
St. Francis, and within days of taking its habit, he began to
despise it. He felt like a man wearing a sack. The sleeves were
wrong, the cowl not to his liking, and the habit was too rough and
too long. It was all unbearable to this boy of gentle upbringing.
He was quickly despising the Order itself, thinking of returning
to the world, because of his disdain for the clothing.

His novice master at the time had taught the youth how to kneel
reverently, when passing before the altar in the friary where the
Blessed Sacrament was stored, uncovering his head and crossing his
hands upon his chest. The boy always did this carefully. And so it
was that on the very night when the youth had decided to leave the
Order, he had to pass through the friary past the altar where the
Blessed Sacrament was stored. As before, he paused to kneel and
bow—and at that moment he was taken up in spirit and a vision of
God was revealed to him.

The boy saw before him a long line of saints, walking in pairs,
dressed in beautiful vestments, their faces and hands shining like
the sun. As they marched before his eyes, they sang, and angels
chanted, adding to the joy. Among those marching saints were
two that stood out more than all of the others; there were two
that shone most brilliantly of all. The boy watched this magical
procession, and when it had passed, he ran up to the saints at the
end of the line and inquired, "Please, tell me who are all of these
beautiful people?"

They turned to him and replied, "We are all Friars Minor in
paradise."

"And who are those two who I saw shining most of all?" the boy
asked.

"That was St. Francis; and with him, the last was St. Anthony, who has just died. He fought like a knight against temptation, enduring until the very end. We are all leading him in glory through paradise.

"These garments that you see us wearing were given to us by God to replace the habits that we wore on earth. And the radiance of our countenance is also God's gift to us, to replace the humility, poverty, obedience, and chastity with which we conducted ourselves in our religious lives. Keep this in mind, son," the saint said, "for if you despise the world now, you will shine in heavenly glory."

With that the vision was ended, and the youth had heard the divine words. He went away encouraged in his vocation and repented to the guardian of the friars for his prior presumptions. From that day forward, this young man accepted rough penance, and by doing so, he became a good man.

[#20 of 53]

CHAPTER 40

When the king of France goes in disguise to see Brother Giles

[1240–1260]

ST. LOUIS, THE KING OF FRANCE, ONCE DECIDED TO go on pilgrimage to see the shrines of the world.* Having heard of the saintliness of Brother Giles, one of the first companions of St. Francis, he decided to visit him personally in Perugia. When he arrived at the friars' gate, with only a few companions, he was dressed as a common pilgrim. He asked the porter if Brother Giles was at home, not saying who he was. So the friar went and found Giles and told him only that a simple pilgrim was looking for him.

Brother Giles knew instantly, through spiritual perception, that it was the king of France who was calling. So he bounded from his cell and ran toward the porter's gate. Once he arrived, he did not say a word but grabbed the pilgrim and hugged him, kissing him, as if the two were long-lost friends. There they remained in silence for some time. Only after a while did they leave one another, and even then, never having spoken a word. St. Louis went along on his journey, and Giles returned to his cell.

Now while the king was in the process of departing, one of the friars asked one of the king's companions who that man was who had just hugged Brother Giles so lovingly. The king's companion answered that it was King Louis IX stopping on his pilgrimage. Then the companion, the king, and the others who were with them, rode away.

The friars went to Brother Giles to complain. "Brother, how could you say nothing at all to the great king who came all this way from France to see you?!" they exclaimed.

"Brothers, don't be so surprised," Giles said, "that neither of us could speak in those moments. God's light revealed who he was

---

* This is the only French monarch in history to be made a saint of the Roman Catholic Church: St. Louis IX (1214–70). While on the throne, he was known to wash the feet of the poor and invite the destitute to dine at his royal table. He was considered a saint throughout the Western world before he died.

to me, and who I was to him, and it was by that light that we saw into each other's hearts.* We heard what we needed to hear without the movement of lips or tongues. Human voices cannot always speak of divine mysteries. Sometimes human conversation is a sad excuse for true communication."

[#34 of 53]

---

* The fame of Brother Giles is mentioned also by Salimbene of Parma (1221–ca. 1290), a thirteenth-century historian.

CHAPTER 41

How St. Clare miraculously travels across
the city on Christmas Eve[*]

[CHRISTMAS 1252]

THERE WAS A TIME WHEN ST. CLARE WAS SO SERIOUSLY
ill at San Damiano that she was unable to get up to say the
Divine Office in church with her sister nuns. It happened to be
the Feast of the Holy Nativity of Our Lord, and the sisters were
to say Matins and then receive Holy Communion at a Nativity
Mass. Clare remained behind in bed, sick, and sad.

But Jesus wanted his faithful spouse to be consoled, and so he
performed a miracle. In spirit, Clare was carried to Matins and
Mass at the church of St. Francis; she enjoyed the entire celebration as done by the friars so that she even heard the organ playing
and the friars' chanting. She received Holy Communion and was
completely consoled. Then, Jesus carried her back to her bed.

The sisters, when they had finished the Divine Office at San
Damiano, returned to see Clare. They said, "Dear mother, Clare,
what beautiful consolation this Feast of the Nativity has been! We
so wish that you could have joined us!"

"My sisters," Clare began, "I thank God, my blessed Jesus
Christ, because I was fully consoled and permitted to attend holy
ceremonies this special night of all nights. In fact, the celebration
that I attended was greater, even, than the one that you have just
come from. By Christ, and through the intercession of St. Francis,
I was there in Francis's church, hearing everything, and receiving
our Lord.

"So praise God with me," she concluded, "who took me there
himself. Whether I was there as you see me now, or in spirit alone,
I don't know. Only God knows."

[#35 of 53]

---

[*] In 1958, during the initial explosion of popularity of the new technology of television,
St. Clare was made its patron saint because of this legend. It was as if she saw the whole
thing on TV!

PART II
STORIES OF FRIARS
FROM THE PROVINCE OF THE MARCHES

CHAPTER 42

When Brother Pacifico saw the soul of his humble
brother flying to heaven

[1230–1250]

I N THE PROVINCE OF THE MARCHES AFTER ST. FRANCIS had
died, there were two brothers who were together in the Order:
Brother Humble and Brother Pacifico.* They were both great in
holiness.

Brother Humble lived at Soffiano,† a long way from where Brother
Pacifico lived in a community of friars. One day, while praying,
Pacifico was touched by the hand of God and he saw his brother's
soul flying directly to heaven. Brother Humble had died.

Years later, Brother Pacifico was himself living at Soffiano, where his
brother had died, when a request came from the house of Brunforte for
the friars to leave Soffiano and move to another place.‡ The friars
needed to move the remains of all of their brothers who had died
in that place, and it was given to Brother Pacifico to transfer the
bones of his brother, Humble. He gathered up the bones reverently and bathed them in wine, wrapped them in a white cloth,
and wept and kissed them. This shocked the other friars. They
looked on him as one who was putting too much care into worldly

---

* Every translator of *The Little Flowers* makes decisions as to when to retain the Italian,
for flavor, and when to render Italian names and words into English for sense and
understanding. This is a case where I'm using "Humble" in place of the Italian *Umile*,
but retaining the Italian original, *Pacifico*, which would be "Peace-Loving" in English.

† Raphael Brown tells us that "Soffiano was a grotto high on the steep slopes of Monte
Ragnolo, three hours' climb from Sarnano—a striking example of early Franciscan
hermitages." (Raphael Brown, ed., *The Little Flowers of Saint Francis: First Complete Edition*
[New York: Image Books, 1958], 341–42.)

‡ This family of Brunforte was likely known to Brother Ugolino, the compiler of these tales.
It seems that the friars were occupying the Soffiano friary only by the good graces of the lords
of Brunforte. The closing of Soffiano is used by scholars today as an indication of when the
original edition of the *Actus* was written—immediately afterward. They say that Soffiano closed
in 1327 and these stories could then have been compiled for the first time in the year or two
following that event. (See *Francis of Assisi: Early Documents*, vol. 3, ed. Regis J. Armstrong et al.
[New York: New City Press, 2001], 429.)

affection and showing too great a devotion to what was merely natural remains. Sensing this, Brother Pacifico explained himself.

"Dear brothers, don't be surprised," he said. "I did what I did because my brother died at a time when I was devoutly in prayer and I clearly saw his soul ascend to heaven. So I have known for certain that these are the bones of a saint and are bound eventually, also, for heavenly glory. If God had graced me with a similar knowledge about any of the other friars who were buried here, I would do likewise with their bones."

With this, the other friars understood Brother Pacifico's intentions, and all were blessed by him. They praised God from whom come all blessings wrought by his holy friars. Amen.

[#46 of 53]

CHAPTER 43

Miracles that God performed through the lives of some of the brothers

[ca. 1240–1290]

I N EARLIER DAYS, THE PROVINCE OF THE MARCHES OF Ancona was like a night sky filled with shining stars representing the holy and worthy friars who shone on earth and in heaven—before God and before their neighbors—in virtue. These men made the Franciscan Order and the entire world brilliant through their example and their teaching. Their memory is a blessing.

Among these there were some who were like the greatest of the constellations, shining most brightly of all. For instance, there was Brother Lucido the Elder, on fire with holiness from God. His preaching was Holy Spirit-inspired and reaped much fruit.

Another was Brother Bentivoglia of San Severino, whom Brother Masseo of San Severino once saw levitating high up in the air while out praying in the woods. It was the witness of this miracle that caused Masseo, who was then a pastor, to leave his work and become a Friar Minor. He then, too, lived a miraculous life, doing many amazing things both before and after his death. His body is buried in Muro.

But back to Brother Bentivoglia. Once when he was by himself taking care of a man afflicted with leprosy, he received instruction from his guardian to leave that place and go to another that was fifteen miles distant. Bentivoglia didn't want to leave the sick man behind, and so with love he carried him on his shoulders from dawn until sunrise the next day, going the whole fifteen miles to the new place, Monte Sancino.* Not even an eagle could have traveled that distance in such a time, and all who heard of this deed admired what he'd done as if it were a miracle.

Another saintly friar was Peter of Monticello, who was once seen by his guardian, Brother Servadeo of Urbino, floating in the air five

---

* A mountain in the Marche region.

or six yards off the ground—or, more precisely, above the floor of the church where he was praying before a crucifix. This Peter was also once overheard talking with the holy Archangel Michael on the final day of the Lent of St. Michael, which he'd been keeping most carefully and with serious devotion. This was overheard by a young friar who had hidden himself under the high altar, spying on the friar. This is what he overheard them say:

"Brother Peter, since you have worked assiduously for me and subdued your body in various ways, I will now bring you some peace. Ask me whatever you desire and I will obtain it," St. Michael said.

"Oh holy prince," Brother Peter answered him, "you defend souls in God's army. I only ask you one thing: ask God to forgive all my sins."

"Something else," the Archangel replied, "for that is already assumed."

But Brother Peter could not ask anything else, and so the Archangel concluded, "Due to your great faith, I will grant your request—but also, many other things to come." And as their conversation ended (it had gone on much of that night), St. Michael the Archangel departed and Brother Peter was left alone, intensely at peace.

Another brother, Conrad of Offida, lived at the same time as Brother Peter. They were members together of the community of friars in Ancona. Once when Brother Conrad left for the woods to pray to God, Peter snuck after him in order to spy. As Conrad started to pray profoundly and with tears to the Blessed Virgin, he asked her to intercede for him before her Son so that he might feel a small measure of the delight that St. Simeon felt on the day of her purification when Simeon held the blessed Savior in his arms.* He was granted this sweet experience and more, as the Queen of Heaven appeared, together with her blessed Son, before Brother Conrad. The splendor of that dazzling Lady

---

* This event took place on the Feast of the Purification of the Blessed Virgin Mary, celebrated on February 2. This feast is also sometimes called Candlemas Day, or the Presentation of Jesus in the Temple. Luke 2:32 has Simeon referring to the infant Christ as "a light for revelation to the Gentiles and for glory to your people Israel."

cleared the darkness from every corner of that place, and she placed her infant Son in Conrad's arms. Conrad took him to himself and kissed him on the lips and embraced him tightly to his heart. He felt as if his soul might melt right there and then.

Brother Peter was watching everything, and he, too, felt a sweetness in his soul. But he remained hidden in those now-illumined woods. When the Blessed Virgin left Brother Conrad, Brother Peter snuck quickly back and was not seen. Later, as Conrad himself returned, beside himself with joyfulness, Peter called to him, "Hey, man of heaven, what love you have had today!"

"What do you mean, brother? What do you know?" Conrad replied.

"I know it well. The Blessed Virgin has come to you with her beloved Son."

But when Brother Conrad heard Brother Peter's words, he begged him to keep it quiet, for he didn't want to brag about such graces. And from that day forward, the charity between those two men was so great that it was as if they were of one heart and soul.

On one other occasion, in Sirolo,* Brother Conrad helped to liberate a young woman from the clutches of the devil by his prayers. The next morning, Conrad fled from there so that the mother of the woman couldn't find him and he wouldn't be praised by any of the crowd who knew what had happened. (Brother Conrad had prayed all the night through and had appeared before the mother in a dream while he was helping free her daughter.)

All to the praise and glory of Jesus Christ.

[#42 of 53]

---

* Another municipality in the Marches—in this case, a beautiful, ancient town that borders the Adriatic Sea.

CHAPTER 44

Brother Conrad shows compassion for a troublesome young friar

[ca. 1240–1290]

THIS BROTHER CONRAD OF OFFIDA LIVED SUCH A saintly
life of faithfulness to the Gospel, to poverty, and to the Rule
of St. Francis that our Lord Jesus honored him with miracle after
miracle while he was with us. Among the many was the time
when he was visiting the friars in Offida and they asked him to
speak with a young friar who was acting foolishly, bothering the
other members of the community, showing little respect for the
Divine Office and the other spiritual practices of their religious
life. Brother Conrad felt great sorrow for that young man and for
the community that he was upsetting. He took the youth aside to
speak with him, and in love said many inspiring things to show
him the better way. It was as if the hand of God came over that
youth, so quickly was he completely changed. It was as if he
turned from one man into another; the child grew quickly into a
man. The youth became obedient, thoughtful, kind, and peaceful,
eager for virtue. If the community was bothered by him before,
now they were joyful in his conversion. He was greatly loved, as
if he were almost an angel.

Now by God's will, it was very soon after this youth's conversion that he became ill and died. The whole community grieved,
and after some days Brother Conrad, while he was praying in the
friary, was greeted by the soul of the young friar. The youth's soul
was coming to Conrad as a son to a father.

"Who are you?" Brother Conrad asked.

"The young friar who just died," the youth's soul replied.

"My son, how are you?" Conrad said.

"Father, by God's grace and your intercession, I am well; I was
not damned. But I have to make amends for my sins and so I am
suffering in purgatory. I beg you, help me by praying for me. God
knows how good your prayers are!" the youth explained.

Brother Conrad agreed and first he prayed an Our Father, followed by a Requiem Mass. When he was done, the youth's soul pleaded, "Keep going, father. I am feeling so much better. Don't stop!" So Conrad went on to say one hundred Our Fathers on his behalf. And when he had finished, the youth said, "Thank you, father, for your love for me. May Our Lord give you rewards in heaven for your kindness to me because by your prayers I am now free! I am right now going to paradise!" he said, and then he was gone.

Brother Conrad told all of this—everything that had happened—to the friars there, in order to bring them joy. To the glory of Our Lord. Amen.

[#43 of 53]

CHAPTER 45

The Mother of Christ and John the Evangelist appear to Brother Peter

[ca. 1240–1290]

THERE WAS ONCE A TIME WHEN THIS SAME BROTHER Conrad and Brother Peter,* two of the brightest stars in the holy firmament of the Province of the Marches, were living simultaneously at Ancona. They loved each other, and were so much of the same heart and mind that they agreed they would always reveal to one another whatever graces God granted to them.

Once, after they had made this agreement, Brother Peter found himself devoutly meditating on Christ's passion. The Blessed Mother and John the beloved disciple together with Blessed Francis with his stigmata were all standing there as well. Peter suddenly wondered, with a holy curiosity, which of those three beloved ones had endured the most because of Christ's passion. Was it the mother who birthed him, or the much-loved one who rested on his breast, or St. Francis who was also "crucified"? While Peter was considering this, the Virgin appeared before him with St. John and St. Francis—they were all dressed in heavenly garments—and Francis's appeared more beautiful even than John's. Peter was afraid of what he saw. But it was St. John himself who reached out to him and said, "Brother, don't be scared, and don't doubt, but know for sure that Christ's Mother and I grieved more than any others over Christ's passion, but after our time it was St. Francis who felt the greatest sorrow. For that reason, you are seeing him so gloriously."

"But most holy apostle, why does Francis's clothing seem brighter than even yours?" Peter asked of John.

"Because he wore simpler clothes than I did while he was here," St. John replied. And he reached out and gave Peter a garment

---

* This is the same Brother Peter of Monticello who appeared for the first time two stories earlier.

that he was holding in his hand. "Take this," he said, "for I brought it to show to you." And John wanted to put it on him.

But at that moment, Brother Peter woke up from his vision. He began to shout, running to Brother Conrad. "Quickly, quickly! See what's happening, here, for it is incredible!" he shouted to him. But the vision was gone. Nevertheless, Brother Peter told Brother Conrad all that had happened.

[#44 of 53]

CHAPTER 46

The holy life of Brother John of Penna

[ca. 1240–1290]

BROTHER JOHN OF PENNA* WAS ALSO ONE OF THE brightest stars in the firmament of the province of the Marches. While he was still a boy living in the world, another, more beautiful lad appeared before him and said, "Go to Santo Stefano, John, where a friar of mine is going to be preaching. Believe all that he has to say. Listen carefully, and afterward you will have a journey before you. Eventually, you will come to me."

John did as he was told and felt a change in his soul before he had even left for Santo Stefano.† But then when he arrived, he saw many men and many women already there, from villages all over, anxious to hear the word of God. The friar-preacher was Brother Philip, one of the first friars who ever came to the Marches of Ancona. Brother Philip got up and began to preach with great fervor, not with great learning, but by simply telling about God's kingdom, the Spirit of Christ, and the path of eternal life. When the sermon ended, the boy (who later became Brother John) went up to Brother Philip and asked, "If you would have me in your Order, I would do penance and serve our Lord."

Philip knew holy innocence when he saw and heard it, as well as readiness to serve the Lord, and so he said to the boy, "Come and visit me in Recanati some day in the future, and I will receive you there." (A chapter of that province was going to be held in Recanati.)

"Surely this will be that long journey that was told to me, the one that I have to make before I may go to heaven," the boy thought to himself, with the innocence that only a youth might have. He was imagining that heaven would come as soon as he was received as a friar. And so he went. And so he was somewhat disappointed.

---

* Penna San Giovanni, a hill-town in the Marches south of Ancona.

† There are more than twenty municipalities in Italy with this name, plus two islands, so it is unclear which one is intended here.

During that provincial chapter, the minister spoke these words: "If there are any here who desire to go to the province of Provence,* I will send them." When Brother John heard this, he wanted to go, thinking that perhaps finally this would be that journey he was to make before going to heaven. But he was shy and kept quiet.

Finally, he whispered to Brother Philip, "Father, can you please ask for me, so that I can go to Provence?" (In those days a friar would offer to travel long distances to unfamiliar places in order to become a true pilgrim and stranger in the world.) Brother Philip asked permission on John's behalf, and John set out joyfully, certain that he was about to finish the long-anticipated journey to heaven.

But in reality, John stayed in Provence twenty-five years, living all the while with this sort of simplicity and simple sanctity, hoping each day would be the one where the promise might be fulfilled in his life. He grew holier and more virtuous and was greatly loved by all in that place, even though he could never quite see where and when his desires might be granted to him.

Until one day when he was praying and crying out loudly to God, complaining that his earthly pilgrimage was taking too long, the blessed Lord Jesus appeared in front of him. Brother John's soul fell to pieces at that moment, and Christ said, "Son, Brother John, you may ask me whatever you desire."

"I cannot speak, my Lord," he stammered. "I don't want a thing from you but one: for you to forgive my sins. And then, allow me to see you again like this when I need forgiving again."

"Your prayer is granted," Jesus said, and then he vanished. Brother John couldn't see him anymore, but he felt completely comforted.

When at long last the friars from the Marches got wind of Brother John's holy reputation, they asked the minister-general that a note be sent to John sending him back to the Marches. When that note arrived, John was delighted to go, and said, "This is surely the

---

* This was truly a long journey, from the Marches region of Italy to the French Riviera.

long journey that was promised to me, by which I shall go to God."
But when he arrived in his home province, no one even recognized
him, not even his closest family. Still, he waited with patience for
God's mercy in fulfilling that old promise.

Still, he lived longer. For thirty more years he stayed in the
Marches and eventually served even as guardian there. Many
miracles were performed through his life.

Among his gifts was the spirit of prophecy, as on one occasion
when he was away and one of his novices was grabbed by the devil
and tempted to leave the Order. That novice yielded but said only
that he would wait to leave until Brother John returned. While he
was away, Brother John's gift of prophecy told him of both the
temptation and the resolution of that novice. "Come with me," John
said to him, upon his return. "I want to hear your confession."

The boy sat down. Then, Brother John began, "First of all, listen
to me," he said. And he told the novice all that God had shown
him. Then he finished by saying, "But because you waited for me
and didn't leave without receiving my blessing, God has shown
his grace to you, in that you will never leave this Order. You will
die as a Friar Minor with God's blessing." With that, the novice
was made strong and indeed, he persevered and became a friar.

It was Brother John himself who told me, Brother Ugolino,
these things.

He was also a man with great peace of mind. He did not
often speak, but was a person of quiet and prayer. After Matins
he would never return to his cell, but would stay bowed in the
church throughout the night until dawn. One night while he
was praying in this way, an angel of God came and said to him,
"Brother John, your journey is soon coming to an end. What you
have desired is coming true. Now you have a decision to make.
Which grace do you choose: one full day in purgatory, or seven
days of suffering here on earth?"

Brother John chose seven days of suffering here. He immediately then felt sick. He had a fever and many pains. He had gout
in his hands and feet. And he had gastrointestinal troubles, suffering greatly from it all. But worse than all of that was a devil that

stood in front of him with a large scroll and read all of John's sins and failings. "These are the reasons why you are going to hell!" the devil said to him. And our ill friar believed him—so much so, that when someone asked him how he was feeling, he said, "Awful! I am damned!"

The oldest friars of the Marches saw what was happening and they sent for Brother Matthew of Monterubbiano, one of Brother John's oldest friends. Matthew came to see him. "How are you doing?" he said, greeting his friend.

"Awful! I am damned!" was Brother John's reply.

"Impossible," Matthew said. "Do you remember confessing your sins? I was your priest and I absolved you completely.

"Also, remember your life. You have served God faithfully. God's mercy is greater than all of the sins in this world, and Jesus paid the price to redeem us of our sins. You can be completely sure of your salvation," Brother Matthew concluded.

Brother John was comforted by this, and also, his seven days of sickness were expiring and so the temptations flew away. "You must be tired," he said to Matthew. "Go lie down and rest." Matthew didn't want to go but John insisted, and so finally, Matthew lay down. Brother John then remained alone, except for the one friar who remained to care for him. While they were there, Jesus Christ came in a brilliant light, wrapped in a sweet fragrance, just as he promised that he would, when John would need him again. It was Jesus who cured John completely that time.

Then Brother John folded his hands and prayed to God with thanks for the long journey that his life had taken, and for the joyful end that was coming. He gave his soul up to God and passed from this life into the next.

His body is buried in Penna San Giovanni. To Christ's glory. Amen.

[#45 of 53]

CHAPTER 47

———

How the Blessed Mother appeared to one of the brothers

[c a . 1 2 4 0 – 1 2 9 0]

IN THOSE SAME MARCHES OF ANCONA, IN THAT SAME lonely place called Soffiano, there was a Friar Minor whose name I cannot recall, but he was so holy that he seemed almost like a god. He was often caught up in the direct experience of our Lord.

On one of these occasions, while his mind was ecstatically wrapped up in God, a flock of birds came and rested upon his head, his shoulders, his arms, and his hands. They just sat there and began to sing melodiously. When he emerged from his contemplation, his face showed forth a joy that seemed angelic, wholly in communion with the divine. It surprised everyone who looked upon him.

This friar was always off alone and spoke on rare occasions. He prayed all the time. Whenever someone asked him a question, he answered with more the quietude of an angel than the bluster of a man. He was always reverent and kind and his words, always divine.

He lived this way, practicing virtues, until his angelic life came to an end. He became sick and could no longer keep food down. He rejected medicine for his sick body, placing all of his faith in Christ his heavenly physician, and in his Blessed Mother. In fact, the Virgin visited and comforted him in many ways in those last days. Once, while he was alone in bed and contemplating his death, the Blessed Mother came to him with a group of angels and holy virgins amid a bright light; she approached him, very close to his bed, and when he glimpsed her, his mind and body were filled with joy.

The friar begged her to pray to her Son that he might leave the prison of the flesh.

"Don't fear, my son," she told him, "your prayer is being granted. Besides, I have seen your tears and have come to bring you a little comfort in your last earth-bound days." Then she revealed the three virgins who had accompanied her, and the electuary boxes that they were carrying.* These were so full of sweetness that the house was filled with their fragrance as the Blessed Virgin opened each one.

With a spoon in her lovely hand, she dipped it into the first box and offered some of the electuary to that sick brother. He tasted it and its sweetness fed his soul and made him want to leave his body behind. "No more, dear Lady, holy physician," he said, "I can't take any more sweetness!" But the Mother of God fed him more, until that first box was completely empty, and she talked with him about her Son, Jesus.

Then, she took the next box and, as she placed the spoon in it, the sick friar said to her, "Blessed Mother of God, I can't take it. My soul will melt away completely!"

"My son," she responded, "you need a little bit from this box." And after a small amount, she said to him, "That's enough. Now, be happy, because I am coming back soon to lead you to my Son and the kingdom that you have desired." Then she said goodbye to the friar, and she was gone. He remained where he was, but completely at peace. The pharmacist of heaven had given him medicine by the hand of the Blessed Virgin.

For his remaining days, the friar took no food, even though he felt strong from the divine medicine that prepared him for heaven. His spiritual vision was enhanced and he could even see the book of eternal life on which were written the names of all who would be saved from final judgment. Only a few days later, he passed from this unhappy place to the Lord Jesus. He was talking with the other friars with joy when it finally happened. To Christ's glory. Amen.†

[#47 of 53]

---

* An *electuary* is just what the story says: a medicinal paste or powder with added sweeteners (usually natural ones, such as syrup or honey), added to help make the taking of one's medicine more pleasant. Today this word is most common in veterinary medicine.

† It is interesting that this unique tale does not even include the most basic of details—the friar's name. Perhaps there was a disagreement on that point, or Ugolino is making the point that it doesn't really matter.

CHAPTER 48

———

When God showed Brother James of Massa true secrets

[1247 – ca.1274]

Brother James of Massa was a man who knew God's secrets because God showed them to him, giving James a perfect understanding of Scripture and all things to come. He was saintly to the point that Brother Giles of Assisi and Brother Mark of Montino knew of no one on earth who would be greater in the sight of God. Brother Juniper and Brother Lucido agreed.

Now while Brother John (the companion of Brother Giles) was my spiritual director, I wanted to see this Brother James. My desire was prompted by a comment of Brother John. He said to me, "If you want an understanding of the spiritual life, you must talk with Brother James of Massa. Even Brother Giles wanted his instruction. Brother James has all the secrets of heaven. All of his words are those of the Holy Spirit."

There was one time when Brother James was so caught up in God that it progressed to the point where he lay unconscious for three days—so long that the other friars began to wonder if he might be dead.* While he rapturously lay there, God gave to him a deep understanding of both Scripture and the future. I heard about this, and my desire to consult with him then grew greater. When that opportunity finally came, by God's grace, I asked Brother James, "Is it true what I have heard, that God gave you knowledge of the future, including the future of our Order? Brother Matthew, whom you told under obedience, said as much." (Brother Matthew was the minister of our province of the Marches, and had forced Brother James to tell him what happened during that three-day rapturous period. Matthew would often say

---

* Readers may have noticed that this theme is repeated several times in the *Fioretti*. Interestingly, St. Francis didn't advocate this sort of prayer as a virtue in itself. See the earlier "Why Brother Rufino has to preach in Assisi in his underwear" (chapter 10).

to the other friars: "I know one of you whom God has shown the future and many unimaginable secrets.")*

Now, this is what Brother James told me. This is what God showed to him: There was a tall and beautiful tree with roots made of gold and fruits in its branches that were made of men. Each of the branches of the tree was a province in our Order, and there was a fruit on each branch for each Friar Minor of that province. He could see there on that tree every member of our Order, including his face and age and virtues and sins.

He saw Brother John of Parma standing tallest in the tree, on the center branch, and near him at the top of the branches closest to the center branch were the ministers of every province. Atop it all was Christ sitting on a large, white throne, speaking with St. Francis and giving him a drink from a chalice filled with life.

"Go visit all of your brothers," Christ said to St. Francis, "for the devil will always attack them and many will fall away." Two angels were given to Francis to accompany him.

After this, St. Francis came down and began to offer the chalice to each of the friars. He started with Brother John, the minister-general, who drank from it quickly and then, as a result, began to glow like the sun. Then Francis offered that chalice with the spirit of life to each of the other friars, one by one, and it became clear that most of them did not drink from it with much reverence or enthusiasm. Those who did glowed as well. And those who did not drink devoutly, or spilled some, began to look dark and deformed and devilish.

More than any of the friars on the tree, Brother John drank most fully and shone most brightly. He seemed to then sense that a storm was coming straight toward that tree, a tempest that would batter those branches, and so he traveled from the top to the bottom and hid himself away in the most solid part of the tree trunk. There, he prayed.

Meanwhile, Brother Bonaventure, who had drunk from the chalice and spilled some of it,† ascended up the tree and took the

---

* By our standards, this would be quite a breach of confidence, but it seems acceptable in the milieu of the early Franciscans!

† This apocalyptic vision reveals the conflicts going on in the Order between the

spot that Brother John had left. And while Bonaventure was there, his fingernails were sharpened like iron razor blades, and he suddenly seemed to want to attack Brother John. Brother John could see this, and cried out to Christ on his throne to help. Hearing his cries, Christ summoned St. Francis, giving him a stone of flint and telling Francis, "Go cut the nails of Brother Bonaventure, for he wants to tear down Brother John!"

St. Francis did as Christ had ordered, and Brother John remained where he was, shining.

Then, a hurricane rose up and hit that tree so strongly that all of the friars began to fall off the branches. Those who had spilled from the chalice were the first to fall, and as they fell, they were carried away by devils. But as the other friars—the ones who had drunk devoutly—fell, they were carried away by angels toward the light of heaven.

He saw all of this clearly in his vision, and remembered carefully all of the details. The hurricane lasted, by God's will, until all the tree was torn up from the roots and scattered into the ground. But when the storm stopped, those golden roots showed forth out of the ground, and a new tree that was golden and full of fruit and flowers grew up beautifully in its place.

I am not omitting anything from my retelling of this vision, for every detail seemed important to me. Brother James remarked that our Order would be reformed in a different way from how it was originally founded. Without a clear leader, the Holy Spirit will use the uneducated, the simple, the plain, and those who are despised by others in order to bring Christ's love again into the world. Christ has increased the number of these in many places, and now they only need a good shepherd who is modeled after their Shepherd, Christ.

[#48 of 53]

Spirituals and the Conventuals. Bonaventure (1221–74) was the minister-general of the Franciscan Order from 1257 (elected at the young age of thirty-six) until his death, which may have been by poisoning. He was canonized, but not until 1482—long after *The Little Flowers* was written down.

CHAPTER 49

Christ appears to Brother John of La Verna

[1275 – 1322]

THE HOLY SPIRIT MADE SO MANY BEAUTIFUL FOLLOWERS of
St. Francis in his Order that we can see the truth of what
Solomon said, that the beauty of a father is seen in his sons.*
Standing among all of these is one other special one, the holy
Brother John of Fermo, who stands out like a brilliant star in the
night sky. Brother John spent so much time associated with the
holy place of La Verna, even dying there, that he is also called
Brother John of La Verna.

When he was but a boy, his heart was like that of a wise old
man. He desired even then a life of penance and began to wear
a breastplate of iron mail and a band on his flesh. By these, he
was carrying a cross of self-denial throughout the day. Especially
while he lived in Fermo, among the canons who were more spiritually lax in their practices, he would strictly avoid all manner of
physical comfort and deny his body with joy. But those companions of his took his breastplate from him and were offended by his
zealous abstinence. In many other ways they hindered him, until
he determined to leave the world behind and offer his holy desires
to the Order of St. Francis, founded by the one of whom he'd
heard saw the wounds of the crucifixion replicated in his body.

He received the habit of a Friar Minor while still a youth, and was
committed for spiritual instruction to a novice master. His fervor
would roast like fire when he heard that master speak of God, and
inside he felt that his young heart would melt like wax in that heat.
He would become so stirred up by the sensation of God's love in his
heart that he would jump up and run around the garden or woods
or church, as God's spirit moved him. Eventually, as he grew older,
his mind was strengthened and his virtue increased, and those

---

* Perhaps Proverbs 17:6, "Grandchildren are the crown of the aged, and the glory of
children is their parents."

ecstatic feelings became like the joyful expressions of an angel in high heaven. At special times, he felt the holy embrace and kiss of Christ and his love, both in his soul and exteriorly, too.

So it happened one day, while on Mt. La Verna, that Brother John's heart was on fire with the love of God in one of these extraordinary ways, and it then lasted constantly for three years. But in God's way of caring for his most special sons, sometimes to keep them humble or to fire their desire for holiness, God decided to take from Brother John that spiritual fire, leaving him lonely and depressed. Suddenly, his soul no longer felt that beloved presence.

Grieving, he ran through the woods, calling out and crying as if for a friend who had left him behind, and without whom he would never again have any peace. He couldn't and didn't find Christ anywhere, and he definitely did not feel any of those holy embraces. He underwent this trial for many days on end until at last—when God knew that he had been tested enough—one day Brother John was sitting in the woods alone, tired and sad, leaning against a beech tree. And as he lifted his face up to heaven with tears running down his cheeks, our Lord stood right there on the path behind him, speaking not at all. When John saw him, he threw himself down at his feet and wept, begging him: "Without you, my Lord, my Savior, there is only darkness and sadness. With you, I have everything: redemption, love, desire. Be my light once again, my loving shepherd. I am your lamb."

But sometimes a man grows in love and virtue even more if and when God does not come easily—and this time, Christ went away, leaving him on the path.

Brother John saw him going, without even answering what he had said. So John jumped up and ran after Christ. Catching up to him, he again threw himself at Christ's feet, holding them fervently, and in tears, saying, "Sweet Jesus, pity me! I am suffering! Please grant my prayer, for the sake of my dark soul," he exclaimed.

But again, the Savior left him on the path, without saying a word. In fact, this time it seemed that Christ was going to leave completely. In reality, Christ was in those moments like a mother breastfeeding her baby, when she takes her breast away for a moment in order to make the child take it more eagerly when it returns.

So Brother John ran after Christ for a third time, crying like that baby seeking its mother. When John reached the spot where he was, Christ turned and looked upon him with such joy and love, holding out arms of mercy, that John saw only light coming from Christ's body. The entire forest around them was lit up with divine luminosity. Then, at that precise moment, the Holy Spirit revealed to John what he should do next: and he threw himself down at the feet of the Savior. There, John wept like a new Magdalene* and said, "I beg you, Lord, reawaken my soul!"

While Brother John was praying, he began to receive the renewal of God's grace and peace—so much that he indeed felt like Mary Magdalene. He felt that fire of God's love and presence returning to him and he gave thanks to God, kissing Christ's feet. Then John lifted up his head to look into the Savior's face. Christ held out his hands, and John kissed them. Leaning even closer, now, he hugged Jesus tightly and kissed his holy breast.

Before long, this rapturous experience of Brother John's was about to be over. The Blessed One disappeared before his eyes, but yet the deep consolation and divine knowledge remained with him. It is not so much that he discovered the human Christ in those special moments, but he discovered his own soul deep within the divine Christ. (It was the one who heard about all of this from Brother John that then told it to me.)

This would be demonstrated in many clear ways to come. For example, Brother John would speak in such luminous words before the curia in Rome and before master theologians and doctors of canon law that it was inexplicable to them where he had gotten such inspiration. John was an uneducated man speaking

---

* A reference to the story told in Luke 7:36–50, when a sinful woman, likely a prostitute, anoints Jesus' feet while he is dining with some Pharisees. Medieval theologians identified this woman as Mary Magdalene, one of Jesus' earliest followers, but most scholars today believe that the woman from Luke 7 is actually someone else.

of the most subtle matters of divine understanding, including the meaning of the Holy Trinity and other matters deeply mysterious in our Scriptures.

If you would like to further understand how Brother John came first to Christ's feet in tears, and then to his hands, and last to his holy breast, read St. Bernard on the Song of Songs. And giving these graces to Brother John without speaking a word shows us what the Good Shepherd does and how God's kingdom is not in external sounds and things but in the inner depths of the heart. As the psalmist says, glory to God comes from within.*

[#49 of 53]

---

* This could refer to many passages, for example, Psalm 84:1–3: "How lovely is your dwelling place, O LORD of hosts! My soul longs, indeed it faints for the courts of the LORD; my heart and my flesh sing for joy to the living God."

CHAPTER 50

—

Brother John of La Verna's saying of Mass frees
many souls from purgatory

[1 3 0 0 – 1 3 2 2]

THERE WAS ONCE AN ALL SAINTS' DAY WHEN Brother John of La Verna was saying Mass for the souls of the dead—who know that nothing is better for them than the Holy Sacrament. Brother John's words were so full of love and compassion that day that his devotion seemed to be completely otherworldly.

When he came to elevate the holy Body of Christ, offering it to God the Father, he suddenly saw innumerable souls rushing out of purgatory like sparks blasting out of a blazing furnace. He saw these human souls fly to heaven by the merits of Christ, who suffered on the cross for the salvation of all humankind. This is the sacrifice that is offered up each day in the most holy Body—for both living and dead. That One is the blessed God-man, light and life, redeemer and judge, who is our Savior now and forever. Amen.

[#50 of 53]

CHAPTER 51

———

The tale of Brother James and Brother John

[1 3 0 0 – 1 3 2 2]

THERE WAS ALSO A TIME WHEN BROTHER JOHN OF La Verna heard about a serious illness of the holy Brother James of Fallerone, who was staying in the friary at Mogliano. From the friary at Massa, John began to pray with all of his heart for James's recovery—that it would be God's will for him to recover, for Brother John loved Brother James as a father loves a son.

While he was praying, Brother John became so caught up in God that he began to see angels and saints in the sky above his head. There, in the woods, he saw them shining brightly, illuminating everything. Among the angels, John saw Brother James, ill, but standing among them in radiant, white clothes. He also saw the blessed Father Francis, with his holy stigmata, also shining in glory. And there were Brother Lucido and Brother Matthew the Elder, too, and other friars whom Brother John had never known in this earthly life, together with the saints, all of them shining above his head.

John just stood there and gazed on them all with delight. And the vision revealed to him that James would indeed die from this illness, but that his soul would be saved. James would not go to heaven right away, but that soul of his would need to be purified in purgatory first.

After seeing all of this, John was full of joy for the salvation of his brother friar—so much so that he didn't even grieve over his impending death. From that moment forward, he began to think of James in these terms, "My dear brother, Christ's faithful servant, God's friend, companion of the angels and saints!"

Soon after this vision, Brother John left the friary at Massa and traveled to the friary at Mogliano, where he found Brother James so weak from illness that he could no longer speak. John told James that by a revelation he knew that he would die, but also that his soul would be saved. This filled James with joy. You could see the joy on his face, for he began to smile, with happy expressions thanking his brother for such wonderful news.

Then, Brother John asked Brother James if he would return to him, after he died, to tell him how it was. James promised that he would, if Christ allowed it. Then, as he died, he began to speak with the words of the psalmist and said, "Ah, in peace . . . Ah, in him . . . Ah, I go to sleep . . . Ah, I now rest!"* Thus, he died, leaving this life to go to Christ. His body was then buried and John returned to the friary in Massa, where he waited for James to come to him someday, as he said he would try to do.

One day, while he was praying, Christ showed himself to Brother John. There were angels and saints all around Christ, but not James, and so John began to quickly praise his brother to Christ.

On the following day, while John was again praying, James came and appeared before John. James was surrounded by angels. John said, "Holy father, you didn't come right away to tell me how it was, as you said that you would!"

"I needed to be purified first," Brother James replied. "It was during the same hour that Christ appeared before you that I showed myself to Brother James of Massa while he was serving at Mass. He saw the host changed into the beautiful face of a boy, and I said to him, 'I am going to God's kingdom today with him, for no one can go there without him!' That was also at the same moment when you were praising me before Christ. Your prayers were heard and I was set free," Brother James concluded.

At this, Brother James of Fallerone returned to the Lord and Brother John was overjoyed. This same Brother James died on the Feast of St. James the Apostle in July and was buried at the friary of Mogliano. To this day, he performs miracles.

[#51 of 53]

---

* See Psalm 3:5, "I lie down and sleep; I wake again, for the LORD sustains me." And Psalm 4:8, "I will both lie down and sleep in peace; for you alone, O LORD, make me lie down in safety." *Death* is often called *sleep* in the Bible.

CHAPTER 52

*When Brother John of La Verna saw how every
created thing relates to its Creator*

[1 3 0 0 – 1 3 2 2]

NOW BROTHER JOHN OF LA VERNA'S HOLINESS was such that he would often receive special revelations upon the greatest feast days of our blessed Lord Jesus Christ. So it happened once as the Feast of the Nativity was approaching that the Holy Spirit gave to him an intense and burning love for Christ. Brother John suddenly glimpsed the love by which the Savior had humbled himself to take on our humanity—so much so that he was frightened to death and felt that he might faint. His heart began to burn intensely to the point where it felt as hot as a furnace inside him. He couldn't help himself: he shouted out loud.

Now at that very moment when he felt this incredible divine love, a powerful surety of salvation flooded over him and he felt that, if he were to die there and then, he wouldn't even need to make his way through purgatory. This supreme love lasted for a half year without any interruptions. The intensity of feeling the love lasted even longer, for more than a year. It took hold of him so much, at times, that Brother John felt he might actually be dying. Even when this time came to an end, he still received many loving kindnesses from God, and countless revelations. I myself observed these with my own eyes on several occasions, as did others.

Among these, there was one night in particular when Brother John was raised to such a level of knowing God that he was able to see the image of the Creator in all created things, in heaven and on earth, each in its own way, including how the choirs of angels are arrayed under God and how the paradise of earth and our blessed humanity are under Christ. He also saw lower realms, and understood how every created thing relates to its Creator and how God is above, within, around, and outside of all of them.

After this God raised him up, above all other creatures, and his soul was completely absorbed in the light of God, and settled deeply into the ocean of God's infinitudes.* Brother John, at this point, was unable to feel or see or think or speak of any of those things that the human heart usually can feel or see, think or speak of. He was so caught up in the divine that it was as if his soul was completely absorbed in the ocean of God. A drop in the sea knows not itself, but only the sea. Even so, Brother John's soul knew this God-sea as three Persons in One.

He could feel the love that caused the Son of God to become man in obedience to the will of his Father, and he meditated on the Incarnation and passion of the Son. Brother John said that there is no way for the soul to be contained in God, or to find everlasting peace, but through the Son, Christ, the way, the truth, and the life.† Everything was shown to him, then, including what Christ did from the time of the very fall of the first man until the God-man ascended into heaven. It is this Christ who is the leader of all of his chosen ones since the beginning of the world until the end of time. Amen.

[#52 of 53]

---

* This image of a drop in the ocean, for the experience of salvation/liberation, isn't found in any of the earliest writings of the Franciscan movement. But curiously, it is present in the mystical writings of many religious traditions throughout the world. Compare to the principle of *moksha* in Hinduism, the stories of the Hasidic masters in Judaism, and the poems of Rumi in Sufism. However, at the end of this paragraph, the author makes it clear that Brother John's experience was thoroughly Trinitarian.

† Cf. John 14:6. This entire story is full of the mystical imagery in John's Gospel.

CHAPTER 53

When Brother John of La Verna fell down while saying Mass

[1300–1322]

SOMETHING INCREDIBLE ONCE HAPPENED TO THAT same Brother John. Some of the friars who were there have told me all about it. This occurred once while he was staying in the friary of Mogliano in the Marches.

It happened during the first night after the eight-day Feast of St. Lawrence (within the eight-day Feast of the Assumption of the Blessed Virgin Mary), when John woke up early before Matins. At the Matins service, as he recited the prayers with the others, the Lord filled his soul with supremely good things. And when Matins was over, he went walking through the garden, filled with God's grace and sweetness, so much so that he began to shout out those words of our Lord, *"Hoc est Corpus Meum!"* "This is my body!" The Holy Spirit had enlightened him through those words.

Brother John's soul could see with clarity Jesus Christ and the Blessed Virgin and all the angels and saints. He clearly understood the words of the apostle that we are all one in the body of Christ, each of us is one with the other, and with the saints we may see and understand the inclusive dimensions and depth of Christ's love.* This love is greater than all knowledge, and we may know it when those words, *Hoc est Corpus Meum*, bring the Holy Sacrament before us.

By dawn, Brother John walked into the church in this passion and fervor brought on by divine grace. He couldn't help himself but shouted it out three times. He thought that no one was there

---

* These are both passages from the Apostle Paul: "For as in one body we have many members, and not all the members have the same function, so we, who are many, are one body in Christ, and individually we are members one of another" (Rom. 12:4–5). And, "I pray that you may have the power to comprehend, with all the saints, what is the breadth and length and height and depth, and to know the love of Christ that surpasses knowledge, so that you may be filled with all the fullness of God" (Eph. 3:18–19).

or would hear him, but there was one friar praying alone in the choir and he heard.

Brother John remained like this until the time came when he was to celebrate Mass. When he put on his vestments and moved toward the altar, the passion of his devotion and Christ's affection swelled within him to the point where he had an overwhelming sense of God's ineffable presence. He was suddenly afraid that these feelings might lead to him interrupting the Mass and so he paused to consider what to do next. Then he recalled that something like this had happened to him once before, and all had gone well, so he thought that he could proceed this time, too. But he was still wary, for the divine can easily interrupt the human.

He got as far in the Mass as the Preface of the Blessed Virgin. Everything was fine, but then the divine sweetness began to overcome him. When he came to the *Qui pridie*,* he felt completely overwhelmed. He came to the consecration itself and began to say those words over the host, repeating *Hoc est* . . . *Hoc est* . . . again and again, unable to continue. He couldn't say the words, for he believed that he saw Christ before his eyes, together with angels and saints. He felt as if he were going to faint.

At this, the guardian of the friary came running to help. He stood beside Brother John, as did another friar with a lit candle. Meanwhile, other friars, and men and women, and many of the most prominent people of the province who were there to hear Mass, stood concernedly around the altar. Some of them were crying, as women are prone to do.†

Brother John was just standing there, consumed with joy and happiness. He'd paused during the words of consecration, but only because he could see that Christ was not entering the host—or,

---

* This is the beginning of the paragraph during the Mass leading up to the *Hoc est Corpus Meum*, when the priest says "*Qui pridie quam pateretur, accepit panem* . . ." or "Who, the day before he suffered, took bread. . . ." In other words, Brother John was coming to that portion of the Mass that had previously so profoundly moved him.

† Such a statement would have been common 100 years ago, let alone 700 years ago, when this was written down.

instead, that the host was not changing into the Body of Christ—because he hadn't yet spoken the second half of the formula . . . *Corpus Meum*.

And so, after what seemed a very long time, unable to bear the majestic, mystical revelation of these things, he loudly exclaimed, ". . . *Corpus Meum!*" Immediately, bread vanished from sight and the host showed only the Lord Jesus Christ. At this, Brother John's humility and adoration left him unable to continue speaking the remaining words of the consecration. He fell backward and was caught by his guardian who was still standing next to him. The others in the church rushed forward, and they all carried John into the sacristy and laid him down. His body had quickly gone cold. He seemed to be dead. His fingers were stiff and bent so that they couldn't be opened or even budged. He laid there as if dead until the time of Tierce.˙

Now, I was among those present that day, and I wanted to know what had truly happened to him. So as soon as he came to, I went and asked him all about it. He used to confide often in me, and by God's grace he told me everything. He told me that both before and after the words of consecration, his heart became inside of him like hot wax, and his body seemed boneless, to the point where he couldn't lift either his arms or hands to make the sign of the cross over the host. Before he ever became a priest, he said, God told him that he would faint like that during Mass. He had said many Masses without it happening and had begun to wonder if the prophecy was not from God. Then, fifty days before this day—before the Assumption of the Blessed Virgin, when all of this happened—it was again revealed to him that it would happen, but he'd forgotten.

[#53 of 53]

---

* Probably about two and a half hours later.

BRIEF BIOGRAPHICAL SKETCHES
OF THE FRIARS

The first three to join Francis . . .

BROTHER BERNARD OF QUINTAVALLE remained a lay brother (not a priest), as did all but one of the first twelve followers of St. Francis. Like many of the earliest followers, Bernard came from a prominent and wealthy family in Assisi. He was the first to become a full-time companion of Francis. This happened in April 1209, and on April 16, 1209, Francis, Bernard, and Peter Catani opened the Scriptures together. Bernard later recruited the first friars in Bologna, in 1211. He died in the early 1240s in Assisi.

BROTHER PETER CATANI joined St. Francis and Bernard to open the Gospels together at the home of the bishop of Assisi on April 16, 1209. They read Matthew 19:21, Luke 9:3, and Mark 8:34 and decided that the words of Christ to the first disciples would also be their rule of life. A well-educated man, Peter was appointed the first minister-general of the Friars Minor in the fall of 1220, when Francis resigned his leadership. Peter died one year later, in 1221, at the Portiuncula, where he is also buried. Strangely, he does not appear as a character in any of the stories of *The Little Flowers*.

BROTHER GILES left the city of Assisi from the east gate that leads down to San Damiano one week after Bernard and Peter had joined St. Francis, seeking to join him, too. When Francis met Giles on the road, he led him to the chapel at Portiuncula and declared him the fourth brother (Francis was himself the first). One of the most legendary and important of the first friars, he traveled the world on early missions, sought martyrdom during the Crusades, and was with Francis when he died. After Francis's death, Giles was visited by popes, cardinals, and Bonaventure, and died an old man in 1262 in Assisi's neighboring town of Perugia, where Francis had assigned him and where Giles lived much of his life.

The primary author of The Little Flowers . . .

BROTHER UGOLINO BONISCAMBI lived a century after the first friars. He was likely born around 1260 in Monte Santa Maria, a municipality in the province of the Marches that is now called Montegiorgio. He died sometime around 1345. He is the primary compiler of the Latin work *Actus Beati Francisci et Sociorum Eius*, or "The Deeds of Blessed Francis and His Companions," from which the Italian *Fioretti di Santo Francesco d' Ascesi*, or "The Little Flowers of Saint Francis of Assisi," is a translation. We know very little about his life except that he spent his novitiate as a Franciscan in Roccabruna in the far northwest corner of Italy and was a friend of the angelic Pope Celestine V, who briefly ruled and then controversially resigned in 1294.

Some other important people mentioned in The Little Flowers . . .

BROTHER ANGELO TANCREDI was a knight before joining St. Francis, and his bearing always remained noble, despite voluntary poverty. He was the fortunate friar to accompany Francis on the walk that became the first sermon to the birds. He kept vigil at Clare's deathbed and testified at her canonization hearings. Angelo died in 1258 and is the third friar to be buried in the crypt of the Basilica. Some scholars have found evidence to suggest that Angelo and Francis may have been biological brothers.

BROTHER ANTHONY OF PADUA was born around 1195 and was a priest and monk of St. Augustine before joining the Franciscans in 1220. We know that Anthony was present at the General Chapter of 1221 when St. Francis presented the second edition of his *Rule*. He was known as a great thinker and theologian and was canonized by the same Pope Gregory IX who canonized Francis, and even more quickly (only one year after his death in 1231).

SISTER CLARE OF ASSISI called herself St. Francis's *pianticella*, or "little plant," who grew to show God's beauty and provide sustenance for the movement he started. By all accounts, she was a woman of great physical beauty and charm. The document known to history as Clare's *Acts*, written to support her canonization, mentions several marriage proposals. She left domestic life behind at the age of eighteen to become the first woman to follow Francis and was the founder of the Second Order of Franciscans, the Poor Clares. She was a woman of wisdom, sensitivity, and strength. She died on August 11, 1253.

BROTHER ELIAS was two years older than St. Francis and knew Francis from childhood. He became minister-general after Peter Catani in 1221, but his rule was controversial. He ruled until 1227, after which he oversaw the building of San Francesco in Assisi, and then once again he was elected minister-general in 1232. He was seen as despotic to some, even the essence of evil; this perspective comes through in *The Little Flowers* in a way that it doesn't always in earlier sources. Pope Gregory IX dismissed Elias from his position in 1239, and one year later, Elias joined Emperor Frederick II, a violent enemy of the Church, as an advisor. After a decade of serving Frederick II (whose mercenaries were famously repelled by St. Clare in an attempt to besiege San Damiano), Elias repented his sins to a priest and the excommunication placed on him was lifted. He died in 1253.

POPE GREGORY IX was Holy Father from 1227 to 1241. As Cardinal Ugolino, he was appointed by Pope Honorius III in 1217 to oversee St. Francis's enthusiastic young movement. He was elected pope just before Francis's death, oversaw his canonization, and brought great changes to his Order.

BROTHER JAMES OF MASSA was a legendary figure in the second generation of Franciscan Spirituals, respected by the prominent Brothers Giles and Juniper according to these stories. Born in the 1220s, he likely died in about 1305.

BROTHER JOHN OF LA VERNA lived from 1259 to 1322. He was born in Fermo in the Marches region, but spent most of his life associated with the mountain most revered in Italy for its associations with St. Francis. It was upon La Verna in the Tuscan Apennines in September 1224 that Francis received the stigmata. Brother John was one of the best friends of Jacopone of Todi, the famous Spiritual Franciscan poet.

BROTHER JOHN OF PARMA was minister-general of the Franciscan Order from 1247 to 1257, the one to serve in this capacity before Bonaventure's term. He resigned in 1257, unable to govern as a Spiritual in the midst of an Order increasingly dominated by Conventuals, and lived the life of a semihermit at Greccio, near Rieti, the place where St. Francis had enacted the first live nativity.

BROTHER JUNIPER was a close friend of St. Clare's, and was among those present at her death. He was a holy fool, and one of the strictest imitators of the life of Christ that the world has ever seen. St. Francis often praised him, believing that he probably possessed the greatest degree of self-knowledge of any of the brothers, and trusted him with various missions and responsibilities. He died in 1258.

BROTHER LEO was, with Angelo, the closest friend of St. Francis among the early friars. He was ordained a priest at some early point in the history of the movement, and seems to have become Francis's confessor, traveling with him all over Italy. Leo was present at the saint's death, and along with Angelo and Juniper, also at the death of St. Clare. He died an old man in 1271, and his burial place in the Basilica of St. Francis may be seen today in the crypt below the lower church.

BROTHER PETER OF MONTICELLO was a friar in the Marches. Born sometime before 1230, he was a leader among the second generation of Franciscans and among the Spirituals. He died in 1304.

BROTHER RUFINO was a cousin of St. Clare and called a saint by St. Francis. He joined Francis in 1210, one year after the first disciples. He was with Francis during the important early days in the caves of the Carceri when the friars were caring for lepers, and he was with Francis on La Verna when Francis received the stigmata. There are many stories of Rufino's having dark visions and temptations from the devil, with Francis counseling Rufino through these trials. Such stories might suggest that he was bipolar. Rufino lived to old age, longer than any of the other original twelve, dying in about 1280.

BROTHER SIMON was an early follower of St. Francis who died in about 1244 to 1245. He was one of the early Spirituals and probably among those who were banished to the Marches in the years after Francis's death.

FOR FURTHER READING

Other Excellent Editions of The Little Flowers
(plus selected secondary sources)

Each of these editions has been consulted in the creating of the present book.

Armstrong, Regis J. et al., eds. *Francis of Assisi: Early Documents*. Vol. 3. New York: New City Press, 2001.

Brown, Raphael, ed. *The Little Flowers of St. Francis: First Complete Edition*. New York: Image Books, 1958.

Doyle, Fr. Eric, OFM, STD, ed. *The Little Flowers of St. Francis, The Mirror of Perfection, and St. Bonaventure's Life of St. Francis*. Introduction by Fr. Hugh McKay. New York: Dutton, 1973.

Gardner, Edmund G. "The Little Flowers of St. Francis." In *St. Francis of Assisi 1226–1926: Essays in Commemoration*, 97–126. London: University of London Press, 1926.

Hopcke, Robert H., and Paul A. Schwartz. *Little Flowers of Francis of Assisi: A New Translation*. Boston: New Seeds, 2006.

Select Sources for Specific Stories

"ST. FRANCIS KEEPS LENT ON AN ISLAND IN PERUGIA" (AND OTHER STORIES ABOUT ST. FRANCIS'S PRAYER LIFE)

Bodo, Murray. *The Way of St. Francis: The Challenge of Franciscan Spirituality for Everyone*. Cincinnati: St. Anthony Messenger Press, 1995.

Sweeney, Jon M. *The St. Francis Prayer Book: A Guide to Deepen Your Spiritual Life*. Brewster, MA: Paraclete Press, 2004.

"ST. FRANCIS TAKES A SHIP TO SEE THE SULTAN"

Cusato, Michael F. "Francis of Assisi, the Crusades and Malek al-Kamil." In *The Early Franciscan Movement (1205–1239): History, Sources, and Hermeneutics*, 103–128. Spoleto, Italy: Fondazione Centro Italiano di Studi Sull'alto Medioevo, 2009.

Moses, Paul. *The Saint and the Sultan: The Crusades, Islam, and Francis of Assisi's Mission of Peace*. New York: Doubleday, 2009.

FOR FURTHER READING

STORIES OF ST. ANTHONY OF PADUA

Cusato, Michael F. "Something's Lost and Must Be Found: The Recovery of the Historical Anthony of Padua." In *The Early Franciscan Movement (1205–1239): History, Sources, and Hermeneutics*, 317–37. Spoleto, Italy: Fondazione Centro Italiano di Studi Sull'alto Medioevo, 2009.

FOR MORE ABOUT ST. CLARE

Armstrong, Regis J., ed. *The Lady: Clare of Assisi—Early Documents*. New York: New City Press, 2006.

Sweeney, Jon M. *The St. Clare Prayer Book: Listening for God's Leading*. Brewster, MA: Paraclete Press, 2007.

Select Books on the Franciscan Spirituals

Burr, David. *The Spiritual Franciscans: From Protest to Persecution in the Century after Saint Francis*. University Park, PA: Pennsylvania State University Press, 2001.

Lambert, M.D. *Franciscan Poverty: The Doctrine of the Absolute Poverty of Christ and the Apostles in the Franciscan Order 1210–1323*. London: SPCK, 1961.

Select Biographies of St. Francis of Assisi

Armstrong, Regis J. et al., eds. *Francis of Assisi: Early Documents*. Vols. 1 and 2. New York: New City Press, 1999, 2000. (These contain all of the earliest biographies of the saint.)

Chesterton, G. K. *Saint Francis of Assisi*. Garden City, NY: Doubleday, 1957. (Originally published in 1924.)

Green, Julien. *God's Fool: The Life and Times of Francis of Assisi*, trans. Peter Heinegg. New York: HarperOne, 1987.

Habig, Marion A. *St. Francis of Assisi: Writings and Early Biographies—English Omnibus of the Sources for the Life of St. Francis*. 4th rev. ed. Chicago: Franciscan Herald Press, 1983. (This also contains all of the earliest biographies of the saint.)

Sabatier, Paul. *The Road to Assisi: The Essential Biography—120th Anniversary Edition*, edited with introduction and annotations by Jon M. Sweeney. Brewster, MA: Paraclete Press, 2014. (Originally published in 1894.)

ACKNOWLEDGMENTS

Many thanks to the Franciscan scholar-saints of blessed memory who laid the foundation for our understanding of these tales today, including Luke Wadding, Paul Sabatier, G. K. Chesterton, Raphael Brown, John Moorman, and David Burr. And thanks, most of all, to Brothers Leo, Angelo, Rufino, Ugolino, and all the men and women who have lived in order to tell the story.

ABOUT PARACLETE PRESS

WHO WE ARE

Paraclete Press is a publisher of books, recordings, and DVDs on Christian spirituality. Our publishing represents a full expression of Christian belief and practice—from Catholic to Evangelical, from Protestant to Orthodox.

We are the publishing arm of the Community of Jesus, an ecumenical monastic community in the Benedictine tradition. As such, we are uniquely positioned in the marketplace without connection to a large corporation and with informal relationships to many branches and denominations of faith.

WHAT WE ARE DOING

PARACLETE PRESS BOOKS | Paraclete publishes books that show the richness and depth of what it means to be Christian. Although Benedictine spirituality is at the heart of all that we do, we publish books that reflect the Christian experience across many cultures, time periods, and houses of worship. We publish books that nourish the vibrant life of the church and its people.

We have several different series, including the best-selling Paraclete Essentials and Paraclete Giants series of classic texts in contemporary English; Voices from the Monastery—men and women monastics writing about living a spiritual life today; award-winning poetry; best-selling gift books for children on the occasions of baptism and first communion; and the Active Prayer Series that brings creativity and liveliness to any life of prayer.

MOUNT TABOR BOOKS | Paraclete's newest series, Mount Tabor Books, focuses on liturgical worship, art and art history, ecumenism, and the first millennium church; and was created in conjunction with the Mount Tabor Ecumenical Centre for Art and Spirituality in Barga, Italy.

PARACLETE RECORDINGS | From Gregorian chant to contemporary American choral works, our recordings celebrate the best of sacred choral music composed through the centuries that create a space for heaven and earth to intersect. Paraclete Recordings is the record label representing the internationally acclaimed choir Gloriæ Dei Cantores, praised for their "rapt and fathomless spiritual intensity" by *American Record Guide*, the Gloriæ Dei Cantores Schola, specializing in the study and performance of Gregorian chant; and the other instrumental artists of the Gloriæ Dei Artes Foundation.

Paraclete Press is also privileged to be the exclusive North American distributor of the recordings of the Monastic Choir of St. Peter's Abbey in Solesmes, France, long considered to be a leading authority on Gregorian chant.

PARACLETE VIDEO | Our DVDs offer spiritual help, healing, and biblical guidance for a broad range of life issues including grief and loss, marriage, forgiveness, facing death, bullying, addictions, Alzheimer's, and spiritual formation.

Learn more about us at our website:
www.paracletepress.com or phone us
toll-free at 1.800.451.5006

SCAN
TO
READ
MORE

THE COMPLETE PARACLETE GIANT SERIES

$29.99, Paperback,
978-1-55725-810-6

$26.99, Paperback,
978-1-61261-235-5

$24.99, Paperback,
978-1-55725-923-3

$29.99, Paperback,
978-1-55725-639-3

$22.99, Paperback,
978-1-61261-620-9

$26.99, Paperback,
978-1-557256706

$26.99, Paperback,
978-1-55725-607-2